C000160995

SINGING A DIFFERENT TUNE

The Slavic Film Musical

IN A TRANSNATIONAL CONTEXT

Film and Media Studies

Edited by Helena Goscilo

SINGING A DIFFERENT TUNE

The Slavic Film Musical

IN A TRANSNATIONAL CONTEXT

BOSTON
2023

Library of Congress Cataloging-in-Publication Data

Names: Goscilo, Helena, 1945- editor.
Title: "Singing a different tune": the Slavic film musical in a transnational context / edited by Helena Goscilo.
Description: Boston: Academic Studies Press, 2023. | Series: Film and media studies | Includes bibliographical references.
Identifiers: LCCN 2022058270 (print) | LCCN 2022058271 (ebook) | ISBN 9798887190204 (hardback) | ISBN 9798887191287 (adobe pdf) | ISBN 9798887191294 (epub)
Subjects: LCSH: Musical films--Slavic countries--History and criticism. | LCGFT: Film criticism. | Essays.
Classification: LCC PN1995.9.M86 S56 2023 (print) | LCC PN1995.9.M86 (ebook) | DDC 791.430947--dc23/eng/20221230
LC record available at https://lccn.loc.gov/2022058270
LC ebook record available at https://lccn.loc.gov/2022058271

ISBN 9798887190204 (hardback)
ISBN 9798887191287 (adobe pdf)
ISBN 9798887191294 (epub)

Book design by PHi Business Solutions
Cover design by Tatiana Melnikova

Published by Academic Studies Press
1577 Beacon St.
Brookline, MA 02446, USA

press@academicstudiespress.com
www.academicstudiespress.com

To my mother, who used to sing Bodo's songs during my childhood
and who introduced me to the pleasures of operetta

and

To Brit, Davey, Elizabeth, and Finn, who for decades have shared my passion for opera

Contents

Acknowledgements ix

Introduction 1
Helena Goscilo

Part One: Polish Film Musicals **37**

1. Early Polish-Language Musicals: The Tug of War between Genre Film and Cabaret 39
Beth Holmgren
2. Between the Market and the Mirror: Stanisław Bareja's *Marriage of Convenience* 82
Helena Goscilo
3. Paweł Pawlikowski's *Cold War*: Music, Space, and Identity 116
Elżbieta Ostrowska
4. The Allure of Agnieszka Smoczyńska's *Lure* (2015) as an Intrepid Feminist Hybrid 141
Helena Goscilo

Part Two: Russian Film Musicals **171**

5. Perplexing Popularity: Ivan Pyr′ev's Kolkhoz Musical Comedy Films 173
Rimgaila Salys
6. The Thaw as Carnival: Soviet Musical Comedy after Stalin 220
Lilya Kaganovsky
7. Constructing the Pop Diva: Alla Pugacheva, Sofia Rotaru, and the Celebrity Musical of the 1970s–1980s 248
Alexander Prokhorov and Elena Prokhorov
8. Postmodernity, Freedom, and Authenticity in Kirill Serebrennikov's *Leto* (2018) 274
Justin Wilmes

Filmography 299
Index 301

Acknowledgements

I am indebted to all the contributors represented in this volume, as well as to the outstanding quartet at the Ohio State University Interlibrary Services personnel: Beth Brown, Brian Miller (department head), Tonya Johnson, and Tranvis Manzione, without whose professionalism and efficiency I would have been up the proverbial creek without a paddle. Various aspects of the volume have benefited from the input of the following individuals, whose generosity saved a part of my anatomy to which I am attached: Bożenna Goscilo, Konrad Klejsa, and especially Elżbieta Ostrowska and Rimgaila Salys, who set aside their own projects to respond to my drafts. As Herodotus observed, "Of all possessions, a friend is the most precious"—a notion confirmed by the friends doubling as authors and respondents in this undertaking, which came together with unexpected speed, but took some time to get into print. Finally, a bow to Kira Nemirovsky at Academic Studies Press for her grace and efficiency at the last stages of this venture.

Introduction

"Without music, life would be a mistake."
—Friedrich Nietzsche, *Twilight of the Idols* (1889)

Hollywood's Favorite Offspring

A multifaceted genre born of 1920s technological innovations—diegetic sound and its synchronization with image—the film musical was a quintessentially Hollywood product of the studio system. Its heterogeneous provenance encompassed revue, vaudeville, operetta, ballet, the minstrel show, Tin Pan Alley, and Broadway stage productions. A combination of studios' competitiveness, commitment to entertainment, and stake in the music publishing, recording, and radio industries[1] prompted Warner Bros. in October 1927 to pioneer a musical as the first talkie—Alan Crosland's *The Jazz Singer*.[2] In September of the following year, the same studio released *The Singing Fool* (directed by Lloyd Bacon). Both starred the immensely popular stage and nightclub singer Al Jolson. Although in the first, he simply adlibbed a few lines of dialogue,[3] while only two-thirds of the second film contained songs and speech, the promise of sound cum music was self-evident, and the films triggered a veritable avalanche of offerings in the genre, by Warner, Fox, and RCA.[4] From 1927 to 1930 an astonishing two hundred-plus musicals appeared on screen, peaking in volume from 1929 to 1930—not coincidentally, during the onset of the Great Depression (1929–1939). In that grim decade the musical's spectacular orientation, upbeat

---

1 John Izod, *Hollywood and the Box Office 1895–1986* (New York: Columbia University Press, 1988), 82; Pam Cook and Mieke Bernink, *The Cinema Book* (London: BFI, 1999), 209.

2 For a detailed survey of the circumstances leading Warner Bros. to make and release the film, see Douglas J. Gomery, "Writing the History of the American Film Industry: Warner Bros and Sound," *Screen* 17, no. 1 (Spring 1976): 40–53.

3 Izod, *Hollywood and the Box Office 1895–1986*, 75.

4 While *The Jazz Singer* fared quite well, *The Singing Fool* proved a genuine blockbuster, strikingly lucrative, as was Jolson's rendition of the song "Sonny Boy," records of which sold more than a million copies. See "A. J. Recordings: The Singing Fool—1928," https://jolson.org/works/film/tsf/singfool.html. Copious information about *The Jazz Singer* is available at "*The Jazz Singer*," Wikipedia, https://en.wikipedia.org/wiki/The_Jazz_Singer.

song and dance routines, espousal of bourgeois heteronormative love, and illusion of community testified to the genre's embrace of fantasy, offering both a welcome respite from, and a reassuring compensation for, the trials of everyday lived reality. Whereas the genre was deemed lowbrow by those indentured to hierarchies and auteur cinema, audiences' enthusiasm for the musical, which reigned as the most popular genre from the thirties into the mid-to-late fifties, stayed undimmed. It elevated singers and dancers such as Fred Astaire, Ginger Rogers, Gene Kelly, Cyd Charisse, and Judy Garland to the rank of screen idols.

The genre's conventions during the thirties and forties remained largely stable—indeed, definitive in such classics as *42nd Street* (1933) and *Footlight Parade* (1933), both with their signature Busby Berkeley extravaganzas, as well as *Flying down to Rio* (1933),[5] *The Gay Divorcee* (1934), *Top Hat* (1935), *Swing Time* (1936), and *Meet Me in St. Louis* (1944). Yet a few individual musicals of the forties such as *The Pirate* (directed by Vincente Minnelli, 1948) at MGM, with Garland and Kelly, modified the model in their portrayal of gender and ironically inflected treatment of those very conventions. Even earlier, such films as *The Wizard of Oz* (1939) and *Ziegfield Follies* (1946) had deviated from the paradigm that scholars such as Rick Altman and Jane Feuer have elaborated in an explicative mode, their purviews marginalizing the distinctive, creative anomalies vis-à-vis the so-called norm so as to make their case for the generic utopian blueprint.[6] Various film scholars have created their own taxonomies for that template, which inevitably appears in a bifurcated form determined by the role of music and choreography within the film's narrative. For instance, Louis Giannetti calls "realist" a musical in which efforts to stage a performance rationalize the song and dance numbers. By contrast, in its "formalist" counterpart characters can burst into song and dance with putative spontaneity at any moment in any situation,[7] giving new meaning to Jacques's observation in *As You Like It*, that "all the world's a stage." Altman labels that distinction as the "show" or "backstage" versus the "integrative" musical, which strives to embed musical numbers convincingly into a narrative structure in which music plays a

---

5 Like Ernst Lubitsch's *Merry Widow* (1934), based on Franz Lehár's 1905 operetta, *Flying down to Rio* antedated the moralistic Production (or Hays) Code, which went into effect later in 1934. Both musicals engage in risqué dialogue and in the latter case show considerably more flesh than the code would approve.

6 Rick Altman, *The American Film Musical* (Bloomington: Indiana University Press, 1987); and Rick Altman, *Film/Genre* (London: BFI, 1999); Jane Feuer, *The Hollywood Musical* (Bloomington: Indiana University Press, 1993).

7 Louis Giannetti, *Understanding Movies* (Upper Saddle River: Prentice Hall, 1999), 218–219.

vestigial, deflective, or irrelevant but audience-pleasing role.[8] His terminology and concepts essentially have codified the critical discourse for three decades.

In the fifties, as the musical inevitably evolved, it gradually absorbed new elements associated with melodrama—hyperbole, heightened emotionalism, suppressed desires, archetypal characters, and the conflict of clear-cut good and evil. These tendencies within the genre hardly conduced to utopianism. Indeed, the impulse to hybridity resulted in musicals that tackled problems less lightly than in the classic versions of the genre; many also bypassed the obligatory happy endings associated with the latter. Alongside more traditional fare such as *An American in Paris* (1951), *Singin' in the Rain* (1952), *Seven Brides for Seven Brothers* (1954), and *Oklahoma* (1955) appeared the refractory, thought-provoking *Love Me or Leave Me* (1955), *It's Always Fair Weather* (1955), *Carousel* (1956), and *Silk Stockings* (1957)—a musical reworking of Ernst Lubitsch's film *Ninotchka* (1939) that concludes without a rousing musical celebration of consensus. Moreover, in the second half of the fifties the widespread prevalence of television, which by 1959 was present in ninety percent of American households,[9] and the dramatic advent of rock'n'roll—with *Rock around the Clock* (1956), *The Girl Can't Help It* (1956), and *Jailhouse Rock* (1957)[10] hitting the screens—destabilized if not outright unseated what had been the standard model of the screen musical's unchallenged sovereignty. Music and dance no longer appeared capable of solving social and personal problems, including violence, crime, pathology, and unzipped sexuality. And while the sixties seemed to revive the genre with such popular "family entertainment" as *The Music Man* (1962) and the "home apple pie" Julie Andrews vehicles, *Mary Poppins* (1964) and *The Sound of Music* (1965),[11] public thirst for the genre dwindled, as did the number of its Hollywood releases, though the Broadway-inspired *My Fair Lady* (1964) made a considerable splash and garnered a plethora of awards. Both films with Andrews restored the efficacy of song as community glue and moral tonic; what rescued them from saccharine banality were the catchy melodies and, in the case of *Mary Poppins,* some clever lyrics.

When film musicals regained a portion of their earlier audiences in the seventies, the aftermath of the preceding decade's volatility inspired a dystopian vision far removed from the conviction during the genre's heyday that "all's well

8 Altman, *The American Film Musical.*

9 Izod, *Hollywood and the Box Office 1895–1986,* 166.

10 Elvis Presley's film debut.

11 *The Sound of Music,* which cost $10 million, benefited hugely from the economically triggered adoption of middle-class values that placed the family on a pedestal, earning approximately $100 million in rentals (Izod, *Hollywood and the Box Office 1895–1986,* 171).

that ends well." The Vietnam War, the civil rights movement, the Watergate scandal, unremitting protests and riots, as well as the assassination of John Kennedy, Malcolm X, Martin Luther King, Jr., and Robert Kennedy created a *Zeitgeist* of retractive disillusionment rather than joyful celebrations of community. Irony and skepticism pervaded a divided and uncertain country in the throes of loss. And in this atmosphere of anomie the versatile, talented Bob Fosse (1927–1987) proved the ideal screen spokesman for a new sense of American life and, accordingly, a new concept of the film musical. An innovative choreographer, dancer, actor, and director who worked in both film and theater, Fosse enjoys widespread fame in cinema primarily on the basis of two landmark film musicals: *Cabaret* (1972), which earned him the Oscar for Best Director,[12] and *All That Jazz* (1979), which won the Palme d'Or at Cannes in 1980. Apart from enjoying a sterling reputation for originality in Broadway shows, Fosse had brought his distinctive choreography to such earlier screen musicals as *The Pajama Game* (1957) and had danced in his inimitable vein in *Kiss Me Kate* (1953). What distinguished the two seventies' outings, however, was not only his new style of dance (with distinctive leg and hand movements), but the replacement of the generic paradigm's carefree atmosphere with the dark, sordid world of entertainment—in 1930s Nazi-ruled Berlin in *Cabaret* and in New York's theater environment in *All That Jazz*—culminating in inevitable doom and death, respectively. The essentially benign, wholesome veneer of Hollywood's early musical has no place in Fosse's dystopian environments, where entertainment rubs shoulders (and other body parts) with sleaze, betrayal, and egotism run amok. Martin Scorsese's *New York, New York* (1977), though commercially and critically much less successful, likewise eschewed the fabled happy ending. Realism in an aporetic vein, in short, invaded utopian fantasies and dissipated them.

Part of this process possibly was aided by the unique, unrestrainedly irreverent British *Rocky Horror Picture Show* (1975). Directed by Jim Sharman, the hilarious cult classic teeming with visual and verbal cinematic intertexts, saturated with multiple modes of unconventional sexuality, and focused on the irrepressible, half-naked *male* body, took the United States by storm. It showcased the rewards of nihilistic parody while exploring the injection of science fiction and horror into what earlier had seemed an impregnably "nice" genre.[13]

---

12 The film also won seven other Oscars.

13 Parody of a genre, of course, normally signals that genre's exhaustion and the need for its rejuvenation by its wholesale reconceptualization or the infusion of transformative elements, frequently from other genres.

Its iconoclastic hybridity recalled that of several fine musicals of the fifties insofar as the latter likewise benefited from the (more cautious) admixture of features from another genre—melodrama. Frank Oz's American pseudo-analogue, *The Little Shop of Horrors* (1986), which drew on Roger Corman's identically titled sci-fi film, likewise courted horror and suggested the benefits of infusing a somewhat tired genre with "alien" elements but paled beside its British predecessor.

Much less revolutionary during the seventies in the United States and abroad was the abrupt, brief explosion of extraordinarily popular disco film musicals, above all John Badham's *Saturday Night Fever* (1977), which propelled its male lead, John Travolta, into stardom and immediately led to his role in the unprecedently profitable teen musical *Grease* (1978).[14] Both subscribed to the "dual focus" that Altman and Feuer attribute to the genre, but the treatment of sexuality, which had been constrained by the puritanical Production Code—adopted in 1930, enforced in 1934, and abandoned in 1968—contains some nasty overtones in both films.[15] What accounts for the originality of *Saturday Night Fever,* however, are the skillful dance routines, which captured viewers' imagination and fueled a veritable craze for disco dancing in numerous clubs in the United States and abroad. Moreover, the single by the Bee Gees issued in advance to promote the film resulted in the best-selling soundtrack album ever after the film's release.[16] Whereas no happy marriage unfolds onscreen, in this case the wedding of cinema and music recording was an ideal union made in Hollywood marketing heaven.[17]

In the ensuing decades, as Hollywood increasingly relied on successful Broadway musicals for transfers onto the screen, the formula that had enchanted audiences for years dissolved almost entirely. Nonetheless, Hollywood largely stayed faithful to the notion of romantic love and a happy ending buttressed by song, for which Europeans often expressed attitudes ranging from envious skepticism to ridicule, with film critics and reviewers in both Poland and Russia adopting the expression "happy end," identified exclusively with the myopic or

---

14 Transferred from Broadway, where it had a record run, *Grease* reportedly "grossed $150 million on its first run alone" and generated sequels and imitations internationally (Jim Hillier and Douglas Pye, *100 Film Musicals* [London: Palgrave Macmillan/BFI, 2011], 92).

15 In 1938, the straitjacketing Production Code had put an end to the hilariously suggestive lines of Mae West (1893–1980), a major creative talent in film during the Depression and popular with audiences from 1932 to 1937. Censorship essentially ended her film career (Izod, *Hollywood and the Box Office 1895–1986,* 105, 107).

16 Hillier and Pye, *100 Film Musicals,* 196.

17 For a glance at *Saturday Night Fever* and other musicals of that period, see J. P. Telotte, "The New Hollywood Musical: From *Saturday Night Fever* to *Footloose,*" in *Genre and Contemporary Hollywood,* ed. Steve Neale (London: BFI, 2002), 48–61.

oblivious optimism that all too frequently renders American mass-addressed films jejune. Even as the traditional film musical faltered, a curious development in the 1990s was the sudden increase in animated film musicals, such as *Beauty and the Beast* (1991), *Aladdin* (1992), and *Hercules* (1997), recalling Disney's pioneering *Snow White* (1937)—a cinematic milestone that became one of Hollywood's greatest moneymakers. It was the film, in fact, "on which the Walt Disney empire was built."[18] The trend in animation, however, weakened in the second half of the 2000s.

By and large, the most memorable and profitable among the few American film musicals to have surfaced in the new millennium evidence the influence of Fosse and continue to depend on the success or failure of Broadway shows as a predictive indicator of screen adaptations' financial viability—currently exampled by the musical biopic *Hamilton* (2020).[19] Notably, the Australian Baz Luhrmann's *Moulin Rouge!* (2001)[20] and Rob Marshall's *Chicago* (2002) have led the way, winning awards and large audiences even as they reconceived both genre and gender. A musical featuring an expensive *cocotte* loved by a naïve writer and expiring of tuberculosis in *fin-de-siècle* Paris (*Moulin Rouge!*)[21] or two female prison inmates guilty of murder in the 1920s (*Chicago*) was unimaginable during the era of the genre's sunny, affirmative phase. *Volens nolens*, sordid realism has crept into the formula and altered it, perhaps for good. Ultimately, the success of individual film musicals notwithstanding, the genre incontestably has declined since its unchallenged supremacy in the thirties. Nostalgic efforts to resuscitate its former status and part of its template, instanced by the inexplicably popular and professionally applauded *La La Land* (directed by Damien Chazelle, 2016), which borrows its ending from Jacques Demy's 1964 sing-through *Les Parapluies de Cherbourg*, demonstrates just how nerveless and clichéd such efforts can be.[22]

---

18 Hillier and Pye, *100 Film Musicals*, 216.

19 The reverse likewise operates in the transfer to Broadway of such popular films as *The Lion King*, *Hairspray*, *Spider-Man*, *Legally Blonde*, and others.

20 Luhrmann's debut feature, *Strictly Ballroom* (1992), was a colorful comedy (bordering on gaudy) that featured dancing competitions, with some remarkably athletic numbers and apostrophes to the audience.

21 The scenario, of course, is familiar from opera, specifically Verdi's *La Traviata* and Puccini's *La Bohème*.

22 *Annette* (directed by Leos Carax, 2021), the latest such outing, met with a stinging review by the *The New Yorker*'s witty, incisive film critic, Anthony Lane (Lane, "The Uncanny Valley of *I'm Your Man*," *The New Yorker*, September 17, 2021, https://www.newyorker.com/magazine/2021/09/27/the-uncanny-valley-of-im-your-man).

Critical Delay and Relay

Until the late seventies, film studies neglected the musical as a genre too frivolous to warrant scholarly investigation. Eventually, however, it drew the attention of the British academic Richard Dyer, followed by Altman and Feuer, among many others.[23] At first glance, Dyer's 1977 article "Entertainment and Utopia" would seem to state the obvious—namely, that musicals provide escapist entertainment, but his examination of precisely what aspects of the genre collectively keep audiences entertained is still one of the most valuable analyses available today. Contending that musicals rely on representational and non-representational signs to purvey utopia, he identifies "colour, texture, movement, rhythm, melody, camerawork" among the non-representational signs before specifying energy, abundance, intensity, transparency, and community as those phenomena that the musical conveys to assuage audiences' anxieties and needs.[24] Dyer's brief, lucid article remains a foundational text. Many years later, Feuer (1993) expanded on the centrality of utopianism in the genre, which works to enlist viewers' cinematically engineered participation in the bracing solution to clashes and contradiction toward which the musical's narrative hurtles. And Altman's various publications, culminating in his monograph (1989; first edition 1987), essentially cover the genre's conventions, based chiefly on early examples from the thirties and forties: a formulaic plot centered on a romantic couple, a dual focus, strong sexual differentiation, a narrative that showcases singing and dancing talents, a display above all of the female body, and a happy ending that reconciles the conflicts featured throughout. As the specialist deemed the foremost authority on the genre, Altman has compartmentalized Hollywood musicals into "show," "folk," and "fairy tale" variants—categories that illuminate the orientation of various films, yet cannot fully accommodate some of the most original and interesting instances of the genre and slight the cultural and industrial context in which they originated.[25] Since, as noted above, the incursion of melodrama into the genre

---

23 For a compact synopsis of the critical literature on the genre, see Steve Neale, ed., *Genre and Hollywood* (London and New York: Routledge, 2000), 104–112.

24 Richard Dyer, "Entertainment and Utopia," in *Genre: The Musical: A Reader*, ed. Rick Altman, 220–232 (London, Boston, and Henley: Routledge & Kegan Paul, 1981). Originally published in *Movie* 24 (Spring 1977).

25 Steve Neale has been one of the few voices raised against Altman's attachment to a canon (Neale, "Questions of Genre," *Screen* 31, no. 1 [Spring 1990]: 45–66). Altman's later work, however, likely in response to Neale's objections, pays greater attention to the effects of temporality and external forces on a genre's evolution (Altman, *Film/Genre*). As Thomas Austin phrases it, more recently "Altman shows how genres are always in process and subject to the interventions of producers, critics (both popular and academic) and (potentially) audiences"

in the fifties resulted in musicals that omitted some of the features ruling earlier films and assimilated new ones, the critical vocabulary became loaded with epithets and other qualifiers, the taxonomical differentiation intended to register what actually was an aspect of the genre's origins.[26]

Categories and subcategories, as Steve Neale has argued, can only go so far when critics' formal emphasis does not take into account historical and sociological, as well as institutional, factors that cannot be separated from the choices made in film production and in one of its favorite genres, which has undergone such significant revisions over the years.[27] As he notes, "Genres do not consist only of films: they consist also, and equally, of specific systems of expectation and hypothesis which spectators bring with them to the cinema, and which interact with films themselves during the course of the viewing process." Sagely pointing out that "genres exist always *in excess* of a corpus of works," Neale (rightly, in my view) criticizes the impulse to establish a canon,[28] and though Altman briefly acknowledges such works as *The Wizard of Oz, West Side Story* (1961), *Grease,* and *Flashdance* (1983), his main interest lies in "canonical" examples of the genre. The typologies he has established are nevertheless useful as a starting point, which one may adopt, develop, or polemicize with, but certainly should not ignore. American film musicals as well as theoretical analyses of them have had an incalculable impact on the genre and its critical reception throughout Europe, including Poland and Russia, where scholarship on musicals is scant.

West to East: A Moveable Feast with Local Seasoning

> "After silence, that which comes nearest to expressing the inexpressible is music."
>
> —Aldous Huxley, "The Rest Is Silence" (1931)

Not all film industries and not all "stars" succumbed immediately to sound and to the heady appeal of song on screen. Sound, in fact, elicited enormous skepticism on the part of such prominent film personalities as Charlie Chaplin, the cornerstone of whose comedies was the singular expressiveness of his body language. And the career of John Gilbert, Greta Garbo's major leading man

---

(Thomas Austin, "*Gone with the Wind* Plus Fangs," in *Genre and Contemporary Hollywood,* ed. Steve Neale [London: BFI, 2002], 296).

26 Cook and Bernink, *The Cinema Book,* 209.

27 Neale, "Questions of Genre"; Neale, *Genre and Hollywood.*

28 Neale, "Questions of Genre," 46, 51.

famous as "the Great Lover," ended with the introduction of sound as well as the machinations of studio politics. Likewise, Hollywood's chief swashbuckler, Douglas Fairbanks, who during the twenties impressed audiences in the sword-wielding roles of Zorro, d'Artagnan, and Robin Hood, found his signature athleticism less in demand with the advent of talkies. Meanwhile, not *The Jazz Singer*, but *The Singing Fool* introduced Europeans to the innovation of sound and musicals, for most cinemas in 1927 still lacked the equipment to project sound. Although not without delay, Europe by and large welcomed the new phenomenon, imitating the Hollywood musical's template or selectively adopting its constitutive features to produce its own versions of the musical during the thirties. Internationalism was the order of the day, and two of Germany's prominent directors—the urbane, witty Ernst Lubitsch (1892–1947) and Fritz Lang (1890–1976), the creator of the single most influential sci-fi film, *Metropolis* (1927)—were responsible for several of Hollywood's most original early musicals: Lubitsch's *The Love Parade* (1929), *One Hour with You* (1932), and the operettish *Merry Widow* (1934), with Maurice Chevalier and Jeanette McDonald; Lang's *You and Me* (1938), with music by Kurt Weill.

England, Germany, and France had no difficulty accepting the new technology. From the thirties through the fifties film musicals proliferated in Germany, but the industry's interest in them petered out at approximately the same time as the genre experienced a slump in Hollywood. Instances of the genre that stand out are G. W. Pabst's *Die Dreigroschenoper* (1931), Erik Charell's *Der Kongress tanzt* (1931), and Reinhold Schünzel's cross-dressing *Viktor und Viktoria* (1933), which a half-century later Blake Edwards reincarnated in the gender-bending British-American *Victor/Victoria* (1982) partly as a vehicle for his wife, Julie Andrews. And France swiftly embraced the genre, contributing *Il est charmant* (directed by Louis Mercanton, 1932), *Antonia* (directed by Jean Boyer and Max Neufeld, 1935), and *Prends la route* (directed by Jean Boyer, 1936) to the international corpus. But the most memorable French film musicals appeared in the 1960s: Demy's sui generis *Les Parapluies de Cherbourg*, followed by his *Les Demoiselles de Rochefort* (1967). England joined its continental counterpart with such works as *Evergreen* (directed by Victor Saville, 1934), which relied on the genre's staple of an assumed identity in its daring plot revolving around an illegitimate child;[29] *Look up and Laugh* (directed by Basil Dean, 1935), and

---

29 One of the few other musicals featuring an unwed mother is Grigorii Aleksandrov's *Tsirk* (Circus, 1936), which contrasts Soviet acceptance of an illegitimate Black child driven out of town with his mother by the intolerant Americans. Indeed, the United States was and continues to be racist, but so was the Soviet Union, as is Post-Soviet Russia.

Everything Is Rhythm (directed by Alfred J. Goulding, 1936)—all three generally adhering to Hollywood precepts and elaborating plots around musical performers. Although the genre never became a firm favorite on the British screen, notable musicals largely independent of the Hollywood model included Richard Attenborough's anti-war *Oh! What a Lovely War* (1969)—which ends with a stunning overhead shot of thousands of crosses on the graves of those killed in World War I—and, six years later, *The Rocky Horror Picture Show*, noted above. In other words, by the end of the thirties, the film musical was firmly established in western Europe, and the ineluctable permutations it underwent over time were fueled mainly by the individual traditions and priorities of each country. As might be expected, cinema at the easternmost end of the continent trod a parallel yet somewhat different path.

Poland's Exuberant Musical Culture of the Thirties

> "My motto is not to educate, but to entertain. What matters most is a film's success with the general public."
>
> —Michał Waszyński[30]

Poland, with cinematic connections closer to Germany and its operetta traditions than to Hollywood, nonetheless had American studios' distributors in Warsaw, Łódź, and Wrocław, which ensured that the Polish public's broad access to foreign films included Hollywood fare. Moreover, Polish film personnel, such as directors Aleksander Ryder, Ryszard Bolesławski, and Emile Reinart and cameramen Piotr Nowicki, Eugeniusz Modzelewski, and Jan Skarbek-Malczewski, collaborated in Austrian, French, Italian, and American projects. The Polish actress Pola Negri enjoyed a successful career in both Germany and Hollywood.[31] These and other sustained interactions meant that the potential of sound and the possibilities of film musicals reached Poland in September 1929, when *The Singing Fool* made its Polish premiere in Warsaw's movie theater

---

30 "Moją dewizją jest nie wychowywać, lecz dawać rozrywkę. Ważne jest przede wszystkim powodzenie filmu u szerokiej publiczności." Cited in Stanisław Janicki, "Michał Waszyński—artysta czy wyrobnik?," *Kino* 5 (2018): 31.

31 For a rundown on Poland's internationalist modus operandi during this period, see Charles Ford and Robert Hammond, *Polish Film: A Twentieth-Century History* (Jefferson: McFarland & Co., 2005), 42–61.

Splendid.[32] Among the array of reactions provoked by both novelties was a strongly negative rejection that assumed a startling form, possibly explained by the country's entertainment traditions. Cosmopolitan interwar Poland boasted a robust cabaret culture that showcased a host of formidably talented composers, singers, and dancers, who became stage stars with devoted fans. Perhaps the popularity of this "live onstage" genre accounted for Poland's initial response to the mediated nature of sound film and the screen musical. In its most extreme form, the strenuous resistance resulted in courts established in Warsaw, Łódź, and Kraków "to publicly denounce the evil of the talkies." Some in the profession viewed sound as "the destruction of the human voice," and others found it inimical to "the lively and dynamic action of the silent film."[33] Yet, during the 1930s, film as a cheap form of entertainment thrived, and eventually the privately owned cinema industry, guided by profits, accepted the arrival of sound and the new genre of screen musicals.

Fiscal considerations explain why during that decade most films on average were shot in a month—the accelerated production keeping pace with audience demand for new movies, some of which were shown briefly, sometimes for less than a month, with most films unable to make a profit.[34] Musical comedies particularly appealed to audiences, who preferred light, frothy fare and above all comedies, with or without music. Scriptwriters, composers, and leading actors and actresses in musicals migrated from the country's richly developed genre of cabaret, which laid the preparatory ground for the screen musical—a transfer that all too often resulted in loose plot development, to put it kindly, but seduced through excellent music, skillful singing, and exuberant dance routines. Recognizability doubtless played a key role in the film musical's popularity when famous cabaret performers appeared in fictional roles instead of themselves on stage.

As chapter one makes clear, the interwar film musical in Poland would be unthinkable without five key individuals: the director Michał Waszyński (né Moshe Waks; 1904–1965); the composer Henryk Wars (1902–1977); the actors Eugeniusz Bodo (1899–1943) and Adolf Dymsza (born Adolf Bagiński; 1900–1975), and the actress/dancer Helena Grossówna (1904–1994).[35] This

32 Sheila Skaff, *The Law of the Looking Glass: Cinema in Poland, 1896–1939* (Athens: Ohio University Press, 2008), 103.

33 Ford and Hammond, *Polish Film: A Twentieth-Century History*, 66–67.

34 Skaff, *The Law of the Looking Glass: Cinema in Poland, 1896–1939*, 156.

35 It was common at that time for assimilated Polish-Jewish public figures to alter their names so as to avoid the stigma of their Jewish origins. By the 1930s, Catholic Poland's earlier indifference to religious and ethnic "otherness" remained but a memory.

cohort—three of them Jewish—deserves much of the credit for the vitality of Poland's thirties musicals, for which audiences seeking visual and aural pleasure but indifferent to lapses in continuity and plotline had a healthy appetite.[36] The supreme director committed to offering the eager public entertainment pure and simple, Waszyński was unprecedentedly prolific, directing thirty-seven features during the thirties—approximately a quarter of that decade's output of 147 films.[37] Adhering to Hollywood conventions of the musical and later of melodrama, he managed to complete some films in a matter of two weeks.[38] His musicals included *Co mój mąż robi w nocy* (What my husband is up to at night, 1934), *Pieśniarz Warszawy* (The songster of Warsaw, 1934), *Będzie lepiej* (It'll be better, 1936), and *Bolek i Lolek* (Bolek and Lolek, 1936), which attracted viewers partly because he favored popular stars and also because he collaborated indefatigably with multiple Polish studios, such as Sfinks (the first Polish studio, owned by Aleksander Hertz), Leo-Film, Blok-Muza-Film, Rex-Film, and Feniks, which widely advertised their offerings.[39] As Stefania Zahorska, a film critic writing in the thirties, phrased it, "his filmmaking was efficient, cheap and popular with . . . audiences."[40] A colorful figure who had a finger on the pulse of the average viewer and became known as The King of Polish Popular Humor, during World War II he joined the peripatetic Anders Army, and after the war ended up as a high-profile, successful producer in Hollywood.[41] In Poland, however, he is best remembered for the country's most durable and fascinating Yiddish-language film, the remarkable *Dybuk* (The dybbuk, 1937).[42]

---

36 On the colossal contribution of Jewish Poles to early Polish film and musicals, as well as music performance during World War II, see Beth Holmgren, "How the Cabaret Went to War," *The Cosmopolitan Review* 6, no. 3 (Fall–Winter 2014), http://cosmopolitanreview.com/how-the-cabaret-went-to-war; and Beth Holmgren, "The Jews in the Band: The Anders Army's Special Troupes," *POLIN* 32 (2020): *Jews and Music-Making in the Polish Lands*, ed. François Guesnet, Benjamin Matis, and Antony Polonsky, 177–191; as well as Janicki, "Michał Waszyński—artysta czy wyrobnik?"

37 Janusz R. Kowalczyk, "Michał Waszyński," Culture.pl., accessed August 31, 2021, https://culture.pl/en/tworca/michal-waszynski.

38 His *Dwanaście krzeseł* (Twelve chairs, 1933), an adaptation of Il'f and Petrov's novel, *Dvenadtsat' stul'ev* (1928), with Adolf Dymsza, testifies to the lively give-and-take across national borders during this period.

39 Kowalczyk, "Michał Waszyński."

40 Ibid.

41 He co-worked with Anthony Mann on the blockbuster costume epics *El Cid* (1961) and *The Fall of the Roman Empire* (1964) (Kowalczyk, "Michał Waszyński"), assisted in Orson Welles's production of *Otello*, and contributed to *Roman Holiday* and *The Barefoot Contessa* (Janicki, "Michał Waszyński—artysta czy wyrobnik?," 31).

42 In 2017, Elwira Niewiera and Piotr Rosołowski released *Książę i dybuk* (The prince and the dybbuk), a documentary about Waszyński's life and works that won the Venezia Classici

No less prolific and versatile than Waszyński, composer Wars (né Henryk Warszawski) attained fame as The Polish King of Jazz. After many years in Warsaw's fabled Qui Pro Quo[43]—a legendary cabaret that lasted from 1919 to early 1932 and incubated a host of formidable talents—Wars composed music for a long string of musicals in the thirties. Allegedly, he was responsible for songs in fifty-two films during that decade, almost a third of all features produced in that span of time,[44] and many of those songs are still cited or sung today. Notably, one of the signature numbers in *Piętro wyżej* (One floor up, 1937), rendered by Bodo, "Umowiłem sie z nią na dziewiątą" ("I've got a date with her at nine"), became a smash hit. Indeed, Wars's music in large measure accounts for the popularity of Waszyński's *Songster of Warsaw*, with Bodo, and his crime drama *Czarna perla* (Black pearl, 1935), also with Bodo; Juliusz Gardan's *Czy Lucyna to dziewczyna?* (Is Lucyna a girl?, 1934/6), with Bodo; Mieczysław Krawicz's *Robert i Bertrand* (Robert and Bertrand, 1937/8), with Bodo and Dymsza; Krawicz's *Paweł i Gaweł* (Paweł and Gaweł, 1938), with Bodo, Dymsza, and Grossówna.[45] After his impressive stint as head of the Tea Jazz Orchestra in the Anders Army in the Middle East,[46] Wars also ended up in Hollywood once the war was over, and (as Henry Vars) composed music for more than fifty films at Warner Bros, Columbia, MGM, and Twentieth-Century Fox, his breakthrough facilitated, quite improbably, by his friendship with John Wayne.[47]

Similarly experienced in cabaret, both Bodo and Dymsza acquired a secondary if greater fame in musical comedies on screen. The unchallenged luminary in cabaret and film in the thirties, Bodo (born Bohdan Eugène Junod) was a celebrity actor, as well as director and entrepreneur, whose songs and skits elevated

---

prize (Kowalczyk, "Michał Waszyński"). For a review, see Joanna Ostrowska, "Książę i dybuk," *Kino* 5 (2018): 32–33. For more on *Dybuk*, see Robert Birkholc, "Dybbuk—Michał Waszyński," trans. Patryk Grabowski, September 2018, https://culture.pl/en/work/dybbuk-michal-waszynski.

43 See Tomasz Mościcki, "Eugeniusz Bodo," November 2010, Culture.pl., March 2017, https://culture.pl/en/artist/eugeniusz-bodo; and Tomasz Mościcki, "Adolf Dymsza," trans. Patryk Grabowski, Culture.pl., August 2018, https://culture.pl/pl/tworca/adolf-dymsza.

44 Juliette Bretan, "Henryk Wars," Culture.pl., August 2018, https://culture.pl/en/artist/henryk-wars.

45 Freud likely could draw weighty conclusions from the fact that in both *Is Lucyna a Girl?* and *Paweł and Gaweł* the protagonist, played by Bodo, uncovers the female disguise by opening her handbag.

46 See Holmgren, "How the Cabaret Went to War"; and Holmgren, "The Jews in the Band: The Anders Army's Special Troupes."

47 Bretan, "Henryk Wars." Throughout his career, The King of Jazz never abandoned his veneration of Karol Szymanowski (1882–1937), the preeminent classical Polish composer of modernist Young Poland.

him to the status of a cultural icon. Readers of *Film* magazine in 1936 voted him King of Style owing to his sartorial fastidiousness.[48] Clearly, fans in the thirties had a penchant for bestowing regal titles on their favorites in the entertainment industry. Bodo's charisma, energy, and requisite skills rendered him the entertainment star par excellence of the 1930s, as made all too evident in *Bodo* (2016), a recent TV biopic that doubles as a musical. Even the lamentable casting of the stolid Tomasz Schuchardt as the quicksilver titular protagonist cannot disguise the multifaceted talent and significance of Bodo in Polish cabaret and film.[49] His gifts in song and dance (honed in Qui Pro Quo), as well as his imaginative and daring ideas, culminated in the film that he scripted, *One Floor Up*, in which a cross-dressing scene—virtually an international commonplace of the genre in the interests of comedy and gender dynamics within this period—famously features him as a robust Mae West.[50] It anticipated Hollywood's humorous challenges to conformity, most engagingly and outrageously in Billy Wilder's inimitable *Some Like It Hot* (1959) and Stanisław Bareja's *Poszukiwany, poszukiwana* (Man/Woman wanted, 1972/3).[51] Unlike Waszyński, Wars, and other colleagues, the ambitious Bodo, tragically, did not live to develop a postwar career, for the Soviets murdered him in one of their labor camps in 1943 on trumped-up charges of espionage.[52]

For Dymsza, "the most important comic actor in Polish cinema" during that era,[53] Qui Pro Quo likewise served as basic training from 1925 to 1931, after which he joined the cabaret Banda (1931–1933).[54] Despite sundry setbacks to what is typically called his "climb to the top," he became the indispensable comic presence in numerous films, as well as the collaborator of Julian Tuwim (1894–1953), renowned iconoclastic poet with a Jewish background involved in cabaret who authored sketches written specifically for Dymsza. Prior to World War II, Dymsza appeared in twenty-eight film roles, five of them in 1930

---

48 Anna Sieradzka, *Tysiąc lat ubiorów w Polsce* (Warsaw: Arkady, 2003).

49 For a brief but vivid summary of Bodo's achievements, see Mościcki, "Eugeniusz Bodo."

50 As illustrated in *Is Lucyna a Girl* and *Paweł and Gaweł*, women more frequently donned the personae of men or of male adolescents than vice versa.

51 Predictably, *Some Like It Hot* was released without the approval of the Production Code (Hays Code), withheld owing to the plot's hilarious play with crossdressing (a typical feature of earlier film musicals) and homosexuality. Its critical and box-office success was one of the many films (notably by Alfred Hitchcock and Otto Preminger) that weakened the Code and contributed to its elimination in the sixties.

52 Bodo's life ended when the Soviets arrested him and sent him to a camp as an enemy of the people, where they killed him—one of the ways Soviets demonstrated their advertised "friendship of peoples" (*druzhba narodov*).

53 Ford and Hammond, *Polish Film: A Twentieth-Century History*, 78.

54 Mościcki, "Eugeniusz Bodo."

alone, for his skills as a singer and versatile comic endowed with acrobatic skills kept him in constant demand. Two of his most well-received outings were with Bodo toward the end of the decade—in *Robert i Bertrand* (1938) and *Paweł i Gaweł* (1938). Though suspended in 1945 for failing to comply with the ban on theatrical performances in theaters administered by Germans, issued in 1940 by the Association of Polish Stage Artists (ZASP), Dymsza returned to the Warsaw stage in 1951 and starred in eight post-World War II films. Amazingly, in the comedy *Sprawa do załatwienia* (A matter to settle, 1953) he played eight different roles.[55] *Pan Dodek* (1970), his last film, comprised a pseudo-fictionalized account of his long career via clips from his earlier films, many of them musicals.

The top three Polish stars in a 1930s survey conducted among Poles in the United States reportedly named Bodo, Dymsza, and Grossówna the winners.[56] Trained in ballet by Bronisława Niżyńska, Grossówna became the prima ballerina and head of the Grand Theater in Poznań ballet, and performed in several cabarets, including Qui Pro Quo. In the space of four years, she starred in seventeen films, including *Paweł and Gaweł, Robert and Bertrand,* and the most lucrative early musical, *Forgotten Melody,* all released in 1938. Not only a remarkable dancer and fine actress, she also shone as a fighter in the struggle against the Nazis, active in the underground and commanding a women's section of a battalion in the Warsaw Uprising of 1944.[57] For her resistance she was interned in the Oberlagen prison camp (Stalag VI-C) in northwestern Germany. Liberated in April 1945 along with other prisoners, upon her return to Poland she became professionally associated in 1948 with the Syrena Theater and continued to appear in films—seven during the sixties—before retiring. A true survivor who never compromised, she graced the Polish stage and screen for four decades. As a condign tribute to her courage, a comics titled *Helena Grossówna. Nigdy nie trać nadziei* (Helena Grossówna. Hope eternal) saw publication in 2019.[58]

The onset of World War II and the invasion from both the West (the Nazis in 1939) and the East (Soviets shortly afterwards) not only foiled Grossówna's (and others') plans to sign contracts offered by Hollywood, but also curtailed Poland's vigorous screen activity. Foremost Polish *Kulturarbeiter,* many of them

---

55 Ibid.

56 Anna Legierska, "Prima Ballerinas, Soldiers & Hollywood Stars: Polish Dancers in the 20th Century," trans. W. F., April 2017, https://culture.pl/en/article/prima-ballerinas-soldiers-hollywood-stars-polish-dancers-of-the-20th-century.

57 Ibid.

58 The comics, with an introduction by Krzysztof Trojanowski, is available in English on the internet at *Helena Grossówna—Hope eternal,* https://issuu.com/kujawsko-pomorskie/docs/komiks_grossowna_ang_m.

Jewish, emigrated (Waszyński, Wars, Hanka Ordonówna, Feliks Konarski,[59] Fryderyk Járosy, Marian Hemar, Nora Ney, Zofia Terné, and many others) or perished in Soviet labor camps (Bodo). And the end, yet again, of an independent Poland coincided with the collapse of the country's film musical.

Screen Musical Famine under the Soviet Regime

In Soviet-era Polish film, musicals were rarer than snowfalls in spring. Despite the success of star-studded interwar musical comedies such as *Zapomniana melodia* (Forgotten melody, 1938), which evoked the Hollywood model, the genre never took off during the postwar era of state socialism—when Poland became the Polish People's Republic/PRL (1947–1989). Just how infrequently it enlivened screens may be deduced from the inventory compiled by Piotr Fortuna, which registers a total of seven musical comedies released from 1954 through the eighties. In common with the formula instituted by Hollywood, they all structured their narratives around the mishaps and misunderstandings that hindered a romantic young couple's happiness until the eventual but wholly predictable resolution culminating in their union: Leonard Buczkowski's *Przygoda na Mariensztacie* (An adventure at Marienstadt, 1954), Stanisław Bareja's *Żona dla Australijczyka* (A wife for an Australian, 1964), *Małżeństwo z rozsądku* (A marriage of convenience, 1966), Jerzy Passendorfer's *Mocne uderzenie* (Big beat, 1966/7), Bareja's *Przygoda z piosenką* (Adventure with a song, 1968/9), Janusz Rzeszewski and Mieczysław Jahoda's *Hallo Szpicbródka czyli ostatni występ króla kasiarzy* (Hallo, Fred the Beard, or The final performance of the king of safebreakers, 1978), and Janusz Rzeszewski's *Lata dwudzieste, lata trzydzieste* (The twenties, the thirties, 1983). Although Fortuna's list is incomplete,[60] that Rzeszewski (1930–2007) and Bareja (1929–1987) alone account for five of the named seven rarities leaves no doubt that directors had scant interest in the genre. Post-World War II audiences' enthusiasm for musical comedies and popular entertainment, however, may be inferred from the enormous crowds that flocked to *Adventure at Marienstadt*, which exceeded the viewership for Andrzej Wajda's *Popiół i diament* (Ashes and diamonds, 1958), the

---

59 Konarski penned the lyrics of the most famous Polish World War II song—the lasting hit "Czerwone Maki na Monte Cassino" ("Red poppies in Monte Cassino").

60 For a discussion of additional musicals, see Ewa Mazierska, *Polish Popular Music on Screen* (Cham: Palgrave Macmillan, 2020), 57–111.

latter's iconic status as the quintessential Polish film—the Holy Grail of national cinema—notwithstanding.

Partly because Buczkowski's *Adventure at Marienstadt* showcases the triumph of Warsaw's reconstruction under the Soviets, features Stakhanovites as the two individuals in the obligatory roles of the genre's romantic duo, and expresses enthusiasm for the "new order," Polish scholars automatically have folded Bareja's three musical comedies of the sixties into the same ideological pigeonhole. That sloppiness doubtless stems from commentators' dismissal of musical comedies as unworthy of meticulous attention. Yet, as chapter two argues, Bareja's *Marriage of Convenience* may be read profitably as an ironic riposte to Buczkowski's film, for it comprises a sophisticated satire on official Soviet propaganda that ridicules not only bombastic Soviet claims of a socialist utopia but also challenges several of the generic conventions that by the sixties had undergone modifications in Hollywood itself. Deriding official slogans about urban progress, Bareja posits independent art as the sole worthwhile cultural value in a society devalued by authoritarian Soviet imposition. As Anthony Lane observed, echoing Stanley Cavell, "it is comedy, rather than tragedy, that is the proper playground for philosophical suggestion"[61]—an aperçu repeatedly confirmed by Lubitsch's comedies.

At approximately the same time the focus on jazz in Passendorfer's *Big Beat* paralleled American cinema's discovery of rock'n'roll in the late fifties. Jazz as a mode of resistance to officialdom (that is, Soviet oversight) played an enormous role in Polish film of this period, leading to a cult of jazz composer and pianist Krzysztof Komeda (1931–1969), perceived as its ultimate embodiment and practitioner. He was responsible for the score in Roman Polański's *Nóż w wodzie* (Knife in the water, 1962), the director's Oscar-nominated debut, which introduced not only a new cinematic vision but also a new sound, one deemed rebellious, modern, and sophisticated.[62] Komeda would go on to supply the scores for three additional Polanski films in the West, and more than twenty by directors such as Jerzy Skolimowski, Andrzej Wajda, and many others in Europe and the United States. A much lesser film than *Knife in the Water, The Big Beat* relied on a script by Ludwik Starski (1902–1984),[63] screenwriter for the best-known musical comedies of the thirties, which accounts for the sense of the film as a musty

---

61 Anthony Lane, "The Uncanny Valley of *I'm Your Man*," *The New Yorker*, September 17, 2021, https://www.newyorker.com/magazine/2021/09/27/the-uncanny-valley-of-im-your-man.

62 In the West, Komeda is perhaps best remembered for his haunting "Rosemary's Lullaby," created for Polański's *Rosemary's Baby*.

63 Starski, however, is not mentioned in the credits. See "Mocne Uderzenie," Film Polski, September 7, 2022, https://filmpolski.pl/fp/index.php?film=121673.

throwback to the earlier period (mistaken identity, romantic competition for the protagonist, and so on). And the music by Andrzej Zieliński and Jerzy Milian lacks the exciting energy of western rock and of arrangements by Komeda, though the choreography in a number danced by a sizable group toward the film's end has both excellent rhythm and effective dynamism.[64] Ultimately, however, *Big Beat* did little for either rock or jazz—or film, for that matter.

In unexpected ways not recognized by the critical literature, it was Bareja's *Marriage of Convenience* that foreshadowed the genre's possibilities once freed from the stranglehold of the Soviet regime. It suggested ways in which the genre could synthesize song and dance with sociopolitical critique so as to engage audiences and prompt them to think about the society in which they lived. Several decades later the dissolution of the Soviet Union and Poland's recovered independence inaugurated the screen musical's dramatic metamorphosis in the new millennium, attracting the attention of Hollywood and winning several international awards.

Exploding Traditions in New Polish Film Musicals

While the film musical, unlike comedy and melodrama, remains a rarity on Polish screens, at least two recent examples of the genre have created a stir, and deservedly so, because of their striking originality. Both films completely overturn the defining features adduced by Altman, Feuer, and, to some extent, Dyer, for they are neither escapist nor celebratory. After his Oscar-winning retrospective *Ida* (2013) Paweł Pawlikowski returned to black-and-white photography for his auteurish *Zimna wojna* (Cold War, 2018)—a musical quite unlike any other. With a narrative that traces the increasingly tragic peregrinations of what chapter three calls "deterritorialized" Poles who have no place to call home anywhere in the world during the political Cold War, the film ends in their suicide within, of all places, a ruined Russian Orthodox church. Although its protagonists—a musician and a versatile singer—fulfill the generic function of a romantic couple, they are constantly separated by the political curtain in addition to their own emotional cold war, and the pleasure of music for audiences for the most part is secondary, if not irrelevant, in the film. Nor is a happy ending amid an integrated community that participates in the couple's final union ever remotely considered as a likelihood. Indeed, the couple die in isolation, hoping to find

64 For an analysis of the film and its lack of credibility, see Mazierska, *Polish Popular Music on Screen*, 85–87.

some form of peace "on the other side." Their loss of life is simply the final act in a narrative of dwindling options and repeated losses—of innocence, country, home, and professional fulfillment. And that trajectory finds expression in the film's major song, performed in diverse venues by the film's strong-willed, gifted heroine. Pawlikowski alters the genre primarily by framing the film in a tragic sociopolitical context, compactly narrativizing Poles' inability to find a "home" in either East or West. The inclusion, however brief, of the male protagonist's stint in a Soviet labor camp and the heroine's pragmatic marriages to other men chart the distance between the upbeat Hollywood musical and its contemporary Polish variant, which casts the genre's romantic couple as the victims and playthings of Poland's disastrous modern history.

Agnieszka Smoczyńska's debut, the colorful film musical *Córki dancingu* (known in English as *The Lure*, 2015), shares little with *Cold War* apart from its non-alignment with Hollywood generic conventions and its political orientation, though the politics it investigates is that of gender. Like many hybrids, *The Lure* is invigorated by its fusion of the musical with horror and folklore, plus a dash of vampirism (see chapter four). Its conclusion shares the bleakness of *Cold War*: it kills off the romantic couple who, contrary to American romantic treatments of the mermaid's terrestrial love, cannot reconcile their profound differences, dramatizes the destruction of at least two familial ties, lacks all sense of community, and offers no hope for the future. As the director acknowledged, Poland's fascination with disco in the eighties and Fosse's musicals, not early Hollywood fare, inspired her. While the film cites several popular American numbers, its hybridity and political dimension distance it from American screen hits in the film genre, preparing the way for future attempts at free-wheeling musicals by Polish directors matching Smoczyńska's self-assured independence.

Russian Sound and Sound Bites in Stalin's Thirties

The Soviet Union shared Poland's initially mixed response to sound. Undoubtedly the most famous reaction to audio was articulated in a document signed by three prominent directors, two of whom in the twenties had pioneered the theory of montage on the basis of pure visuality: Sergei Eisenstein, Vsevolod Pudovkin, and Grigorii Aleksandrov, who had worked with Eisenstein. Their collective notice (*zaiavka*), published in *Zhizn' iskusstva* on August 5, 1928, claimed to welcome sound, but averred that film was an artistic medium of visual images organized by montage; sound, instead of superfluously "repeating" the image, should serve a "contrapuntal" [sic] function within the overarching principle of montage.[65] Composer/conductor Vladimir Messman (1898–1972) pointed out that the three directors misunderstood the concept of musical counterpoint and that sound film would require directors to work jointly with composers,[66] while documentarian Esfir' Shub in *Kino* (1929) welcomed the new invention and urged Soviet technicians to work on the requisite technology so that directors and cameramen could learn its usage from them.[67] When Pudovkin returned to the issue shortly thereafter, he echoed Eisenstein's concept of "collision" within montage and explicitly advocated a kindred collision of sound and image.[68] The debate dragged on, with the participation of Viktor Shklovsky, Yuri Tynianov, Boris Shumiatskii (head of the film industry from 1930–1937), and others as the contributors essentially tried to rationalize the primacy of their specializations, even after the Soviet adoption of sound became a reality.

In 1931, the first bona fide full-length talkie, Nikolai Ekk's *Putevka v zhizn'* (Road to life), hit the screens,[69] earning an unprecedented fifteen million rubles.[70] That year also saw the release of Grigorii Kozintsev and Leonid Trauberg's appreciably less profitable yet popular sound film *Odna* (Alone)—initially planned as a silent—with orchestral music by Dmitrii Shostakovich. Yet studios went on making silent films until 1935[71] owing to the dearth of sound projectors in cinemas across the country: in mid-1931 only one movie theater had the capacity to play sound films, and in 1933 only 300 of the 32,000 projectors were able to do so. By 1938, silent projectors still outnumbered those equipped with sound.[72] An inadequate technological infrastructure exacerbated whatever apprehensions film personnel may have harbored about the deleterious consequences of the new technology. And Soviets' practice of making silent versions of sound films until decade's end was "without parallel in other film-producing

---

65 Richard Taylor and Ian Christie, eds., *The Film Factory: Russian and Soviet Cinema in Documents, 1896–1939* (London and New York: Routledge, 1988), 234–235.

66 Messman's objection was particularly relevant for musical comedies, which would dominate audience preferences in the thirties.

67 Ibid., 235–237, 271.

68 Ibid., 264–267.

69 The advent of sound in the Soviet Union receives a thorough, book-length treatment in Lilya Kaganovsky, *The Voice of Technology: Soviet Cinema's Transition to Sound, 1928–1935* (Bloomington: Indiana University Press, 2018).

70 Denise J. Youngblood, *Movies for the Masses: Popular Cinema and Soviet Society in the 1920s* (Cambridge: Cambridge University Press, 1992), 173.

71 Peter Kenez specifies the year 1936 (Peter Kenez, *Cinema and Soviet Society, 1917–1953* [Cambridge: Cambridge University Press, 1992], 138).

72 Ibid., 137.

European countries."[73] That the partial transition to sound coincided with a steady intensification of censorship explains why the mid-thirties witnessed a significant decline in the number of films produced, from 109 in 1928 to forty-three in 1935, forty-six in 1936, and twenty-four in 1937.[74]

Opinions regarding sound may have varied, but the film musical inarguably was manna from heaven for the Soviet regime. As the state struggled to negotiate among the various classes of a huge, ethnically diverse population in a sprawling empire, with more than forty percent of citizens still mired in illiteracy in the late twenties, a genre focused on the body's infectious mobility and emphasizing collectivity, unanimity, and, above all, utopia was the ideal propaganda tool to disseminate the "voice of state power" (see chapter six) in an accessible form. Stalin—an apparently fine singer and devotee of opera—quickly grasped how musical comedies as mass entertainment could reinforce the official vision of the Soviet Union as a nation of contented, industrious citizens celebrating the values proclaimed by the Kremlin. Exhorted to create "movies for the millions"[75] according to the principles of Socialist Realism instituted in 1934, astute directors abandoned the aesthetic experimentations of the 1920s, which audiences had failed to appreciate in their preference for American imports, and turned to what would become "the greatest favorite with Soviet moviegoers in the late 1930s"—the musical.[76]

Beginning in 1934, a handful of musicals appeared in rapid succession, most notably Igor' Savchenko's kolkhoz comedy *Garmon'* (The accordion, 1934) and Boris Barnet's *U samogo sinego moria* (By the bluest of seas, 1936). As Richard Taylor phrased it, *The Accordion* illustrates how "even popular song is a legitimate weapon in the struggle against enemies of the people, saboteurs, and wreckers."[77] Savchenko's film pioneered the popularity of the Russian accordion as a transportable emblem of national identity, which became a staple of Soviet

---

73 Youngblood, *Movies for the Masses*, 172. For a detailed description of the impracticalities see Richard Taylor, "Boris Shumyatsky and the Soviet Cinema in the 1930s: Ideology as Mass Entertainment," *Historical Journal of Film, Radio and Television* 6, no. 1 (1986): 448.

74 Taylor, "Boris Shumyatsky and the Soviet Cinema in the 1930s," 60; and Kenez, *Cinema and Soviet Society, 1917–1953*, 134.

75 The phrase gained considerable traction after the articulation at the Party conference on cinema in March 1928 that movies should be "intelligible to the millions," which prompted debates about films' purpose, caught between the Scylla of entertainment and the Charybdis of political enlightenment (propaganda). See Taylor and Christie, *The Film Factory: Russian and Soviet Cinema in Documents 1896–1939*, 191–194.

76 Neya Zorkaya, *The Illustrated History of Soviet Cinema* (New York: Hippocrene Books, 1989), 159.

77 Richard Taylor, "Singing on the Steppes for Stalin: Ivan Pyr'ev and the Kolkhoz Musical in Soviet Cinema," *Slavic Review* 58, no. 1 (Spring 1999): 146.

cinema, in both peace and war—a ubiquity that *Stiliagi* (Hipsters, 2008), one of the few post-Soviet musicals, resuscitates. But the genre only took flight when two directors adopted and sovietized the Hollywood formula in a string of movies that became classics of the Stalinist era: Grigorii Aleksandrov (1903–1983) and Ivan Pyr'ev (1901–1968). Regardless of the fundamental ideological differences between the governments of the Soviet Union and the United States, during the blighted decade the popular tastes of the two nations converged.

Tuneful Travels and Tractors amid Mass Murder

After his visit with Eisenstein to the stronghold of capitalism, the adroit Aleksandrov understood exactly how to adjust the American musical to the needs of Soviet audiences and the regime's priorities. With Stalin's approval and with Liubov' Orlova as the singing star in all his major musicals, his increasingly politicized and decreasingly comic screen narratives became the period's blockbusters: *Veselye rebiata* (Jolly fellows or Happy guys, 1934), *Tsirk* (Circus, 1936), *Volga-Volga* (1938), and *Svetlyi put'* (The radiant path, 1940). Loaded with infectious music composed by Isaak Dunaevskii (1900–1955) to lyrics by Vasilii Lebedev-Kumach (1898–1949), they conceived of the capital as the radiant sun to which all Soviets (and in *Circus*, even Americans escaping their country's racism) allegedly aspired, since the adulated source of enlightenment, wisdom, and happiness was Stalin, not coincidentally the nation's primary exterminator and chief enthusiast of the genre.[78] Lilting and exuberant melodies, waltzes, marches, and elements of jazz glorifying the life of Soviet citizens—even as the Great Terror (*ezhovshchina*) of 1937–1938 claimed countless victims—drew viewers to Aleksandrov's success-story scenarios, which blended tuneful numbers with familiar bodily comic devices borrowed from slapstick, vaudeville, and the circus.[79] In Altman's taxonomy, those comedies belonged to the fairy-tale subgenre of musicals (with Orlova incarnating variations on

78 For an impeccably researched analysis of Aleksandrov's films, career, and relevance in the era's political-historical context, see Rimgalia Salys, *The Musical Comedy Films of Grigorii Aleksandrov: Laughing Matters* (Bristol: Intellect, 2009).

79 Because jazz was favored by some of the political elite, it was more or less accepted by the Soviet regime, though its American origins accounted for the vagaries in its fate over decades. Associated with novelty and youth, it regularly encountered acidulous criticism by older members of the cultural establishment. For an excellent, comprehensive survey of jazz in the Soviet Union, see the monograph by Starr, which contains an informative chapter on Utesov and reactions to *Jolly Fellows* (Frederick S. Starr, *Red and Hot: The Fate of Jazz in the Soviet Union* [New York: Limelight Editions, 1985], 130–156).

Cinderella), which, in the words of Neia Zorkaia, showed humble workers' "road to glory,"[80] culminating in arrival at some of the capital's most famous landmarks: the Bolshoi Theater in *Jolly Fellows,* the Kremlin, VDNKh (All-Union Agricultural Exhibition), and the skies in *Radiant Path.*[81]

Stalin, who personally monitored the film industry to ensure that the masses were entertained and convinced of the Soviet Union's supremacy as a Panglossian "best of all possible worlds," even suggested to Aleksandrov the title of *Radiant Path* as a trope for the radiant future toward which the Soviet Union was advancing, just as later he had Pyr'ev replace the title of his comedy *Veselaia iarmarka* (The jolly fair) with *Kubanskie kazaki* (Cossacks of the Kuban'), possibly to avoid the implication of frivolity through iteration.[82] Vladimir Nil'sen (1906–1938), the versatile cameraman for *Jolly Fellows, Circus,* and *Volga-Volga,* used copious tracking shots that caught protagonists' bodies in constant motion. Dynamism, humor, and seductive melodies proved irresistible to a public eager for relief from everyday trials. Just as Americans during the Depression found psychological relief in movie theaters, so Russians in the lethal thirties flocked to tuneful onscreen fairy tales of Soviet joy and upward mobility. And though the number of films released in the twenties shrank dramatically in the thirties, the number of sold tickets increased, partly because some viewers apparently went to see the same movie repeatedly.[83]

As Wolfgang Thiel has noted, the heterogeneous music in these comedies admixed elements from revue, operetta, and Viennese waltzes with Russian urban songs, *chastushki,* and modified jazz, while relying on the singing talents of Orlova, a graduate from the realm of operetta. The comedies also incorporated classical music, whether by Chopin, Liszt, or Verdi, for comic effect. In a programmatic number in *Jolly Fellows,* the jazzman Leonid Utesov (as the shepherd Kostia, no less) encapsulates the appeal of the musical in a *mise en abyme* when he sings the song "Nam pesnia stroit' i zhit' pomogaet" ("A song helps us to live and laugh . . . We can sing and laugh like children amid the existing struggle and ongoing work").[84] As in the United States and Poland, the

---

80 Zorkaya, *The Illustrated History of Soviet Cinema,* 161.

81 On the indivisibility of cinematography and ideology in *The Radiant Path,* see Anna Wexler Katsnelson, "The Tramp in a Skirt: Laboring the Radiant Path," *Slavic Review* 70, no. 2 (2011): 256–258.

82 After all, how much titular jolliness did the Soviet screen need? Aleksandrov's *Jolly Fellows* already had established the population's cheerful laughter.

83 Kenez, *Cinema and Soviet Society, 1917–1953,* 133.

84 For the lyrics in Russian, see "Tekst pesni Leonid Utesov—Nam pesnia stroit' i zhit' pomogaet," Alllyr, https://alllyr.ru/lyrics/song/83812-leonid-utesov-nam-pesnya-stroit-i-zhit-pomogaet/.

symbiosis between cinema and the recording industry facilitated the transfer of songs in screen musicals onto records, and the film's song "Kak mnogo devushek khoroshikh" ("Such a lot of nice/pretty girls") became an independent mega-hit. Throughout Aleksandrov's musical comedies zestful demilitarized marches and waltz rhythms carried along not only the screen characters but also audiences susceptible to catchy tunes.[85] Music served both comic and—especially in the marches—ideological functions, the lyrics promoting Soviet propaganda and establishing a class hierarchy, as classical music (associated with bourgeois tastes) either became "lowered" through slapstick gags or trumped by popular songs of "the people." Yet, true to the generic model, endings invariably embraced cheerful reconciliation of all elements. In short, Aleksandrov and his talented team knew precisely what would capture the affection of the "millions" tirelessly invoked in pronouncements and critical publications during the thirties.[86]

Whereas Aleksandrov consistently favored the urban milieu, Pyr'ev's province was the countryside. Otherwise, both opted for a kindred fusion of official propaganda and escapist fantasy, the two indistinguishable in Pyr'ev's "tractor musicals," which glossed over the ravages of agricultural collectivization—the official depredations of private farms to ensure food supplies for cities and Stalin's industrial projects. Launched with the First Five-Year Plan of 1928 and lasting until 1937, at its worst and most intensive it peaked in 1929–1933. Pyr'ev assumed the role of the radiant future's secular John the Baptist, inasmuch as his musicals projected not the empirical conditions on collective farms, but a future bucolic utopia. Contemporary reality had no place in Pyr'ev's musicals, though the verisimilitude of his *mise en scène* testified to his knowledge of agriculture and folk culture. His musicals generally adhered to the genre's syntax: the proliferation of songs performed individually and in chorus, rivalry and misunderstandings temporarily thwarting the union of a romantic couple, and the elimination of conflicts at a festive conclusion: *Traktoristy* (Tractor drivers, 1939), *Svinarka i pastukh* (The swineherdess and the shepherd, 1941), and *Kubanskie kazaki* (Cossacks of the Kuban', 1947), among others.[87]

Pyr'ev wisely followed Aleksandrov's example by relying on the combined talent of Dunaevksii and Lebedev-Kumach for the music in his *Bogataia nevesta*

---

85 Wolfgang Thiel, "The Musical Film Comedy, or, 'Be Embraced, Millions,'" *East European Film Bulletin* 110 (December 2020), https://eefb.org/retrospectives/motivic-merrymaking-in-the-musical-films-of-grigori-aleksandrov-and-ivan-pyryev/?pdf=7847.

86 Richard Taylor offers a "blow by blow" summary of the plot accompanied by some useful commentary in his "Veselye rebiata: The Happy Guys," in *The Cinema of Russia and the Former Soviet Union*, ed. Birgit Beumers (London and New York: Wallflower Press, 2007), 79–87.

87 For an overview of Pyr'ev's screen career see Taylor, "Singing on the Steppes for Stalin."

(The rich bride, 1937). Dunaevskii also provided the music for *Cossacks of the Kuban'*, with lyrics, however, by various hands. Some of the songs entered the repertoire of independent hits, still sung to this day (see chapter five). Tikhon Khrennikov (1913–2007), the composer for *The Swineherdess and the Shepherd,* lacked comparable creative abilities. He would become the head of the Union of Soviet Composers (1948–1981), with Andrei Zhdanov's endorsement, just as the purging of "undesirable" forces in music got under way (*zhdanovshchina*). Khrennikov's vilification of Sergei Prokofiev, Dmitrii Shostakovich, and Aram Khachaturian accorded with his desire to please the powers that be and simultaneously to promote the "accessible" music of the sort typified by his own harmless folkish compositions. Although his goal coincided with those of Pyr'ev, whose musicals reassured rural viewers that future collective farms would comprise a paradisial environment where the entire population sang, smiled, and praised the Soviet Union as a haven of milk and honey, even amid starvation, World War II, and the hardships of its aftermath, Khrennikov's contributions did little to construct an aural paradise on a par with Pyr'ev's visuals.

It seems likely that a combination of factors—Shumiatskii's failure to revitalize the film industry in conformity with his unrealistic plans, the paucity of new films, the expensive investment in those that remained uncompleted, and the debacle of his overly ambitious Soviet Hollywood project (Cine-City) in the Crimea, as well as his complaints to Stalin—brought about his downfall.[88] Inability to achieve desired results in any industry in the late thirties and forties, when only success was acceptable to Stalin as a testament to his omnipotent image, could incur severe penalties.[89] Both Shumiatskii and the gifted cinematographer Nil'sen, so influential in the early thirties, were executed in 1938 during the purge that eliminated various members of the film industry, despite their allegiance to the state. With a fine command of understatement, Zorkaia refers to Pyr'ev's penchant for hyperbole,[90] but in fact his popular musicals simply depicted a pastoral Eden that utterly ignored the tragedy of death, dearth, and brutality on the collective farms; they followed the fairy-tale formula of "*skazano, sdelano,*" inasmuch as they were generated by Stalin's enunciations as

---

88 Taylor, "Boris Shumyatsky and the Soviet Cinema in the 1930s: Ideology as Mass Entertainment," 60.

89 For an analogous phenomenon in art, see Helena Goscilo, "Luxuriating in Lack: Plenitude and Consuming Happiness in Soviet Paintings and Posters, 1930s–1953," in *Petrified Utopia*, ed. Marina Balina and Evgeny Dobrenko (London and New York: Anthem Press, 2009), 53–79, 268–273. Given Stalin's paranoia, the immediate reason for numerous executions during this era is almost impossible to establish.

90 Zorkaya, *The Illustrated History of Soviet Cinema*, 163.

diktats. Once Stalin proclaimed a false reality, *Kulturarbeiter* realizing what was at stake raced to depict it on page or screen, and Pyr'ev numbered among the obedient. What astounds one about his films, which outstrip the imagination behind futuristic sci-fi movies, is that naïve audiences credited their empirical accuracy,[91] as, reportedly, did Stalin, who was ignorant of real conditions in the countryside, from which he remained remote, gleaning his information from films.[92] Even more remarkably, Pyr'ev, as chapter five contends, apparently had unflagging faith in the veracity of his screen vision as a glimpse into the glorious Soviet future. That viewers appreciated melodious reassurance onscreen, especially in the aftermath of World War II, may be deduced from the fact that his *Cossacks of the Kuban'* and Aleksandrov's *Vesna* (Spring) proved two of the biggest box office hits of 1947.

The Short Goodbye: The Demise of the Model

While musical comedy did not die together with Stalin in 1953, it went into recession; its status diminished irreversibly during the Khrushchev and Brezhnev eras. Of the various forays into the genre in the fifties and sixties, few were memorable other than perhaps those by a recognized master of Soviet comedy, El'dar Riazanov (1927–2015): *Karnaval'naia noch'* (Carnival night, 1956) and *Gusarskaia ballada* (A hussar ballad, 1962).[93] Released during the Thaw, both have a retrospective dimension: the latter idiosyncratically so, for it adapts Nadezhda Durova's memoirs about the Napoleonic War, *Zapiski kavalerist-devitsy* (The cavalry maiden, 1836), mediated by Aleksandr Gladkov's (1912–1976) first play, *Davnym-davno* (A long time ago, 1940), subtitled

---

91 Ibid., 159.

92 Khrushchev in his speech at the Twentieth Congress of the Communist Party (February 1956) was the first to expose Stalin's complete ignorance of the countryside from January 1928 onwards—and ever since historians have echoed that criticism (Jay Leyda, *KINO: A History of the Russian and Soviet Film* [Princeton: Princeton University Press, 1983], 400). For the disappearance of Nil'sen, see ibid., 344.

93 The musical comedy of this period emphasized situational comedy at the expense of spectacle and song-and-dance numbers, as illustrated by Andrei Tutyshkin's *Svad'ba v Malinovke* (Wedding in Malinovka, 1967) and *Shel'menko-denshchik* (Shel'menko the orderly, 1971). Their historical settings sooner link them to the theatrical operetta than to the typical film musical. Georgii Shengelaia's Georgian *Melodii Veriiskogo kvartala* (Melodies of the Veriiskii quarter, 1973), based on old Georgian vaudevilles and plays, in its lively songs and exuberant dancing comes closer to the Hollywood musical. See "Soviet Comedy," Wisconsin Center for Film and Theater Research, https://wcftr.commarts.wisc.edu/exhibits/rzhevsky-collection-soviet-films/soviet-comedy.

A Heroic Comedy in Verse in Four Acts. Conceived to commemorate the 150th anniversary of the Battle of Borodino, with music by Khrennikov, the film for much of its dialogue adopts Gladkov's verses, favors light operettish cadences, and generally observes the conventions of musical comedy.[94] Despite or because of its rather old-fashioned style and broad humor, it won favor with the public, attracting forty-nine million viewers.[95]

By contrast, *Carnival Night*—Riazanov's Pyr'ev-mentored first feature, with singer Liudmila Gurchenko's (1936–2011) debut in the major female role of Lena, which catapulted her to fame overnight—is retrospective in another sense, inasmuch as it may be viewed profitably as a remake of Aleksandrov's *Volga-Volga*. Chapter six examines it as such, contending that Riazanov's musical comedy decrowns its predecessor.[96] The most lucrative film of 1956, with music by Anatolii Lepin (1907–1984), *Carnival Night* doubles as a musical and a New Year's Eve film, a peculiarly Russian/Soviet genre repeatedly aired on TV on New Year's Eve, with Riazanov's *Ironiia sud'by* (The irony of fate, 1976) renowned as the exemplar of the genre. The music of *Carnival Night* benefited from the contribution by the jazz band under the leadership of Eddie Rosner, the trumpeter known as The Polish Louis Armstrong, who earlier languished in Kolyma after his arrest in 1946.[97] The twenty-one-year-old Gurchenko sang only two songs, "Five Minutes" and "Song of Love with a Boy," but completely won over viewers and instantly became one of the most sought-after Soviet singers. To capitalize on her acclaim, Aleksandr Faintsimmer cast her in his musical *Devushka s gitaroi* (Girl with a guitar, 1958). Her success with the public, however, clashed with official disapproval of her "western" style, which may account for the film's limited distribution and box-office failure.

The vogue for mass songs was over, whereas film musicals for children steadily gained currency: *Novogodnie prikliucheniia Mashi i Viti* (The New Year

---

94 The persona of the crude, intellectually challenged male lead, Lieutenant Rzhevskii, played by Iurii Iakovlev, generated countless *anekdoty* (jokes).

95 Alexander Prokhorov, "Cinema of Attractions versus Narrative Cinema: Leonid Gaidai's Comedies and El'dar Riazanov's Satires of the 1960s," *Slavic Review* 62, no. 3 (Fall 2003): 456.

96 In their excellent monograph, Alexander and Elena Prokhorov designate *Carnival Night* a remake and contextualize it within Riazanov's general predilection for parodying genre conventions of both earlier Soviet and American movies. See Alexander Prokhorov and Elena Prokhorova, *Film and Television Genres of the Late Soviet Era* (New York and London: Bloomsbury, 2017), 117. In a somewhat self-contradictory article inspired by Bakhtin's theory of carnival, Evgeny Dobrenko sees *Carnival Night* as a continuation of *Volga-Volga*, yet dissimilar (Evgeny Dobrenko, "Soviet Comedy Film: or, the Carnival of Authority," *Discourse* 17, no. 3 [Spring 1995]: 49–57).

97 For a fascinating account of Rosner's musical life, see Starr, *Red and Hot: The Fate of Jazz in the Soviet Union*, 194–203, 214–215, 225.

adventures of Masha and Vitia, directed by Igor' Usov and Gennadii Kazanskii, 1975), Mikhail Iuzovskii's *Posle dozhdichka v chetverg* (After the rain, on Thursday, 1985). Some of the most popular musicals appeared on television, as, for instance, *Pro krasnuiu shapochku* (About Little Red Riding Hood, directed by Leonid Nechaev, 1977) and the classic animation *Prikliucheniia Buratino* (Buratino's adventures, directed by Aleksei Nechaev). Adventure as both motif and structural principle characterized many of the offerings, in which fantasy and fairy tales figured prominently. And animations such as the delightfully original *Dereza* (directed by Aleksandr Davydov, 1985) received international recognition.

Late Stagnation under Brezhnev changed the configuration of film musicals for adults, shifting the focus from the masses to the talented individual in the biopic. As Vladimir Sorokin pointed out in an interview, "[I]n the ironic seventies . . . nobody believed in Communism at all anymore."[98] Traditional Soviet musical comedies still appeared, such as Tat'iana Lioznova's *Karnaval* (Carnival, 1981), in which Irina Murav'eva retraced Orlova's formulaic journey from the provinces to Moscow—a progression also familiar from Murav'eva's role of Liudmila in Vladimir Men'shov's (1939–2021) Oscar-winning *Moskva slezam ne verit* (Moscow doesn't believe in tears, 1979). Increasingly, however, the genre favored other directions and itineraries.

My iz dzhaza (We're from jazz, 1983),[99] the cinematic debut of Karen Shakhnazarov (b. 1952), proved somewhat iconoclastic and augured a concern with youth that would become central during the Gorbachev years.[100] Once again opting for a retrospective temporal setting—the 1920s—it mined the identification of youth with jazz as it was being introduced to the Soviet Union while simultaneously being anathematized by embattled conservatives. Just as later in *Stiliagi* (Hipsters, 2008), vibrant colors marked the proponents of jazz, contrasting with the more nondescript appearance of its detractors.[101] While Mark Minkov (1944–2012) composed the songs and Anatolii Kroll (b. 1943) conducted the Sovremennik orchestra as well as playing a piano

98 Vladimir Sorokin, "Vladimir Sorokin on Supernatural Encounters," interview with Deborah Treisman, *The New Yorker*, October 4, 2021.

99 The title most often was translated as *Jazzman* or *Jazzmen*, which lost its identity (whether intended or not) as a riposte to Efim Dzigan's *We're from Kronstadt* (1936), a film that celebrated the early Communist, not the musical, struggle.

100 Anna Lawton, *Kinoglasnost: Soviet Cinema in Our Time* (Cambridge: Cambridge University Press, 1992), 181–195.

101 Herbert Eagle. "Socialist Realism and American Genre Film: The Mixing of Codes in *Jazzman*," in *The Red Screen: Politics, Society, Art in Soviet Russia*, ed. Anna Lawton (London and New York: Routledge, 1992), 257.

solo, Shakhnazarov was clever enough to use archival recordings from the earlier period and to include stylizations that recalled thirties' musicals, especially *Jolly Fellows*. Released shortly before Mikhail Gorbachev's policy of perestroika (1985) and glasnost' (1986), the zany film not only received positive reviews in the West, but attracted a sizable domestic audience, no doubt because jazz was no longer perceived as a decadent capitalist invention.[102] And though Pavel Lungin's *Taxi Blues* (1990) was not a musical, it created a stir by its portrayal of a jazz saxophonist, accurately connecting jazz with both Black Americans and talented Jewish musicians while dramatizing his conflict with an unreconstructed Soviet proletarian.

Late Stagnation, as chapter seven maintains, witnessed the rise of two pop divas—Alla Pugacheva and Sofia Rotaru—as the stars of biopics that modified the terms of the film musical by structuring the narrative around the female personality as singer and object of desire. Both women relied on their screen personae as a means of promoting their offscreen careers in recordings and revues. From the outset their rivalry operated on unequal terms: the unacknowledged Soviet policy of relegating all fourteen republics to an inferior periphery vis-à-vis the Russian republic accounted for the difficulties the Moldovan Rotaru encountered in competing with Pugacheva. And as early as in the screen musical *Zhenshchina, kotoraia poet* (The woman who sings, 1978), Pugacheva's independence and willfulness were in full display both onscreen and behind the scenes; they presaged the uncompromising qualities that would elevate her to the position of the premier Soviet female pop performer on stage and television. Endowed with a fine voice and the ability to color emotionally anything she sang, Pugacheva proved a star confined to both the Soviet Union and post-Soviet Russia, for her tours in the West left audiences bewildered at her media eminence on home terrain. Yet in *The Woman Who Sings* and elsewhere she transformed the image of the professional songstress along feminist lines, and though Russia remains indifferent, at best, to feminism, for decades it has championed a blowsy singer with vulgar taste who nonetheless incarnates agency and disciplined determination. More importantly, *The Woman Who Sings* paved the way for the Russian biopic variant of a film musical—which had flourished decades earlier in the United States in such movies as *The Great Caruso* (directed by Richard Thorpe, 1951), *The Glenn Miller Story* (directed by Anthony Mann, 1954), *The Benny*

---

102 The year 2013 witnessed the release of the sequel, *We're from Jazz 2*.

Goodman Story (directed by Valentine Davies, 1956), and *The Helen Morgan Story* (directed by Michael Curtiz, 1957).

Last Gasps or a New Life in the Post-Soviet Era?

As everywhere else, musicals in Russia during the new millennium have been few and, perhaps predictably, tend to portray a bygone era. Of the recollective musicals that have proved most successful it is worth singling out the prize-winning, engaging *Hipsters* (2008) by Valery Todorovsky (b. 1962). Like Smoczyńska in Poland, Todorovsky in an interview after the film's premiere observed that Russia lacked a tradition of the genre.[103] And, like her, he turned to an earlier era—that of the late fifties—the brief, liberating years of the Thaw, when censorship weakened, Stakhanovism evaporated, and men were no longer made of steel. *Hipsters* portrays the conflict between vestiges of Stalinist repression and the attempt by Soviet youth's counterculture to forge an individual identity through popular music and a Westernized dress code as a statement of rebellion against the status quo.[104] Unusually for a Russian film, music, camerawork, set design, and savvy use of color combined to convey the heady atmosphere of the period and its indebtedness to American sources, which *Hipsters* deftly thematized instead of trying to camouflage. Although the unexpected conclusion—after dispiriting betrayals, psychological breakdowns, and arrests—explicitly acknowledges Soviet youth's idealizing ignorance of real American life, it simultaneously portrays the protagonist's passionate faith in a Soviet appropriation of rock, jazz, and dance as a mode of Russian self-expression and inclusive resistance to official ideology. Contrary to expectations generated by a series of eventual disappointments, the film's conclusion (filmed, as was most of *Hipsters*, in Minsk) accords with the standard Hollywood musical.

While the plot contains a series of intriguing themes and characters, what ultimately emerges as the heartbeat of the film is popular music and dance—vividly conveyed in many dynamically shot, swiftly cascading sequences.

---

103 "Stiliagi (2008). Istoriia sozdaniia," Kinorium, accessed May 1, 2020, https://ru.kinorium.com/449067/info/.

104 On the politico-historical implications of the group's sartorial choices see Rimgalia Salys, "*Hipsters/Stiliagi*," in *The Contemporary Russian Cinema Reader*, ed. Rigmaila Salys (Boston: Academic Studies Press, 2019), 114–135. For the film's layered musical aspects see Lilya Kaganovsky, "Russian Rock on Soviet Bones," in *Sound, Speech, Music in Soviet and Post-Soviet Cinema*, ed. Lilya Kaganovsky and Masha Salazkina (Bloomington: Indiana University Press, 2014), 252–272.

Hipsters' political dimension allies it partly with less overtly political Polish musicals of the new millennium, though its abruptly optimistic finale seems somewhat forced and takes viewers back to an earlier time of mandatory reconciliation within the genre. Nonetheless, the spirited zest of the film recalls the kinetic energy of *Saturday Night Fever* and communicates the irresistible seduction of music and dance—moreover, not only among the young, given the male protagonist's extraordinary accordion-playing father (Sergei Garmash) and the privileged older diplomat (Oleg Iankovskii), who pleasurably recalls his youthful days of swing. Humor enhances the appeal of a film that addresses weighty issues—political repression, the Cold War, anti-Semitism, racism, and moral integrity—while demolishing the political claims of Aleksandrov's *Circus,* to establish its own place in the genre's Russian repertoire.[105]

Leto, a more recent (2018) retrospective screen musical by the stage and film director Kirill Serebrennikov (b. 1969), attracted considerable attention on home territory and debatably qualified as the cinematic event of the year.[106] It hybridizes the genre with the biopic or, perhaps more accurately, oscillates between the two—a strategy that prompted heated reactions in Russia. Since the advent of color, film musicals have depended on bright hues for projecting an atmosphere of joyful vivacity as an intrinsic component of entertainment. Serebrennikov's decision to shoot *Leto* in black and white likely suggested to some detractors—chiefly aging rock movers and shakers—that the weight leaned on the documentary/biographical aspects of the relationships that form the core of the film: the friendship between the cultural icon Viktor Tsoi (1962–1990) and musician Mike Naumenko (1955–1991), dubbed the "Dylan from Leningrad," and the interaction of both with the latter's wife, Natasha (b. 1960), caught between the two men. The film's reliance on her memoirs reinforced that viewpoint. Some of the objections to the film's "inaccuracies" betrayed carelessness, for the director forestalled such readings by repeatedly breaking down the fourth wall to address the audience with the disclaimer that various episodes never occurred. Combined with selections from concerts by Tsoi and performances by the groups Kino and Zveri, as well as covers of well-known Western hits, this deconstructive device, currently much in vogue, added to the film's youthful appeal, though its impact cannot carry the punch it did in one of cinema's earliest and most effective invocations of it—Tony Richardson's rollicking *Tom Jones* (1963). *Leto* also unobtrusively affords glimpses of the difficulties

105 Regarding *Hipsters'* intertextual engagement with *Circus,* see Salys, "*Hipsters/Stiliagi,*" 131–133.

106 For the soundtrack, composer Roman Bilyk won both a Cannes award and a Nika.

faced by young rockers vis-à-vis conservative older citizens as well as powerful politicized institutions, and the music makers' stratagems for overcoming them. As chapter eight argues, despite its downbeat conclusion,[107] the film by and large complies with the principles of the classic film musical, reworked, however, in a postmodernist vein.

The elimination of the fourth wall took an unexpected turn in one of the more anodyne post-Soviet releases in the genre that, atypically, engages contemporaneity: Zhora Kryzhovnikov's kitschy *Samyi luchshii den'* (The very best day, 2015). The highest-grossing film of 2015, this festival of stereotypes illustrates the tendency in recent Russian cinema to feed off prior films of appreciably better quality—in this instance, Riazanov's *Irony of Fate,* repeatedly recycled through remakes. Derivative and devoted to the cliché of Russian masculinity as inebriation, Kryzhovnikov's musical incorporates songs from the seventies to the 2010s and doubles as a New Year's Eve film. The slapstick comedy places the spineless male protagonist between two females and runs through the tired peripeteia of the typical musical, concluding with a wedding and a reconciliation of various decades in Russia's history couched in music of the relevant period. One of the few interesting aspects of this brew is the karaoke address to the viewers inviting them to join in the songs onscreen.[108] Otherwise, the film relies on their pleasure in recognizing familiar songs,[109] timeworn situations, and aging stars who have appeared in considerably finer screen fare: Inna Churikova (1943–2023), a stellar actress who graced numerous major Soviet films, and Elena Iakovleva (b. 1961), best known for her roles in *Intergirl* (1989) and the wildly popular TV series/police procedural, *Kamenskaia* (1999–2011). The film's box office profits indicate the lucrative rewards for directors seeking mass approval from unsophisticated audiences—a fact that doubtless will generate similar musical comedies in the future.

---

107 The early death of Tsoi, at the age of twenty-eight, and Naumenko, at thirty-six, resembled the youthful demise of numerous American rock singers, notably Kurt Cobain, Jimmi Hendrix, Janis Joplin, and Jim Morrison—all four at twenty-seven and the last three of a drug overdose.

108 Churikova appears in the thankless role of the protagonist's (Dmitrii Nagiev) mother, and actor cum singer Mikhail Boiarskii (b. 1949), famous for his swashbuckling roles onscreen, as his father. Rachel Stauffer's review kindly omits evaluation of the film. See Rachel Stauffer, "A Traditional Karaoke Musical: Zhora Kryzhovnikov's *Best Day Ever* (*Samyy luchshiy den'*)," *East European Film Bulletin* 110 (December 2020), https://eefb.org/perspectives/zhora-kryzhovnikovs-best-day-ever-samyy-luchshiy-den-2015/?pdf=7859.

109 Ibid.

Contents and Contentions

Philosophers from Plato through Schopenhauer to Nietzsche have proclaimed music the most direct, immediate, and affective communicator of all the arts, accentuating its capacity to articulate what words cannot express. With the addition of eloquent body movement, a romantic narrative, and an affirmation of happiness in the world, the film musical could not do otherwise than thrive when cinema acquired sound. From the outset associated with American popular culture, it instantly found universal favor with audiences. With time it established itself worldwide as a genre sufficiently flexible to accommodate satire, tragedy, and explicit political agendas. While Hollywood remains the most prolific producer of musicals, some of the most intriguing Slavic films over the last near-century have adapted the genre in unexpected and creative ways, particularly (though sparsely) in the new millennium.

Singing a Different Tune: The Slavic Film Musical in a Transnational Context reflects the diversity of musicals in Polish and Russian cinema, from the American-indebted 1930s (chapters one and five), through the more independent sixties (chapters two and six), seventies, and eighties (chapter seven), to the present day (chapters three, four, and eight). The temporal trajectory illustrates the genre's evolution from imitation to, finally, a dramatic departure from the generic Hollywood model. Although the volume's balance in favor of contemporary works may appear capricious, the dearth of musicals during sundry former eras and especially the innovative nature of the three recent selections under analysis justify that choice. In all three instances, the narrative culminates in death instead of communal celebration—a denouement that replaces "happy ends" with "dead ends"—a choice doubtless rooted in Slavs' historical experiences.

Both cultural context and individual preference determined the various authors' approaches to the films under discussion, some highlighting the music, others the thematic content, the narrative, or the works' relationship to the model of the genre established by Anglophone scholarship based on early Hollywood musical comedies. From the outset our intention has been to familiarize readers with a genre that consistently has drawn millions of viewers to movie theaters yet has received little scholarly examination in Slavic Studies. We hope that *Singing a Different Tune* stimulates further investigation into specific instances of film musicals excluded here owing solely to limitations of space.

* * *

Whereas each chapter in our collection contains its own bibliography, a filmography comprising the films analyzed at length throughout the volume appears after the final chapter. For films discussed briefly or merely mentioned readers should consult the index.

Helena Goscilo, August 2021

Bibliography

Aleksandrov, Grigorii, Sergei Eisenstein, and Vsevolod Pudovkin. "Statement on Sound." In *The Film Factory: Russian and Soviet Cinema in Documents 1896–1939*, edited by Richard Taylor and Ian Christie, 234–235. London and New York: Routledge, 1988.

Altman, Rick. *The American Film Musical*. Bloomington: Indiana University Press, 1987.

———. *Film/Genre*. London: BFI, 1999.

Austin, Thomas. "*Gone with the Wind* Plus Fangs." In *Genre and Contemporary Hollywood*, edited by Steve Neale, 294–308. London: BFI, 2002.

Birkholc, Robert. "Dybbuk—Michał Waszyński." Translated by Patryk Grabowski. Culture.pl., September 2018. Accessed February 1, 2019. https://culture.pl/en/work/dybbuk-michal-waszynski.

Bretan, Juliette. "Henryk Wars." Culture.pl., August 2018. Accessed January 12, 2020. https://culture.pl/en/artist/henryk-wars.

Cohan, Steven, ed. *Hollywood Musicals: The Film Reader*. London and New York: Routledge, 2002.

Cook, Pam. *The Cinema Book*. New York: Pantheon Books, 1985.

Cook, Pam, and Mieke Bernink. *The Cinema Book*. London: BFI, 1999.

Dobrenko, Evgeny. "Soviet Comedy Film: or, the Carnival of Authority." *Discourse* 17, no. 3 (Spring 1995): 49–57.

Dyer, Richard. "Entertainment and Utopia." In *Genre: The Musical: A Reader*, edited by Rick Altman, 220–232. London, Boston, and Henley: Routledge & Kegan Paul, 1981. Originally published in *Movie* 24 (Spring 1977).

Eagle, Herbert. "Socialist Realism and American Genre Film: The Mixing of Codes in *Jazzman*." In *The Red Screen: Politics, Society, Art in Soviet Russia*, edited by Anna Lawton, 249–263. London and New York: Routledge, 1992.

Feuer, Jane. *The Hollywood Musical*. Bloomington: Indiana University Press, 1993.

Ford, Charles and Robert Hammond. *Polish Film: A Twentieth-Century History*. Jefferson: McFarland & Co., 2005.

Giannetti, Louis. *Understanding Movies*. Upper Saddle River: Prentice Hall, 1999.

Gomery, J. Douglas. "Writing the History of the American Film Industry: Warner Bros and Sound." *Screen* 17, no. 1 (Spring 1976): 40–53.

Goscilo, Helena. "Luxuriating in Lack: Plenitude and Consuming Happiness in Soviet Paintings and Posters, 1930s–1953." In *Petrified Utopia*, edited by Marina Balina and Evgeny Dobrenko, 53–79, 268–273. London and New York: Anthem Press, 2009.

Grant, Barry Keith, ed. *Film Genre: Reader II*. Austin: University of Texas Press, 1995.

Hillier, Jim, and Douglas Pye. *100 Film Musicals*. London: Palgrave Macmillan/BFI, 2011.

Holmgren, Beth. "How the Cabaret Went to War." *The Cosmopolitan Review* 6, no. 3 (Fall–Winter 2014). Accessed September 1, 2021. http://cosmopolitanreview.com/how-the-cabaret-went-to-war.

———. "The Jews in the Band: The Anders Army's Special Troupes." In *POLIN* 32 (2020): *Jews and Music-Making in the Polish Lands*, edited by François Guesnet, Benjamin Matis, and Antony Polonsky, 177–191.

Izod, John. *Hollywood and the Box Office 1895–1986*. New York: Columbia University Press, 1988.

Janicki, Stanisław. "Michał Waszyński—artysta czy wyrobnik?" *Kino* 5 (2018): 27–31.

Kaganovsky, Lilya. *The Voice of Technology: Soviet Cinema's Transition to Sound, 1928–1935*. Bloomington: Indiana University Press, 2018.

———. "Russian Rock on Soviet Bones." In *Sound, Speech, Music in Soviet and Post-Soviet Cinema*, edited by Lilya Kaganovsky and Masha Salazkina, 252–272. Bloomington: Indiana University Press, 2014.

Katsnelson, Anna Wexler. "The Tramp in a Skirt: Laboring the Radiant Path." *Slavic Review* 70, no. 2 (2011): 256–258.

Kenez, Peter. *Cinema and Soviet Society, 1917–1953*. Cambridge: Cambridge University Press, 1992.

Kowalczyk, Janusz R. "Michał Waszyński." Culture.pl. Accessed August 31, 2021. https://culture.pl/en/tworca/michal-waszynski.

Lane, Anthony. "The Uncanny Valley of *I'm Your Man*." *The New Yorker*, September 17, 2021. Accessed September 17, 2021. https://www.newyorker.com/magazine/2021/09/27/the-uncanny-valley-of-im-your-man.

Lawton, Anna. *Kinoglasnost: Soviet Cinema in Our Time*. Cambridge: Cambridge University Press, 1992.

Legierska, Anna. "Prima Ballerinas, Soldiers & Hollywood Stars: Polish Dancers in the 20th Century." Translated by W. F. Culture.pl., April 2017. Accessed July 28, 2021. https://culture.pl/en/article/prima-ballerinas-soldiers-hollywood-stars-polish-dancers-of-the-20th-century.

Leyda, Jay. KINO: *A History of the Russian and Soviet Film*. Princeton: Princeton University Press, 1983.

Mazierska, Ewa. *Polish Popular Music on Screen*. Cham: Palgrave Macmillan, 2020.

Michałek, Bolesław, and Frank Turaj. *The Modern Cinema of Poland*. Bloomington: Indiana University Press, 1988.

Mościcki, Tomasz. "Adolf Dymsza." Translated by Patryk Grabowski. Culture.pl., August 2018. Accessed August 27, 2021. https://culture.pl/pl/tworca/adolf-dymsza.

———. "Eugeniusz Bodo." November 2010. Translated by N.S. Culture.pl., March 2017. Accessed August 22, 2021. https://culture.pl/en/artist/eugeniusz-bodo.

———. "Qui Pro Quo." June 2010. Translated by Marcin Gozdanek. Culture.pl., August 2018. Accessed April 17, 2019. https://culture.pl/en/artist/qui-pro-quo.

Neale, Steve, ed. *Genre and Contemporary Hollywood*. London: BFI, 2002.

———. "Questions of Genre." *Screen* 31, no. 1 (Spring 1990): 45–66.

———. *Genre and Hollywood*. London and New York: Routledge, 2000.

Ostrowska, Joanna. "Książę i dybuk." *Kino* 5 (2018): 32–33.

Prokhorov, Alexander. "Cinema of Attractions versus Narrative Cinema: Leonid Gaidai's Comedies and El'dar Riazanov's Satires of the 1960s." *Slavic Review* 62, no. 3 (Fall 2003): 455–472.

Prokhorov, Alexander, and Elena Prokhorova. *Film and Television Genres of the Late Soviet Era*. New York and London: Bloomsbury, 2017.

Replewicz, Maciej. *Stanisław Bareja. Król krzywego zwierciadła*. Poznań: Zyski Spółka, 2009.

Salys, Rimgaila. "*Hipsters/Stiliagi*." In *The Contemporary Russian Cinema Reader*, edited by Rigmaila Salys, 114–135. Boston: Academic Studies Press, 2019.

———. *The Musical Comedy Films of Grigorii Aleksandrov: Laughing Matters*. Bristol: Intellect, 2009.

Schatz, Thomas. *Hollywood Genres: Formulas, Filmmaking, and the Studio System*. New York: Random House, 1981.

Sieradzka, Anna. *Tysiąc lat ubiorów w Polsce*. Warsaw: Arkady, 2003.

Skaff, Sheila. *The Law of the Looking Glass: Cinema in Poland, 1896–1939*. Athens: Ohio University Press, 2008.

Sorokin, Vladimir. "Vladimir Sorokin on Supernatural Encounters." Interview with Deborah Treisman. *The New Yorker*, October 4, 2021.

Starr, S. Frederick. *Red and Hot: The Fate of Jazz in the Soviet Union*. New York: Limelight Editions, 1985.

Stauffer, Rachel. "A Traditional Karaoke Musical: Zhora Kryzhovnikov's *Best Day Ever* (*Samyy luchshiy den*." *East European Film Bulletin* 110 (December 2020). Accessed July 1, 2021. https://eefb.org/perspectives/zhora-kryzhovnikovs-best-day-ever-samyy-luchshiy-den-2015/?pdf=7859.

"*Stiliagi* (2008). Istoriia sozdaniia." Kinorium. Accessed May 1, 2020. https://ru.kinorium.com/449067/info/.

Taylor, Richard. "Veselye rebiata: The Happy Guys." In *The Cinema of Russia and the Former Soviet Union*, edited by Birgit Beumers, 79–87. London and New York: Wallflower Press, 2007.

———. "Singing on the Steppes for Stalin: Ivan Pyr'ev and the Kolkhoz Musical in Soviet Cinema." *Slavic Review* 58, no. 1 (Spring 1999): 143–159.

———. "Boris Shumyatsky and the Soviet Cinema in the 1930s: Ideology as Mass Entertainment." *Historical Journal of Film, Radio and Television* 6, no. 1 (1986): 43–64.

Taylor, Richard, and Ian Christie, eds. *The Film Factory: Russian and Soviet Cinema in Documents, 1896–1939*. London and New York: Routledge, 1988.

Telotte, J. P. "The New Hollywood Musical: From *Saturday Night Fever* to *Footloose*." In *Genre and Contemporary Hollywood*, edited by Steve Neale, 48–61. London: BFI, 2002.

Thiel, Wolfgang. "The Musical Film Comedy, or, 'Be Embraced, Millions.'" *East European Film Bulletin* 110 (December 2020). Accessed August 22, 2021. https://eefb.org/retrospectives/motivic-merrymaking-in-the-musical-films-of-grigori-aleksandrov-and-ivan-pyryev/?pdf=7847.

Youngblood, Denise J. *Movies for the Masses: Popular Cinema and Soviet Society in the 1920s*. Cambridge: Cambridge University Press, 1992.

Zorkaya, Neya. *The Illustrated History of Soviet Cinema*. New York: Hippocrene Books, 1989.

Part One

POLISH FILM MUSICALS

CHAPTER 1

Early Polish-Language Musicals: The Tug of War between Genre Film and Cabaret

Beth Holmgren

To understand the halting, yet eventually distinctive evolution of Polish-language musical comedies between the world wars, we must know how well-established, sophisticated, and engaging Polish-language cabarets and revue theaters were in Warsaw when the talkies burst onto the entertainment scene.[1]

---

1 In using the term "Polish-language" musicals, I distinguish these films from the Yiddish-language musicals produced in Poland primarily by Łódź-born Joseph Green—films that include *Yidl mitn Fidl* (directed by Jan Nowina-Przybylski, 1936), *Der Purimshpiler* (directed by Green and Nowina-Przybylski, 1937), and *Mamele* (directed by Green and Konrad Tom, 1938). My distinction implies no ban on Jewish participation in the creation of Polish-language musicals, for the opposite was the case. Acculturated Jewish artists—screenwriters, directors, composers, lyricists, cinematographers, cast members—were central to the production of Polish-language musical films, just as they were in the creation of Polish-language cabaret and revue theater, though the metropolitan cabaret was far more open in acknowledging Jewish talent and representing Jewish-gentile equality onstage. While Yiddish-language musical films starred imported American and domestic Yiddish-speaking stars, some bilingual Jewish artists such as the acculturated and bilingual Konrad Tom also contributed substantially to their making. For more on Yiddish-language musicals, see J. Hoberman, *Bridge of Light: Yiddish Films between Two Worlds* (New York: Museum of Modern Art and Schocken Books, 1991) and Joshua Walden, "Leaving Kazimierz: Comedy and Realism in the Yiddish Film Musical *Yidl mitn Fidl*," *Music, Sound, and the Moving Image* 3, no. 2 (Autumn 2009): 159–193. For information on the Jewish foundations of Polish-language cabaret, see Beth Holmgren, "Cabaret Nation: The Jewish Foundations of Kabaret Literacki, 1920–1939," *POLIN* 31 (2019): *Poland and Hungary: Jewish Realities Compared*, ed. François Guesnet, Howard Lupovitch, and Antony Polonsky, 273–288.

Most film historians assume that the production of good Polish-language musical comedies was hindered by the general state of the national film industry—its lack of stable studios and production financing, state-of-the-art camera and recording equipment, and a national distribution system as compared with the resources at the disposal of contemporary Hollywood studios and Germany's dominant Universum Film AG (UFA).[2] Yet when fledgling directors such as Jan Nowina-Przybylski, Mieczysław Krawicz, Michał Waszyński, and others began to film comedies, a genre far less prestigious than film adaptations of Polish literary classics or the ever popular "somber nationalist melodrama,"[3] they faced high viewer expectations in Poland's big cities precisely because Warsaw's versatile, comedic cabaret stars had become, to a great extent, national idols. These stars' songs and sketches were recorded in the capital and sold nationwide; their photos, interviews, and notes about their work and lifestyle filled the pages of big-city newspapers; and a number of cabaret luminaries toured provincial Poland during the summer months to supplement their income in the off-season. No one in metropolitan Poland (or parts of Poland aspiring to that status) doubted that the bobbed, curvaceous Zula Pogorzelska was the sexiest woman in the nation as well as a terrific, audacious comedienne, or that the compact, athletic Adolf Dymsza (Bagiński) was one of the funniest men and best impersonators on the planet. Nor could anyone imagine a more charismatic, dapper showman than Eugeniusz Bodo (Bohdan Eugène Junod), who could sing, dance, and convincingly play lover, villain, or clown depending on the contents of a sketch.

Film directors eagerly featured these stars in their productions, yet they possessed neither the ingenuity nor the right kind of equipment to make a movie of an actual cabaret show. They also may have feared the competition. Alas, filmmakers and cabaret producers and directors seemed incapable of imagining a time when this cabaret would cease to be, leaving future generations of Polish audiences (and theater historians) to piece together its representation from memoirs, reviews, photos, and fleeting glimpses of cabaret stars in films of mainly inferior quality. As Tadeusz Lubelski observes, almost no film documentation of the live cabaret has survived, with the exception of *Parada gwiazd Warszawy* (Warsaw's parade of stars, directed by Konrad Tom, 1937), which, ironically enough, flopped at the box office.[4]

---

2 Sheila Skaff, *The Law of the Looking Glass: Cinema in Poland, 1896–1939* (Athens: Ohio University Press, 2008), 67.

3 Ibid., 108.

4 Tadeusz Lubelski, *Historia kina polskiego* (Kraków: Universitas, 2015), 105.

Genre Film Character and Story Formulae

The industry's initial foray into comedy films and the subset of musical comedies (in Poland, those that included a few songs and perhaps a dance number) was slapdash in terms of writing, casting, cinematography, and acting. These early 1930s films were usually romantic comedies and therefore drew from the conventions of operetta and theatrical productions as well as those being readjusted for mass consumption onscreen in Hollywood.[5] In both early American and Polish-language musical films, thwarted romance between two young, good-looking, bland lovers usually served as the plot's axis. As Richard Altman argues, what enriched the musical was the (often antagonistic) dualities that proliferated in the plot and could only be reconciled with the romance's successful resolution in marriage-as-grand-production-finale.[6] Altman also singles out the musical's frequent reliance on the integration of "a secondary couple in order to relieve the monotony and—just as important—to provide work for their older stars or create an image for a new face."[7] Such hierarchical romantic pairings frequently recurred in the earliest Polish film musicals.

Clinging to set genre elements in comedy and musical comedy film, however, Polish producers, directors, screenwriters, and the actors themselves at first stymied the most effective casting of their best national stars. Renowned Warsaw cabaret actors were in their late twenties or early thirties when the talkies came to town. They were neither "older stars" nor "new faces." Because these performers' talents were so wide-ranging—from moving audiences with touching melancholy solos to delighting them with wild, nonsensical comedy sketches—no one knew where they belonged or which part they should play in a traditional comedy film. This meant that cabaret actors, and especially actresses, were too often wasted in secondary, grotesque comedy parts since the directors/screenwriters deemed them too funny or sexy to serve as female leads.

---

5 Thomas Schatz, *Hollywood Genres: Formulas, Filmmaking, and the Studio System* (Philadelphia: Temple University Press, 1981), 186. It seems odd that Thomas Schatz, a foremost expert on American film genres, assumes that the film musical was an "unprecedented—and peculiarly American—genre [that] emerged during the late 1920s and early 30s from its roots in vaudeville, music hall, and theater, and reached a remarkable level of artistic and cultural expression by the 1940s." In fact, there was far more overlap in features between the early American film musical and a wide array of light comedic forms on the stages of Europe as well as North America.

6 Richard Altman, *The American Film Musical* (Bloomington: Indiana University Press, 1987), 22, 27; Jane Feuer, *The Hollywood Musical* (London: The Macmillan Press, 1993), 71.

7 Altman, *The American Film Musical*, 31–32.

By 1933, the writers for the burgeoning Polish press on film were complaining bitterly about this miscasting and the consequent loss of "charm, beauty, and poetry" in comedies. Though critics applauded the growing success of Adolf Dymsza as "our lone genuine comedic-grotesque artist," they disliked the degradation of Mira Zimińska, Dymsza's frequent partner in clever cabaret sketches, when she was paired with the actor in *Każdemu wolno kochać* (Everyone is free to love, directed by Mieczyław Krawicz, 1933).[8] One of the film's reviewers confessed his disappointment that Zimińska, "a talent so subtle, quick-witted, and full of piquant charm, should be squeezed into the crude part of 'clumsy servant.'"[9] Another critic took his cue from a female moviegoer's outrage, demanding that Polish directors stop sidelining the marvelous, multi-talented Zula in the role of doltish, working-class sidekick allotted a single character song.[10] He could not understand why Polish directors were incapable of showcasing Zula as an at once beautiful and comic actress in an appropriate star vehicle, following the lead of American and French screenwriters and directors: "Wouldn't the sort of roles that Clara Bow, Colleen Moore, Annabella, and others play be more suited to [Zula]?"[11]

Such concerns were not easily remedied, given the film industry's inexperience and desperate need to make money with each movie during a decade riddled with economic crises.[12] The studios' insistence on churning out genre films for mass consumption militated against investment in nuanced character creation and coherent, well-paced story lines. The most prolific director in this period, Waszyński, produced a whopping forty talkies from 1929 to 1939. He earned a reputation for making movies economically and very quickly, usually completing a feature in two to three weeks and instantly undertaking the next project.[13] Such an astonishingly tight schedule allowed little to no time for script readthroughs or technical rehearsals, to say nothing of discussing characterizations. All the actors actively recruited for the early talkies, whether they were stars on the dramatic stage or in sophisticated cabaret, were accustomed

---

8 "Romeo i Julcia," *Kino*, January 22, 1933, 10.

9 Leon Blum, "*Każdemu wolno kochać*: trochę poezji w grotesce," *Kino*, March 12, 1933. 3.

10 "Pokażcie na filmie ładną Zulę!" *Kino*, March 12, 1933, 4.

11 For more on American attempts to develop such star vehicles for lovely comediennes, see, for example, Sara Ross, "'Good Little Bad Girls': Controversy and the Flapper Comedy," *Film History* 13, no. 4 (2001): 409–423; and Angela Latham, *Posing a Threat: Flappers, Chorus Girls, and Other Brazen Performers of the American 1920s* (Hanover: University Press of New England, 2000).

12 Ewa Mazierska, *Polish Popular Music on Screen* (Cham: Palgrave Macmillan, 2020), 29.

13 Janusz R. Kowalczyk, "Michał Waszyński, 29.09.1904–20.02.1965," Culture.pl., April 2018, https://culture.pl/pl/tworca/michal-waszynski.

to being given the time to memorize their lines and/or songs and rehearse intensively. The ad hoc, mechanical approach to film acting forced actors to fall back on caricature, improvisation, and broad reactions, often performed out of sequence vis-à-vis the plot.

At the same time, it was not clear that most cabaret stars could have convincingly incarnated a movie-length leading role. Many cabaret performers were hired for their skills as singers, dancers, or comedians. Some stars, among them Michał Znicz, Mira Zimińska, and Jadwiga Andrzejewska, proved able to alternate between cabaret performances and acting on comic and even dramatic stages. A chosen few—Zula, Zimińska, Dymsza, Bodo—could carry the weight of an entire show when a larger revue theater produced special performances celebrating their hit songs and acts, though such shows were not shaped by any sequential story. But most cabaret performers had no dramatic training at all and acting in front of the camera was the great unknown. Konrad Tom, a talented cabaret writer and comedian who aimed to write good screenplays and eventually direct, stated the situation best in a 1932 interview. Tom could envision Polish film's "marvelous future," but remained dissatisfied with the utter chaos of its present: "It seems to me that if our cinematography has not yet reached the level of American, French, or German production, this mistake mainly lies with our inability to think through our material . . . I repeat: we are at fault in our unpolished screenplays, directing, and acting."[14]

The Influence of Cabaret and Warsaw Nightlife

Ambitious professionals involved in every aspect of creating cabaret and revue shows quickly became interested in the "marvelous future" of Polish film—writers such as Tom, Napoleon Sądek, and Jan Fethke; lyricists such as Ludwik Starski and Emanuel Schlechter; and composers and bandleaders such as Henyrk Wars and Jerzy Petersburski.[15] German-Polish screenwriter Fethke joined Sądek and Tom in developing more imaginative, coherently unfolding screenplays. Starski and Schlechter expanded their professional portfolios from writing song lyrics to producing clever, animated dialogue; the Polish-language

---

14 "Konrad Tom nie chce być artystą filmowym, ale . . .," *Kino*, October 30, 1932, 3.

15 For an excellent review of Ludwik Starski's life and work, see Barbara Milewski, "Hidden in Plain View: The Music of Holocaust Survival in Poland's First Post-War Feature Film," in *Music, Collective Memory, Trauma, and Nostalgia in European Cinema after the Second World War*, ed. Michael Baumgartner and Ewelina Boczkowska (New York: Routledge, 2020), 111–137.

literary cabaret was famed for its pithy, witty sketches. The dance and jazz music composed by Wars, Petersburski, Artur and Henryk Gold, among others, was both a hallmark and a staple of cabaret and revue theaters as well as late-night eating and dancing venues in downtown Warsaw. These composers' numbers signaled to listeners and, eventually, to moviegoers, that metropolitan Poland had arrived in the modern Western world of swing. In Polish-language musical comedies, as in American musicals, swing music usually triumphed over classical music and traditional songs; in Jane Feuer's words, swing "represent[ed] youth, community, warmth, personal expression and spontaneity."[16]

Lubelski correctly points out that no Polish film replicated the standard progression of cabaret and revue shows—that is, quickly paced sequences of unconnected sketches, songs, and dances.[17] Yet quite a few musical comedies either take place in Warsaw's well-known sites of entertainment or refer to similar, sometimes inferior venues. Since the city functioned as Poland's capital of popular entertainment *and* film, it is no surprise that many movies included scenes of protagonists rendezvousing at night clubs, playing for big radio broadcasts, and dancing to the music of swing bands. Warsaw studios did not develop the subset of backstage musicals, but films such as *Papa się żeni* (Papa is getting married, directed by Michał Waszyński, 1936), and Poland's lone "serious" musical, *Strachy* (Dread, directed by Eugeniusz Cękalski, 1938), include scenes of cabaret and revue show rehearsals and backstage melodramas.

In this chapter, I argue that the tug of war between genre formulae and cabaret influence in Polish musical comedies was on the verge of being won by cabaret artists who had retooled for filmmaking but was halted forever by the Nazi and Soviet invasions in 1939. I trace how that cabaret influence increased and adapted to a new medium by analyzing a series of four films, the first premiering in 1934, and the other three produced in the late 1930s. *Co mój mąż robi w nocy* (What my husband is up to at night, directed by Waszyński, 1934) features six well-known cabaret artists and locates the action mainly in the Alhambra, a fictional name given the Adria, interwar Warsaw's premier restaurant and dance floor. (See chapter four on the Adria's role in a recent Polish musical.) All secrets and problems are ultimately revealed and resolved in this modern space of malleable identity. *Zapomniana melodia* (Forgotten melody, directed by Fethke and Tom, 1938), written and filmed to attract a mass audience, is enlivened by Wars's excellent musical soundtrack and featured songs and demonstrates how deeply

16 Feuer, *The Hollywood Musical*, 53–57.
17 Lubelski, *Historia kina polskiego*, 105.

swing music had permeated everyone's life in the big city, wherever they lived, studied, or worked.

The other two films—*Piętro wyżej* (One floor up, directed by Leon Trystan, 1937), and *Paweł i Gaweł* (Paweł and Gaweł, directed by Mieczysław Krawicz, 1938)—star Bodo, the most successful cabaret crossover into the role of onscreen romantic lead. In the first movie, Bodo also served as producer, co-screenwriter, and artistic director, and largely carried the film with a performance that approximates American screwball comedy with realistically integrated songs (music by Wars, lyrics by Schlechter and Starski). In the second film, the title roles of Paweł and Gaweł were performed by Bodo and Dymsza, respectively—two cabaret stars who were old hands at delivering the quick back-and-forth of comic sketches. Their duo is fundamentally enhanced by Helena Grossówna, a highly talented actress, dancer, and comedienne who had learned to shine onscreen as well as onstage.[18] The three performers had proved to be a winning trio in the Krawicz-directed *Robert i Bertrand* (Robert and Bertrand), filmed earlier in 1938. The screenplay for *Paweł and Gaweł*, however, is superior to that of its "prequel": less contrived and pandering to Dymsza's talent for the grotesque, yet elastic enough to alternate rapidly between comic and character-building scenes. By the film's end, it is not completely clear whether the well-balanced ensemble incarnates the happy end of joined couple plus stalwart friend or three characters who have learned to love playing together.

What My Husband Is Up to at Night: Take Your Troubles to the Alhambra

What My Husband Is Up to at Night is initially linked to Warsaw's best cabarets by featuring that institution's most famous director and conferencier, Fryderyk Járosy. With his lively, handsome face, debonair dress, excellent rapport with the audience, and witty, accented Polish patter (half-Croatian and half-Austrian, he learned Polish in his thirties), Járosy figured as guarantor of a night of top-notch entertainment. In lieu of rolling credits, the film cleverly positions him before the closed curtain, using him to introduce the film and its makers just as he would announce live performers onstage. Járosy accompanies each

---

18 Grossówna was also the female romantic lead in *Forgotten Melody* and *One Floor Up*, though her roles in both were quite circumscribed—as either dreamy schoolgirl or modern girlfriend-sidekick.

announcement with funny gestures and comments about the aforementioned's weight and height. He completes his readout of the cast by presenting himself as "Mr. Pickwick," a visitor from London whom Varsovians revere as "the king of fashion." Járosy's bit part as the visiting trendsetter underscores the class-leveling role of cabaret stars in Warsaw and *My Husband*. In the capital's press, cabaret performers competed with the fashion balls of Polish aristocrats, hosting their own versions and crowning various actors and actresses the kings and queens of fashion. Yet their "royalty's" actual pedigrees—working-class or middle-class, Catholic or Jewish—simply did not matter.

Járosy's baring of this device serves as an excellent epigraph for *My Husband*, because the film's plot hinges on the hero's sudden reversal of fortune and mad efforts to adapt in identity and behavior. The primary husband and wife in this movie are not young lovers, but an established, older, wealthy couple—the industrialist Roman Tarski, whom the superb character actor Michał Znicz (Feiertag) transforms from order-loving businessman into an adroit, unabashed schemer, and Tarski's extravagant, but still loving spouse, Stefa, played by the dramatic actress Maria Gorczyńska. Tarski's plans to redecorate their posh apartment while Stefa is vacationing on the Riviera fall apart when he discovers that his business partner has absconded with their firm's funds, his so-called friends refuse him loans, and he desperately hunts for work.

As Tarski paces a now empty apartment (its new furnishings have been repossessed), his lone resource is the maid, Kazia Fafułówna, and the company she keeps. Kazia, played by Tola Mankiewiczówna, a cabaret performer renowned for her operatic mezzo-soprano, good looks, and vivacious stage persona, is a curious and opinionated servant, and notably younger and sexier than Stefa Tarska (fig. 1.1). In this case, the female cabaret star's "secondary" casting does not degrade her, as in the cases of Zula and Zimińska, the more so because her soon-to-be fiancé Walery (Wojciech Ruszkowski) helps her employer Tarski land a job at his workplace, waiting tables in the Alhambra's nightclub. Kazia is also entrusted with the film's best song, "Odrobinę szczęścia w miłości" ("A bit of happiness in love"), which became a much-reprised hit thereafter (music by Jerzy Petersburski, words by Emanuel Schlechter). Soon after Kazia finishes her dreamy song in the maid's quarters off the kitchen, she, Walery, and Tarski ease the class tension in the kitchen itself (the symbolic "downstairs" in a luxury apartment) by polishing off a bottle of cognac and joining together in contemplating what they might accomplish if they had four legs instead of two. Schlechter assigned a verse of the comic "Cztery nogi" ("Four legs") to each one of this motley trio, including Znicz, who only ventured to sing in *My Husband*, just one of the twenty-seven films in which he appeared between the wars.[19] The upper-class/working-class ensemble seems most comfortable imagining themselves as a distinctly nonhuman species.

Figure 1.1. The maid Kazia (Tola Mankiewiczówna) helps Tarski (Michał Znicz) welcome his spouse (Maria Gorczyńska) home to their noticeably emptier apartment. *Co mój mąż robi w nocy* (What my husband is up to at night), 1934, dir. Michał Waszyński.

Kazia's genial Walery trains Tarski on the job, where the former industrialist works all night serving customers who were once his peers. Muddling Tarski's class status further is the fact that the Alhambra's assistant head waiter, his immediate superior, is Kazia's protective father, Mr. Fafuła. In his review of *My Husband,* Leon Blum, then editor of the major film magazine, *Kino,* declared that Romuald Gierasieński, the cabaret comedian playing Fafuła, bests everyone in the cast in his small role as an "irascible fat man," constantly exploding with anger over every misperceived slur on his or his daughter's honor.[20]

The other two cabaret comedians cast in the film—Tom as the detective who literally searches the globe for Tarski's fugitive partner, and Kazimierz Krukowski as Count Carolescu, who serenades Stefa in a ridiculous lounging robe on the Riviera and then follows her to Warsaw—are mired in broadly stereotyped parts

19 Michał Pieńkowski, "'Cztery nogi,' 1934," Stare-kino, accessed July 22, 2022, https://stare-kino.pl/cztery-nogi/.

20 Blum, "*Każdemu wolno kochać*: trochę poezji w grotesce," 3.

that they do little to improve. Tom's progress is conveyed by a recurring cartoon of him wearing a Sherlockian deerstalker, with pipe in mouth, gun in one hand, and leash in another, while his dog sniffs the ground. In each case, the cartoon feeds into pat newsreel footage of Africa (dancing tribes), Japan (citizens under fire), and India (a huge crowd of Muslims bowing down in worship), and then a close-up of Tom ostensibly on the scene. For Polish audiences in 1934, such sequences likely seemed innovative; today they are embarrassingly dated. Krukowski, most loved in the cabaret (and several lackluster films) as the character Lopek, a lower-middle-class Jewish shopkeeper both bewildered and seduced by a modern Warsaw, here exercises the cabaret freedom to play a distinctly different role, that of a mustachioed, monocle-wearing Romanian seducer. The part of Count Carolescu, memorable only for his three comically foiled suicide attempts and his classical rendition of the Petersburski/Schlechter song "Najpiękniejsza signorina" ("The most beautiful signorina"), might have worked well in a short sketch. But Krukowski's caricature grows tiresome over the course of a film in which he alone must help Stefa understand (or undermine) a husband who seems disaffected because he just wants to sleep and refuses to tell his wife why.

The real star of this film, apart from Znicz as quick-change artist and Gierasieński as explosive comedian, is the bedazzling, transformative location of the Alhambra. This set is no Hollywood facsimile, but Warsaw's Adria itself. The Adria's complex of eateries (restaurant, cafe, American bar) and dance hall, which boasted a revolving floor resembling a phonograph record, was widely regarded as the most elegant entertainment establishment in the capital. Studios with invariably limited budgets were pleased to be able to use its different venues as sets.[21] Jerzy S. Majewski remarks that almost half of *My Husband* was filmed in the Adria, either in its dance hall or the backrooms reserved for private parties.[22]

Waszyński or his casting coordinator accentuated the Alhambra's more general entertainment identity by filming its dance band under the baton of Ivo Wesby (Ignacy Singer), the well-known conductor of a smaller orchestra

---

21 Wojciech Herbaczyński, *W dawnych cukiernicach i kawiarniach warszawskich* (Warsaw: Państwowy Instytut Wydawniczy, 1983), 161. Other films, such as the 1933 *Jego ekscelencja subjekt* (His majesty, the shop clerk) were shot in various sections of the Adria complex.

22 "Świat kina jest tylko ułudą, jednak obraz szalonych dansingów warszawskich lat 30. XX wieku był jak najbardziej prawdziwy. Do niektórych filmów robiono dekoracje, ale ponieważ kino polskie nie dysponowało dużymi budżetami, często kręcono je w autentycznych wnętrzach" (Jerzy S. Majewski, "Przedwojenne warszawskie dancingi: najsłynniejsza była Adria," *Gazeta Wyborcza*, July 19, 2015).

for the cabaret. Petersburski, the composer of the film's score, who typically shared conducting the Adria's famous band with Artur Gold, elected not to be screened at his post in *My Husband*. The film's makers also advertised the Alhambra as an international venue. They easily could have hired local singing and dancing pairs to perform a number on the revolving parquet, but they chose to engage an American team who sang in English and featured a male dancer who showed off markedly Black jazzy breakout moves and borrowed Wesby's baton to whip up the band into "real swing." It is intriguing that in a musical comedy in which no star's Jewish identity is marked (for example, Znicz, Tom, Krukowski), this imported American team of Miriam Kressyn and Hymie Jacobson primarily performed in Yiddish-language theater on both sides of the Atlantic and just happened to be touring Poland when the film was underway.[23] In any event, their prerequisite American English and "authentic" (or convincingly appropriated) jazziness bestowed a world-class imprimatur on the Alhambra.

Much like American film musicals, *My Husband* features the Alhambra to emphasize the value of entertainment, which is one of the genre's main messages and *raison d'être*.[24] Yet the scenes at the Alhambra also easily cross the boundaries between those consuming and those laboring to produce entertainment that the American musical usually skirted.[25] The Alhambra provides the atmosphere for the characters—whoever they may be—to drop their inhibitions and put on new masks or be unmasked. Examples abound. Arriving late for work at the Alhambra, Tarski simply replaces his missing tuxedo jacket by swiping Mr. Picknick's finer model when he helps the Londoner remove his coat. Without noticing his state of relative undress, Picknick strides onto the dance floor in white shirt and vest, and soon all the male patrons are doffing their jackets to emulate "the king of fashion" (fig. 1.2). In another instance, Kazia, all dressed up and waiting for Walery, behaves as an entitled patron rather than a maid on her night off. When Tarski, her employer/waiter, talks furtively with the girl to avoid engaging with his wife and Carolescu on the other side of the

---

23 In fact, the singer Miriam Kressyn was born in Białystok in 1911 and emigrated to the United States when she was twelve. Kressyn and Jacobson were married when they performed in *My Husband*. Both of them also appeared in Joseph Green's 1937 Yiddish film, *Der Purimshpiler*, which was made in Poland.

24 Feuer, *The Hollywood Musical*, 91.

25 As Feuer argues, "We are never allowed to realize that musical entertainment is an industrial product and that putting on a show (or putting on a Hollywood musical) is a matter of a labor force producing a product for consumption" (ibid., 12).

floor, Stefa immediately stops worrying about her husband's alienated affections and concludes that his fatigue results from a romance with Kazia. For the first time, she contemplates cheating on him with the Count.

Figure 1.2. Mr. Picknick (Fryderyk Járosy) unwittingly models a new fashion in evening wear for smart young men. *Co mój mąż robi w nocy* (What my husband is up to at night), 1934, dir. Michał Waszyński.

Yet once the key players move to the Alhambra's discreet backrooms, they prevent rather than pursue illicit romance. After devising rather tasteless comical revenge on Carolescu, with Kazia's help, Tarski ultimately confesses the awful truth to Stefa, Stefa declares her love for him regardless, and Tom, the private detective, miraculously appears with the stolen funds stuffed inside his coat, so that both confession and declaration are moot. The older primary couple are reunited by their love for each other rather than the money they almost lost, and they imply their equality with Kazia and Walery when all four join in a champagne toast (fig. 1.3). At the Alhambra, both couples find their happy end, and the moviegoers are treated to not one, but three entertaining shows—the first performed by bona fide Americans onstage, the second at the expense of a foreign dandy and his upper-class sycophants on the dance floor, and the third backstage, where the lovers at first scheme and squabble, then reconcile, and finally join together in celebrating their good fortune.

Figure 1.3. The two pairs of lovers drink a champagne toast with the detective (Konrad Tom) on the far left, the singing count (Kazimierz Krukowski) in the middle, and Kazia's happy father (Romuald Gierasieński) on the far right. *Co mój mąż robi w nocy* (What my husband is up to at night), 1934, dir. Michał Waszyński.

Forgotten Melody: Melodies that No One Forgot

In *Forgotten Melody*, the love of just one couple is repeatedly threatened by the fact that the lovers differ a great deal in terms of worldly experience. Helenka Roliczówna, the daughter of a wealthy businessman, Bogusław Rolicz (Antoni Fertner, usually cast as the portly, befuddled, widowed patriarch), is presented as a sheltered girl in her late teens, an age that actress Grossówna projects convincingly even though she was thirty-four during the film's production. Her male counterpart, Stefan Frankiewicz, played rather woodenly by the fine singer Aleksander Żabczyński, is gradually revealed to be a ladykiller and a passionate fan of swing and jazz. Stefan chases Helenka despite the fact that he has not yet broken off his romance with a dancehall singer, Lila Fontelli (Alina Żeliska), whom he has showered with expensive gifts. Stefan literally bumps into Helenka near the campus of the latter's private school. When he returns on foot to get a better glimpse of his next conquest, he discovers that his paternal uncle, who bears his surname, is a professor of singing and the lone male faculty member living on campus. Professor Frankiewicz, incarnated initially as a prejudiced pedant by the excellent Znicz, first alerts the audience to Stefan's rakishness (fig. 1.4). He pleads with his nephew to leave because Stefan's visits always "compromise" him.

Figure 1.4. The "rakish" Stefan (Aleksander Żabczyński) posed with his guitar. *Zapomniana melodia* (Forgotten melody), 1938, dir. Jan Fethke and Konrad Tom.

Stefan attempts to comply, but when an indignant Helenka stalks him into the Vistula and her eager schoolmates "save" him from drowning, he is carried to his uncle's lodging to recover from his ordeal. There he wins Helenka's love as well as the promise of an indoor pool for the school from her father, who is the institution's chief patron and proud of the girls' apparent lifeguarding skills. A few days later, after the professor, upset by his nephew's loud performances of swing on the guitar and the piano, throws him out, the impatient, infuriated Lila Fontelli arrives in Warsaw, hot on Stefan's trail. Confused about her lover's whereabouts, she returns Stefan's gifts to the professor's address, scandalizing the school's female administrators. Somewhat later Lila's meeting with Stefan in person is accidentally spotted by Helenka, who tearfully renounces her love for him until the finale corrects all painful misperceptions.

The other actors who deserve mention here are female. Jadwiga Andrzejewska, a highly gifted cabaret performer and dramatic actress, is cast as Jadzia Pietrusińska, Helenka's closest friend, the school comedienne, who at first mercilessly teases their boring professor of singing, and the leader who subsequently rallies her colleagues to rescue the dismissed Professor Frankiewicz and to convince Helenka's father to resume sponsoring their school.[26] Though none of the other students is singled out, these school girls play a seminal role in the plot, and it is important to know that they were all recruited as extras for the film from the respected dancing institute of Tacjanna Wysocka.[27] Wysocka, who had trained in "rhythmic gymnastics" in prerevolutionary St. Petersburg and founded the School of Musical Education and Theatrical Dance in interwar Warsaw, agreed to let her ensemble perform primarily artistic numbers in Qui Pro Quo, Warsaw's best and most ambitious cabaret. On this stage, the "Tacjann-Girls," as they came to be called, proved that young female dancers could wow audiences with serious repertoire rather than be demoted to the role of erotic stage decoration.[28] In the film, these extras appear as normal, high-spirited girls, not Lila Fontellis in the making.

Over the last several decades, a number of Polish film scholars have come to agree that *Forgotten Melody* represents the best national musical of the interwar era.[29] Its screenplay is cleverly constructed and fast-paced; its leading actors, for the most part, deliver fine performances; and its two hit songs and the soundtrack's masterful play with recurring variations on their refrains raises this Polish film to contemporary Hollywood's reigning gold standard in terms of its musical score. As Leszek Armatys noted in his 1988 retrospective review, *Forgotten Melody* demonstrated how well its makers had absorbed what was most effective in American musicals, distancing their work from operetta conventions.[30] Wars was not the only quick study contributing to the film's excellence; his lyricist Starski should be given equal credit. Most important, Tom joined Fethke in directing *Forgotten Melody,* and at this point in his career he had honed his skills as director of at least a half-dozen Polish-language and Yiddish-language movies. Compared with the musical comedies of the early 1930s, *Forgotten Melody* definitely reflected its creators' greater ability to "think through [their] material."

---

26 See Roman Włodek's excellent biography of Andrzejewska.

27 Grzegorz Rogowski, "Kim jest ostatnia statystyka z 'Zapomnianej melodii?,'" *Rzeczpospolita,* August 10, 2017, rp.pl/Rzecz-o-historii/308109880-Kim-jest-ostatnia-statystka-z-Zapomnianej-melodii.html.

28 Tacjanna Wysocka, *Wspomnienia* (Warsaw: Czytelnik, 1962), 134, 197.

29 Lubelski, *Historia kina polskiego,* 112; Jerzy Toeplitz, *Historia sztuki filmowej,* vol. 4, *1934–1939* (Warsaw: Wydawnictwa Artystyczne i Filmowe, 1969), 390; Marek Haltof, *Kino polskie* (Gdańsk: słowo/obraz teritoria, 2004), 48.

30 L. Armatysz and W. Stradomski, *Od "Niewolnicy zmysłów" do "Czarnych diamentów": Szkice o polskich filmach z lat 1914–1939* (Warsaw: Centralny Ośrodek Metodyki Upowszechniania Kultury, 1988), 230–233.

Contemporary reception of *Forgotten Melody* was more mixed. Anna Zahorska, one of its harshest critics, faults the film for its projection of the "low values" associated with swing music and dance: "[Its] trifles, amoralisms, exhibitions of human inferiority, outrageously vulgar level of the characters, trashy atmosphere conveyed in the screenplay, and the mixing together of school with the dance hall characterize all the films being made in Poland."[31] Her parting shot skewers the lowness of the music itself, which, in her words, was composed "for revue theaters rather than concert halls."[32]

Paradoxically, Zahorska's criticism misses the fact that such "low associations" are precisely what the screenplay and character development in *Forgotten Melody* seek to dispel, since the filmmakers focus on the potentially incendiary relationship between innocent girl and man about town and the suspect "new music" that they both thoroughly enjoy (fig. 1.5). Though this film never explicitly locates its action outside of Warsaw, the opening shots of young women

Figure 1.5. Singing, kayaking schoolgirls on the Vistula. *Zapomniana melodia* (Forgotten melody), 1938, dir. Jan Fethke and Konrad Tom.

31 Anna Zahorska, "Recenzje filmowe," *Kultura*, December 11, 1938, 8.
32 Ibid.

paddling kayaks down the Vistula and singing Wars and Starski's new hit "Ach, jak przyjemnie" ("Oh, how delightful") present viewers with a sugarcoated vision of impressionable virgins under the spell of a revue song extolling the joys of nature. The girls' school that they attend, which boasts its own dock, boathouse, and fenced-in, forested campus, suggests a cloistered oasis in the big city. Indeed, when Stefan's stalled motorboat drifts into the kayak flotilla's way, the kayaking team of Helenka and Jadzia descends on the hapless sailor like angry birds. Whatever the genesis of their song, these two girls are filled with righteous indignation when a man intrudes on their territory.

In addition, the (im)moral influence of swing music is raised at the very beginning of the film. Professor Frankiewicz complains to the headmistress that the kayaking students are late for his singing class and the song he has heard them warbling disturbs him with "its frivolous words," "Negro jazzband melodies," and "wild Negro rhythm."[33] (In its words, melody, and rhythm, the song "Oh, How Delightful" sooner resembles a summer camp hiking song than anything like a swing dance tune or a jazz number.) Professor Frankiewicz's condemnation echoes that of right-wing nationalists in Poland (and in all of Europe and the United States) with its trumped-up claim of the allegedly pernicious influence of Black music on young white people. But the motherly headmistress pleasantly dismisses the professor's accusation, opining that their song is simply good fun.

Forgotten Melody does not engage in the fight against fascism, in large part to assure its mass appeal, particularly for Polish moviegoers in the provinces. Its screenwriters, composers, and lyricists were intent on normalizing swing. In contrast to *My Husband,* this film no longer presumes that its viewers would know and appreciate the model of the Alhambra, let alone believe that it could cure one's troubles. The plot eventually leads us to a tawdrier place of entertainment, a dance hall named the Imperial. We view its stage, backstage, and bar in the company of a clearly second-rate, nasty Lila as she finishes her set, thanks a befuddled Professor Frankiewicz for returning his nephew's gifts to her, and then goads the teetotaler to try a cocktail for her own amusement. When Stefan appears, he cynically confides in a friend that he plans "a great farewell scene with Lila," not foreseeing that Helenka will witness only the scene's prelude and run sobbing into the arms of her father, who happens to be socializing with his board members at the Imperial. Whereas the Alhambra was showcased as a most

33 "Frywolne słowa," "melodie murzyńskie jazzbandowe," and "dziki murzyński rytm." Unless otherwise indicated, all translations from Polish into English are mine.

desirable destination offering first-rate entertainment in *My Husband,* the dance hall in *Forgotten Melody* features neither fine performers nor classy patrons. Instead, the decent people who happen to be at the Imperial are damned by association in the eyes of respectable society—specifically, those of the hypocritical Bogusław Rolicz and the school's prim staff. The sight of Helenka and Professor Frankiewicz on its premises so infuriates Rolicz that he withdraws Helenka as well as his patronage from the school and causes Stefan's uncle, once again "compromised" by his nephew, to be dismissed.

Forgotten Melody instead strives to prove the positive, infectious power of swing and jazz in morally untainted settings and interactions. This goal is pursued through the film's editing, production numbers, and the doubled thematic importance of its best song. The plot cleverly progresses through scenes instantly linked by the same musical motif. These may involve Stefan and Helenka playing the same song on the piano (with close-ups focused on their hands moving over the keys) or an orchestral number followed by its piano rendition. The music moves from one set of hands to another and does not bring the bodies of the lovers together in a dance or an embrace. The film editing thus accentuates the fact that Wars's and Starski's songs travel to school, apartment, and home, and their "repetition" is magically inevitable.

It is no accident that the three production numbers in *Forgotten Melody* all feature the female students as amateur singers and dancers. The film opens on the kayak flotilla, with panoramic shots, mid shots, and close-ups of girls happily singing and exercising in the great outdoors. *Forgotten Melody* closes with a reprise of its other Wars/Starski hit, "Już nie zapomnisz mnie" ("You'll never forget me"), in which Stefan sings the lead and the girls, strangely seated up in the trees, provide him with an angelic chorus. The most thrilling production number, however, spontaneously erupts in the classroom of Professor Frankiewicz. While the girls wait for their instructor, the comedienne Jadzia assumes his place at the podium, and loosens up her audience with a funny, exaggerated impersonation of their pedantic teacher. Helenka then launches a jazzy "call-and-response" version of "Frère Jacques," the one unsullied song that Frankiewicz invariably forces the girls to sing. The students quickly push their desks together to form a makeshift dance floor, on which they arrange themselves as a singing, swaying chorus line (in school uniform) while Helenka struts back and forth to the rhythm, waving jazz hands, and occasionally launching into a short tap dance. Implied here is the fact that these cloistered female students already know jazz well enough to improvise such a performance on their own. They do not need to sully themselves by frequenting the Imperial (fig. 1.6).

Figure 1.6. Helenka (Helena Grossówna) surrounded by her chorus line after their improvised jazz number. *Zapomniana melodia* (Forgotten melody), 1938, dir. Jan Fethke and Konrad Tom.

Thematically, the forgotten melody of the film's title endows a "revue" song with two higher purposes in 1930s Warsaw. On the one hand, as Stefan tells Helenka after she has rebuffed his attempts to explain his breakup with Lila, forgetting or remembering this melody reflects either the death or the resurrection of their love. He therefore revives their romance when he sings "You'll Never Forget Me" in the finale. On the other hand, this melody also functions as "a song of business," for Rolicz could only memorize the chemical formula of his firm's latest, greatest invention by setting it to the rhythm and tune of Wars's composition.[34] Stefan's performance literally enables Rolicz to recall his bombshell report before his board of directors and thus ensures his company's financial boon.[35] Both bourgeois love and capitalism triumph here, as in so many American musicals.

Though *Forgotten Melody* seeks to convince its mass audience that swing and jazz qualify as respectable music for ordinary people, be they adults or adolescents, it cannot purge this music of its roots in and references to cabaret and revue theater. Not only did the creators of the film's music emerge from these still popular venues, but also the cabaret's best performers—Grossówna,

---

34 "[P]iosenka interesu."

35 Mazierska, *Polish Popular Music on Screen*, 38.

Andrzejewska, and Znicz—make the most effective case for this music's general appeal *as well as* ordinary people's tolerance of a broader range of acceptable musical tastes and pastimes. For example, Grossówna incarnates a defiant virgin holding out for true romantic love, yet her passions include jazzy songs and tap dancing. Andrzejewska's Jadzia deftly impersonates Znicz's dull, sing-song mode of lecturing as she plays before the class, but her contrition over her role in the professor's dismissal is rendered with equal skill; as Frankiewicz prepares to leave, Jadzia cues the class to sing "Frère Jacques" traditionally in his honor. Znicz, in turn, manages the transition from racist pedant to tender consoler of the weeping Jadzia in a very moving scene. The close-up of his transformed face projects an expression close to saintliness (fig. 1.7). Most important, *Forgotten Melody* elevates and, to a great extent, "bourgeoisifies" "the chorus girls" used in cabaret and revue theaters, assigning them a central collective role as wholesome, boisterous middle-class young women with open hearts that readily encompass a love for swing songs and dances.

Figure 1.7. Professor Frankiewicz (Znicz) as saint, and Jadzia (Jadwiga Andrzejewska) as supplicant. *Zapomniana melodia* (Forgotten melody), 1938, dir. Jan Fethke and Konrad Tom.

One Floor Up: The Showman Carries the Show

Though *Forgotten Melody* qualifies as the best interwar Polish musical in the opinion of a number of Polish film scholars, I contend, along with another group, that *One Floor Up* takes first place for its excellence and distinction.[36] The success of *One Floor Up* stemmed not only from its male lead, Bodo, whose reign as the king of interwar Polish film, beginning in 1932, was only temporarily threatened by a press-prompted rivalry between the reigning monarch and Żabczyński. The romantic lead in *Forgotten Melody*, whose voice was classically trained, sang more beautifully than Bodo, but no one could deliver a popular song as well as Bodo did, with impeccable diction, irresistible verve, and the personal, natural rapport he invariably established with his audience, whether they were on the set, in the theater, at the cinema, or at home listening to the radio or the phonograph.

The box office and critical success of *One Floor Up* depended on Bodo's many talents as a performer; his artistic and managerial control over this particular film; and his collaboration with other excellent artists, especially his close friend Wars, the greatest Polish film composer of his era. Bodo was the rare cabaret and revue theater star who absolutely thrived in film, with thirty-one movies to his credit before the war. (His death in a Soviet labor camp in 1943 put paid to a postwar career.) The young Bohdan Eugêne Junod had been raised literally in the entertainment business, exposed to both popular theater and film in his childhood. His Swiss father, Theodore Junod, was an engineer fascinated by cinema in its infancy and chose to make a living exhibiting moving pictures throughout the Russian empire in the 1900s. The cinema-smitten Junod eventually settled his business and family in Łódź, the economically thriving "Polish Manchester," in 1907, where his new theater, dubbed the Urania, combined moving pictures with circus and revue shows.[37] Predictably, Bodo grew up addicted to the stage, though his father and Polish mother pressed him to pursue a respectable career in medicine. He ran away in his teens and made his theatrical debut in Poznań. By his early twenties, he had become a promising star at Qui Pro Quo, the best Warsaw Polish-language cabaret, and, subsequently, Morskie Oko, the capital's best revue theater. As his biographer Ryszard Wolański observes, Bodo's great

36 Łukasz Budzik, "*Piętro wyżej.* 80 lat od premiery," Film.org.pl, February 18, 2017, https://film.org.pl/r/pietro-wyzej-80-lat-od-premiery-101499.

37 Ryszard Wolański, *"Już nie zapomnisz mnie": Opowieść o Henryku Warsie* (Warsaw: MUZA SA, 2010), 16.

versatility made him stand out from his talented peers: "Like nobody else, he was able to combine singing, dancing, and acting onstage with natural humor and exceptional physical dexterity."[38]

Qui Pro Quo trained Bodo to perfect his performance skills and comic timing, play well with others, and establish a knowing connection with his audience even as he incarnated a quite separate character onstage. Morskie Oko, under the direction of song and sketch writer Andrzej Włast (Gustaw Baumritter), was much less concerned than Qui Pro Quo about the originality and local topicality of its material, and most intent on delivering a splashy show about the metropolis and its celebrities in the tradition of Casino de Paris and The Ziegfeld Follies. At Morskie Oko, Bodo grew accustomed to being the star attraction, a handsome leading man dressed in a tuxedo with his mop of dark hair swept back from his brow or clad in a Chevalier-style suit with a straw boater tipped over one eye, projecting tremendous sex appeal and a showman's grace and largesse. The hit songs he performed were at first those that Włast stole and translated from Parisian revues and subsequently those composed by Wars, another artist whom Włast shrewdly recruited for his big stage. To a great extent, Bodo and Wars's experience at Morskie Oko not only cemented their friendship and initial creative partnership, but also prepared them for their respective leading roles in film—as durable screen idol and most prolific, ingenious composer.

Given Bodo's longevity, popularity, and earnings in film (he first appeared in the silent *Rywale* [Rivals, directed by Henryk Szaro, 1925]), the movie star was able to retrace his father's path as an entertainment entrepreneur, founding the studio Urania-Film in 1933, so named to pay tribute to his father's entertainment mecca in early-twentieth-century Łódź.[39] According to Wolański, Bodo was the first and only interwar Polish actor to produce his own films, the best of which was *One Floor Up* (1937).[40] In his role as this movie's producer, Bodo assembled the cast and other creative talent he most preferred. For the role of his starring character's sardonic pal and foil, he chose Ludwik Sempoliński, a friend from his early years on the Warsaw stage and a well-known cabaret performer. His character's love interest was played by Grossówna, the actress whom he had auditioned with the goal of launching her as a star in a previous romantic comedy, *Dwa dni w raju* (Two days in paradise, directed by Leon Trystan, 1936).[41]

38 Ibid., 24.

39 Tomasz Mościcki, "Eugeniusz Bodo," Culture.pl., 2010, culture.pl/pl/twórca/eugeniusz-bodo.

40 Ibid., 242.

41 Unfortunately, no copy of this film has survived.

Bodo even managed to feature Wars onscreen—camouflaged somewhat with Groucho Marx's trademark bushy hair and greasepaint mustache—as the piano player for his character's hot jazz band.

After working with the inventive Wars in such films as *Czy Lucyna to dziewczyna?* (Is Lucyna a girl?, directed by Juliusz Gardan, 1934), and *Pieśniarz Warszawy* (The songster of Warsaw, directed by Waszyński, 1934), Bodo was especially keen for his favorite composer to produce and arrange the songs for this new film, which openly celebrated jazz. Wars rose to the challenge enthusiastically: "With extensive deliberation, [Wars] showed what he could do, what he had heard and committed to memory . . . demonstrating the wealth of his jazz inspirations."[42] The three hits that Wars composed were entrusted to Bodo as solo singer and Wars's selected jazz instrumentalists. While Bodo left the writing of song lyrics to the expert Schlechter and Starski, he decided to collaborate with the two on the screenplay, though his specific contribution is unclear. Bodo ceded the director's chair once again to Leon Trystan (Chaim Lejb Wagman), who had first occupied that seat for *Two Days in Paradise.* According to a press report, Trystan's knowledge of cinema and use of cinematic "impressionism" allegedly awed the star.[43]

Altman would be thrilled with the proliferation of dualities in the plot of *One Floor Up,* the more so because their abundance renders the convention self-ironizing and delightfully nonsensical. The primary lovers—Bodo as Henryk Pączek and Grossówna as Lodzia Pączkówna—meet by accident because Lodzia, on her first visit to Warsaw, mistakes Henryk's apartment for that of her paternal uncle, Hipolit Pączek (Józef Orwid), since only the young man's door sports a card with a first initial and a surname. The young woman has no prior knowledge of the ongoing feud between these two unrelated, temperamentally antagonistic Pączeks. Hipolit, an elderly landlord who cherishes order and the old days, likes to play the most tedious repertoire of classical music in an amateur quartet. In vivid contrast, the zany, mercurial Henryk, who earns a living as a radio announcer, mainly enjoys rehearsing with and writing songs for his jazz group, in hopes of performing in public. The more Hipolit longs to evict the chaos-creating Henryk, the more Henryk determines to entrench himself. Hipolit lives to be outraged, while Henryk lives to provoke (fig. 1.8).

---

42 Wolański, *"Już nie zapomnisz mnie,"* 102.
43 Ibid., 249.

Figure 1.8. Henryk's jazz band provokes Hipolit to rush into his apartment and complain about the noise. Henryk Wars half-stands at the piano, Henryk (Bodo) rises above the rest with maracas in hand, and Hipolit (Józef Orwid) wields his umbrella impotently at the far right. *Piętro wyżej* (One Floor Up), 1937, dir. Leon Trystan.

Lodzia, a resourceful, modern young woman, discovers an extra key to what she thinks is her uncle's apartment under the hall carpet and lets herself in, awaiting her relative's return. When Henryk rolls home drunk, wearing a fez and depositing a live goose he won in some contest on an armchair, Lodzia is more indignant than frightened, and then amused when Henryk begins to break various items of his own to disprove her claim that he is in the wrong apartment. The two fall in love with each other after Henryk plays her a song that he wrote and she clearly adores; the lovely Lodzia shares neither the taste nor the temperament of her uncle (fig. 1.9). Henryk gallantly offers her his bedroom for the night while he bunks in his bathtub.

Once Lodzia leaves before breakfast the next morning, and Henryk launches one of his frantic searches for his "princess," other dualities crop up. Instead of integrating a formal secondary couple, this musical comedy exploits the confusion created by the lovers' two friends/foils—Henryk's gold-digging pal Kulka-Kulkiewicz (Ludwik Sempoliński), whose desired lifestyle means that he keeps a little black book of rich bachelorettes, and Lodzia's dull friend,

Figure 1.9. Henryk enchants Lodzia (Grossówna) with his new song. *Piętro wyżej* (One Floor Up), 1937, dir. Leon Trystan.

Anita Bonecka (Alina Żeliska), whose calling card Lodzia left in Henryk's place and therefore the woman whose name Henryk persistently attaches to Lodzia. A much later scene in which Henryk insists that the Bonecka standing before him cannot *be* Bonecka because she is not the woman to whom he intends to propose echoes the scene in which Lodzia insists that Henryk's apartment cannot be his because her uncle's "card" is tacked on his door. Both of these scenes are comical largely due to Henryk's crazy insistence on his "truth," even when that truth is false. Lodzia's second misunderstanding almost ends in tragedy, very likely because she has lost direct contact with Henryk, the playful lover whose character she is still learning to read. When Lodzia overhears Henryk recount Kulka-Kulkiewicz's mercenary marrying strategy to another companion, she mistakes it for Henryk's own, and ends their relationship without explanation. This impasse rouses another, lesser, duo to action—the feckless servants of the two Pączeks, Henryk's Damazy (Czesław Skoneczny) and Hipolit's Protazy (Stanisław Woliński), who thoroughly muddle the exchange of explanatory letters between the two lovers. Yet the misunderstanding is cleared up, the lovers passionately embrace, and a suddenly sanguine Hipolit predicts their wedding at the film's end.

That Henryk is impetuous, uninhibited, and prone to fall madly in love with a woman, a song, or an act of crazy provocation equips him to be an excellent lead in a musical. Bodo's character possesses what Martin Sutton defines as the key qualities of the musical's protagonist: "the romantic/rogue imagination and its daily battle with a restraining, 'realistic' social order."[44] Feuer expands on this liberatory function in the genre: "Musicals are unparalleled in presenting a vision of human liberation which is profoundly aesthetic. Part of the reason some of us love musicals so passionately is that they give us a glimpse of what it would be like to be free."[45] Indeed, Henryk in some cases provides his own buoyant soundtrack (albeit with unseen orchestral accompaniment). He is first prompted to do so after he discovers Lodzia's clue about her feelings for him—specifically, her revisions of his song title to indicate that its protagonist will love the same woman day after day: "Dzisiaj ta, i jutro ta" ("This girl today, and the same girl tomorrow"). Henryk immediately pounds out the new version on the piano and then takes to a crowded Warsaw street, singing this song loudly, walking swiftly to its rhythm, and pushing other pedestrians on the sidewalk out of his way to maintain both the rhythm and the rush of ecstasy that the music gives him. The camera, loaded on a truck bed or a very long dolly, keeps pace with him coursing through what seems to be an authentic crowd, with some boys in the background running along to stay in the moving shot. Henryk's song conveniently ends when he reaches the radio station where he works.

In a similar fashion, Henryk cannot refrain from sharing the thrilling news of his impending first date with Lodzia while he is on air, even though his boss has already warned him not to use the radio to locate his missing princess. As Henryk announces upcoming events by the hour, he suddenly puts down his news sheet and slips easily into the song "Umówiłem się z nią na dziewiątą" ("I've got a date with her at nine"), a lovely light number that Bodo confides to the big studio microphone and embellishes with just a few hand gestures (fig. 1.10). The camera cuts to several radio listeners (more women than men) who seem enchanted by this impromptu love song. When the boss rushes into his cubicle, he does not fire Henryk, but compliments him on his fine voice and invites his band for an audition.

---

44 Martin Sutton, "Patterns of Meaning in the Musical," in *Genre: The Musical. A Reader*, ed. Rick Altman (London: Routledge, 1981), 91.

45 Feuer, *The Hollywood Musical*, 84.

Figure 1.10. Henryk sings on-air about his date with Lodzia. *Piętro wyżej* One Floor Up), 1937, dir. Leon Trystan.

The success of both of these somewhat unorthodox numbers relies on Bodo's particular talents. In the street scene, his fame as well as his showmanship helped clear the way for his music-driven passage down a crowded Warsaw sidewalk, though credit is due Trystan for resisting any conventionalized setup in which the singer stops and crowds surround him. Instead, Trystan uses the camera to convey how an "ordinary" man in love strides along in his private bubble of music-accompanied happiness. Henryk's sudden song about his anticipated date with Lodzia works so well because of Bodo's emotional openness, spot-on diction, and gestural restraint. This scene resembles a little gem of a cabaret sketch.

The other two musical numbers in *One Floor Up* present a striking juxtaposition of genre film convention and cabaret influence. The final performance not only untangles the misunderstandings separating the lovers, but also fulfills the musical's set requirement of reconciliation in the larger community—in this case, resolving the feud between the two Pączeks. Since the radio station mistakenly has invited both men's ensembles to perform, Henryk "suddenly" realizes what Wars had planned all along—that the amateur quartet's rendition of Antonín Dvořák's *Humoresque* be blended with the jazzy third hit of the film, "Sex appeal to nasza broń kobieca" ("Sex appeal is our defense as women"). As Henryk conducts, Hipolit's fellow players "heat up" under the influence of the jazz band's performance, and the radio station manager declares the joint session a success that he wants to feature regularly in his programming. In this instance, jazz does not so much trump classical music as inspire classical players to try out jazz riffs. Henryk's conciliatory gesture towards the quartet wins him Hipolit's good will and clears the path to his and Lodzia's restored romance and predicted marriage.

The other number constitutes one of the most famous performances in Polish film to date. It takes place during a masked ball, where guests dress in costumes ranging from giant animal heads placed atop suits to Hipolit's unfortunate, yet highly appropriate choice of a knight's armor. In addition to the masks and costumes that play with identity and propriety, other social rules are disregarded at the ball as a line of dancers holding hands sweeps up and down the stairs of the two-story ballroom and pulls random people into the melee. Lodzia is one of the last to be chosen, and she seems at once helpless and happy to be swept away. We suddenly learn that Henryk's jazz band will be the evening's feature entertainment, at last performing in full the tune of "Sex Appeal" that they have been rehearsing so long one floor up. Missing in the rehearsals was Henryk's key role as singer. Sebastian Jagielski describes Henryk-Bodo's stunning reveal in useful detail:

> "And now our evening's star attraction, our lovely national version of Mae West!" . . . The curtains part and she appears, a star with oversized female attributes, before both diegetic and non-diegetic viewers. Everything in her image is too large, intense, and expressive. She is dressed in a close-fitting evening gown, a satin number that highlights her curves (mainly her monstrously large bust). She wears long black gloves decorated with sequins, is draped with necklaces, bracelets, earrings, and rings, and holds a fan of ostrich feathers. All her female attributes have been hyperbolized.[46]

Jagielski notes the different global valences of a Mae West impersonation in the 1930s. West herself was rumored to be a drag queen and had emerged as an important symbol of inclusiveness in gay male clubs from Berlin to New York City. The Polish scholar argues that Bodo's costuming and performance as Mae West secretly signals his own homosexuality—a revealed self-portrait—that would be clear and gratifying to the initiated and a comic romp for the general

---

46 Sebastian Jagielski, "Teoria *queer* a kino polskie," *Przegląd kulturoznawczy* 13, no. 3 (2012): 267–270.

public. This performance continues after the show and offstage, when Bodo-Henryk's Mae West bewitches and ridicules an adoring Hipolit, his longtime opponent, who is literally encased in a construct of old-fashioned masculinity (fig. 1.11).

Figure 1.11. Bodo-Henryk as "the Polish" Mae West. *Piętro* wyżej (One Floor Up), 1937, dir. Leon Trystan.

Within the context of the film, however, Henryk's astonishing impersonation of a big woman playing an alternately brazen and affected coquette (his performance does not attempt to capture West's sardonic delivery and stagey burlesque poses) represents his greatest, most layered act of provocation. Up to this point in *One Floor Up*, he has sung about his feelings of being in love with a certain girl. Henryk's "Sex Appeal" is a much more aggressive, complex number in terms of its implied persona, message, and singing style. It requires a clever, angry female performer—or someone convincingly imitating such a performer—to convey all it contains. This song equates masculine strength primarily with violence (physical strength, a punch, a slap) and women's power with their "grace, style, charm, and chic." Yet the singer drawing these equations and arguing for "the weaker sex's greater strength" underscores the sheer performativity of "her sex" because Henryk's large, obviously cross-dressed body and emphatic, fast-paced singing indicate otherwise. Schlechter's lyrics, shifting from battle tactics to explosive cries, pose an obstacle course for any Polish singer. Henryk's version of Mae West cannot help but suggest a fusion of the male and female powers that the song lays out: aggression and blandishment. Furthermore, Henryk crosses another line of identity, accompanying his band's final instrumental refrain with markedly Black scat singing and exclamations. His bravura performance indulges in the transformations that the innately liberatory, transgressive qualities of early jazz seemed to afford all of its performers—crossing conservatively defined binaries of gender, sexuality, and race.

Henryk's bravura performance also smuggles a cabaret/revue theater bombshell into a genre film that leaves the viewers longing for more. In comparison with the imported American act at the Alhambra in *My Husband* or Grossówna dancing across desktops in *Forgotten Melody, One Floor Up* literally showcases one of Poland's greatest cabaret/revue stars delivering one of his most challenging, magnetic stage numbers onscreen. Suddenly the madcap Henryk in love is unveiled and unleashed as Bodo the magnificent. This number does not even fit into the maximally stretched character and plot conventions of the film. It barrels in from the cabaret, where cross-dressing was a staple source of edgy sexual comedy, as was the ability to incarnate a famous celebrity onstage—for example, Marlene Dietrich of *The Blue Angel* (Zula Pogorzelska), or the wildly self-aggrandizing operatic tenor Jan Kiepura (Adolf Dymsza). In consequence, Bodo's performance as Mae West proved to be too good to be relegated to film and wasted on a mass audience. Five months after the premiere of *One Floor Up,* the best Warsaw cabaret in business in 1938, Cyrulik Warszawski (The barber of Warsaw), engaged Bodo to reprise his daring "Sex Appeal" number before live appreciative theatergoers, who welcomed him with thunderous applause.[47]

In contrast, the sequence of scenes following "Sex Appeal" in the film are anticlimactic in their resumption and eventual reconciliation of the lovers' plot. Bodo subsides into the smitten Henryk and utilizes "Sex Appeal" as an inspiring instrumental number, not an occasion for a second reveal of his power. As much as *One Floor Up* succeeds in enriching its musical romantic comedy with Henryk's mostly well-developed characterization, Kulka-Kulkiewicz's sardonic partnering, and Lodzia's swift, smart responsiveness to her lover, Bodo, Wars, Schlechter, and Trystan let a cabaret genie out of the bottle in a set piece that steals the show. Nonetheless, most contemporary reviewers praised the film for

---

47 Wolański, *Eugeniusz Bodo: "Już taki jestem zimny drań,"* 264.

its ensemble and plot coherence, while the right-wing press predictably singled out Bodo's cross-dressed performance as vulgar and unnecessary. After the screening of *One Floor Up* at the Eastern Trade Fairs in Lwów, the film won an award from the Chief Council of the Film Industry, and Wars netted a separate award from the same body for his jazz ensemble's performance, integration of classical music into the film, and three hit songs.[48]

Paweł and Gaweł: An Unconventional Cabaret Family

As mentioned above, the 1938 *Paweł and Gaweł* was made to capitalize on the box office success generated by *Robert and Bertrand* shot earlier the same year. Unfortunately, neither film was produced by Bodo's Urania Film, and their director was Mieczysław Krawicz, whom both Bodo and various critics deemed sloppy in his work. On a happier note, Wars composed each film's two songs, for which Starski and Schlechter wrote the lyrics. Sądek and Fethke worked on both screenplays, drawing on a comic sketch by Viennese writer Jan Nestroy for *Robert and Bertrand;* in the case of *Paweł and Gaweł*, Sądek and Fethke, joined by Starski, based their script very loosely on a fable by the great Polish playwright Aleksander Fredro. What sold both movies to the public was their pairing of Bodo and Dymsza—the two most successful film stars who had trained and performed together in the capital's cabarets. Dymsza, who appeared in twenty-five films between the wars, excelled as a dancer and an acrobat; an expert at nonsensical patter songs and monologues; an impersonator of political and artistic celebrities as well as unsavory city types; and a "grotesque" comedian—that is, a specialist in slapstick, mugging, and any kind of physical comedy he could improvise. Dymsza was a Varsovian born and bred, who, "thanks to his exceptionally original style, created the figure of a Warsaw rascal and most appealing smartass."[49]

Yet in both films the performer who at once grounded and energized this comic pair was the much less-known Grossówna. Bodo claimed to have "discovered" her in 1936, but Grossówna had already appeared in five films, steadily ascending in terms of her importance in the cast, before she starred in the 1936 *Two Days*

48 Ibid., 265; Wolański, *"Już nie zapomnisz mnie,"* 105.

49 Joanna Sławińska, "Adolf Dymsza, najlepszy cwaniak polskiego kina," Polskie Radio/Jedynka, August 22, 2015, https://www.polskieradio.pl/7/4457/Artykul/1492205,Adolf-Dymsza-najlepszy-cwaniak-polskiego-kina. See also Dymsza's biography in Roman Dziewoński, *Dodek-Dymsza* (Łomianki: Wydawnictwo LTW, 2010).

in Paradise. The preceding films had connected her to other influential figures in the industry such as Fethke, Sądek, Tom, Wars, Schlechter, and Dymsza himself. Grossówna was only four years younger than Bodo and Dymsza, but her path to Warsaw stage and screen stardom was more circuitous—in part due to her starting point as a working-class girl born in the provincial city of Toruń, in part because she first pursued the career of dancer and choreographer. Grossówna trained as a ballerina for several years in Paris with Bronisława Niżyńska (sister of the famous Vaclav Nijinsky). Upon her return to her hometown, she had graduated to the position of first-tier dancer in Toruń's newly revived Teatr Miejski (City Theater), performing a wide array of works as needed in operettas and dramas—classical ballet, Polish folk dances, and "grotesque" dances that integrated stunning acrobatic moves.[50]

Grossówna at last moved to Warsaw in the early 1930s, where she performed in those cabarets that maintained the standards and the key staff of Qui Pro Quo after it closed: Little Qui Pro Quo and The Barber of Warsaw. Once the newly minted cabaret artist was cast in film in the mid-1930s, her fresh, vivid features, slim athletic build, and relative obscurity allowed her to pass as much younger heroines than were possible for her contemporaries. But what most enabled her string of successes from 1937 until the beginning of the war were her learned abilities as a film actress. Grossówna not only knew how to move her body for the camera, but also had learned how to project rapt attention and ardent enthrallment—the sort of still expressions that hold the viewer's gaze, especially if one performs the part of the silent female lover. Grossówna's appeal thus matched Bodo's and Dymsza's in ways that accomplished cabaret actresses such as Zula and Zimińska could not or perhaps would not project.

The plots of *Robert and Bertrand* and *Paweł and Gaweł* are highly contrived, to a point of absurdity that privileges spontaneous play over verisimilitude. The stars and their lively onscreen interactions proved much more important than a conventional plot. The screenwriters for *Robert and Bertrand* shrewdly inserted a special fanfare for their most famous players, at last brought together on the silver screen. The film introduces Bodo (Bertrand) and Dymsza (Robert) by themselves, as two traveling salesmen who fortuitously meet when they are down on their luck. After Robert attempts to train a despairing Bertrand with his ridiculously fast, funny sales pitch (already an injection of cabaret), the two sing a duet celebrating their partnership, assuring moviegoers that these comic stars will be sharing the screen throughout. Despite the fact that Grossówna was

---

50 Artur Duda, "'Purpurowy płomień': Helena Grossówna w Operze Pomorskiej i Teatrze Toruńskim," *Pamiętnik teatralny* 1–2 (2017): 128–131, 133.

already a familiar face to moviegoers from *Forgotten Melody* and *One Floor Up,* the screenwriters chose to represent her gradual initiation into this famous pair's company. She is cast as Irena, an upper-class young woman who longs for personal fame rather than an advantageous marriage arranged for her by her father (Fertner in his traditional role). Yet Irena seems perfectly happy to fall in love with the unsuitable Bertrand. Excited about writing a detective novel, Irena hires the two as criminal consultants for her research, not realizing that their credentials consist of a short stint in jail for vagrancy. Robert-Dymsza inevitably eclipses the two lovers through his impersonations: first, as an experienced Warsaw thief and, second, as a recently arrived Chinese specialist on expensive "Oriental" ceramics. Both comic characterizations qualify as cabaret imports. Towards the film's end, the entire trio performs an utterly unexpected, outrageously exaggerated Apache dance, with Grossówna matching the moves of both men as well as Dymsza's peculiar acrobatic verve. The film closes with an absurd three-way scene as Bertrand and Irena kiss in his jail cell, and Robert, in the cell above, lowers himself through a hole in his floor to smile his blessing on their union.

In *Paweł and Gaweł,* therefore, the reconstitution of the trio is a foregone conclusion, prompting audiences to renew their contact with Bodo, Dymsza, and Grossówna together as if these reunited stars are their old friends.[51] In this film, Grossówna's role is that of plucky runaway rather than dabbling socialite. Her character and relationships with both male characters are complicated and rendered ambiguous by the fact that she plays Violetta Bellami, a talented violinist, at three different interchangeable ages—the authentic Violetta, who is a nineteen-year-old longing for love and an adult life, the thirteen-year-old violin prodigy whom she must impersonate in order to pay off her dead father's debts to her demanding impresario, Hubert (Józef Orwid), and the much younger brat persona she devises to manipulate Bodo and Dymsza's characters.

In contrast to *Robert and Bertrand,* in which Dymsza enjoyed more comedic latitude with his impersonations, Bodo's character in *Paweł and Gaweł* is delineated and motivated more specifically, and Dymsza's agenda is fluid. Bodo plays Paweł Gawlicki, an ambitious engineer/inventor who sells radios in his shop one floor above the household goods store owned and operated by Dymsza's Gaweł Pawlicki. As Robert Birkholc observes in his recent review of the film, the Fredro fable from which the movie derives presents a story of two neighbors who live on top of each other and constantly quarrel, yet this plotline quickly disappears

51 Altman, *The American Film Musical,* 297.

in the film because "Paweł and Gaweł here are essentially sympathetic."[52] Early on, Paweł decides to travel to Warsaw in hopes of selling his new invention, which looks like a precursor of the transistor radio. The film opens on his enthusiastic, highly technical pitch of this wonder to an older couple who simply want a traditional radio that will complement their furniture. Whereas Dymsza's pitch in *Robert and Bertrand* sounded more improvised, Bodo-Paweł's pitch demonstrates his mastery over technology and word-perfect memorization of a script packed with technological jargon. The playful Gaweł at first seems devoted to playing irritating practical jokes on the serious Paweł, but over the course of the film he gravitates towards the role of his neighbor's indispensable, funny sidekick, especially as the two try to manage the problem that is Violetta.

The trio soon reunite on the train to Warsaw. Gaweł has made sure that he is booked in Paweł's compartment, the better to torment him. A close-up of Violetta through the compartment window as she stares with wonder at Paweł effectively spotlights Grossówna's return and fulfills the viewers' expectations. Here Violetta is dressed as a thirteen-year-old and eventually is hauled away by Hubert, who is angered by her show of independence as she wanders down the train corridor. But Hubert is too late. Paweł accidentally bruised her nose when he opened the compartment door too quickly, and by the time he kisses it "to make it better" and put an end to her complaints, Violetta is already longing for him.

The screenwriters deliberately booked Paweł, Gaweł, Violetta, and Hubert in the same Warsaw hotel, where the plot thickens with romance, scandal, and comedy. Here Violetta escapes her keeper once more, borrows a shoulder-baring evening dress with the help of a light-fingered bellboy, and boldly enters the hotel restaurant, with its fancy bar and modest dance floor, hoping to bump into Paweł. Not recognizing the girl from the train in the beauty standing before them, both Paweł and Gaweł play tricks on each other so as to monopolize her attention. In both instances, the film smartly focuses on the action of play rather than romantic plot—that is, the resulting comic sketches rather than the wooing of Violetta. Gaweł arranges for Paweł to be called urgently to a telephone booth in the hotel lobby, where he engages in a furious, nonsensical argument with another man whom Gaweł has conned into the adjacent booth. When Paweł returns, Violetta is in Gaweł's arms on the dance floor. Paweł then outwits his pesky neighbor by surreptitiously marking him as a waiter, attaching a numbered pin to his lapel and stuffing a white napkin into his pocket (fig. 1.12). Sent

52 Robert Birkholc, "*Paweł and Gaweł*, reż Mieczysław Krawicz," Culture.pl., June 2018, https://culture.pl/pl/dzielo/pawel-i-gawel-rez-mieczyslaw-krawicz.

off to get more drinks for the trio, Gaweł is accosted by diners on all sides to take orders, clear tables, bring checks, and, in one case, dispose of a check for a drunk who cannot pay his bill. Paweł has launched Gaweł into one of Dymsza's best roles, for he responds to all of these diners like a Warsaw smartass, with arrogance, backtalk, and the sudden performance of a miraculous balancing act with a loaded tray in a crowd. When Gaweł finally resurfaces after his lengthier sketch, Paweł and Violetta are no longer there, for Paweł has strategically moved his prize out onto the terrace.

Figure 1.12. Paweł (Bodo) on the right transforms Gaweł (Dymsza) into a waiter. *Paweł i Gaweł* (Paweł and Gaweł), 1938, dir. Mieczysław Krawicz.

This relatively brief, touching scene just outside the hotel expeditiously establishes Paweł and Violetta as the film's lovers (fig. 1.13). As in *One Floor Up*, but in a more intimate way, Bodo-Paweł easily, eloquently declares his love to Violetta in the Wars/Starski song "Moja królewna" ("My princess"), portraying her as the sleeping beauty he has sought the world over and whom he will wake "with the most ordinary kiss that will leave us breathless."[53] Once again rendering her passive part alluring, Grossówna basks in Paweł's tender address as he draws

53 "[N]ajzwyklejszym pocałunkiem / Takim do utraty tchu."

closer to her and then kisses her on the hand and the lips. Before they part, Paweł purchases two copies of the silhouettes that a roving artist has made for them, thereby providing them both with tangible proof of their love.

Figure 1.13. Paweł and Violetta (Grossówna) on the terrace. *Paweł i Gaweł* (Paweł and Gaweł), 1938, dir. Mieczysław Krawicz.

What thwarts these lovers, unleashes an avalanche of nonsensical, slapstick comic scenes, and reconfigures the enchanted couple into an oddball cabaret trio is the false public announcement of Paweł as the thirteen-year-old Violetta's father. Hubert had paid someone to play the (actually deceased) dad of his prodigy at a press conference, but Paweł, duped into believing that the press has gathered to hear about his amazing new radio, unwittingly steps into the paid pretender's place. It now beggars belief that neither Paweł nor Gaweł recognizes the incredible similarity between the prodigy and the princess pursued the night before. Instead, they join forces in trying to flee the bratty girl, who, in turn, wants to flee Warsaw with them. The clever Violetta quickly realizes that a loud shriek, the signal of an oncoming tantrum, will bend both men to her will. One of the funniest sequences involves Paweł locking a shrieking Violetta in his wardrobe and Gaweł rescuing the shrieker after he has had to flip both wardrobe and girl upside down. (Violetta is braced in a headstand when he opens the door [fig. 1.14].) When Gaweł learns that his neighbor wants to let his alleged "daughter" escape, he decides to stop her in the most abrupt, cartoonish way, hanging her on a coatrack by the bow on the back of her dress. Both Dymsza and Grossówna perform this grotesque feat effortlessly.

Figure 1.14. Gaweł unlocks the wardrobe door on an upended Violetta. *Paweł i Gaweł* (Paweł and Gaweł), 1938, dir. Mieczysław Krawicz.

Once the three arrive in Paweł and Gaweł's provincial hometown, the relationship among them grows more confused. On the one hand, Violetta is now adamant about revealing her adult identity to Paweł and reclaiming his love. She conspires with his shop clerk, Stefek (Tadeusz Fijewski), to steal out to a Roma encampment at night and purchase a love potion. On the other hand, Gaweł and, especially, Paweł remain puzzled about her identity since Paweł and Violetta's "father and daughter" photos have been splashed across the pages of the Warsaw press, and Hubert has posted a substantial reward for Violetta's return to her supposedly anguished impresario. Public opinion seems to be eroding Paweł's private conviction. In the meantime, Violetta's shrieks force the trio to act like an awkward family. When Violetta demands that her "papa" sing her to sleep and Paweł, in turn, demands Gaweł's assistance, the two perform the greatest musical hit of the film, Wars/Starski's slow foxtrot imitating a lullaby, "Ach, śpij, kochanie" ("Oh, sleep, my darling"). As the two men sing at her bedside—just as Paweł sang on the hotel terrace—Grossówna conveys both rapture and deep contentment, incarnating an onscreen audience with which the viewers can ally (fig. 1.15).[54] She projects how deeply her character wants to be absorbed into a duo—or, perhaps, a trio. Paweł and Gaweł, however, react first with anxiety and then irritation. Gaweł cannot decide whether he should sing beside Paweł in solidarity or leap to the other side of the bed to function as a kind of co-parent. He therefore leaps over her bed twice, trying out both positions. The men's increasing irritation with Violetta's wakefulness resonates in their harsher singing. Yet they prove to be most childlike as the repeated song puts *them* to sleep, allowing Violetta to escape. Thus, the three performers have come to match one another in wielding power, succumbing to vulnerability, and, above all, garnering laughs.

Figure 1.15. Gaweł (left) and Paweł (middle) prepare to sing Violetta to sleep. *Paweł i Gaweł* (Paweł and Gaweł), 1938, dir. Mieczysław Krawicz.

54 Feuer, *The Hollywood Musical*, 26–29.

The film's shift to the Roma encampment initially seems an ill-judged side trip into cliched exotica. Most of the performers in this strange scene did belong to the Zespół Cygańskich Kwieków (The Kwieks's Gypsy ensemble), a Roma group that professionally performed their ethnic music and dance. Unfortunately, those Roma characters with speaking parts were Poles mimicking Roma accents and reinforcing contemporary negative stereotypes of Roma as sham fortune tellers and actual thieves. Nevertheless, the separate forays of Violetta and Stefek, and then Paweł and Gaweł on a rescue mission, bring about three important character and plot developments. First, Violetta, clad in Roma dress, is entranced by Roma songs and simply takes over playing the violin from a young Roma man, thereby demonstrating her more capacious musicality as an adult. A non-Polish "elemental" venue liberates her from the proscriptions inhibiting her as a child prodigy in a Polish concert hall. Second, Violetta soon finds herself performing Roma dances with the disguised Paweł and Gaweł, her eyes once more shining with joy. Cast together for the first time, the trio plays wonderfully well, though Dymsza-Gaweł cannot resist some comic embellishments. Third, after the two men rescue Violetta from a Roma plot to return her to Hubert and win the reward, Paweł unexpectedly discovers the silhouettes among the sleeping Violetta's things and recognizes her at long last as his sleeping beauty.

A few more comical escapades follow, but the encampment segment has prepared us for the delightful ambivalence of the film's final scene. The lovers are reunited, and the previously unsettled Paweł has slipped into a state of blissful acceptance. A joint Paweł and Gaweł team has repelled Hubert in his attempt to re-enslave Violetta financially and psychologically. In the concluding scene, Grossówna has drifted off to sleep between Bodo and Dymsza, after which the two actors face the camera, break the fourth wall, and bid the viewers beyond to hush. By demonstrating their awareness of the moviegoing audience, they acknowledge that they are actors rather than the characters they have been incarnating. At the same time, as actors, they openly invite the audience to join them as they "hush" in Paweł's room and the show itself. In short, Bodo and Dymsza are behaving like cabaret performers, underscoring the artifice of their sketch and welcoming patrons to join in their game. Instead of concluding the film with the lovers' kiss, Bodo and Dymsza disregard the genre convention and present themselves and the sleeping Grossówna as three adept comedians who have reached what they deem to be the most appropriate end to their play, in both senses of the word.

Conclusion

Hundreds of Polish-language films were produced in the interwar period, after Poland regained its status as a sovereign state. Yet the developing Polish film industry had, at most, nine years to mold anything resembling a national cinema in genres ranging from nationalist melodrama to Polish-language musical comedy. While an eager, gifted group of composers, lyricists, and musicians quickly mastered the skills for writing songs and scores for the onscreen musical comedies, the Polish film industry did not possess the financial or human resources for an American-style Busby Berkeley extravaganza or even soundstages adequate for shooting a glamorous star vehicle focused on renowned singers and dancers. As I have argued in this essay, the greatest distinction in Polish-language musical comedies derived from the talent and freewheeling style that they transferred and integrated from Warsaw's cabarets and revue theaters, a process that gained momentum from roughly 1934 to 1939. Cabaret artists and writers invested in the new medium quickly learned that cabaret stars could not simply appear in film, mugging their way through scenes without time for preparation and adjustments to new film genre conventions that they themselves found silly and constraining. Even the relatively successful film *What My Husband Is Up to at Night*, which literally showcased cabaret stars and sites, suffered from cabaret sketch conceptions that grew tiresome when they were drawn out onscreen.

But by the late 1930s, directors and screenwriters had learned a great deal about maintaining the film plot's pacing and coherence—often tightening exposition using dovetailing visual and musical links—and cabaret stars had absorbed the right techniques for performing effectively in front of the camera. While *Forgotten Melody* did imitate some Hollywood-style scenes of a group of pretty girls adept at coordinated kayaking or teasing and giggling at male visitors to their school, the real magic of the movie relied on Wars's score, Grossówna's dancing, Żabczyński's singing, and Andrzejewska and Znicz's acting. *One Floor Up* and *Paweł and Gaweł*, in turn, represented a distinctive fusion of musical comedy film with cabaret artistry: in the first case, through the synergy of Wars's songs and scoring, Trystan's direction, the efforts of multiple screenwriters, and Bodo's crossover talents; and, in the second, through the combination of a screenplay that cleverly embedded cabaret sketch comedy in the plot and that comedy's expert execution by film/cabaret stars Bodo, Dymsza, and Grossówna.

Indeed, I maintain that it is impossible to fully appreciate these last two movies without understanding the interaction between filmmaking and sophisticated cabaret performance in Warsaw up to the outbreak of World War II. While various Polish musical comedies echo or parallel those of Hollywood with plots that reconcile class and generational differences, the most interesting later films mainly provide the best conditions (oddball characters, numbers, dialogue) for talented stars to romp easily with each other at an upbeat pace. The carefully unaccented, yet insurmountable difference here privileges neither class nor political stance, but qualified, charismatic showfolk. This artistically exciting interdependence between stage and screen was literally destroyed by the two-pronged invasion of Poland by German troops on 1 September 1939 and Soviet troops on 17 September 1939. The Nazis' prosecution of the Holocaust murdered the vast majority of the acculturated Jews who had formed the foundations of the film and entertainment industry and who remained in Warsaw. Znicz, Schlechter, Włast, Trystan, and Artur Gold were just a few of several thousand such victims. As Bodo's death in a labor camp examples, the Jewish and Christian directors, writers, performers, and musicians who fled into Soviet-held territory also suffered, albeit to varying degrees. Even those lucky enough to be attached to the "revue units" included in General Władysław Anders's Army—which left the Soviet Union in 1942 and trekked through the Middle East to the Italian front in 1944—discovered that they were denied reentry into Poland after the war due to the "anti-reactionary" policies of the new Moscow-allied government.[55] If we are to assess the surprisingly rich popular culture that arose in interwar, independent Poland, then theater and film historians today must attempt to reconstruct what so many talented Polish Jewish and gentile artists succeeded in creating and finetuning together onstage and onscreen, before their exceptional collaboration was torn apart.

Bibliography

Altman, Richard. *The American Film Musical.* Bloomington: Indiana University Press, 1987.

Armatysz, L., and W. Stradomski. *Od "Niewolnicy zmysłów" do "Czarnych diamentów": Szkice o polskich filmach z lat 1914–1939.* Warsaw: Centralny Ośrodek Metodyki Upowszechniania Kultury, 1988.

Birkholc, Robert. "*Paweł and Gaweł*, reż Mieczysław Krawicz." Culture.pl., June 2018. https://culture.pl/pl/dzielo/pawel-i-gawel-rez-mieczyslaw-krawicz.

Budzik, Łukasz, "*Piętro wyżej*. 80 lat od premiery." Film.org.pl, February 18, 2017. https://film.org.pl/r/pietro-wyzej-80-lat-od-premiery-101499.

Blum, Leon (L. B.). "*Każdemu wolno kochać*: trochę poezji w grotesce." *Kino*, March 12, 1933, 3.

55 For a study of the cabaret artists serving in Anders's Army, see Beth Holmgren, "The Jews in the Band: The Anders Army's Special Troupes," *POLIN* 32 (2020): *Jews and Music-Making in the Polish Lands*, ed. François Guesnet, Benjamin Matis, and Antony Polonsky, 177–191.

———. "*Co mój mąż robi w nocy?* Kilka dobrych pomysłów i ładna piosenka." *Kino,* November 11, 1934, 3.

Duda, Artur. "'Purpurowy płomień': Helena Grossówna w Operze Pomorskiej i Teatrze Toruńskim." *Pamiętnik teatralny* 1–2 (2017): 122–133.

Dziewoński, Roman. *Dodek-Dymsza.* Łomianki: Wydawnictwo LTW, 2010.

Feuer, Jane. *The Hollywood Musical.* 2nd ed. London: The Macmillan Press, 1993.

Haltof, Marek. *Kino polskie.* Gdańsk: słowo/obraz teritoria, 2004.

Halvi/Hyman Encyclopedia of Jewish Women. s.v. "Miriam Kressyn." December 31, 1999. www.jwa.org/encyclopedia/article/Kressyn-miriam.

Herbaczyński, Wojciech. *W dawnych cukiernicach i kawiarniach warszawskich.* Warsaw: Państwowy Instytut Wydawniczy, 1983.

Hoberman, J. *Bridge of Light: Yiddish Films between Two Worlds.* New York: Museum of Modern Art and Schocken Books, 1991.

Holmgren, Beth. "Cabaret Nation: The Jewish Foundations of Kabaret Literacki, 1920–1939." *POLIN* 31 (2019): *Poland and Hungary: Jewish Realities Compared.*, edited by François Guesnet, Howard Lupovitch, and Antony Polonsky, 273–288.

———. "The Jews in the Band: The Anders Army's Special Troupes." *POLIN* 32 (2020): *Jews and Music-Making in the Polish Lands,* edited by François Guesnet, Benjamin Matis, and Antony Polonsky, 177–191.

Jagielski, Sebastian. "Teoria *queer* a kino polskie." *Przegląd kulturoznawczy* 13, no. 3 (2012): 256–272.

"Konrad Tom nie chce być artystą filmowym, ale. . . ." *Kino,* October 30, 1932, 3.

Kowalczyk, Janusz R. "Michał Waszyński, 29.09.1904–20.02.1965." Culture.pl., April 2018. https://culture.pl/pl/tworca/michal-waszynski.

Latham, Angela. *Posing a Threat: Flappers, Chorus Girls, and Other Brazen Performers of the American 1920s.* Hanover: University Press of New England, 2000.

"Lives in the Yiddish Theatre, 1931–1969. Miriam Kressyn." Accessed July 20, 2022. www.museumoffamilyhistory//ex/K/Kressyn-Miriam.html.

Lubelski, Tadeusz. *Historia kina polskiego.* Kraków: Universitas, 2015.

Majewski, Jerzy S. "Przedwojenne warszawskie dancingi: najsłynniejsza była Adria." *Gazeta Wyborcza,* July 19, 2015.

Mazierska, Ewa. *Polish Popular Music on Screen.* Cham: Palgrave Macmillan, 2020.

Milewski, Barbara. "Hidden in Plain View: The Music of Holocaust Survival in Poland's First Post-War Feature Film." In *Music, Collective Memory, Trauma, and Nostalgia in European Cinema after the Second World War,* edited by Michael Baumgartner and Ewelina Boczkowska, 111–137. New York: Routledge, 2020.

Mościcki, Tomasz. "Eugeniusz Bodo." Culture.pl., 2010. culture.pl/pl/twórca/eugeniusz-bodo.

Pieńkowski, Michał. "'Cztery nogi,' 1934." Stare-kino. Accessed July 22, 2022. https://stare-kino.pl/cztery-nogi/.

"Pokażcie na filmie ładną Zulę!" *Kino,* March 12, 1933, 4.

Rogowski, Grzegorz. "Kim jest ostatnia statystyka z 'Zapomnianej melodii?'" *Rzeczpospolita,* August 10, 2017. https://www.rp.pl/historia/art2518041-kim-jest-ostatnia-statystka-z-zapomnianej-melodii.

"Romeo i Julcia." *Kino,* January 22, 1933, 10.

Ross, Sara. "'Good Little Bad Girls': Controversy and the Flapper Comedy." *Film History* 13, no. 4 (2001): 409–423.

Schatz, Thomas. *Hollywood Genres: Formulas, Filmmaking, and the Studio System*. Philadelphia: Temple University Press, 1981.

Skaff, Sheila. *The Law of the Looking Glass: Cinema in Poland, 1896–1939*. Athens: Ohio University Press, 2008.

Sławińska, Joanna. "Adolf Dymsza, najlepszy cwaniak polskiego kina." *Polskie Radio/ Jedynka*. August 22, 2015. https://www.polskieradio.pl/7/4457/Artykul/1492205,Adolf-Dymsza-najlepszy-cwaniak-polskiego-kina.

Sutton, Martin. "Patterns of Meaning in the Musical." In *Genre: The Musical. A Reader*, edited by Rick Altman, 190–196. London: Routledge, 1981.

Toeplitz, Jerzy. *Historia sztuki filmowej*, vol. 4, *1934–1939*. Warsaw: Wydawnictwa Artystyczne i Filmowe, 1969.

Walden, Joshua. "Leaving Kazimierz: Comedy and Realism in the Yiddish Film Musical *Yidl mitn Fidl*." *Music, Sound, and the Moving Image* 3, no. 2 (Autumn 2009): 159–193.

Włodek, Roman. *Jadwiga Andrzejewska na scenie i ekranie*. Warsaw: Księgarnia Akademicka, 2019.

Wolański, Ryszard. *"Już nie zapomnisz mnie": Opowieść o Henryku Warsie*. Warsaw: MUZA SA, 2010.

———. *Eugeniusz Bodo: "Już taki jestem zimny drań,"* Poznań: Rebis, 2012.

Wysocka, Tacjanna. *Wspomnienia*. Warsaw: Czytelnik, 1962.

Zahorska, Anna. "Recenzje filmowe." *Kultura*, December 11, 1938, 8.

CHAPTER 2

Between the Market and the Mirror: Stanisław Bareja's *Marriage of Convenience*

Helena Goscilo[1]

"I think the very reason I became a director was to make comedies."
—Stanisław Bareja, interview in *Kino* (1967)

A Genre for the Multitudes

During the extended postwar period of the PRL (the Polish People's Republic, 1947–1989) the discrepancy between the Polish populace's tastes and those of the critics yawned wide; and the latter's denigration of comedy explains the entrenched practice of overlooking or belittling the works of Stanisław Bareja (1929–1987), sometimes dismissing them altogether. Yet, "[o]f the twenty films shown in 1967, [his] *A Marriage of Convenience* and *Westerplatte* [dir. Stanisław Rózewicz] . . . [were] the most popular, with 57% of the total capacity of movie houses."[2] That audiences for specifically these two films topped attendance

---

1 I am indebted to Konrad Klejsa, professor of film and audio-visual media at the University of Łódź, who generously supplied me with his valuable survey of Bareja's oeuvre, and especially to the Interlibrary Loan service at the Ohio State University, the few but outstanding librarians of which located and provided access to materials critical for this chapter. And my warmest gratitude goes to Ela Ostrowska, who saved me from the errors peppering an earlier version of this chapter.

2 Charles Ford and Robert Hammond, *Polish Film: A Twentieth-Century History* (Jefferson and London: McFarland & Co., 2005), 107.

figures for that year suggests a polarization of domestic viewers' predilections: whereas *A Marriage of Convenience* belongs to the genre of musical comedy, the somber *Westerplatte* is a historical war feature dramatizing outnumbered Poles' fierce resistance against the Germans in the first battle (1939) of World War II. Unlike audiences, critics remained consistent insofar as they regularly privileged "serious" films and scorned the screen entertainment that the population craved and voted for with their złotys.[3] In that respect the situation differed little from that in the United States, where "cultural status often seemed in inverse proportion to mass appeal."[4] Such was also the case in the Soviet Union's early years, when audiences preferred popular fare imported from the United States—comedies starring Charlie Chaplin, adventures with Douglas Fairbanks, and the inimitable call of Tarzan—to the works of Sergei Eisenstein.

Accordingly, Bareja's exclusive focus on comedies,[5] which made him a favorite with cinemagoers, militated against his status within the professional cinematic hierarchy. In a corseted either/or approach, critics perceived him as insignificant vis-à-vis touted auteurs such as Andrzej Wajda and Krzysztof Zanussi, who tackled moral or historical issues from an intellectual standpoint, often in an elevated or melodramatic vein. Because Bareja, undisputedly the foremost figure in screen comedy of that period,[6] brought situational and visual humor, even occasional slapstick, to the weighty questions he tackled—and tackle them he did—he was deemed a lightweight.[7] Yet laughter, as Mikhail Bakhtin astutely maintained, has enormous subversive potential and may overturn the established order[8]—a concept of the comedic shared by the novelist Evgenii Zamiatin in his dystopian novel *My* (We, 1920), whose protagonist discovers that "laughter [i]s the most

---

3 For 1960s Polish reviews of *A Marriage of Convenience*, see Zygmunt Lichniak, "*Małżenstwo z rozsądku*, czyli film z ciuchów," *Słowo powszechne* 3 (1967); and Stanisław Grzelecki, "Bal na ciuchach," *Życie Warszawy* 2 (1967), both of whom apply the word *ciuchy* (secondhand or foreign-made clothes) to the film so as to denigrate it.

4 Jim Hillier and Douglas Pye, *100 Film Musicals* (London: Palgrave Macmillan/BFI, 2011), 5.

5 Apart from the crime drama *Dotknięcie nocy* (The touch of night, 1961/1962), all of Bareja's films are comedies.

6 Probably one of the more positive assessments of his oeuvre, though far from laudatory, concluded that he was "gifted with an exceptional inventiveness, but . . . [was] a careless scriptwriter and without any great talent at directing. His productions therefore suffered, although they abounded in excellent ideas that combined satire with absurdity" (Bolesław Michałek and Frank Turaj, *The Modern Cinema of Poland* [Bloomington: Indiana University Press, 1988], 55).

7 At the same time, the government encouraged the production of genres for the masses (Piotr Zwierzchowski, "Socialist Content, Hollywood Form: Crime Films and Musicals in the Polish Cinema of the 1960s," *Panoptikum* 17 [2017]: 198–200).

8 See Mikhail Bakhtin, *Rabelais and His World*, trans. Hélène Iswolsky (Bloomington: Indiana University Press, 1984).

potent weapon: laughter can kill everything—even murder."[9] And that conviction, of course, fuels Charlie Chaplin's films, in particular his sendup of Hitler in *The Great Dictator* (1940), as well as Mike Nichols's screen adaptation (1970) of Joseph Heller's *Catch-22* (1961), and many other anti-establishment films, such as *La Cage aux folles* (directed by Édouard Molinaro, 1978). Although Bareja understood all too well the dissentious possibilities of comedy, critics patently did not, their condescension presumably based on an animus against entertainment, which they mistook as incompatible with genuine political and social critique. Rimgaila Salys states that the Russian director Ivan "Pyr′ev made films for the people, not for film critics, so that his cinema is neither esoteric nor refined and should be judged as an artefact of popular culture (chapter five of this volume)." Bareja also made films "for the people," but, as my chapter contends, several aspects of his *Marriage of Convenience*—especially his meticulous attention to structure as well as his engagement with aesthetics—may sooner be identified with art films than popular movies. That fact, however, eluded most critics, who lambasted his comedies from the word go. While audiences laughed, critics sneered. Titles of two recent items devoted to Bareja explicitly pinpoint this division: "Audiences loved him; the critics didn't."[10] and "Critics couldn't tolerate him; censorship gave him no rest."[11] An active supporter of anti-Communist organizations, Bareja had to contend not only with censorship and limited budgets, but also with colleagues' envy.[12]

Those circumstances changed radically once Poland regained independence (1989). Recent years have witnessed a reassessment of Bareja's contribution to Polish cinema, ranging from director Juliusz Machulski's hyperbolic, apodictic assertion, "The entire cinema of moral concern isn't worth as much as one film by Bareja," to the more measured admission by Maciej Pawlicki, "We harmed Bareja. We: a horde of film scribblers . . . There was only one Bareja. The only one in his astounding pertinacity of recording the absurdities of everyday life."[13] Not only has the film community belatedly acknowledged Bareja as one

---

9 Evgenii Zamyatin, *We*, trans. Mirra Ginsburg (New York: The Viking Press and Bantam, 1972), 210.

10 Maciej Gąsiorowski, "Stanisław Bareja: Widzowie go kochali, krytycy nie," *Super Express Chicago*, December 11, 2020.

11 Paweł Piotrowicz, "Krytycy go nie znosili, cenzura nie dawała spokoju. 34 lata temu zmarł Stanisław Bareja," Onet, June 14, 2021, https://kultura.onet.pl/film/wywiady-i-artykuly/34-lata-temu-zmarl-stanislaw-bareja-kim-byl-rezyser-sylwetka/mb3vqx2.

12 Gąsiorowski, "Stanisław Bareja: Widzowie go kochali, krytycy nie"; Maciej Replewicz, *Stanisław Bareja. Król krzywego zwierciadła* (Poznań: Zyski Spółka, 2009), 123–126.

13 Bartozs Staszczyszyn, "Masters of Polish Comedy," Culture.pl., January 9, 2015, https://culture.pl/en/article/masters-of-polish-comedy.

of its most astute commentators on the foibles of pseudo-communism,[14] but in 2005, a street in Warsaw was named after him; a year later, then President Lech Kaczyński awarded him the Commander's Cross of the Order of Polonia Restituta; and in 2008, he was the posthumous recipient of a special Golden Duck Award as the country's comedy director of the century.

Poland today recognizes him as a master of comedy,[15] a genre that, like Bareja, has been rehabilitated and continues to attract multitudes.[16] Reportedly, his films shown on TV attract the most enthusiastic viewers.[17] A BAREJADA festival has come into being, and the director Kazimierz Kutz's term "Bareisms," which carried exclusively pejorative connotations when it originally entered the cinematic lexicon,[18] has transformed so fundamentally over the last five decades as to denote, admiringly, "expressions or scenes using a specific kind of humour invented" by him.[19] Moreover, as Konrad Klejsa has observed, the formerly neglected Bareja was the first Polish filmmaker whose entire body of works

---

14 Jerzy Eisler in his review of Dorota Skotarczak's volume *Obraz społczeństwa PRL w komedii filmowej*, points out that today Bareja's comedies, "so harshly greeted by critics . . . have become one of the most important sources of information about that period [PRL]," especially for the young generations (Jerzy Eisler, "*Obraz społczeństwa PRL w komedii filmowey*, 2004," review of *Obraz społczeństwa PRL w komedii filmowej*, by Dorota Skotarczak, *Pamięć i Sprawiedliwość* 3–2, no. 6 [2004]: 88).

15 Beata Pieńkowska, "Stanisław Bareja," Polish Film Academy, accessed August 9, 2022, https://akademiapolskiegofilmu.pl/en/historia-polskiego-filmu/directors/stanislaw-bareja.32.

16 Some of the biggest recent moneymakers in Poland have been comedies, notably those of Machulski, but also such franchises as *Planeta Singli* (Planet of singles), a romantic comedy lucrative enough to have prompted one sequel after another. In 2019, the romantic comedy *Miszmasz czyli Kogel Mogel* (A mishmash, or, A mess-up) topped the list of highest-grossing screen offerings, and *Planeta Singli 3* was in seventh place. The only other Polish film among the top ten was the drama *Polityka* (Politics), which was in sixth position. The remaining seven films were all Anglophone imports (Polish Box Office for 2019, Boxofficemojo, https://www.boxofficemojo.com/year/2019/?area=PL). The preceding year likewise saw two romantic comedies in the top ten, with *Planeta Singli 2* occupying third place (Polish Box Office for 2018, Boxofficemojo, https://www.boxofficemojo.com/year/2018/?area=PL&grossesOption=calendarGrosses). And in 2017, the romantic comedy *Listy do M.3* (Letters to Santa 3), yet another sequel, reigned as number 1, while 2020 ushered in *Letters to Santa 4* (Polish Box Office for 2017, Boxofficemojo, https://www.boxofficemojo.com/year/2017/?area=PL&grossesOption=calendarGrosses).

17 Gąsiorowski, "Stanisław Bareja: Widzowie go kochali, krytycy nie."

18 Bareja unhesitatingly admitted that Kutz's derogatory term wounded him, since they were supposedly friends at school and later. See Piotrowicz, "Krytycy go nie znosili." See Daniel Olbrychski's belated praise of Bareja and his remorseful confession that he joined the chorus of the director's detractors (Daniel Olbrychski, *Anioły wokół głowy* [Warsaw: BGW, 1992], 84).

19 Joanna Rożen-Wojciechowska, "The Phenomenon of Polish Independent Cinema in 1989–2009," in *Polish Cinema Now!: Focus on Contemporary Polish Cinema*, ed. Mateusz Werner (London and Warsaw: Adam Mickiewicz Institute and John Libbey Publishing, 2020), 148.

was released on DVD, clearly, with an eye on the market. These now enjoy cult status,[20] especially among the young, for whom his comedies provide invaluable insights into an era they never knew firsthand. Such a sea change, ironically, instances precisely the sort of ideological *volte-face* that the director satirized in his works. Yet it is a welcome development, for the belated reassessment of Bareja as an auteur should prompt substantive, unjaundiced studies of his oeuvre, not unlike the biography by Maciej Replewicz (2009) and his subsequent publications about the director.

Animated Credits as Condensed Preview

"I don't wish to scare viewers."
—Stanisław Bareja, interview (1967)

From the very first frame Bareja's vastly underrated *Marriage of Convenience* relies on an unusual filmic technique to supply a visual network of motifs on which the subsequent narrative expands. At first unobtrusively, a red thread extends against a white frame even before the animated credits unroll at manic speed against a luridly colored background to the rom-pom-pom of lively, swiftly changing music. Such a thread also separates each of the names identifying all participants in the production of the film. Interspersed among entries in this list are what seem to be arbitrary objects: a mirror onto which two hearts are superimposed, subsequently flanked by a pack of dollars to the right and a wad of złotys on the left, later followed by a separate shot of a bright red knit shirt (fig. 2.1). A painting oddly "framed" by several rows of red thread and, then, a circular labyrinth composed of red thread emerge. Both threads start to unravel (fig. 2.2). Additional images of a sizable red wall and a childlike drawing of five musicians with red mouths emphasize the ubiquity of the hue that reticulates throughout the film's preliminaries. The music accompanying these seemingly random but, in fact, carefully selected items likewise imperceptibly transitions from one stylistic register to another—muzak, jazz, Charleston—in a seamless partial mix of the numbers accompanying the narrative that ensues.

20 Konrad Klejsa, "Stanisław Bareja—nadrealizm sojalistyczny," in *Autorzy kina polskiego*, vol. 2, ed. Grażyna Stachówna and Bogusław Zmudziński (Krakow: Jagiellonian University Press, 2014), 79–128.

Figure 2.1. Bareja condenses the film's major themes—here, money and art—in a series of images as the credits unfold. *Małżeństwo z rozsądku* (A marriage of convenience), 1966, dir. Stanisław Bareja.

Figure 2.2. The red thread that frames a depiction of a neighborhood in Warsaw and provides structure as it runs throughout the film.

Given the year of the film's release and the period it portrays, the red patently adverts to the color ineluctably associated with the Soviet Union and its ideology. Its constant presence, however, concurrently urges the viewer to infer another, more subtle connection, facilitated by the initially puzzling appearance of the mirror and the recurrence of the red thread. Whereas critics and reviewers have focused on the more obvious evocation of Polish post-war society under imposed Soviet socialism, most have failed to grasp the metaphorical significance of the mirror and the thread, which direct viewers to the imbricated and universal theme of art that Bareja addresses through the film's artist-hero, relying on two "high culture" intertexts, which I analyze later in the chapter. Within the credits the devices of visual metonymy and synecdoche incorporated by Bareja signal, with impressive concision, the axes around which the comic "surface" plot and the compressed exploration of art will turn. While the hearts adumbrate the genre's obligatory love story (the heroine), the image of contrasting currencies establishes the centrality of money (all secondary characters) that the narrative's opening sequence confirms. It does so via sound as an overhead shot introduces a quintet of strolling musicians—a diegetic "real life" version of the five two-dimensional music makers shown in the credits (fig. 2.3).

Figure 2.3. An overhead shot of the singing quintet, located in Warsaw's Old Town, which serves as a chorus commenting on developments in the city.

As the camera pans over Warsaw's New and Old Town, including the sixteenth-century Barbican (*barbakan warszawski*), with a display of paintings along its walls, the itinerant band's song focuses on the country's distribution of wealth, thereby linking the film's two focal concerns of art and money through sight and sound. Slowly moving lower, the camera halts on a male in a loft looking out of the window through binoculars at a young brunette running among the rooftops before shedding her dress and lying down with a book to sunbathe. When the camera shifts back to the male figure and enters his apartment, we realize that he is an artist in the process of painting the woman. At this point the music stops and the "money plot" is launched.

Bareja introduces music and its performers at the earliest opportunity to evoke genre conventions, but, more importantly, through the lyrics to refine verbally on the monetary motif already prefigured in the credits as part of the narrative. Although the film's music, by composer and jazz musician Jerzy Matuszkiewicz (1928–2021),[21] is not particularly memorable—to compare it with Leonard

21 Matuszkiewicz also composed the music for Bareja's *Poszukiwany–poszukiwana* (1972/3), a comedy that involves cross-dressing—popular in earlier instances of the genre (see

Bernstein's compositions for *West Side Story*, which had appeared five years earlier, would be grotesque—what matters is less the music per se than the incisive lyrics. Written by the tireless and talented Agnieszka Osiecka (1936–1997), they explicitly address the absurd socioeconomic conditions in 1960s everyday Poland, the target of Bareja's comic critique.

Laughter and Lyrics about Lucre and Love: Malfeasance in a Self-Defeating System

O tempora, o mores!
—Cicero, *First Oration against Catiline* (63 BCE)

As John Darnton, chief of the *New York Times* bureau in Warsaw wrote in 1981, "Satisfying the basic needs of the population [in Poland] was given low priority when it came to allocating investment in the national budget, but it was given lip service in public propaganda and highlighted in the speeches from the podiums on May Day celebrations."[22] Such circumstances explain how, as the quintet of musicians moves along, the song "Panie Kwiatkowski, Panie Kowalski" ("Mr. Kwiatkowski, Mr. Kowalski") performed by their vocalist (the *estrada* and cabaret singer Tadeusz Chyła [1933–2014] as himself) confirms Darnton's words, delineating an obstructive background that clarifies the rebellious antics within the plot. The mild melody cannot disguise the lyrics' scathing attitude toward a centralized economy, when, after noting how initiatives in construction have altered Warsaw, the singer poses a series of pointed questions to the hypothetical titular addressees about their housing, car, clothes, possessions, and possible private business. What structures the lyrics' queries is the contrast between haves ("the lord") and have-nots ("the mouse"). Manifestly ironic, the stinging chorus of rhymed couplets iterated throughout the song undercuts the official claim via statistics that the new socialist order guarantees all citizens economic equality in a proclaimed collective utopia.[23] In fact, it merely has worsened their

---

introduction to this volume)—in light of which the title may best be translated as *Man/Woman Wanted.*

22 John Darnton, "Communism and Better Life: Poles Found Wait Too Long," *New York Times*, December 14, 1981, https://www.nytimes.com/1981/12/14/world/communism-and-better-life-poles-found-wait-too-long.html.

23 Amazingly, Ewa Mazierska fails to detect the irony in these lyrics and interprets the film as supportive of the national economy under Soviet supervision. See Ewa Mazierska, *Polish Popular Music on Screen* (New York and Oxford: Berghahn Books, 2020), 76. Not only film critics during the sixties, it seems, paid insufficient attention to Bareja's subversiveness.

wellbeing in addition to breeding envy and acrimony: "How can one get resentful at these things / when in general it's not bad / and statistically we live super-well, / everything is common property."[24] The false slogan that "everything is common property" renders the very concept of theft logically impossible, as if justifying the sundry devious acts that we subsequently witness. Such patent absurdity, of course, invalidates the authorities' spurious pronouncements echoed in the sly song, and points to the chief source of comedy in the film.

At song's end the lyrics, in counterpoint to the skeptical couplets about possessions and statistics, prepare viewers for what the film genuinely champions—a loving young couple as the sole meaningful value: "When two young people are in love / then in principle it's not bad / and one lives super-well in that configuration / and that's the most important secret."[25] This dismissal of the promulgated socialist principles in the country's development not only inscribes the theme of "then versus now" as change through time—incorporated in official directives about class, and briefly recuperated in the "furniture duet" close to film's end—but also undermines the political ideology ushered in by the Soviet regime. Furthermore, the primacy of the individual over the collective and of love over material goods leads naturally to the genre's story of the romantic couple, who in their mutual love are contrasted to all other personae in the film. The initial song, in other words, skillfully establishes the agenda, for it signposts the trajectory of the plot, simultaneously ensuring that the identity of the quintet as roaming street musicians integrates them credibly into the narrative, for they respond to whatever scene they witness as they walk through the town—the purchase of cars, factory production, and so on. They constitute a remnant of the city's bona fide street musicians in pre-war (that is, pre-socialist) Poland,[26] and in reprising that cultural phenomenon they represent genuinely Polish urban values at ironized odds with the Soviet ideology ushered in after World War II.

Importantly, they are the chief purveyors of the film's songs, and, unlike the few other singing personae in the narrative, whose lyrics articulate subjective desires and reactions, their viewpoint functions as an ironic, objective voice in various settings, paralleling the omniscient narrator in literature or a chorus in a classical drama. In that role, they crop up sporadically to offer brief observations and to participate in the wedding celebrations at film's end. *In toto*, they return seven

---

24 "Czy mogą gniewać rzeczy te, / kiedy ogólne nie jest źle / i statystycznie żyje się fest, / to wszystko wspólna własność jest." All translations from the Polish are mine, with the exception of those film titles whose English equivalents have been established.

25 "Gdy dwoje młodych kocha się, / to już w zasadzie nie jest źle / i w takim składzie żyję sie fest / to najważniejszy secret jest."

26 Thank you, Ela.

more times, playing topical variations on the lyrics connected to plot developments, usually concluding with the ironical refrain that juxtaposes statistics with individual experience and at film's end iterates the couplets about young lovers. Notably, while comedy, ranging from verbal and situational irony to complete absurdity and slapstick, is omnipresent, musical numbers by characters other than the quintet are few and far between: one duet by the romantic couple; one serenade by the artist that is partially reprised more than halfway through the film, one by his rival/friend; and the two pseudo-rivals' brief, sequential summary of their past romantic lives at the wedding, followed by that of the quintet's vocalist on the same topic of a past life. In other words, two solos, a duet, and a short "round." Since none of the other personae in the film engages in song, one may legitimately claim that *A Marriage of Convenience* is more comedy than musical, which holds true for all of Bareja's musical comedies.

With the stage set by the quintet, viewers may anticipate what follows. Apart from the idealistic young painter Andrzej (Daniel Olbrychski) and his love interest, Joanna Burczykowa (Elżbieta Czyżewska), whose crass parents (Hanka Bielicka, Bolesław Płotnicki) sell clothing (*ciuchy*)[27] at a market (the Różycki Bazaar), everyone pursues prestige or simply lucre. All devise unscrupulous or outright illegal schemes to achieve their goals, for, as Bareja pointed out, "the real protagonist of the film is money."[28] The inveterately shifty individuals include the well-to-do but low-class Burczyk and spouse—traders whose ill-gotten profits cannot legally improve their social status owing to the private nature of their "labor"; Andrzej's indolent aristocratic friend, Edzio Siedlecki (Bohdan Łazuka), who despises work and aspires to marry Joanna only to acquire her parents' wealth and restore the family villa that his aunt (Janina Romanówna) owns but cannot afford to maintain; the so-called "engineer" Kwilecki (Bogumił Kobiela), who fakes enthusiasm for "folk" handicrafts but steals material from the textile factory across the street and peddles knit shirts illegally produced by him and his wife (Alicja Bobrowska), even as he pronounces all domestic goods shoddy and pockets other people's foreign currency (*waluta*);[29] Andrzej's unnamed friend and fellow artist (Andrzej Zaorski), who dreams of buying a Jaguar and whose threads for his creations suspiciously

---

27 *Ciuchy*, originally meaning secondhand clothes or clothes sent from abroad, as here, became the vernacular for clothing, especially among the young, reminiscent of the Anglophone "glad rags."

28 Stanisław Bareja, "'Nie chcę płoszyć widzów,'" interview with Maria Oleksiewicz, *Film* 7 (1967): 10–11.

29 During this period the word referenced foreign currency, that is, money with buying power, unlike złotys.

resemble those pilfered by Kwilecki; and the good-natured but ignorant street art peddler (Jarema Stępowski), who distinguishes schlock from fine art by the fact that with the former, one always knows "which side is up and which is down." This gallery of secondary characters, who sacrifice integrity for material benefit along a sliding scale of ethics, underscores the ludicrous contradictions of the centrally managed national economy, and simultaneously illustrates the film's polarities of East and West, socialism and capitalism, new and old, the collective and the individual.[30] These country-specific binaries parallel but, as several commentators have remarked, are distinct from the various dualities that characterize American musicals.[31] Nor does the realignment and altered status of the three separate classes portrayed in the film—a consequence of Poland's forced membership in the Eastern Bloc—correspond to American structures: the old aristocracy impoverished by the new social order; average citizens, who violate socialist injunctions so as to make a comfortable living; and artists, who occupy a paradoxical niche both within and outside the new system.[32]

Bareja's Visual Metaphors: Moralized Chronotopes and Polysemous Mirrors

The young couple's romance unfolds in this context of rampant misconduct/corruption and, after the requisite retardation inherent in comedy, inevitably culminates in their wedding. Yet the ensuing celebrations, rather than functioning as part of a "happy-ever-after" ending, are disrupted by an unpleasant scene when Andrzej learns that his new father-in-law was the sole buyer of his paintings, using his accomplices as surrogates to purchase them. Furious at the deception, he throws the money he has received at Burczyk and then storms out of the villa bought ostensibly for him and Joanna by part of those very funds. Art collides with acquisitiveness, and the configuration of the conflict's *mise en scène* establishes the disparity in morals between the artist and his newly acquired,

---

30 For useful comments about the role of the Polish economy in the film and how it actually functioned during this period, see Mazierska, *Polish Popular Music on Screen*, 76–78.

31 Notably Piotr Fortuna, "'Muzykol'—A Cultural Metaphor of the Polish People's Republic," *Kwartalnik Filmowy* 91 (2015); and Piotr Zwierzchowski, "Socialist Content, Hollywood Form: Crime Films and Musicals in the Polish Cinema of the 1960s," *Panoptikum* 17 (2017).

32 One could argue, of course, that the differentiation between "old money" and "new money" in works by Edith Wharton and Henry James, so poignantly portrayed in F. Scott Fitzgerald's novel *The Great Gatsby* (1925), approximates the European reversal of financial/social power ushered in by such sociodemographic changes as the rise of the nouveau riche and its incursion into what formerly was the enclave of aristocratic wealth.

manipulative relative through the chronotope of the staircase, which, as Mircea Eliade and numerous others have pointed out, represents spiritual ascent or superiority.[33] Andrzej, consistently associated with a higher plane, stands midway up the stairs as he tosses the banknotes down at Burczyk, located near the bottom. In the social and moral hierarchy, as a wheeler-dealer the affluent Burczyk belongs to moneyed "lowlife," whereas the penniless artist occupies the elevated position of someone who, as he himself phrases it, "lives on air"—a dichotomy dating from Romanticism passionately promoted by the intelligentsia in both Poland and Russia. Here, as elsewhere, Bareja skillfully translates several characters' moral or situational standing through their spatial associations onscreen. Stairs constitute the same visual chronotope for superiority during the couple's musical number in the furniture store when Andrzej leaps onto them, whereas Joanna, whose probity is compromised by her complicity with her deceitful parents, remains at floor level.

This sort of contrast and morally inflected placement along the vertical axis likewise operate in the musical interaction between Joanna and the two rivals for her hand. When Andrzej's lazy, supercilious foil, Edzio, arrives at the Burczyk apartment to inveigle her into marriage, singing "Miłość złe humory ma" ("Love has its bad moods") so as to smooth over her impatience with him, she proves unresponsive. As Fortuna notes, after a few minutes he ignores her and continues to serenade—not Joanna, but his own reflection in triplicate in the mirror, in "a sterile exaltation of the self in isolation from other selves."[34] While this striking image illustrates Edzio's class narcissism, the camera concurrently registers in the background her parents' plebeian tastes in the stifling clutter of their apartment: "superfluous little tables, tablecloths, vases, tapestries, paintings, and other bibelots."[35] This synecdochic evidence of tasteless wealth, filmed in closed form, not only creates a claustrophobic environment, but also redoubles the self-satisfied Edzio's desire for a "marriage of convenience," even as his snobbery prompts him to present Joanna to others as the daughter of "our Polish ambassador" or of "the Consulate General in Hawaii" (fig. 2.4). At film's conclusion, he again pleasurably examines himself in a floor-length mirror during the couple's nuptial festivities, and soon afterwards manages to snag a "convenient"

33 Mircea Eliade, *Images and Symbols: Studies in Religious Symbolism* (Princeton: Princeton University Press, 1991), 51.

34 Mary Douglas, *Natural Symbols: Explorations in Cosmology* (New York: Pantheon Books, 1983), 141.

35 Fortuna, "'Muzykol,'" 131–132.

Figure 2.4. Amid the tacky clutter of the moneyed Burczyks' apartment, the pragmatic, unemployed aristocrat, Edzio Sedlecki (Bohdan Łazuka), attempts to cajole Joanna (Elżbieta Czyżewska) into marriage so as to improve his financial situation.

future bride, Magdalena (Wiesława Kwaśniewska), whose well-to-do father (Kazimierz Wichniarz) operates a shoe business.

The comic episode of Edzio's proposal could hardly contrast more eloquently with Andrzej's musical declaration of love, which takes place in the loft that serves as his studio and apartment—the chronotope of "higher being." So indifferent to material phenomena that he does not even require Joanna's presence to apostrophize her in the serenade "Wyrzeźbiłem Twoją twarz w powietrzu (Bo jesteś taka ładna)" ("I've sculpted your face in the air [because you're so beautiful]"), he conjures up her physical self seemingly at will. Memory of her so inspires his imagination that it suffices to bring her to life,[36] and for a moment Bareja leads the viewer to believe that she has appeared magically in the apartment (fig. 2.5). This lyrical number is one of two dream sequences in the film, both stemming from Andrzej, and it ends with the sudden interruption by Edzio the pragmatist, which instantly dispels the romantic daydream and enables the viewer to see that Andrzej has been embracing not Joanna, but a garment associated with her by his powers of fantasy.[37] However brief, the illusion of her actual physical presence is nonetheless significant, for it allows the audience to appreciate the

36 Andrzej's instant attraction to Joanna is bolstered by the picture the street art seller gives him, which features her in a travel advertisement.

37 Joanna later wears the garment as she paints the walls of their apartment, thereby demonstrating the capacity of artistic imagination to create reality. During Edzio's song she is filmed in close-up, briefly appearing in a bridal veil and gown, duplicating the picture on the wall of a married couple; but Edzio's desire is practical, not romantic.

Figure 2.5. In a fantasy sequence, the idealistic Andrzej (Daniel Olbrychski) imagines Joanna in his artist's loft.

generative richness of Andrzej's romantic imagination and to share in his vision, thereby bolstering identification with his point of view.

Once the couple reach an understanding and plan to marry, Bareja conveys the suitability of their union through a nicely choreographed duet—the only one in the film—in the furniture store where they are supposed to shop. Instead, under the impact of what they find, they dance and sing "Tak bardzo zmienił się świat" ("The world has changed so much"), reprising the introductory motif of change summed up in the musicians' lyrics as they initially extol the new Poland's ability to offer newlyweds modern furniture ("good, cheap, and functional") that may be purchased quickly on the installment plan because the government allegedly has bettered the population's lives by eliminating the prolonged delay thwarting couples in the past. Just as in the 1930s musicals built around Fred Astaire and Ginger Rogers (*Top Hat*, 1935, *Shall We Dance*, 1937, and others) the compatibility of the two lovers finds expression in the excellent coordination between them, here buttressed by the precision of their movements in a Charleston on and around the table and chairs that serve as props, to the accompaniment of an extradiegetic orchestra (fig. 2.6).[38] And the obliging acceptance by unsuccessful suitors in musicals featuring romantic triangles improbably finds Edzio in one of the store's wardrobes, inanely repeating "Kochana" ("Beloved") when its door abruptly opens.

38 See Elżbieta Czyżewska and Daniel Olbrychski, "Tak barzdo zmienił się świat," Youtube, August 9, 2019, 2:39, https://www.youtube.com/watch?v=43J_Ji1yFKg.

Figure 2.6. Andrzej and Joanna pay a prenuptial visit to a furniture store, where they dance the Charleston and encounter stylish furniture on display but unavailable for purchase—one of the many instances in the film that expose the hollowness of socialist claims about a thriving economy.

Edzio's ridiculous genre-specific whereabouts, of course, occasions humor, in tune with the film's repeated orchestration of his appearance in slapstick, body-centered routines,[39] but the chronotope of carceral confinement also suggests that his aristocratic inflexibility "boxes him in," for the new sociodemographic order has left him behind. Whereas Bareja emphasizes Andrzej's mobility in multiple venues and in interaction with diverse individuals, he tends to situate Edzio in closed spaces—such interiors as his small apartment, a room in his aunt's villa, and a part of Andrzej's loft.[40] His emergence also diminishes his already flawed image by analogizing him with a mechanical cuckoo's sudden popping out from a cuckoo clock. Above all, the logical impossibility of Edzio's presence in the furniture store transforms the duet's message of marvelously enhanced opportunities for consumers into a potential joke. And that tonal switch is reinforced by the indifferent salesman paring his nails, who informs the couple that the minimalist furniture ostensibly illustrating the new order's advances in supplying goods is purely for display. What the store has available for sale is the ponderous, garish furniture of clashing colors and hideous design

---

39 These include his setting fire to Andrzej's pants, knocking him down on the rooftop, banging Andrzej's painting against Joanna, squeezing Magda into the pull-out couch, and other instances of basic bodily humor common in vaudeville and converted into more sophisticated forms by Charlie Chaplin, an icon of comedy in Poland, as elsewhere.

40 Exceptions include his early promenade down the street with Joanna and his visit to the bazaar to request the Burczyks' permission to marry Joanna.

in a separate section.[41] This information completely discredits the musical number's lyrics praising the socialist economic reforms, unmasking them as mere rhetoric, intended to camouflage lack.

The Artist as Acrobatic Idealist and Ideal

"An artist is not paid for his labor but for his vision."
—James Whistler[42]

From the first to the last, the individual who holds the film together is the artist Andrzej, with whom the film opens and closes and who invariably resides at the center of major episodes (fig. 2.7). He embodies the dominant concept of the film—that art alone merits pursuit, for it engages eternal, transcendent values and brings incalculable rewards, though not necessarily of a monetary nature. Notably, Andrzej is devoid of the ubiquitous mercantilism that infects those around him; he sells Joanna the painting that catches her eye for the negligible

Figure 2.7. Andrzej in his studio/loft, amid his modernist paintings.

41 Such is precisely the furniture found in the Burczyks' apartment. For a different emphasis and different reading of this sequence see Klejsa, "Stanisław Bareja—nadrealizm sojalistyczny," 95–97.

42 "Famous Quotes by James Abbott McNeill Whistler," Jameswhistler.org, accessed August 15, 2022, http://www.jameswhistler.org/quotes/.

sum of five złotys (then approximately twelve dollars) and he advises the street art peddler to move the paintings he is hawking unsuccessfully to the Barbican—Warsaw's traditional venue for selling artworks—even though that relocation means competition for his own efforts to attract buyers. While such lack of self-interest may seem fanciful, from the outset Andrzej's uncompromising principles contrast with those of the various money-chasing swindlers and initially with those of Joanna as his eventual "life's partner."

Quite apart from her reluctant complicity in her parents' shady dealings, Joanna is a somewhat ambiguous character, one who lacks a solo—an omission that is extraordinary and unique for the genre. Given her role of the female romantic lead, her lack of an individual musical voice intimates a more significant lack, that of firm moral principles. Unprotestingly benefiting from her parents' illicit trading, she is nonetheless ashamed of them, though, as Andrzej states at one juncture, she has become used to a materially privileged life. Moreover, she dishonestly colludes in Edzio's misrepresentation of the Burczyks as governmental officials in Hawaii, and like him, offers Andrzej a false account of his proposal. And whereas Andrzej's profession of artist calls for creativity and the imagination that he repeatedly demonstrates, her part-time work is in the glitzy world of advertising—a profession that trades in surfaces and thereby suggests superficiality. Adding to these discrepancies in the two leads' ethical standards and values is the film's delineation of Andrzej as not merely idealistic but as a peerless ideal in virtually all respects. He is a larger-than-life Romantic hero in an environment of lesser beings—"among them, but not of them," as Byron characterized his exceptional protagonists.[43]

Andrzej's lofty status, from his studio amid rooftops to his placement on ascending staircases, reaches its apogee in the chronotope of one particularly dramatic sequence devised to establish his superiority. Devoid of song, but strong in dynamic, jazz-accompanied choreography, it occurs early in the film when five bottle-carrying hoodlums accost Joanna outdoors, neatly contrasting with the four benign but anonymous motorcyclists who escort her up the street in the segment that introduces her to the viewer. Feeling threatened by the ominous crew, she seeks help by unexpectedly calling out Andrzej's name, and the camera's abrupt shift dramatically aggrandizes his image as a celestial savior. A radical low-angle shot of his immediate materialization on a rooftop in response to her summons creates the impression that he has descended from heaven to rescue her (fig. 2.8). This startling shot recalls the DC and Marvel

43 Although that phrase comes from *Childe Harold's Pilgrimage* (1812–1818), it applies to all Byron's heroes as personifications of exceptionalism.

comics franchises, in which Superman, Batman, Spiderman, Captain America, and other characters all dwell in the stratosphere of those endowed with the miraculous powers of ancient Greek and Roman divinities. Making his agile way down to street level through a series of daring jumps, Andrzej proceeds to disarm and send the gang packing by his quick, impressive twirls, leaps, and dynamic balletic movements that illustrate Olbrychski's fabled athleticism.[44] Only the strange, rather hollow sound of his voice as he calls to the group, "Leave the girl alone!" hints at what the conclusion of his victory reveals: the entire episode has been his wish-fulfillment dream, interrupted, this time, by his nameless artist friend.[45] Yet viewers have witnessed Olbrychski's/Andrzej's effortless acrobatic skills and though the episode has proved imaginary, its impact remains, aureoling his image. Such is especially the case because the same talent is on full display in the couple's visit to the furniture store (Andrzej performs splits, walks on his hands, leaps onto the stairs,[46] and so on), which, as Fortuna accurately points out, recalls Gene Kelly's formidable prowess in a series of landmark Hollywood musicals: *On the Town* (1949), *An American in Paris* (1951), and *Singin' in the Rain* (1952).[47]

Figure 2.8. A dream sequence comprising Andrzej's romantic scenario of heroically rescuing Joanna from a group of hoodlums.

---

44 In his youth, Olbrychski's roles in various films benefited from his legendary physical skills, as shown dramatically in Jerzy Hoffman's *Potop* (The deluge, 1974). Knowledge of his physical prowess became so famous in the world of Polish film that it prompted jokes and anecdotes (Sławomir Koper, *Gwiazdy kina PRL* [Warsaw: Czerwone i Czarne, 2014], 247).

45 This and other pairings of scenes indicate Bareja's fine sense of rhythm, thematic unity, and character contrasts and parallels.

46 Several of Olbrychski's colleagues, including actor Stefan Friedmann and actress Małgorzata Braunek, recall his offscreen tendency to show off by walking on his hands, largely to attract attention. Here, that skill fulfills a useful function. See Koper, *Gwiazdy kina PRL*, 246–247.

47 Fortuna, "'Muzykol,'" 132.

Space and perspective likewise come into play in Bareja's ascription of breadth and original vision to Andrzej, shown invariably looking outward at the world. The plenitude of Andrzej's expansive inner world enables him to embrace a concept of art that is inaccessible to other characters, for only three people seem capable of appreciating his paintings: Edzio, who assures Burczyk that Andrzej is very talented; to an extent, Joanna (since she purchases one of them upon their first encounter), and a little girl (whose innocence may be analogized with his), supervised by her philistine mother when the two pause to glance at his canvasses.[48] His aesthetics contravenes the official demands of Socialist Realism, which may be equated with mediocre representative art accessible to the masses and dedicated to ideologically approved subjects—not unlike the style of dreadful, kitschy paintings sold by the ignorant but good-natured street vendor. Andrzej embraces a range of styles that may be called modified avant-gardism and, in several cases, engage full-fledged abstraction, at odds with an aesthetics premised on mass taste. Through Andrzej's artwork, in short, Bareja smuggles into the film a challenge to the mandatory mode of cultural production under state socialism.

Gender-Bending and the Body

> "There is more wisdom in your body than in your deepest philosophy."
> —Friedrich Nietzsche, *Thus Spoke Zarathustra* (1883–1885)

One of the most fascinating and original aspects of *A Marriage of Convenience* is that, although Joanna fulfills the genre's traditional function of the female attracting two radically dissimilar suitors, it is Andrzej who unquestionably incarnates the object of romantic/sexual desire, and that identity owes an incalculable debt to Olbrychski's performance, remarkable athletic talent, and physical appearance. In one sense, the film retains the immemorial notion of the male as the active force, while females are to be displayed as beauty and inspiration—Joanna and the brunette who removes her clothes to sunbathe naked on the roof in full sight of Andrzej through his window and who finds amorous rapport with his artist friend. Bareja deviates from this gender stereotype and generic topos, however, by presenting women from more than one perspective (in imitation of the artist's versatile mirror): while the sunbather unwittingly serves as Andrzej's model, her body on his canvas becomes deindividualized and abstracted, identified solely by the dress she sheds; the astounding immobility of the model's

48 Fortuna's claim that no one appreciates Andrzej's paintings is inaccurate. Ibid., 136.

naked body in Joanna's art class suggests a statue, devoid of eroticism; Joanna is portrayed as desirable only insofar as her face sells advertisements for travel, bubble baths, and toothpaste, yet she has no sexual appeal whatever for the cynical, oily scion of an impoverished aristocratic family, for whom she merely represents a means of enrichment. Similarly, in the domestic environment, her crude, overbearing parents treat her simply as cook, dishwasher, and potential conduit to social legitimacy through marriage. Admittedly, Andrzej is instantly attracted to her, but his vaunted ability to penetrate beneath the surface suggests that for him her allure is not sexual, especially since his serenade to her, which voices his long wait for a woman whom he can love, corroborates the primacy of emotion over sexual allure in his choice of a romantic partner.

In general, the film's treatment of Joanna, supposedly beautiful and inspirational, makes it difficult for audiences to share onscreen men's instant, if fleeting, response to her purported irresistibility. Although Czyżewska (1938–2010) enjoyed the reputation of a versatile beauty who could play virtually any part, here she is completely outclassed by Olbrychski, whose fresh, captivating looks make her look much older than the seven years separating their ages, especially given his slim, well-proportioned body and its capacity for impressive feats of athleticism.[49] His ability to project impassioned innocence is abetted by his angelic looks: at the age of twenty-one, with his rosy cheeks and curly blond hair, he is much prettier than his female counterpart, a bottle blonde with obtrusively false eyelashes and a frequent air of sulky, frowning dissatisfaction about her, not to mention surprisingly unflattering clothes that do Czyżewska as Joanna no favors. Bareja, in fact, focuses not on her body, but on Olbrychski's as an object of desire. In a reversal of genre conventions, *A Marriage of Convenience* features not a trophy bride, but a trophy groom—a revision that makes mockery of the typical fairy-tale plot.

The film introduces Andrzej to the viewer in his loft, his lower body clad only in briefs that fully expose his legs. Forced to buy a pair of pants when Edzio's carelessness sends his only pair up in flames,[50] he purchases new ones at the Różycki market from his future bride's parents, in a prolonged sequence as he tries them on for size, then makes sure that they stay on with a belt around his narrow waist. Unlike hers, his outfits unfailingly outline his trim form. Furthermore, one of the film's surprising sequences overturns traditional gender relations in a scenario manifestly intended to enhance his erotic seductiveness. When Joanna angrily

---

49 For colleagues' admiration of Czyżewska's looks, sense of style, and effect on men, see Koper, *Gwiazdy kina PRL*, 201–204.

50 Owing to his poverty, Andrzej has cleaned his pants with benzine, a highly flammable substance.

moves out of her parents' apartment and spends the night at his, upon preparing to leave the next morning, she (and unavoidably the viewer with her) pauses to gaze at Andrzej as he lies sleeping, naked, under a blanket in a hammock.[51] Without waking him, she pulls up and tucks around him the blanket that conveniently has slipped off his coyly exposed shoulder and upper chest. This unusual scene casts the man as Snow White, the latter's famous coffin replaced by his hammock, with Joanna as the transgendered voyeur-prince. Whereas Andrzej's body is constantly revealed and filmed in a variety of positions from diverse angles, hers is far from elegantly or glamorously clothed for much of the film. In fact, Bareja bypasses the opportunity to display her naked form in the sequence devoted to her TV commercials for bubble baths and toothpaste: the bubble bath in which she reclines covers her up to the face, and after she partially lifts a leg, her sneeze blows bubbles onto her face, turning the episode into a comic interlude. The focus on the female body in American musicals has no place whatever here. Given Olbrychski's physical endowments and the persona he inhabits, it is Andrzej who seems to signify untouched, beautiful virginity waiting to be claimed. Not only visually, but through the inseparability of his persona with historically self-identified Polish traits (honor, decency, generosity, love of beauty), Andrzej in Olbrychski's enactment of the role incarnates a national ideal in both inner and outer form.

What Is Art? Redux

Aesthetics, in fact, constitutes the musical comedy's dominant issue, strategically implanted to appear subordinate to the all too blatant focus on money. At key moments Bareja resorts to the venerable trope of the mirror, for which the playful image of a mirror inserted among the opening credits has prepared the audience. A natural part of an apartment's furnishings, the mirror recurs visually and verbally in the film, but its associations change according to different situations and sundry characters' use of it. As noted above, in Edzio's case the mirror comically reveals his narcissism—in triplicate. In the case of the Burczyks, as he lies in bed and she curls her hair in front of the mirror, it reflects (likewise in triplicate) not only both of them, but also their tastelessly appointed bedroom, which indexes their indifference to aesthetics. In Andrzej's case, the mirror carries an antithetical valency: instead of gazing into a mirror he impractically spends the money paid for his painting to buy one—an unusual rococo mirror,

---

51 Scenes such as these leave no doubts about the gross oversimplification of Laura Mulvey's initial generalizations about the male gaze, for which she and others subsequently provided a corrective.

as he points out when he triumphantly brings it to the apartment he now shares with Joanna. By then the mirror has acquired a meaning inseparable from the film's engagement with art, and the definition of art proposed early in the film has cropped up at regular junctures in the narrative as a verbal *ostinato*.

Upon his first visit to Andrzej's studio early in the film, Edzio cites a maxim attributed to his great grandfather, who during a conversation with Tolstoy supposedly announced, "Art is a mirror that roams along roofs," adding that the mirror may be placed at various angles, depending on the individual artist's intent.[52] This idea, later echoed verbatim by Joanna in her art class to the instructor's (Wojciech Rajewski) startled bemusement—though he later repeats it to Edzio's aunt—reprises the mirror's longstanding equation with art derived from the classical theory of *mimesis*.[53] Modern *Kulturarbeiter* have modified or rejected the seeming oversimplification of such a definition, subjectivizing/internalizing the mirror to take into account the modern creator's perspective, which delves beneath surfaces. Hence the Surrealist André Breton's objection, "The eye is not open when it is limited to the passive role of a mirror . . . if it has only the capacity to reflect"[54] and Paul Klee's declaration, "My mirror probes down to the heart . . . My human faces are truer than the real ones."[55] What such ostensible correctives ignore is that the mirror may be concave, convex, cracked, positioned remotely from the subject or overly close to it—all variations that connote refraction rather than a rudimentary reflection. Tellingly, the triple reflections that are cast back at Edzio and the Burczyks testify to the mirror's complexity, for it may display more than what is projected onto it—a notion that ideally suits the film's reliance on it as a trope for art.

In light of Andrzej's profession, the definition of art as a mobile mirror, echoed throughout the film, merits attention, particularly if one keeps in mind the

---

52 Despite his foolish image of lecherous indolence, Edzio is articulate, quick on his feet, and a former student of art history at the university; he understands enough about art to recommend Andrzej's works to Burczyk.

53 For instance, in the segment preceding "the play within the play" in Shakespeare's *Hamlet*, the protagonist advises the actors "to hold the mirror . . . up to nature"; and Stendhal's *Le Rouge et Le Noir* (The Red and the Black, 1830) famously designates the novel "a mirror carried along a main road."

54 André Breton, "The Manifesto of Surrealism" [1924], Obelisk: A New History of Art, accessed August 9, 2022, https://arthistoryproject.com/artists/andre-breton/the-manifesto-of-surrealism/.

55 Ed Newman, "Imaginary Interviews #1: Five Minutes with Artist Paul Klee," Medium.com, last modified December 27, 2018, https://ennyman.medium.com/imaginary-interviews-1-five-minutes-with-artist-paul-klee-92dfd5674023. Leonardo da Vinci maintained that "The mind of a painter should be a mirror which is filled with as many images as there are things placed before him" (Leonardo da Vinci, *The Notebooks* [Mineola: Dover Publications, 1970], 253).

refinements and modifications built into the idea of *mimesis*. While expressed by Edzio, the concept pertains specifically to Andrzej, who iterates the specular definition, averring that he can position his mirror at any angle. Indeed, he seems to favor no subject for his works, but paints cityscapes, female bodies, and rather cryptic entities in which empirically verifiable features, significantly, are transfigured by his creative perception of them. The sunbathing brunette's unclothed body, for example, becomes anonymous through its transformation into a study of proportion and quasi-geometric shapes. His praxis and implied philosophy of art constitute an aesthetic meta-statement, which manifestly belongs to Bareja himself, inasmuch as his film reflects the everyday reality of average Poles in their country's era of socialist deprivation but refracted by his comic gift. Here, as in his later comedies, Bareja criticizes the system, but in what critics have called a "light, entertaining" vein—one that actually requires closer scrutiny than his more obvious satires of the seventies and early eighties.

Bareja and Western Conventions of the Musical

"The sight of movement gives happiness: horse, athlete, bird."
—Robert Bresson, *Notes on the Cinematograph* (1975)

How useful is it to assess the extent to which *A Marriage of Convenience* adheres to the constitutive features of the classic Hollywood musical—specifically in comparison with Polish musical comedies of the thirties (chapter one) as well as post-socialist musicals (chapters three and four), which in multiple ways simply circumnavigated the template? For a start, as in most of Bareja's musical comedies, the film contains surprisingly few songs, the majority performed by a group of strolling musicians and only three of the many characters involved in the "love and money" plot, with no solo by the female lead. In addition to constructing the narrative around the heterosexual romantic couple and including a rival for the heroine's affections, Bareja adopts the paradigmatic "happy ending" and the reconciliation of incompatible forces that the narrative ultimately irons out by restoring harmony—but only temporarily, for after the wedding ceremony a rancorous separation of the generations remains intact, and the loaded question of art is unresolved. True to the Hollywood paradigm, Bareja relies on music and choreography to reinforce character traits, clarify situations, and sustain the narrative, but through the itinerant musicians he creates a partial frame that embeds these functions in a national context. Inasmuch as the film presents issues and conflicts that preoccupied Poland at the time of the film's release, these unavoidably sprang from the sociopolitical situation in Central Europe of the mid-sixties, which accounts for the specifically Polish elements in a genre that during the period made no attempt to acquire the status it enjoyed in Hollywood. Accordingly, the film examines tendencies and dilemmas critical for Poland but tangential, if at all relevant, to the west: the illogicality of socialist economics and the impact of Soviet politics on class distinctions; impoverishment of a formerly privileged class; consumerism in a country blighted by a dearth of quality goods; a domestic currency that had scant buying power by comparison with the omnipotent dollar (possession of which was illegal and indivisible from the shadow economy); the anomalous role of the artist, and so forth. Furthermore, the utopia to which the early Hollywood musicals aspired could be treated only ironically in postwar Poland, onto which the Soviet blueprint of a communist utopia was imposed, and which is the very object of the film's sociopolitical irony.

By and large, the Eastern Bloc's problems were incomprehensible to western cinemagoers, though the non-musical romantic comedy *Ninotchka* (1939) by Ernst Lubitsch familiarized anglophone audiences with them through its polarization of socialist and capitalist values, which *A Marriage of Convenience* satirizes above all in the segments featuring the Kwileckis. Their fraudulent, clandestine manufacture of men's knit shirts—not the folk items Kwilecki falsely endorses as his supposed hobby—are peddled at the Różycki Bazaar by the Burczyks and bring in money, even as in private the false "engineer" vocally insists on the inferiority of domestic goods to the prohibited imports from the west. Kwilecki's motif is the incessant query whether something—indeed, anything, including the handcuffs that the secret agent (Wojciech Pokora) places around his wrists upon arresting him—is imported or domestically produced.[56] Similarly, the mandated conventions of Socialist Realism implemented by Soviet oversight profoundly politicized the role of art and the financial position of the artist in society, though, as Andrzej's status paradoxically illustrates, impecunious artists had a cachet as members of the creative class, for their funds were not subject to inspection. Such considerations, of course, were remote from the concerns in Hollywood musical comedies, though they illuminate such musical numbers in *A Marriage of Convenience* as the introductory song by the quintet of musicians and the young couple's song and dance routine at the furniture store, both of which target a problematic consumerism.

The only other significant musical number by a group occurs at the film's conclusion, when several dozen performers in coordinated outfits at the young couple's wedding celebration dance to a rousing orchestral rhythm. As an overhead

---

56 Pokora subsequently played the art historian in *Man/Woman Wanted.*

shot replaces the eye-level introduction of the dancers, we see them forming two chains as their movements adjust to the lively music, but the performance bears little relationship to the spectacular numbers choreographed by Busby Berkeley (1895–1976) (fig. 2.9). Those maximally, even mathematically, organized displays overwhelmingly featured women and were interpolated independently of the narrative;[57] they existed specifically to exhibit skills that, in Berkeley's addiction to kaleidoscopic geometric arrangements, from the 1930s on lacked any individual element. Impressive as they were, they reduced dancers to proverbial cogs in a musical machine. In contrast, Bareja's dancers, both male and female, are convincingly rationalized as part of the wedding revelry, and their robust performance induces the newly married couple and guests to take to the floor. Indeed, the only audible echo of American musicals within the film is the dynamic, percussion-dominated orchestration of Andrzej's dream about rescuing Joanna from the five hoodlums, which recalls Bernstein's exciting orchestration accompanying the superb mambo "Dance at the Gym" in *West Side Story*. But Fortuna's conviction that *West Side Story*—based, as it is, on the tragic plot of Shakespeare's *Romeo and Juliet*—inspired *A Marriage of Convenience* (an opinion repeated by Zwierzchowski, who detects an [understandably unspecified] reference to the American film) strikes me as somewhat fanciful.[58]

Figure 2.9. The chain of dancers at the wedding as a modest counterpart to the spectacles choreographed by Busby Berkeley.

57 An exception to the all-female participants is the number "My Forgotten Man" in Mervyn LeRoy's *Gold Diggers of 1933* (1933), which features two tiers of men—one military, the other civilian. This all-male ensemble is typical of Berkeley's choreography, so at odds in a genre that emphasizes gender difference.

58 Fortuna, "'Muzykol,'" 123; Zwierzchowski, "Socialist Content, Hollywood Form: Crime Films and Musicals in the Polish Cinema of the 1960s," 203.

Polish critics during the 1960s found the film derivative, dependent on but vastly inferior to Hollywood models, and likened it to the kitsch that Bareja derides. Yet, in addition to the various differences inventoried above, the film's final sequence, unlike that of the Hollywood model, ends on a highly ambiguous note. Were it intended to imitate the Hollywood musical's solution to all contradictions and conflicts, then it would fail ignominiously. I contend, however, that Bareja here makes an unorthodox and supremely un-Hollywoodian choice, as he does throughout the film. After both Joanna and Andrzej abandon the celebration of their wedding and engage in mutual recriminations, viewers suddenly see them kissing outdoors in the darkness. This hasty shift to the classic ending of the genre, however, leaves suspended the issue of where and how the couple will live, for Edzio now intends to buy his aunt's villa with funds from his anticipated entrepreneurial father-in-law. Moreover, the abrupt, fantastic materialization in the darkness of the street art vendor injects an original and startling element.

Delighted to have found them, as his wedding gift he has brought a new "work of art," which he demonstrates in the evening's murk: a refrigerator with a saccharine image of the couple in wedding clothes painted on one side, and a kitschy depiction of a deer on another. These decorated refrigerators, he proudly announces, are the showpieces of a new business masterminded by him and his colleagues and have been selling well. The idea for such a monstrosity was voiced much earlier by Andrzej's artist friend, who pessimistically speculated that such items would find favor among a population inured to authentic art. What the success of such an item portends remains an open question, for the third side of the refrigerator bears the word *koniec* ("the end"), surrounded by traditional floral cutouts—domestic, not foreign, as Kwilecki would observe (fig. 2.10).

Figure 2.10. Announcement of the film's ending and potentially of the end in store for genuine art, inasmuch as refrigerators decorated with kitschy paintings are now selling successfully as works of art.

Such an open ending, with no resolution on the familial *or* artistic front, is a far cry from Hollywood musicals' utopian finales and bodes nothing positive for art's future. Though the ironic conclusion could hardly be more remote from that of the Hollywood generic configuration, it prepares the way for Bareja's subsequent comedies, which essentially show a People's Poland irredeemably mired in wholesale, catastrophic corruption.

The Odd Couple: Entertainment and The Red Thread

> "X demonstrates a great stupidity when he says that to touch the masses there is no need of art."
>
> —Robert Bresson, *Notes on the Cinematograph* (1975)

The entertainment built into a musical comedy that Richard Dyer has pinpointed derives mainly from the pleasure of hearing songs, witnessing hilarious situations, seeing honed, expressive bodies in (often spectacular feats of) movement, and delectating colorful costumes and sets.[59] *Pace* Polish critics in the sixties, providing such an experience is quite compatible with onscreen sociopolitical satire and the inclusion of profound issues cast in a comic vein that does not lessen their weight.[60] Indeed, *A Marriage of Convenience* makes a strong case for the fusion of entertainment with aesthetic and sociopolitical engagement—partly through unobtrusively embedded cultural intertexts. The early reference to Tolstoy, though casual, is freighted, for linking his name to a definition of art automatically raises the specter of his notoriously pedantic thesis, *Chto takoe iskusstvo*? (What is art?, 1897). An unambiguous precursor of Socialist Realism in its reductive concept of art as a mode of cultural production that should infect its readers and viewers with "correct feelings," Tolstoy's post-crisis publication presumably is what prompts the riposte by Edzio's great grandfather, which advances the less prescriptive aesthetics of *mimesis* that the film adopts. It transparently adverts to Andrzej's painterly manner, while the reported exchange from the past certifies Bareja's familiarity with Tolstoy's text. Unlike Wajda's

59 Richard Dyer, "Entertainment and Utopia," in *Genre, the Musical: A Reader*, ed. Rick Altman (London: Routledge, 1981), 175–189.

60 Steve Neale, in one of his many articles on genre, contends that "it is often the generically verisimilitudinous ingredients of a film . . . which are often least compatible with regimes of cultural verisimilitude—singing and dancing in the musical . . . that constitute its pleasure, and that thus attract audiences to the film in the first place" (Steve Neale, "Questions of Genre," *Screen* 31 [1990]: 48). Bareja's film, I believe, is "verisimilitudinous" in both spheres.

last film, *Powidoki* (Afterimages, 2016), for example, which directly dramatizes the nonconformist artist's fate under socialism as a protracted melodrama cum tragedy, Bareja's approach is more aleatory. He leaves it up to the viewer to draw connections between apparently casual statements in the diegesis and the protagonist's aesthetic choices, which, given the political circumstances prevailing in Poland at the time, are also ethical. Paradoxically, such a difference in handling narrative merely calls upon audiences of Wajda's film to watch in dismay, whereas Bareja's films necessitate viewers' active ability to make connections that are not immediately apparent and, evidently, not anticipated in musical comedies or noticed by reviewers. Unfortunately, few specialists in film rose to the occasion, and, seemingly needing the unambiguous explicitness of such later films as *Miś* (Teddy bear, 1980/1), projected their incomprehension onto the director's alleged "lack of clarity"—a response sooner expected from proponents of Socialist Realism.

Furthermore, Bareja's unusual reliance on red threads in the film evokes, quite extraordinarily, Goethe's novel *Die Wahlverwandtschaften* (Elective affinities, 1809). Most probably drawing on the thread in Greek mythology that enables Theseus to find his way out of the Minotaur's maze (the labyrinth of red thread displayed in the film's credits), Goethe elaborates it into a trope for a work's coherence or unity.[61] *A Marriage of Convenience* creatively literalizes the trope, which links a series of separate scenes: early in the film, as Andrzej watches, his nameless friend uses red thread for his enigmatic creations on the rooftop; the textile factory, of which Bareja offers a brief glimpse that captures workers at machines, manufactures it; Kwilecki cannily steals the red thread across the street from the factory, suspended like an elevated bridge between the two buildings (linking national and private enterprise); and Burczyk's burly assistant, Kiełkiewicz (Cezary Julski), delivers to him a large hold-all of fifteen red knit shirts produced by the Kwileckis; finally, Andrzej depicts that thread stretching above the street in his painting (likewise shown in the opening credits)—a detail that leads to Kwilecki's eventual arrest. In other words, Bareja adopts and materializes Goethe's metaphor for coherence to connect different entities at various stages in the film, and all instances tie it to creativity or production.

As noted earlier, the film more generally favors ingenious literalization of tropes and idioms, and these also serve structural ends. They include not only the red thread, but also the colloquial expression "dirty money" for illegal funds. At one juncture Burczyk and his wife crouch on the floor, contemplating their

---

61 Johann Wolfgang von Goethe, *Elective Affinities*, trans. R. J. Hollingdale (Harmondsworth: Penguin Books, 1978), 163–164.

booty, and lament how the dollars they have accumulated are wet and malodorous: fearing that their possession of foreign currency would be discovered, they had buried it in the ground, with predictable consequences. As in the past, Burczyk seeks help from Kwilecki, who restores the dollars to sanitized respectability—for a hefty price, of course (fig. 2.11). Conversely, Bareja treats some commonplace parts of the *mise en scène* symbolically, such as the mirror, the staircase, and elevated spaces (Andrzej's loft, rooftops). In the film's hierarchical differentiation even for petty crime, Burczyk, the street-level dealer, has to ascend to Kwilecki's apartment, for the mendacious engineer is a more educated, skillful crook, able to launder funds literally. Such devices lend a degree of unity to the film, connecting themes, characters, and locations.

Figure 2.11. Kazimierz Burczyk (Bolesław Płotnicki), who peddles *ciuchy* at the market, brings his ill-gotten dirty cash to the crooked Kwilecki (Bogumił Kobiela) for literal laundering, while Kwilecki's wife, Anna (Alicja Bobrowska), works on the loom with their stolen red thread.

In kindred vein, even strikingly dissimilar individuals repeat the same statements verbatim, as when defining art as a mirror (Edzio, Andrzej, Joanna, and her art teacher, Professor Lipski). And in sequences devoted to monetary transactions, in response to the standard query about the price, the answer is the typical salesman's pitch, "For you, five hundred złotys," which elicits the potential buyer's question, "And for everyone else?" The frank response is "Also five hundred." Burczyk automatically invokes this formula with Andrzej, a man purchasing a jacket, and most probably all customers; Andrzej, not without irony, repeats it when Burczyk's surrogate buyers inquire about the cost of his paintings. Gags function in a kindred way to optimize cohesion.[62]

62 Bareja faulted his own films for lacking sufficient gags (Bareja, "'Nie chcę płoszyć widzów,'" 10).

All these leitmotifs lend unity to a film that lasts only ninety minutes yet boasts a fairly large cast, diverse locations, and several subplots. These devices demonstrate Bareja's careful attention to structure, just as his literary intertexts testify to his incorporation of fundamental issues of aesthetics. Yet a fine scholar such as Klejsa, who authored a smart, lengthy article on Bareja (2007), acknowledges that *A Marriage of Convenience satirizes* kitsch, then proceeds to categorize Bareja's three early musical comedies as camp *or* kitsch[63] and accuses the director of a sloppy professional technique (*niechlujność warsztatowa*).[64] Like practically all Poles speaking or writing about Bareja until recently, he echoes the unexamined perception of a decisive break in the *quality* of Bareja's output, whereby the supposedly weak, retrograde three musical comedies of the sixties unaccountably yielded to successful films in the seventies and early eighties. The purported pinnacle of this upswing was the universally lauded *Teddy Bear*, which is disappointingly straightforward and lacks the structure and discipline of *A Marriage of Convenience*. Ewa Mazierska seems the only scholar to have noticed the multiple weaknesses in this '80s film, and her minority opinion about its deficiencies, which I fully share, is worth citing in full: "It is very fragmented; many episodes do not move the action forward. . . . The dialogue is crude and often the criticism of social reality is obvious or forced, somewhat mirroring the crude propaganda of the socialist state; in addition, its production values are low, giving the impression that it was made on the cheap."[65] Furthermore, the narrative's sweeping satire of all aspects of Polish society under socialism is completely undifferentiated, and the rote repetition wears thin, especially since the film lasts almost two hours.

Accordingly, swimming against the current, I contend that *A Marriage of Convenience* provides an incomparably more subtle critique of socialist Poland and evinces a vigorous, original talent for comedy, even though some of the slapstick falls flat. Additionally, Bareja's instincts in his choice of actors were inspired, above all in casting the unfailingly hilarious Kobiela as Kwilecki and Olbrychski as the *schöne Seele*. Additionally, apart from the overly hasty conclusion, which, however, admirably refuses to provide closure (and how many

---

63 Here Klejsa seems to be hedging his bet, for the distinction between camp and kitsch is quite significant. See Susan Sontag's oft-quoted essay on camp (Susan Sontag,"Notes on 'Camp,'" in her *Against Interpretation and Other Essays* [New York: Dell Publishing Co., 1969], 277–293).

64 Klejsa's uncertainty recalls Edward Bonusiak's bewilderment, cited by Fortuna, as to what the film satirizes. See Edward Bonusiak, "Z czego się śmiejemy?," *Głos Olsztyński* 12 (1967); and Fortuna, "'Muzykol,'" 135.

65 Ewa Mazierska, *Poland Daily: Economy, Work, Consumption and Social Class in Polish Cinema* (New York and Oxford: Berghahn Books, 2017), 246.

musical comedies dare/d to forgo that *sine qua non*?),[66] the film is cleverly organized and briskly paced.[67] Inability to parse the film's meaning springs from critics' inadequacies, not Bareja's.

Conclusion: Denigration as Liberation

Ultimately, Bareja's *Marriage of Convenience* validates age-old Polish ideals even as it paints a humorous but dismaying picture of a society maimed by a patently absurd socioeconomic system. At first glance, critical animosity toward the film during the sixties seems puzzling inasmuch as the film upholds those beliefs and standards enshrined by the critical corpus and by such lionized directors as Wajda, Jerzy Hoffman, and Andrzej Munk. Moreover, Bareja's comic exposés of moral frailties fully coincided with those aspects of Polish life targeted for opprobrium by the directors loosely grouped under the rubric of *kino moralnego niepokoju* (cinema of moral anxiety/unease)—Feliks Falk, Agnieszka Holland, Krzysztof Kieślowski, and Krzysztof Zanussi. Bareja's animosity to the socialist establishment was unmistakable, and it found expression in such activities as smuggling into Poland books published by Kultura, the émigré Polish press in Paris anathematized by Soviet authorities, and his support of KOR—the Committee for Social Self-Defense, which led to the establishment of Solidarność.[68] That his favorite director was René Clair (1898–1981), whose elegant challenges to social conventions combine with an original approach to sound, should have alerted critics and reviewers to the subtexts of Bareja's early musical comedies. The relegation of comedy to a lowly position nonetheless enabled Bareja, film after film, to ridicule, despite censorship, the society in which he lived and which he cinematically reproduced with impressive acuity, sometimes accompanied by song.[69] As he noted in an interview with a belligerent and ignorant interviewer, the Lumière brothers established the paradigm for all future comedies—the genre, he insisted, that ages the least and that he

---

66 The ending parallels that of an outstanding romantic comedy, Billy Wilder's *Some Like It Hot* (1959).

67 One flaw, however, concerns continuity—which seems to be most directors' Achilles heel. In Andrzej's dream, after his Superman rescue of Joanna, his white shirt (shining armor!) is visibly soiled, but almost immediately afterwards appears pristine. The inconsistency belongs not to the painter's wish fulfillment, but to Bareja's lapse.

68 Gąsiorowski, "Stanisław Bareja: Widzowie go kochali, krytycy nie."

69 Censorship, however, prevented the realization of countless Bareja-envisioned film projects. Ibid.

deemed optimal for spotlighting with laughter the awfulness of life under Soviet oversight without, as he phrased it, frightening the audience.[70]

As in the case of Alfred Hitchcock, the broad popularity of whose films for decades elicited critical disdain, the disparagement of comedy and entertaining movies impeded Bareja's acceptance by film scholars and critics, who ignored the dynamism and serious concerns of his savvy musical comedies. Coincidentally, Bareja also shared Hitchcock's penchant for popping up in cameo roles in his own films. He turns up in *A Marriage of Convenience* as a customer in a red knit shirt in the process of buying from the Burczyks an ugly checkered jacket, much too small for his stocky body. As usual, the couple launch into their oblivious sales talk, which, contrary to what is all too painfully obvious, persuades him to buy the ill-fitting garment. The episode confirms Bareja's ability to laugh not only at the ridiculous aspects of Polish life, but also at himself.[71] Perhaps that disarming trait accounts to some extent for Polish audiences' affection then and now for his unabashedly hilarious comedies, among which *A Marriage of Convenience* demonstrates formal skills and a clever defense of art that should gratify any critics unencumbered by snobbish or ideological baggage.

Bibliography

Altman, Rick, ed. *Genre: The Musical: A Reader*. London: Routledge, 1981.

———. *The American Film Musical*. Bloomington: Indiana University Press, 1989.

Bakhtin, Mikhail. *Rabelais and His World*. Translated by Hélène Iswolsky. Bloomington: Indiana University Press, 1984.

Bareja, Stanisław. "'Nie chcę płoszyć widzów.'" Interview with Maria Oleksiewicz. *Film* 7 (1967): 10–11.

Bonusiak, Edward. "Z czego się śmiejemy?" *Głos Olsztyński* 12 (1967).

Breton, André. "The Manifesto of Surrealism." [1924]. Obelisk: A New History of Art. Accessed August 9, 2022. https://arthistoryproject.com/artists/andre-breton/the-manifesto-of-surrealism/.

Darnton, John. "Communism and Better Life: Poles Found Wait Too Long." *New York Times*, December 14, 1981. https://www.nytimes.com/1981/12/14/world/communism-and-better-life-poles-found-wait-too-long.html.

da Vinci, Leonardo. *The Notebooks*. Mineola: Dover Publications, 1970.

Douglas, Mary. *Natural Symbols: Explorations in Cosmology*. New York: Pantheon Books, 1983.

70 Bareja, "'Nie chcę płoszyć widzów,'" 10–11.

71 For a clip of all appearances by Bareja in his films (as a loud, nagging woman in one!), see Poznac kino, "Wszystkie występy Stanisława Barei w swoich filmach lub serilach," Youtube, August 9, 2017, 6:05, https://www.youtube.com/watch?v=BFAJB55hdlc&list=PLnzfYRIEk1uVsa_PF7GNfIBSBZ99mO-YH.

Drozdowski, Bogumił. "Kopciuszek-malarz i księżniczka bazaru." *Film* 4 (1967): 4.

Dyer, Richard. "Entertainment and Utopia." In *Genre, the Musical: A Reader*, edited by Rick Altman, 175–189. London: Routledge, 1981.

Eisler, Jerzy. "*Obraz społczeństwa PRL w komedii filmowey*." Review of *Obraz społczeństwa PRL w komedii filmowey*, by Dorota Skotarczak. *Pamięć i Sprawiedliwość* 3–2, no. 6 (2004): 386–390.

Eliade, Mircea. *Images and Symbols: Studies in Religious Symbolism*. Princeton: Princeton University Press, 1991.

Ford, Charles, and Robert Hammond. *Polish Film: A Twentieth-Century History*. Jefferson and London: McFarland & Co., 2005.

Fortuna, Piotr. "'Muzykol'—A Cultural Metaphor of the Polish People's Republic." *Kwartalnik Filmowy* 91 (2015): 121–140.

Gąsiorowski, Maciej. "Stanisław Bareja: Widzowie go kochali, krytycy nie." *Super Express Chicago*, December 11, 2020.

Goethe, Johann Wolfgang von. *Elective Affinities*. Translated by R. J. Hollingdale. Harmondsworth: Penguin Books, 1978.

Grzelecki, Stanisław. "Bal na ciuchach." *Życie Warszawy* 2 (1967).

Haltof, Marek. *Polish Cinema: A History*. 2nd ed. New York and Oxford: Berghahn Books, 2019.

Hillier, Jim, and Douglas Pye. *100 Film Musicals*. London: Palgrave Macmillan/BFI, 2011.

Klejsa, Konrad. "Bareja i bareizm—twórczość reżysera." Akademia polskiego filmu. June 2, 2014. 2:56. https://www.youtube.com/watch?v=WeY_-Yh8K0k.

———. "Stanisław Bareja—nadrealizm sojalistyczny." In *Autorzy kina polskiego*, vol. 2, edited by Grażyna Stachówna and Bogusław Zmudziński, 79–128. Krakow: Jagiellonian University Press, 2014.

Koper, Sławomir. *Gwiazdy kina PRL*. Warsaw: Czerwone i Czarne, 2014.

Lichniak, Zygmunt. "*Małżenstwo z rozsądku*, czyli film z ciuchów." *Słowo powszechne* 3 (1967): 3.

Mazierska, Ewa. *Polish Popular Music on Screen*. New York and Oxford: Berghahn Books, 2020.

———. *Poland Daily. Economy, Work, Consumption and Social Class in Polish Cinema*. New York and Oxford: Berghahn Books, 2017.

———. *Masculinities in Polish, Czech and Slovak Cinema*. New York and Oxford: Berghahn Books, 2008.

Michałek, Bolesław, and Frank Turaj. *The Modern Cinema of Poland*. Bloomington: Indiana University Press, 1988.

Neale, Steve. "Questions of Genre." *Screen* 31 (1990): 45–66.

Newman, Ed. "Imaginary Interviews #1: Five Minutes with Artist Paul Klee." Medium.com (blog), last modified December 27, 2018. https://ennyman.medium.com/imaginary-interviews-1-five-minutes-with-artist-paul-klee-92dfd5674023.

Olbrychski, Daniel. *Anioły wokół głowy*. Warsaw: BGW, 1992.

Pieńkowska, Beata. "Stanisław Bareja." Polish Film Academy. Accessed August 9, 2022. https://akademiapolskiegofilmu.pl/en/historia-polskiego-filmu/directors/stanislaw-bareja.32.

Piotrowicz, Paweł. "Krytycy go nie znosili, cenzura nie dawała spokoju. 34 lata temu zmarł Stanisław Bareja." Onet, June 14, 2021. https://kultura.onet.pl/film/wywiady-i-artykuly/34-lata-temu-zmarl-stanislaw-bareja-kim-byl-rezyser-sylwetka/mb3vqx2.

Replewicz, Maciej. *Stanisław Bareja. Król krzywego zwierciadła*. Poznań: Zyski Spółka, 2009.

Rożen-Wojciechowska, Joanna. "The Phenomenon of Polish Independent Cinema in 1989–2009." In *Polish Cinema Now!: Focus on Contemporary Polish Cinema,* edited by Mateusz Werner, 139–149. London and Warsaw: Adam Mickiewicz Institute and John Libbey Publishing, 2020.

Słodowski, Jan, ed. *Leksykon polskich filmów fabularnych.* Warsaw: Wiedza i Życie, 1996.

Sontag, Susan. "Notes on 'Camp.'" In her *Against Interpretation and Other Essays,* 277–293. New York: Dell Publishing Co., 1969.

Staszczyszyn, Bartosz. "Stanisław Bareja." Culture.pl. Accessed August 9, 2022. https://culture.pl/en/artist/stanislaw-bareja.

———. "Masters of Polish Comedy." Culture.pl, January 9, 2015. https://culture.pl/en/article/masters-of-polish-comedy.

———. "The Most Powerful Films beyond the Iron Curtain." Culture.pl, July 17, 2014. https://culture.pl/en/article/the-most-powerful-films-from-beyond-the-iron-curtain.

Zamyatin, Yevgeny. *We.* Translated by Mirra Ginsburg. New York: The Viking Press and Bantam, 1972.

Zwierzchowski, Piotr. "Socialist Content, Hollywood Form: Crime Films and Musicals in the Polish Cinema of the 1960s." *Panoptikum* 17 (2017): 198–206.

CHAPTER 3

Paweł Pawlikowski's *Cold War*: Music, Space, and Identity

Elżbieta Ostrowska

Although Paweł Pawlikowski's *Zimna wojna* (Cold War, 2018) won the Palme d'Or at the 2018 Cannes Film Festival and was nominated for three Oscars, not all Polish film critics were enthusiastic about the film, which features two lovers—Zula, a singer, and Wiktor, a musician—who for many years travel across Europe, divided by the Iron Curtain and unable to settle down on either side of it. When they eventually decide to return to Poland, it is only to commit suicide together. For Iwona Kurz, one of the most prominent Polish film scholars, the film is disconnected from the Polish reality of the 1950s and 1960s.[1] Agnieszka Morstin compares *Cold War* to Krzysztof Kieślowski's *Podwójne życie Weroniki* (The double life of Veronique, 1991), arguing that Pawlikowski also uses a clichéd image of the relationship between the West and the East, with Poland presented as a space of sacrifice and death. According to Morstin, Pawlikowski aestheticizes Poland's backwardness in the 1950s and 1960s in a similar way to Kieślowski's handling of the period of late state socialism.[2] Apparently, Polish

---

1 Iwona Kurz, "Wychłodzone obrazy," *Dwutygodnik* 239 (June 2018), https://www.dwutygodnik.com/artykul/7865-wychlodzone-obrazy.html.

2 Agnieszka Morstin, "Kieślowski versus Pawlikowski. *Podwójne życie Weroniki* i *Zimna wojna* jako opowieści o świecie dwudzielnym," *Kwartalnik filmowy* 103 (2018): 79. I strongly disagree with such a claim, for *The Double Life of Veronique*, unlike *Cold War*, establishes a very strong visual contrast between the Polish and French parts. For the former, Kieślowski uses a predominantly sickly greenish-yellowish palette with diffused lighting, whereas the latter is consistent in its employment of warm brownish-reddish hues, with a crispy blueness for the Parisian sky. In contrast, Pawlikowski throughout his film uses a black-and-white photography

film critics prefer to focus on how the film depicts Polish reality, while not paying much attention to the visual and generic stylization of the film's fictional reality, or regarding it at best as an aesthetic veil covering the "truth" of the past.

Interestingly enough, film scholars and critics abroad focus on how the film plays with the conventions of popular cinema, especially the genre of the musical. Ewa Mazierska examines *Cold War* as an example of the Polish postcommunist musical, claiming that the film demonstrates a more general tendency in world cinema: the recent attraction of the genre for arthouse independent directors, such as Quentin Tarantino, the Coen Brothers, and Danny Boyle.[3] Joanna Rydzewska claims that *Cold War* originates in the tradition of popular genres as well as European art cinema.[4] Unlike Mazierska, she performs a detailed analysis of how the film fits in and departs from the classical model of the genre as analyzed by Rick Altman.[5] She believes that this inconsistent approach to generic conventions is a sign of Pawlikowski's hybrid perspective, which draws on the myths of the Romantic artist and of the neoliberal entrepreneur (Rydzewska, in press).

In this chapter, I examine both approaches as I discuss how *Cold War* revisits and revises the generic formulas of the musical, integrating them into the mode of art cinema in order to engage with Polish postwar reality. Jerry White perceptively remarks about the film's narrative scope, "There is something of the epic in this film, even an anti-epic, a sense throughout that Pawlikowski is trying to tell the story not just of two lovers but of Eastern Europe itself, and to tell it through the perspective of those who were crushed by its repressive tendencies: the musicians, the intellectuals, the romantics."[6] In what follows, I discuss how music contributes to this "epic" dimension of the film. Specifically, I focus on the leitmotif song "Dwa serduszka, cztery oczy" ("Two hearts and four eyes"), which *Cold War* presents in four renditions in various localities and temporalities. It is my contention that the symbolic trajectory of the song from the south-Carpathian village through the communist concert hall to trendy

---

that produces the effect of aesthetic consistency in representing various spaces and places, suggesting their equality.

3 Ewa Mazierska, *Polish Popular Music on Screen* (Cham: Palgrave Macmillan, 2020), 114. However, she does not explore how Pawlikowski's film employs the generic conventions of the musical, but, rather, focuses on how the songs used in the film demonstrate certain strategies of communist culture, especially its effort to create a "new Polish folklore" (ibid., 137–145).

4 Joanna Rydzewska, "Art and the Musical in Paweł Pawlikowski's *Cold War*" (paper presented at the Fifty-First Annual Conference of the Association for Slavic, East European and Eurasian Studies [ASEEES], San Francisco, November 2019).

5 Rick Altman, *The American Film Musical* (Bloomington: Indiana University Press, 1989).

6 Jerry White, "'*Cold War* Contexts': Pawlikowski in Film, Television, and European History," *Film Quarterly* 72, no. 3 (2019): 48.

cafés and salons in Paris parallels the actual and imagined movement of the Polish postwar self-migrating from the countryside to cities, simultaneously dreaming about the West. Specifically, the "traveling" song signifies the Polish self's displacement in Cold War Europe and Poland as well. While tracing the changes to a Polish self, the film sets up binaries that are signaled in the leitmotif song's title, yet these are not reconciled toward the end, but, rather, demolished.

"Two Hearts" denotes two lovers living in two countries separated by the Iron Curtain. Their "togetherness" is only possible through the "nothingness" of their death, non-represented in the film's ending. The symbolic cinematic gesture of locating their death off-screen and, thus, liberating it from the scrutinizing camera's gaze, relocates the unhappy romance into the sanctuary of a transcendent, non-territorial and non-contemporary venue that is the suitably ruined Orthodox church. The entry into the realm of the spiritual through their death is the only possibility to overcome the binaries of the social and political order. Finally, the film's ending ultimately undermines the myth of a "return home."

Generic transactions

Cold War's use of black-and-white film stock, academic ratio, episodic narrative, unclear motivation for the characters, and open ending locates it within the realm of art cinema. Yet the film also displays an affinity with the musical genre as elaborated by Altman: it features a "narrative" of a "romantic couple in society" and "a combination of rhythmic movement and realism" as well as a "mixture of diegetic music and dialogue." However, another key characteristic identified by the American film scholar—"parallelism between male and female"—is absent from Pawlikowski's film, as is a "mystic marriage" and a "romantic triumph over limitations."[7] As current research on the musical explains, the genre has been constantly evolving and its corpus has been changing accordingly. Beth Carroll and Kevin J. Donnelly note, "Since 2000, a kaleidoscopic range of musicals has been made . . . there has been a simultaneous return to known musical models, demonstrably illustrated through a reliance on the West End and Broadway theatres, and an exploration into unconventional modes."[8] With all of its departures from the classical musical, *Cold War* is a good example of the

---

7 Altman, *The American Film Musical*, 110.

8 Beth Carroll and Kevin J. Donnelly, "Introduction: Reimagining the Contemporary Musical in the Twenty-First Century," in *Contemporary Musical Film*, ed. Kevin J. Donnelly and Beth Carroll (Edinburgh: Edinburgh University Press, 2017), 3.

constant fluctuations in the genre's corpus, for its first part adheres to the model of "integrated musical," whereas its second part diminishes the importance of music, as if paralleling the impossibility of the "romantic triumph" considered by Altman as a part of the genre's syntax.[9] With this eventual rejection of the generic formula, Pawlikowski seems to share the viewpoint articulated by Jean-Luc Godard about his *A Woman Is a Woman* being "nostalgia for the musical."[10] Accordingly, *Cold War* can be seen as nostalgia for the socialist musical, discussed below, and at the same time as its cultural critique.

Nostalgia permeates most contemporary Hollywood musicals, such as *La La Land* (directed by Damien Chazelle, 2016), yet in the context of the Eastern European and especially the postsocialist musical, it gains special importance. The genre belongs to the realm of popular cinema that flourished after the fall of communism. However, as Mazierska and Zsolt Győri note, "Ironically, many of them [popular genres—E. O.], instead of praising the new system, convey nostalgia for bright moments from the history of state socialism, whose traces were obliterated by a new, Western-style consumerism."[11] In his analysis of nostalgia for communism in contemporary Eastern European comedies, Balázs Varga notes that postcommunist popular cinema frequently participates in the process of "retrospective mythmaking (idealizing the socialist past as an antidote to the disturbing postsocialist present)," which would exemplify Svetlana Boym's concept of "restorative" nostalgia as opposed to "reflexive" nostalgia, which interrogates the past to deconstruct it rather than commodify it.[12] *Cold War* defies such a dichotomy, as it employs "musical moments" to revive the hopes emerging after World War II and then to show their gradual erosion and ultimate destruction.

While discussing generic negotiations of the classical model of the musical, it is also necessary to approach *Cold War* as a contemporary transnational meta-musical—a sub-genre that, according to Björn Norðfjörð, "share[s] a certain distance from the classical Hollywood musical [. . . It is] transnational in being both American and something other, and the gap between the two manifests the tension in both form and content. . . . This gap is both geographical and

---

9 Altman, *The American Film Musical*, 110.

10 Björn Norðfjörð, "The Post-Modern Transnational Film Musical," in *The International Film Musical*, ed. Corey K. Creekmur and Linda Y. Mokdad (Edinburgh: Edinburgh University Press, 2012), 245.

11 Ewa Mazierska and Zsolt Győri, "Introduction: Popular Music and the Moving Image in Eastern Europe," in *Popular Music and the Moving Image in Eastern Europe*, ed. Ewa Mazierska and Zsolt Győri (New York: Bloomsbury Academic, 2019), 15.

12 Balázs Varga, "Worlds That Never Were: Contemporary Eastern European Musical Comedies and the Memory of Socialism," in *Popular Music and the Moving Image in Eastern Europe*, ed. Ewa Mazierska and Zsolt Győri (New York: Bloomsbury Academic, 2019), 63.

aesthetic."[13] This distance is frequently established through self-reflexive references to musicals and aesthetic traditions other than Hollywood's. *Cold War* introduces this aesthetic distance from its opening.

In Search of (Authentic) Folk Music

Cold War begins with a black silent screen and a few captions with the names of film production companies and studios. When the last inscription, "a film by Paweł Pawlikowski," appears, the initial silence is rapidly interrupted with the loud, squeaky sound of a bagpipe. Soon, a close-up of rough hands playing the instrument follows. Black-and-white film stock makes the image as bare and rough as the played music. The shot lasts long enough to let the viewer see the rugged fingers, dirty nails, and well-worn clothes of the musician before the camera tracks upward and we see a close-up of a man against an out-of-focus background of a wintry rural landscape (fig. 3.1). He sings the first verses of the song "I knocked, I cried / She wouldn't open up" while looking straight into the camera with a blank stare. At some point his eyes twitch as if to signal his discomfort at being put on display.[14] A "merciful" camera pans left to show another musician, who is playing a violin and also singing. His demeanor is as opaque as the first man's. When the camera pans and tilts down, a little boy appears, looking suspiciously at the camera.

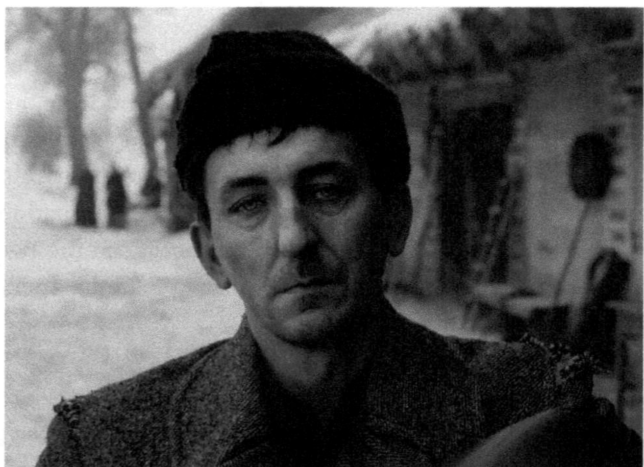

Figure 3.1. The opening shot of *Cold War.*

13 Norðfjörð, "The Post-Modern Transnational Film Musical," 253.
14 The musician is played by Tomasz Kiciński, a bagpipe player from Bukówiec Górny.

The first song is not "properly" integrated into the narrative and there is no clearly executed "politics of the gaze" attributing the image of the musician to any of the characters' perspective. Therefore, it resists unproblematic inscription into the narrative structure. Yet the camerawork, specifically its frontal position and the relatively long duration of the first shot, emphasizes the staginess of the performance and transforms the musicians into "objects on display." Thus, it might be seen as a metaphor of postwar exploitation of folk art that is removed from its natural habitat of peasant festivities celebrated by whole communities. The use of shallow focus in the opening shot, which blurs the background populated by other people, visually separates the two musicians from their fellows. They do not sing for them but for this somewhat mysterious and disembodied camera "eye" whose agency is unknown. The musicians look into this disembodied "eye," confronting it or perhaps resisting its power. It is not revealed, however, what or whom they see, as the shot abruptly ends and is replaced with the black screen displaying the film's title, *Cold War*. The way in which the film's first song appears and disappears on the screen does not facilitate the emergence of a consistent and continuous narrative. Instead, there is a brief explosion of sound that establishes fragmentary, yet distinctly rhythmical structures. This principle of repeated disconnectedness seems to form the film's aesthetic pattern.

The opening song does not return in the film's later conversations and there is no record of its being played again. Instead, the viewer sees an extended sequence of Irena and Wiktor recording various folksongs.[15] As it turns out, they are on a kind of ethnographic mission assigned by the new communist authorities. Kaczmarek, an *apparatchik*, takes care of the "political correctness" of the enterprise. The montage sequence of recordings consists of single and frequently static shots of the musicians, with occasional "response shots" of Irena and Wiktor to show their appreciation of and sometimes delight at the impromptu performances. Interestingly, they do not talk about the music, but only look at each other and occasionally share a cigarette as if trying to find a gestural expression for their emotions. Mazierska observes that initially the couple appears as musical ethnologists trying to preserve vernacular folklore. Yet, as she notes, "[t]he act of recording places the ethnomusicologists in a position of power over the folk artists, who seem unaware of the purpose of this

---

15 The following folk artists and ensembles appear in the film: Roman Wojciechowski's band from Opoczno, Wiesława Gromadzka's band from Kamień Duży, Katarzyna Majerczyk-Bobak from Chabówka, Stefania Bortniczak, the Kapela Manugi band from Bukówiec Górny, Tadeusz Tarnowski's band, Ryszard Piecyk's band from Wir, and Gabriela Kmon from Krosno. Pawlikowski organized a professional casting session for the folk artists who participated in a folk music festival in Kazimierz Dolny.

exercise."[16] She also adds that it soon transpires that the real object of their field trip is "to create a 'new Polish folklore': one which would be appreciated not so much by people from the countryside, but by those living in the cities, as well as beyond Poland's borders. Wiktor and Irena's goal is thus changing folklore into what in Poland was described as folklorism: an 'arbitrary, artificial, spectacular representation of folk culture fabricated for a mass audience.'"[17] Bruce Bennett and Katarzyna Marciniak interpret the characters of Irena and Wiktor similarly, as "agents engaged in the same patriotic project of cultural appropriation."[18] Indeed, it is legitimate to say that the very act of recording folk culture (whether it be visual or audio, or both) is an act of appropriation. Yet the significance of musical recordings in *Cold War* is more complex than the critics suggest, and the motif of musical recordings and the relationship between original and copy are at the center of the film's narrative.

Ambiguity of the concepts of "authentic" and "inauthentic" music is evoked in the scene introducing the female protagonist, Zula. Along with many young peasants, she comes to an old, dilapidated country estate (its owners most likely having been forced to leave it by the communist authorities) to participate in an audition for the Mazurek group. Waiting for her turn, she asks a girl sitting nearby about what she plans to sing for the jurors. When the fellow competitor sings a couple of verses in a high-pitched voice characteristic of highlander music, Zula suggests that they collaborate in part-singing. Soon, they sing the song for Irena and Wiktor. That sequence presents the traditional folk song as a rather sophisticated performance. Wiktor is visibly fascinated with Zula and asks her to sing "something more personal." She thinks for a while and starts singing in Russian "Tak mnogo devushek khoroshikh" ("Such a lot of nice/pretty girls"), a famous song, covered as "Serdtse" ("Heart"), from the Soviet movie *Veselye rebiata* (Jolly fellows, directed by Grigorii Aleksandrov, 1934).[19] The auditioning couple is visibly dumbfounded and understandably so. After all, the girl has selected as "something personal" a song from a Soviet movie shown to Polish

---

16 Mazierska, *Polish Popular Music on Screen*, 138.

17 Ibid. Mazierska is citing Józef Burszta, *Kultura ludowa, kultura narodowa* (Warsaw: Ludowa Spółdzielnia Wydawnicza, 1974), 299.

18 Bruce Bennett and Katarzyna Marciniak, "Close Encounters with Foreignness," *Transnational Cinemas* 10, no. 2 (2019): 95. Both interpretations overlook the fact that Irena and Wiktor are presented as in conflict with Kaczmarek who, indeed, can be seen as an agent of the new folklorism as envisioned by the communist project. In contrast, they frequently manifest affinity with the musicians representing multiethnic and multicultural prewar Poland. The most radical expression of Irena's ideological stance is her later decision to leave Mazurek to protest its political appropriation.

19 The title is also translated as *Happy Guys*.

audiences as a part of communist propaganda. And she sings it wholeheartedly. They try to stop her, yet she continues, saying she needs to sing the refrain as well. When they ask her how she has heard the song, she answers that a mobile cinema came to her village and showed the movie featuring it. Tellingly, Lenin was right when he reportedly said, "Film for us is the most important of the arts."

Admittedly, the brief scene lends itself to be understood as a metaphor of postwar Soviet colonization of Poland in both a literal and a figurative sense. Yet it is unclear whether the girl's selection of the song is an opportunistic act aimed at convincing the "cultural envoys" of the new socialist state that she supports the new political system or whether she is, indeed, sincerely infatuated with it. Either way, Zula's performance of both songs—the highlander music piece and the Soviet "Heart," "deterritorializes" the musical works, since they are removed from their original habitat and performed in different localities.

Musical Moments: The Trajectory of the Postwar Polish Self

Four different renditions of the song "Two Hearts and Four Eyes" epitomize the concept of dislocation while also problematizing the concept of "authentic" folk music and culture. As I argue here, each of these renditions symbolically marks the trajectory of a Polish postwar self as it traverses various geopolitical formations. I approach these four variants of the song as "musical moment[s]" that are defined by Estella Tincknell and Ian Conrich as "musical performances" that may appear not only in musicals but a whole range of other types of movies. Importantly, as they argue, these "musical moments" create a "particular point of disruption, an isolated musical presence in a non-musical film which is most notable for its potential to disturb the text through its unexpectedness or at times excessiveness."[20] To address this disruptive potential of musical moments, I take inspiration from Amy Herzog's examinations of non-classical musicals as also featuring musical moments.[21] Unlike numbers in classical musicals, she argues, musical moments do not constitute autonomous audio-visual spectacles but work as moments of rupture: "the musical moment . . . occurs

---

20 Estella Tincknell and Ian Conrich, "Introduction," in *Film's Musical Moments: Music and the Moving Image*, ed. Ian Conrich and Estella Tincknell (Edinburgh: Edinburgh University Press, 2006), 1–2.

21 Amy Herzog, *Dreams of Difference, Songs of the Same: The Musical Moments in Film* (Minneapolis: University of Minnesota Press, 2010), 6.

when music, typically a popular song, inverts the image–sound hierarchy to occupy a dominant position in a filmic work."[22] These moments always produce a rupture within a film on many different levels. Most importantly, they destroy spatio-temporality established by the narrative and, thus, open the cinematic text to alternative readings and interpretations, and, finally, produce affective responses from the viewers. Herzog emphasizes that the aim of her close analysis of selected musical moments is not to "decode" them, but, rather, to approach them as "dynamic events, distinct temporal occurrences that are always open to the outside."[23] Following this line of reasoning, I look at musical moments in *Cold War* as establishing their own spatio-temporal structures that relate to various forms of post-World War II cultural production.

As musical moments are frequently embedded within structures of repetitiveness, Herzog employs Gilles Deleuze's theoretical concepts of refrain and its close connection with "territory."[24] Looking at non-standard musicals from this perspective, Herzog argues, "Musical moments can serve to propagate certain types of representational strategies. The repetitions evidenced on a formal register (musical structures, narrative formulas, characterizations) speak to a far-reaching tendency to reproduce, standardize, and codify certain cultural fictions."[25] Following Herzog's line of argument, I contend that *Cold War* engages with Polish postwar reality more efficiently through its musical moments than its narrative content and cinematic image. In this section, I examine the four renditions of "Two Hearts and Four Eyes" as musical moments to argue that each of them engages with various cultural fictions. I contend that they serve as symbolic instances of rupture marking fractures and displacements of the postwar Polish self.

Repetitive appearances of "Two Hearts and Four Eyes" transform the song into a "musical refrain" as conceptualized by Deleuze and Guattari.[26] As they note in *A Thousand Plateaus*, musical refrains—which may be compared to birdsongs that delineate territories—always evoke the concept of territoriality. In the broadest sense, as Ronald Bogue explains, Deleuze and Guattari "extend the notion of the refrain to refer to any kind of rhythmic pattern that stakes out a territory . . . The elements from which territories are formed are milieus and rhythms, which themselves are created out of chaos."[27] The narrative structure of *Cold War* develops into rhythmically organized sequences of the protagonists'

---

22 Ibid.
23 Ibid., 9, 16.
24 Ibid., 8.
25 Ibid., 9.
26 See Ronald Bogue, *Deleuze On Music, Painting, and the Arts* (New York: Routledge, 2003), 13.
27 Ibid., 16–17.

encounters, separations, and reunions that occur in diverse milieus and these are marked by different performances of "Two Hearts and Four Eyes." Instead of narrative progress and change, *Cold War,* like Jacques Demy's *The Umbrellas of Cherbourg* (1964), is marked by various losses and disappointments.[28] As Herzog states, these structures of repetitions lead to the process of fabulation that ultimately demonstrates how "the musical's cultural fictions can multiply and destabilize the past."[29] In other words, fabulation creates fictions that interpellate the individual and write him or her into the narrative of the larger social order.[30] Likewise, Pawlikowski's film relocates the leitmotif song across diverse spatio-temporalities as if suggesting a potential for multiplicity of Bakhtinian chronotopes within which polyphonic narratives can develop. In consequence, the song (de)territorializes Polishness, which emerges as defined by various sets of values and ideals. As Bogue notes, "[a]rt, as the disposition of expressive qualities, is the active agent in the formation of territory and the establishment of its occupant's proprietary identity."[31] Arguably, the song serves as such an active agent in the formation or negotiations of the territory of Polishness and its occupants' identity. Moreover, it is not only the song that negotiates the narrative variants of Polish identity, as there are also numerous intertextual references to Polish postwar cultural production that also undermine linear progression.

Folklorist Mash-Ups

The first performance of the song occurs during the "ethnographic recording" sequence. In a dark room of a rural cottage, a dark-haired and dark-eyed girl[32] sings it with an audible Eastern (possibly Lemko) accent (fig. 3.2). Although not mentioned in the dialogue, it is implied that the girl represents an ethnic minority. While recording her *a capella* singing, Irena looks at the girl with tender admiration and a kind of nostalgia, as if having a premonition that this kind of song and singing—authentic folklore—will vanish, or, in the best (or worst?) case, will be transformed into a postwar communist "folklorism," participating

---

28 Herzog, *Dreams of Difference, Songs of the Same: The Musical Moments in Film,* 126. Herzog writes, "The narrative development of *Les parapluies,* though chronological, is marked less by action and progression than by loss, delay, and the failure to overcome difficulties."

29 Ibid., 18.

30 Ibid., 132.

31 Bogue, *Deleuze On Music, Painting, and the Arts,* 20.

32 The song is performed by Gabriela Kmon from Korczyna near Krosno, whom Pawlikowski spotted at a folklore festival in Kazimierz Dolny in 2018.

Figure 3.2. The first performance of the song "Two Hearts and Four Eyes."

in the fabrication of the "new" Polish nation based on ethnic unity.[33] However, "Two Hearts and Four Eyes" is anything but an authentic traditional song originating in the nostalgically evoked multi-ethnic Poland. In fact, it was composed by Tadeusz Sygietyński, who founded Mazowsze, the real ensemble that the filmic Mazurek was shaped after. Inspired by a piece of folk music, he arranged it into a song, while his wife, Mira Zimińska-Sygietyńska, adapted the folk lyrics. As if to hide its fabricated nature, the scene's *mise en scène* of a poorly lighted cottage sparsely decorated with a few basic pieces of furniture fits cultural stereotype of remote locations where traditional music is still alive. One could say that the visual design of the song performance is an effort to recreate an authentic "aura" that is to be inevitably lost in the "era of mechanical reproduction," as claimed by Walter Benjamin in his seminal essay.[34] The visual emphasis on the recording equipment may suggest that the camera captures the very exact

33 Audrey Kichelewski, "Poland's Postwar Trauma and Identity in Pawel Pawlikowski's Films: Reflections on *Ida* and *Cold War*," *Central European History* 52, no. 3 (2020): 653. In this article, Kichelewski comments on the issue as "the ambiguities of the new regime promoting popular folklore in order to gain legitimacy and thus helping to promote a new elite, yet also politicizing these issues and depriving the official image of Poland of the remnants of the ethnic diversity lost in the war."

34 Walter Benjamin, "The Work of Art in the Age of Its Technical Reproducibility: Second Version," in his *Selected Writings*, vol. 3, *1935–1938*, ed. Howard Eiland and Michael J. Jennings, trans. Edmund Jephcott and Harry Zohn (Cambridge: The Belknap Press of Harvard University Press, 2006), 103.

moment when the "aura" of the song performance is vanishing and the couple (and simultaneously the viewers) is listening to the original, not a copy of the music. However, the black-and-white photography, the chiaroscuro effect, and the careful deep-space composition produce an effect of aesthetic excess in opposition to the typical aesthetic of field recording. The soundtrack does the same in a less noticeable, yet more profound way, as it eliminates all "nonmusical sounds [that] reinforce associations between the rural past and definitions of authenticity."[35] Thus, despite the narrative content of recording "authentic" traditional music in a remote peripheral region of postwar Poland, the visual and sonic properties of the episode present the song as already being deterritorialized from its natural habitat. In fact, there was no original song at all.[36]

The visual aspect of the first musical moment and the whole "ethnographic" sequence of recording traditional folk music can also be seen as reinvention and reappropriation of the Polish tradition of documentary cinema and photography. On the one hand, images of folk musicians call to mind sociological documentaries made by Kazimierz Karabasz, one of the most renowned and respected Polish filmmakers of non-fiction cinema, who authored *Muzykanci* (The Sunday musicians, 1960), among others. In this film, the "patient eye"[37] of the camera registers a rehearsal of an amateur orchestra of retired tram-drivers. The restrained camera work employs a composition of careful long shots, while the sound equipment records the many awkward and discordant sounds that are ultimately synchronized in a beautiful musical piece. Likewise, *Cold War* features in isolated brief shots or episodes the sounds of traditional music that are eventually linked in a unique soundscape that in its roughness recalls the bare landscape of a wintry countryside.[38] Pawlikowski's predilection for a static frontal camera setup and long shots that are weakly integrated into the narrative

---

35 Michael A. Young, "Hi-Fi Heritage: Recording Technology, Audio Engineering, and the Mediation of Authenticity in the Polish Revival of Traditional Music," *Journal of Folklore Research* 57, no. 1 (2020): 34.

36 See Karolina Kosior, "Niejedna słowiańska dusza," *Pismo folkowe* 140–141 (2019), https://pismofolkowe.pl/artykul/niejedna-slowianska-dusza-5358.

37 Karabasz explains his concept of documentary cinema in his book *Cierpliwe oko* (Patient eye, 1979).

38 Furthermore, Pawlikowski's film extensively uses static close-ups or medium close-ups of the musicians that, when linked to one another, form a film album like those in the photographic cycles of Bogdan Dziworski or Zofia Rydet. In his photographs, especially of children and musicians, the former combines realism and poetry: mundane subject matter is illuminated by mysterious lighting and composed in a picturesque fashion. Similarly, Rydet in her photographic cycle *Sociological Records* (1978–1989) blends ethnographic realism with aesthetic patterns of naive paintings fusing frontal composition and shortened perspective.

establish the opening sequence as an anthology of musical moments rather than a narrative exposition that includes musical numbers. Furthermore, the static images of the landscape, interiors of cottages, and musical performances visually contrast with the official ideology of social mobility and progress during that period. Instead of the politically endorsed postulates of the dynamic change identified with communism, Pawlikowski's film shows the stasis of post-World War II rural Poland.

The static images of the opening "ethnographic" sequence are gradually replaced with more dynamic segments. The transition is marked by a long extreme high-angle shot of trucks bringing young people to the palace intended to serve as a site of the new folklore Mazurek group. The *apparatchik* Kaczmarek welcomes the candidates with a speech describing the chance of a lifetime being offered to them. Pointing to the door of the former palace, he says: "This is your new home. Through this door you will enter a world of music, song, and dance. Music born in the fields. The music of pain and humiliation . . . Under the careful supervision of our tutors you will step onto our nation's stages and the stages of our fraternal nations." The rhetoric of the speech clearly indicates the ideological underpinnings of the previous "ethnographic" sequence and suggests the prospects of social mobility for those who will be selected for the group. The speech is filmed with a static camera alternating between low-angle shots of Kaczmarek and high-angle shots of the motionless young people, firmly establishing the power relationship.

The following sequence of the audition is also devoid of on-screen movement, for it is filmed with a mostly static camera. Eventually, when the core team of the Mazurek ensemble is selected, there is a long shot of young women and men dancing and singing. Admittedly, the prospect of social mobility is visually evoked in their frantic movements. However, the camera records the impromptu dance from a significant distance and it does not move to follow the movements, as if implying skepticism about their hopes and excitement.

Cultural Advancement and Political Subordination

The first performance of Mazurek is similarly ambiguous in terms of the correlation between camera movement and on-screen performances. It starts with the second rendition of the song "Two Hearts and Four Eyes," performed by Zula and another female singer in a concert hall. They are shown in a medium shot taken from behind, so that we do not see them actually singing. Arguably, this non-standard camera setup for shooting musical numbers ruptures or prevents the emergence of the standard mode of cinematic representation based on synchronous sound and image. This subtle yet perceptible departure from the conventional rendition of musical numbers symbolically marks "deterritorialization" of the film's "musical refrain." Furthermore, the concert hall contrasts with the previous habitat in which the song was performed for the first time. The following shots of the two soloists standing in front of a choir also defies the spatial arrangement of traditional music singers, which involves fluid changes of positions and configurations. For the dance sequence, the camera stays relatively static, only dissecting it into smaller segments and movements. There is no dynamic editing either. As a result, the performance is not shown as a spectacular dynamic musical number that transcends the limits of physical space and time. Instead, it is frequently presented as subordinated to the controlling look of Kaczmarek, who is vigilantly observing the ensemble from off-stage. Finally, there are also some extreme long shots utilizing deep staging composition that show the singers in the foreground and the political leaders sitting in the balcony in the background (fig. 3.3). The static camera symbolically locks the dancers within the space controlled by their authoritarian gaze.

Figure 3.3. Deep staging composition demonstrating ideological inscription of the second performance of the song "Two Hearts and Four Eyes."

Cinematic "Refrains" and "Territories"

The first performance of Mazurek is also firmly rooted in Polish cinematic tradition. First and foremost, the folklore ensembles (also played by members of Mazowsze as in *Cold War*) earlier appeared in two popular Polish film musicals, *Przygoda na Mariensztacie* (Adventure at Marienstadt, directed by L. Buczkowski, 1954) and *Żona dla Australijczyka* (A wife for an Australian, directed by S. Bareja, 1963). Both of these films represent what Thomas Schatz calls genres of social integration such as musicals, melodramas, and comedies.[39] In Buczkowski's film, a flagship of Socialist Realist popular cinema, a female protagonist comes to Warsaw with a folklore musical group and, enchanted with the charm of both the newly rebuilt city and one of its builders, she decides to stay there and find a job in construction. Her trip with the folklore group to the city made this transition possible. Tellingly, *Adventure at Marienstadt* presents membership in the ensemble as indeed a symbolic "door"—as Kaczmarek announces it in the aforementioned scene in *Cold War*—to social advancement. Yet it also means a socio-cultural displacement.

Cold War presents a similar deterritorialization of traditional music in the scene of Mazurek's first concert. The event occurs in a large concert hall that traditionally was reserved for classical music representing highbrow culture. Thus, the location may symbolically signify the radical sociodemographic changes occurring in postwar Poland and, more specifically, massive migration from the countryside to cities. The folklore ensemble performs its music in a city as an autonomous spectacle instead of being an integral part of the festivities and family rituals celebrated by peasants in their natural habitat. It is tempting to view traditional folk culture as "authentic," and its ideologically appropriated version, called "folklorism," as "inauthentic." Such a judgement has been shared by a significant sector of Polish society, mostly the intelligentsia, who claimed that Mazowsze destroyed "real" folk music.[40] However, the opposition of "authentic" and "inauthentic" traditional music is more than ambiguous and, even if

---

39 Thomas Schatz, "Film Genre and the Genre Film," in *Film Theory and Criticism*, ed. Leo Braudy and Marshall Cohen (Oxford: Oxford University Press, 2009), 571.

40 As Chrzanowski discusses in his article on the folk musicians who appear in *Cold War*, "Paweł Pawlikowski's film was a good opportunity to return to the beginnings of the Mazowsze ensemble, which was received very well after the war. Crowds of people would join Mazowsze, as it was an opportunity to leave poverty behind and achieve artistic success. The most popular folk group supported whole villages, where costumes for it were woven and tailored. For example, women from Kołbielszczyzna literally lived off Mazowsze. The music that was initially performed by the group was created by authentic musicians from the countryside. They would sing and dance the way people from villages did. With time, it became polished and

detectable, it cannot serve as a criterion for aesthetic judgement. Instead, I contend that the socialist folklore ensembles marked the transitional stage between prewar and postwar socio-political and cultural formations. Their performances, blending traditional music with classical instrumentation and a choir singing in four voices, can be seen as attempts at a "cultural advancement" of folk music, as if reflecting the social and economic advancement of a huge sector of Polish society also migrating, like this music, from the countryside to cities. The happy endings of *Adventure at Marienstadt* and *A Wife for an Australian* convince the viewer that the experience of displacement is only temporary and an individual can be (re)integrated into the new political system of communism.

Cold War is far from following the positive scenario presented by popular cinema during the earlier stages of state socialism in Poland. It presents an ironic perspective on social and national integration in that it perversely plays with the social backgrounds of the Mazurek ensemble and does not offer a positive resolution of the romance. Zula is not a peasant and she represents everything but the innocence and purity often ascribed to the inhabitants of the countryside. She originates from urban poverty and has a criminal past, as she attempted to kill her father, who tried to have sex with her. Thus, it is evident that for her, joining Mazurek is not an opportunity to cultivate and preserve her cultural heritage, but rather to improve her socio-economic condition. In turn, Wiktor is an upper-class professional musician for whom the ensemble was, most likely, the only accessible artistic option. Both want a better life, which, however, means two different things for them: prosperity and freedom respectively. Therefore, when Wiktor decides to use the opportunity of the Mazurek concert in Berlin to defect and stay in the West, Zula does not join him. Yet she is unable to persuade him to do otherwise. Pawlikowski's film refuses to reiterate the female allegory of Poland and faith in national unity symbolized by a positive resolution of the heterosexual romance (for a less radical stance on this issue see the discussion of Stanisław Bareja's musical comedy in chapter two of this volume).

Years later, Zula comes with Mazurek for an artistic tour to Dubrovnik. Owing to the special status of Yugoslavia in the Eastern Bloc, Wiktor, now a Polish immigrant in France, can visit the country to reunite with her. He comes to the concert and watches her dance, yet the secret police detain him during the performance, preventing him from meeting his beloved. When she sings "Two Hearts and Four Eyes" with another female singer and a small choir, she looks at Wiktor's empty seat in the audience, which evocatively marks his absence. Though the song's

---

appropriated to the needs of performance and the audience's expectations" (Przemysław Chrzanowski, "Kapele z *Zimnej Wojny*," *Witryna wiejska*, February 22, 2019.)

rendition is identical to the one delivered during the first concert, its cinematic presentation significantly modified. There are no long or extreme longs shots; instead, the camera is closer to the singers and the audience. With the radically reduced *mise en scène*, the space in which the song is performed is not a site of ideological inscription as it was in the earlier concert, but an abstract, lyrical space of two lovers' impossible encounter. The aesthetic of this musical moment can be seen as evoking some hope emerging in Poland after 1956 that art, at least to a certain extent, can be liberated from ideological pressure to express individual subjectivities. Yet secret agents' forceful detention of Wiktor at the concert hall proves otherwise. In a similar vein, the concept of a neutral ideological space in a Europe divided by the Iron Curtain is questioned. Tellingly, the Dubrovnik performance of the song marks another cultural and political rupture. Nevertheless, years later, after succeeding in communist folklorist show business, Zula abandons it and marries an Italian man to be able to move freely across Europe. Ultimately, she decides to reunite with Wiktor in Paris, where the third and the fourth renditions of the song "Two Hearts Four Eyes" take place.

French "Bastard"

The third rendition of the song differs from the previous ones in every possible way. In a simple black dress and a simple hairstyle, Zula performs the song in the smoky, cramped space of a trendy Parisian café (fig. 3.4). Its jazzy score de-territorializes the song from its vernacular cultural milieu.[41] In its instrumentation and performance style this version of "Two Hearts and Four Eyes" marks a radical departure from both the folk musical tradition and its communist appropriation. It marks a significant rupture in traditional national culture and epitomizes the various cultural and political aspirations of Polish artists that could not be fulfilled in communist Poland. And jazz represented these phenomena. Arguably, the emergence of jazz music on the Polish musical stage in the mid-1950s was one of the most important signals of the end of the Stalinist era. Krzysztof Komeda, one of the country's most original jazz musicians and composers, was beloved by the young generation of Polish filmmakers, who were more than eager to have him write scores for their films. His score for Roman Polański's *Nóż w wodzie* (Knife in the water, 1962) is as memorable as the film's sophisticated cinematography and ambivalent characters, who were everything

41 This rendition of the song is very similar to the version recorded by Anna Maria Jopek, one of the most popular Polish singers, whose father was a soloist in the Mazowsze ensemble.

but communist heroes.[42] Zula's performance for the Parisian bohemia evokes the Polish artist's dream of making a career in the West.[43]

Figure 3.4. "French" performance of the song "Two Hearts and Four Eyes."

The last rendition of the song, this time with French lyrics, appears in the film not as live performance, but in a recording played during a private party celebrating the release of the "authors'" artistic project—that of Zula and Wiktor, now both "artists in exile." She listens to herself singing, as does everybody else. This

42 In her blog Film Comment, Imogen Sara Smith compares *Cold War* with *Red Boogie*, a Slovenian movie made by Karpo Godina in 1982, as both explore how cultural production, specifically music, was complicit and subversive of political regimes of postwar Poland and Yugoslavia. Both films feature a jazzy rendition of a folk song that becomes an act of political dissent (Imogen Sara Smith, "Blues for the Iron Curtain: *Cold War* and *Red Boogie*," Film Comment, October 30, 2018, www.filmcomment.com/blog/blues-iron-curtain-cold-war-red-boogie/).

43 One of these artists was Ewa Demarczyk. She was often called the Polish Edith Piaf and was also compared to Juliette Greco. There were some hopes that she would share their international fame. In 1963, Bruno Coquatrix, director of the Paris Olympia Music Hall, saw Demarczyk's performance in Poland and invited her to Paris. However, the singer declined the offer, as she wanted to graduate from the Theatre Academy first. Eventually, she performed at Olympia to great acclaim from both audiences and critics. Later, she gave concerts in many European countries, as well as in the States, where she performed at venues including Carnegie Hall. Importantly, she insisted on singing only in Polish. Her insistence on doing so is echoed in *Cold War* in Zula's eventual refusal to accept the French version of "Two Hearts and Four Eyes."

separation of her voice from her body symbolically marks the ultimate deterritorialization of the song, for it loses its identity. As Kichelewski notes, "Zula is made to understand that she needs to sing in French in order to gain success and is compelled to perform the expected stereotypes of the Slavic lady [*sic*]."[44] Eventually, she refuses to fulfill these expectations. After they leave the "opening night" party, Wiktor demands that a sullen Zula be pleased with the record's release. When he calls it their "first child," she retorts that it is a "bastard" and forcefully takes it from his hand, throwing it into a garbage can. The next day she leaves Wiktor for Poland.

Arguably, the trajectory of the song "Two Hearts and Four Eyes" from the south-Carpatian village through the communist concert hall to a trendy café in Paris parallels the actual and imagined movement of the Polish postwar self's migration from the countryside to the city and its dream about the West, only to be disappointed by it. Pawlikowski's film mobilizes what John Connell and Christopher Gibson call "cartographies" of music, which refer to the symbolic relationship between music and space.[45] The stylized photography in *Cold War* is used not only to interrogate "imaginative" but also "affective" geographies of postwar Poland and Paris, the latter being a place every Pole dreamed of. As Kichelewski aptly notices, "The song illustrates the possibilities of cultural transfers but also their impossibility because it works best in Polish reality rather than as a jazzy adaptation."[46] With this statement, the author implies that any Polish rendition is "authentic," thereby "better," whereas non-Polish versions are inevitably "inauthentic" and, thus, worse. However, as explained above, none of the film's renditions of the song is original and all of them are appropriations. Kichelewski sees only its "foreign" versions as such.

I contend that the inauthenticity of the song wherever and whenever it is performed signifies the Polish self's displacement in Cold War Europe. Pawlikowski presents this displacement, whether geographical, social, or cultural, through musical cartographies. The song "Two Hearts, Four Eyes" as it is featured in *Cold War* travels across many borders, between rural and urban, original folk music and its socialist appropriation, popular and jazz music, its renditions adding up to a series of deterritorializations without the possibility to mark the original habitus. Thus, the film never implicates the binaries of "here" and "there" or authentic and inauthentic. Gina Arnold, in her brief yet insightful essay on the

---

44 Kichelewski, "Poland's Postwar Trauma and Identity in Pawel Pawlikowski's Films: Reflections on *Ida* and *Cold War*," 655.

45 Connell and Gibson, *Sound Tracks: Popular Music Identity and Place*, 12.

46 Kichelewski, "Poland's Postwar Trauma and Identity in Pawel Pawlikowski's Films: Reflections on *Ida* and *Cold War*," 655.

film, notes the "tension—hovering between a critique of the original group's work and its celebration of folk as a way back to authenticity."[47] Arguably, *Cold War* undermines the concept of authenticity, yet it also demonstrates that so-called inauthentic cultural production expresses authentic life experience in its affective dimension.

"Bajo Bongo," or the Impossibility of Polish National Culture

Admittedly, Zula's return to Poland is not a reclamation of her "true" self and the genuine art of music. The last musical moment in the film ostentatiously demonstrates the failure of the project of genuine socialist as well as national art. To contextualize this moment: After Zula leaves for Poland, Wiktor decides to follow her, but is accused of treason and put into a communist jail, where he is tortured. Zula marries the *apparatchik* Kaczmarek, most likely to use his political connections to get Wiktor out of prison. After his release, Wiktor comes to Zula's performance, which is a part of a commercial music event, "Summer with a Song," apparently managed by her husband. When Wiktor shows up, Zula is on the stage. The first extreme long shot of her is taken from the perspective of the audience, remarkably presenting her as an "object to look at" that is facilitated by her appearance. She wears a long, sequined, low-cut dress, black opera gloves, and high-platform sandals. Instead of her natural blond hair, she wears a dark wig. Surrounded by an all-male band whose exoticism is marked by huge sombreros, she sings the song "Bajo Bongo" (fig. 3.5), whose titular refrain sounds exotic although it does not originate in any real language. The song was one of the biggest popular hits in postwar Poland during the late fifties and it also exemplifies the de-territorialized musical refrain of vernacular musical culture. With music composed by the German Heinz Gietz, and lyrics by Zygmunt Sztaba, a prominent Polish author of popular crime stories, it was performed by Natasza Zylska, a Jewish singer, whose real name was Natasza Zygelman. She was unquestionably the biggest star of popular Polish music in the 1950s, yet she decided to emigrate to Israel in the 1960s. In light of all these intertextual references, Zula's performance of the song emerges as a palimpsest of various musical traditions that by no means add up to a coherent project of vernacular culture under state socialism.

---

47 Gina Arnold, "Love in a Cold Climate: *Cold War*, Music, and the Limits of Authenticity," *Journal of Popular Music Studies* 31, no. 3 (2019): 2.

Figure 3.5. Zula's performance of the song "Bajo Bongo."

The episode may also be seen as an intertextual reference to Andrzej Wajda's *Człowiek z marmuru* (Man of marble, 1977), especially in terms of presenting an erstwhile *apparatchik* from the 1950s who makes a career in show business in the 1970s. In *Cold War*, Kaczmarek undergoes precisely that metamorphosis from political activism to entrepreneurship. Furthermore, Pawlikowski shows Zula as an alcoholic trapped in a marriage of convenience in which she recalls Hanka Tomczyk, the treacherous wife of Mateusz Birkut, the eponymous man of marble in Wajda's film. Arguably, Zula's performance of the "exotic" "Bajo Bongo" song marks the total failure of authentic national art, whether created under the auspices of the communist authorities or the democratic systems of the West.

The Sound of Silence

Various renditions of the leitmotif song represent the successive tribulations of Polish postwar collective identity. As none of these versions is "original," *Cold War* puts into question the concept of genuine and authentic national culture. Pawlikowski invests in a musical "local" idiom to reveal that it does not originate from one singular tradition but instead is an effect of an ongoing process of appropriation and reworking. *Cold War* avoids "romanticizing of the local . . .

as inherently 'subversive', 'oppositional' and 'authentic.'"[48] The song is appropriated for the propagandistic agenda of the communist authority but then is "reclaimed" in its jazz version that is subversive of the former. Arguably, all three Polish renditions of the song are equally "authentic" in that they represent various sectors of Polish postwar culture reflecting rapid tectonic movements of displacements and erosions. However, once the song is displaced outside the vernacular that is revised through the addition of French lyrics, Zula abrasively criticizes it for being "empty" in both its semantic and affective aspect. The song establishes the imaginative and affective geography of the local and its borders. When Zula throws her French record as "inauthentic" into the garbage can it is a symbolic rejection of the possibility of a hybrid or global identity that could be accommodated in various localities.

Zula and Wiktor's return to Poland re-immerses them in the realm of the vernacular, which does not offer inhabitable space either. The only stable spatiality is, as the ending shows, the space of Orthodox spirituality, thus not "Polish"—the abandoned church where they decide to commit suicide together (fig. 3.6). In *Cold War,* Pawlikowski, a transnational filmmaker, displays distrust in the transformative potential of travel, without, however, believing in the restorative power of a "return home."[49] The return brings about death rather than atonement. And there is no music or song to accompany the final scene of their private wedding, without priest, witnesses, or guests, followed by their suicide. Their death is not marked by a musical moment. Nor is it visualized as they leave the frame to see "the better view from the other side." If the musical moment marks ruptures in the (national) narrative, its final absence is significant in that it suggests that to "seal" and "heal" the fractured Polish self is only possible through death. Thus, *Cold War,* which employs musical moments to subvert the idea of

---

48 Ian Biddel and Vanessa Knights, *Music, National Identity and Politics of Location: Between the Global and the Local* (New York: Routledge, 2007), 3.

49 In his article, Jerry White overlooks the fact that the suicide scene takes place in an abandoned Orthodox church, and therefore interprets the film's ending as a regressive return to "nationalized" Catholic religion: "This doomed romance is consecrated through a kind of purified Catholicism, once seen (and now again) as a *sine qua non* of a certain kind of conservative Polishness, no longer suppressed by a communist government keen to ape the antinationalism and secularism of its Soviet parent state. The scene seems calculated to communicate that the two lovers have fully returned not only to each other but also to Poland, using images of spirituality, commitment, and persistence through ruin that are, without a doubt, viscerally evocative of the transcendence of love and of cultural belonging" (White, "'*Cold War* Contexts': Pawlikowski in Film, Television, and European History," 50). Locating the scene in a ruined and desolated Orthodox church "exiles" the lovers from the "national community" that symbolically has been marked by the Catholic Church, which is why the ending shows that for them there is no return home.

authentic national culture, unexpectedly subscribes to the most persistent myth of death as the only accessible existential project in Polish national culture established by Polish Romanticism. The ending, as the most radical departure from the generic convention of the musical genre, signifies the impossibility of social integration in the project of communism.

Figure 3.6. Zula and Wiktor's "wedding" in the abandoned Orthodox church.

Conclusion

Cold War does not subscribe to a dichotomous model of nostalgia as defined by Boym. Although it aestheticizes the communist past by means of a stylized black-and-white photography that presents postwar Poland as image rather than reality, the film simultaneously establishes a complex network of intertextual cinematic references, thereby foregrounding its self-reflexivity. The music used in the film, especially the song "Two Hearts and Four Eyes," unveils the tension between affective memory and historical knowledge. Performed in huge concert halls, the song is dignified, yet also exiled from its habitat. A symbol of folk culture is simultaneously elevated and annihilated. In its origins it evokes the feelings of home, yet its ideological adjustments to the needs of communist propaganda estranges the song from it. The film's ending proves that the process of leaving home cannot be reversed. There is no return home for the Polish postwar self. The couple's death is a radical departure from the generic convention of the musical's happy ending; instead of the celebration of social integration, *Cold War* ends up with the irreversible annihilation of the couple's and the nation's romance.

Acknowledgments

My gratitude to Helena Goscilo for her insightful comments and generous help in writing this chapter.

Bibliography

Altman, Rick. *The American Film Musical*. Bloomington: Indiana University Press, 1989.

Arnold, Gina. "Love in a Cold Climate: *Cold War*, Music, and the Limits of Authenticity." *Journal of Popular Music Studies* 31, no. 3 (2019): 3–5.

Benjamin, Walter. "The Work of Art in the Age of Its Technical Reproducibility. Second Version." In his *Selected Writings*, vol. 3, *1935–1938*, edited by Howard Eiland and Michael J. Jennings, translated by Edmund Jephcott and Harry Zohn, 101–122. Cambridge: The Belknap Press of Harvard University Press, 2006.

Bennett, Bruce, and Katarzyna Marciniak. "Close Encounters with Foreignness." *Transnational Cinemas* 10, no. 2 (2019): 89–102.

Biddel, Ian, and Vanessa Knights. *Music, National Identity and the Politics of Location: Between the Global and the Local*. New York: Routledge, 2007.

Bogue, Ronald. *Deleuze On Music, Painting, and the Arts*. New York: Routledge, 2003.

Burszta, Józef. *Kultura ludowa, kultura narodowa*. Warsaw: Ludowa Spółdzielnia Wydawnicza, 1974.

Carroll, Beth, and Kevin J. Donnelly. "Introduction: Reimagining the Contemporary Musical in the Twenty-First Century." In *Contemporary Musical Film*, edited by Kevin J. Donnelly and Beth Carroll, 2–9. Edinburgh: Edinburgh University Press, 2017.

Chrzanowski, Przemysław. "Kapele z *Zimnej Wojny*." *Witryna wiejska*, February 22, 2019.

Connell, John, and Chris Gibson. *Sound Tracks: Popular Music Identity and Place*. New York: Routledge, 2003.

Herzog, Amy. *Dreams of Difference, Songs of the Same: The Musical Moments in Film*. Minneapolis: University of Minnesota Press, 2010.

Karabasz, Kaziemierz. *Cierpliwe oko*. Warsaw: Wydawnictwa Artystyczne i Filmowe, 1979.

Kichelewski, Audrey. "Poland's Postwar Trauma and Identity in Pawel Pawlikowski's Films: Reflections on *Ida* and *Cold War*." *Central European History* 52, no. 3 (2020): 652–656.

Kosior, Karolina. "Niejedna słowiańska dusza." *Pismo folkowe* 140–141 (2019). Accessed August 9, 2022. https://pismofolkowe.pl/artykul/niejedna-slowianska-dusza-5358.

Kurz, Iwona. "Wychłodzone obrazy." *Dwutygodnik* 239 (June 2018). https://www.dwutygodnik.com/artykul/7865-wychlodzone-obrazy.html.

Mazierska, Ewa, and Zsolt Győri. "Introduction: Popular Music and the Moving Image in Eastern Europe." In *Popular Music and the Moving Image in Eastern Europe*, edited by Ewa Mazierska and Zsolt Győri, 1–24. New York: Bloomsbury Academic, 2019.

———. *Polish Popular Music on Screen*. Cham: Palgrave Macmillan, 2020.

Morstin, Agnieszka. "Kieślowski versus Pawlikowski. *Podwójne życie Weroniki* i *Zimna wojna* jako opowieści o świecie dwudzielnym," *Kwartalnik Filmowy* 103 (2018): 79–90.

Norðfjörð, Björn. "The Post-Modern Transnational Film Musical." In *The International Film Musical*, edited by Corey K. Creekmur and Linda Y. Mokdad, 241–255. Edinburgh: Edinburgh University Press, 2012.

Rydzewska, Joanna. "Art and the Musical in Paweł Pawlikowski's *Cold War*." Paper presented at the Fifty-First Annual Conference of the Association for Slavic, East European and Euroasian Studies (ASEEES), San Francisco, November 2019.

———. "Neoliberal Authorship: Auteur Theory and European Art Cinema in 2021—The Example of Paweł Pawlikowski." In *The Routledge Companion to European Cinema*, edited by Gábor Gergely and Susan Hayward. New York: Routledge, 2022.

Schatz, Thomas. "Film Genre and the Genre Film." In *Film Theory and Criticism*, edited by Leo Braudy and Marshall Cohen, 691–702. 7th ed. Oxford: Oxford University Press, 2009.

Smith, Imogen Sara. "Blues for the Iron Curtain: *Cold War* and *Red Boogie*." Film Comment, October 30, 2018. www.film comment.com/blog/blues-iron-curtain-cold-war-red-boogie/.

Tincknell, Estella, and Ian Conrich. "Introduction." In *Film's Musical Moments: Music and the Moving Image*, edited by Ian Conrich and Estella Tincknell, 1–12. Edinburgh: Edinburgh University Press, 2006.

Varga, Balázs. "Worlds that Never Were: Contemporary Eastern European Musical Comedies and the Memory of Socialism." In *Popular Music and the Moving Image in Eastern Europe*, edited by Ewa Mazierska and Zsolt Győri, 63–82. New York: Bloomsbury Academic, 2019.

White, Jerry. "'*Cold War* Contexts': Pawlikowski in Film, Television, and European History." *Film Quarterly* 72, no. 3 (2019): 44–51.

Young, Michael A. "Hi-Fi Heritage: Recording Technology, Audio Engineering, and the Mediation of Authenticity in the Polish Revival of Traditional Music." *Journal of Folklore Research* 57, no. 1 (2020): 33–71.

CHAPTER 4

The Allure of Agnieszka Smoczyńska's *Lure* (2015) as an Intrepid Feminist Hybrid

Helena Goscilo

"In Poland there's no tradition of musicals."
—Agnieszka Smoczyńska in interview

Agnieszka Smoczyńska's initial forays into film attested equally to her gynocentrism and her passion for music. Created while she was still enrolled in Wajda's Master School, her unusual thirty-minute feature, *Aria Diva* (2007)—an adaptation of Olga Tokarczuk's short story "Ariadna na Naksos" ("Ariadne on Naxos")—dramatized a young housewife's fascination with the titular diva, for whom classical singing appears to constitute her entire existence. Three years later, Smoczyńska's seventeen-minute documentary, *Viva Maria!* (2010), likewise completed during her studies, traced the life and master class of Maria Fołtyn (1924–2012), Poland's premier operatic soprano of her generation, internationally applauded for her performance of the major role in Stanisław Moniuszko's *Halka* (1847). Given these two outings, Smoczyńska's full-length feature debut, *Córki dancingu* (The lure, 2015), seemed a predictable culmination of her earlier works inasmuch as it belongs to the genre of a film musical. Predictable, however, is precisely what *The Lure* itself is not. Its premiere at the Sundance Film Festival, where it received a much-publicized award, and its screening amidst enthusiastic accolades at the Fantasia Film Festival sparked not only rave but also stunned and uncomprehending reviews. The film proved hugely profitable, entered the prestigious Criterion Collection, and eventually won the director and her scriptwriter, Robert Bolesto, a grant from the

Sundance Institute for her next musical—provisionally titled *Deranged,* with music by David Bowie.[1]

No one could gainsay *The Lure*'s originality. Sui generis on multiple fronts, it imaginatively synthesizes the genre of film musical with horror and folkloric adaptation, features sequences brutal and grotesque enough to distress many viewers raised on anodyne Hollywood "sing along" fare and could hardly have a more devastating conclusion. One laudatory reviewer declared, "*The Lure* puts to shame any notion that something as bland as *La La Land* is the future of the movie musical. . . . The film's messages are cleverly wrapped in Smoczynska's entertaining, original vision. It's sexy, fearless, fun, and unrepentantly nasty."[2] Another called the film "A delirious, kaleidoscopic cannibal mermaid musical."[3] In short, the film made an indelible impression on critics and viewers alike, winning more than twenty awards.[4]

Yet puzzled or "unknowing" commentators, to invoke Linda Hutcheon's handy term, found the film excessive or bewildering, largely because they seemed unaware that it challenges a Hans Christian Andersen fairy tale, and their ignorance automatically circumscribed their understanding and appreciation of how *The Lure* treats that universally acclaimed text. Hutcheon's "Knowing and Unknowing Audiences"[5] proposes a "palimpsestic doubleness" that encapsulates a largely overlooked distinction between viewers possessing cultural knowledge and those lacking it. The "knowing" not only may derive additional pleasure from citations that bypass other viewers, but also may nurture specific expectations and 'read' the adaptation differently from the "unknowing," who experience "the work for itself"—*an sich.*[6] The "knowing" instantly recognize the "citation" in *The Lure* as the Andersen hypotext—a fact that eluded various uninitiated commentators who therefore detected no polemic in the film, probably because Smoczyńska deviated from many adapters' habit of reproducing

---

1 *The Lure* received the World Cinema Dramatic Special Jury Award for Unique Vision and Design at Sundance and three prizes during the Thirty-Six International Film Festival Fantasporto. See "Sundance Grant for Poles to Film David Bowie 'Science-Fiction Opera,'" Culture.pl, February 1, 2017, https://culture.pl/en/article/sundance-grant-for-poles-to-film-david-bowie-science-fiction-opera.

2 Odie Henderson, "Polish Mermaid Musical 'The Lure' Gets Joyously Nasty," Village Voice, January 31, 2017, https://www.villagevoice.com/2017/01/31/polish-mermaid-musical-the-lure-gets-joyously-nasty/.

3 Russ Fischer, "'The Lure' Is a Delirious, Kaleidoscopic Cannibal Mermaid Musical," Playlist, February 1, 2017, https://theplaylist.net/lure-delirious-kaleidoscopic-cannibal-mermaid-musical-review-20170201/.

4 See "*The Lure,*" IMDB, https://www.imdb.com/title/tt5278832/awards/?ref_=tt_awd.

5 Linda Hutcheon, *A Theory of Adaptation* (New York and London: Routledge, 2006).

6 Ibid., 127.

the title of Andersen's fairy tale.[7] Unlike the spate of reviews incapable of moving beyond their confusion at the film's generic cocktail,[8] Angela Lovell's insightful commentary numbered among the few to recognize *The Lure*'s status as a feminist response to Andersen's complacently sexist "Little Mermaid" (1837)—an awareness that probably accounts for the inclusion of her commentary in the Criterion Collection.[9]

Andersen's "Little Mermaid" on Page and Screen

The Lure is a *rara avis*—a feminist musical that subverts one of the world's most popular narratives revisited in sundry cultural genres for almost two centuries. Anyone without a thorough knowledge of the Danish literary fairy tale, however, cannot grasp how cleverly *The Lure* overturns its ideology and constitutive features while literalizing some of its tropes.[10] Andersen's text typifies the author's proclivity to moralize and indulge his sadomasochistic tendencies even while giving free rein to his vivid imagination. "The Little Mermaid" delves into the underwater world, where a lovely young mermaid, unlike her five sisters, yearns to acquire a soul and join the human race. After rescuing a shipwrecked prince with whom she becomes infatuated at first sight she has a water-witch perform

---

7 Yet even a "knowing" viewer, such as Ewa Mazierska, seemed puzzled by what the film attempts and by and large achieves. Her opinion that "the connections between episodes in *The Lure* are so tenuous that it is almost impossible to extract any message from the film" is startling. See Ewa Mazierska, *Polish Popular Music on Screen* (London: Palgrave Macmillan, 2020), 133–137, specifically 134.

8 Perhaps the most myopic review appeared in *Variety*: "Smoczyńska's deeply dippy story of vampire mermaid sisters wreaking havoc above water gleefully shows off its cluttered collection of whosits and whatsits galore." Not a word about Andersen's "Little Mermaid" (Guy Lodge, "The Seaweed is Always Grislier in Agnieszka Smoczyńska's Unbalanced but Enticing Vampire-Mermaid Musical Fable," Variety, March 7, 2016, https://variety.com/2016/film/festivals/the-lure-review-1201722757/).

9 Angela Lovell, "The Lure: One is Silver and the Other Golden," Criterion Collection, October 10, 2017, https://www.criterion.com/current/posts/5030-the-lure-one-is-silver-and-the-other-Golden.

10 For an earlier satirical debunking of Andersen's literary fairy tale, see the clever story by Joanna Russ (1937–2011), "Russalka, or, The Seacoast of Bohemia" (1978), excerpted from her children's text, *Kittatinny: A Tale of Magic* (1978), and reprinted as a stand-alone text. It is one of many narratives by women that revise or ironize traditional fairy tales. For a brief discussion of it, see the rather weak study by Lucy Fraser, which cites numerous theorists and works without managing to arrive at convincing analyses of the verbal and visual texts she references in the pursuit of her slippery thesis of pleasure. See Lucy Fraser, *The Pleasures of Metamorphosis: Japanese and English Fairy Tale Transformations of "The Little Mermaid"* (Detroit: Wayne State University Press, 2017), 135–137.

dark magic on her body to transform her into a pseudo-human. The price for replacing her fishtail with legs is constant pain and a loss of voice that proves catastrophic. To become genuinely human, she needs to marry the prince; otherwise, she will die, transformed into seafoam. Tolerated by him as a mute, amusing child, she docilely serves him, only to see him marry a princess. When offered a last-minute choice of killing the happy honeymoon couple or accepting death, she opts for the latter, dissolves into seafoam, and joins the "daughters of the air"—invisible do-gooders who will earn a soul if they faithfully perform charitable deeds throughout the world for three centuries. That period of probation will be reduced by "good" children and extended by "naughty" ones. Presumably, this prolonged service will earn the mermaid and her aerial companions a human soul.

The pedagogical tale smugly propounds a repressive ideal of femininity that comprises an improbable brew of beautiful innocence, patience, silence, self-sacrifice, unquestioning steadfast love, and complete subordination to a male, including readiness for self-mutilation to win his love—exactly those gendered attributes against which feminism has battled since the late 1960s. Whereas for Andersen muteness, invisibility, and self-immolation are women's admirable lot, Smoczyńska, after two shorts about talented, self-reliant professional women specializing in voice production, turned his notions on their head, rescripting his scenario to uphold female agency while retaining but transvaluating the basic aspects of the fairy-tale plot. In so doing she swam against the current of multiple screen versions of Andersen's bathetic narrative. These include Russian adaptations ranging from Ivan Aksenchuk's animated *Rusalochka* (1968) to Anna Melikian's *Rusalka* (2007),[11] and, most notoriously, Disney's saccharine animated musical, *The Little Mermaid* (1989), with its red-haired Ariel as the heroine who interacts with sundry "cute" underwater creatures and, in a stereotypical Hollywood "happy ending," actually snags Eric, her prince, with whom she sails off into the proverbial sunset. Clearly calculated to appeal to credulous children (the producer initially worried that the film would attract only girls and therefore yield smaller profits), the expensive movie boosted animation in the film industry, won two music awards at the Oscars, proved vastly lucrative for the studio, and spawned a number of forgettable sequences. Characteristically, in its relentless pursuit of commodification, the Disney conglomerate hawked

11 For an examination of the many Russian screen adaptations, see Helena Goscilo, "The Danish Little Mermaid vs. the Russian Rusalka: Screen Choices," in *Hans Christian Andersen in Russia*, ed. Mads Sohl Jessen, Marina Balina, Ben Hellman, and Johs. Norregaard Frandsen (Odense: University Press of Southern Denmark, 2020), 319–349.

endless other products to increase its profits.[12] As Jack Zipes observed, "Whereas Andersen's tale is disturbing and ambivalent about the meaning of happiness, the Disney films about the Little Mermaid are sentimental, romantic, and one-dimensional."[13] And the notorious Hollywood "happy ever after" scenario is exactly what Ron Howard's earlier lightweight "fantasy romantic comedy," *Splash* (1984), likewise peddled—unsurprisingly, given that the film launched Disney's Touchstone Pictures, which the studio devised to market films targeting (immature?) adult audiences incapable of tolerating any ending that fails to transform life's trials into a pastel paradise. Predictably, *Splash,* too, generated myriad marketable items.[14] These technically slick but hackneyed screen offerings could hardly be more remote from *The Lure,* which anticipated a genuinely adult audience unhampered by formulaic, rosy visions of romantic bliss. In one respect, however, Smoczyńska's unique adaptation resembles all others. It ignores what for Andersen was arguably primary: the acquisition of a soul.

Polarizing Womanhood: The Cliché and the Feminist Antidote

Whereas during the reign of the omnipotent studio system the early American film musical, as Rick Altman, Jane Feuer, and others have contended, relied on a romantic heterosexual couple to bring about the obligatory reconciliation of paradoxes and seemingly irreconcilable differences at film's end,[15] Smoczyńska's *Lure* complicates that simplistic model by presenting two asymmetrical couples:

---

12 For more information about the film, see the comprehensive article "The Little Mermaid," Wikipedia, https://en.wikipedia.org/wiki/The_Little_Mermaid_(1989_film). During its early, more adventurous days, Disney produced Hollywood's first animated musical, *Snow White and the Seven Dwarfs* (1937), which had the distinction of being the first color animated film worldwide.

13 For a scathing and accurate analysis of Disney's animated films as formulaic pablum, see Jack Zipes, *The Enchanted Screen: The Unknown History of Fairy-Tale Films* (New York and London: Routledge, 2011), 86–89.

14 For more about screen versions of Andersen's tale, see ibid., 254–261. Strangely, Zipes seems ignorant of *Splash*. An unusual study of Andersen's tale as adapted in English and Japanese culture is Fraser, *The Pleasures of Metamorphosis: Japanese and English Fairy Tale Transformations of "The Little Mermaid."*

15 See Rick Altman, *The American Film Musical* (Bloomington: Indiana University Press, 1989); and Jane Feuer, *The Hollywood Musical* (Bloomington: Indiana University Press, 1993). Feuer's study concentrates on the early Hollywood musical, which, Steven Cohan logically contends, "is now impossible to take seriously except as an artifact of nostalgia" (Steve Cohan, ed., *Hollywood Musicals: The Film Reader* [London and New York: Routledge, 2002], 2).

the romantic duo of the mermaid Srebrna/Silver (Marta Mazurek) and Mietek, a young, blond, far from intelligent musician (Jakub Gierszał), and the contrastive sisters, Silver and Złota/Golden (Magdalena Olszańska). The dramatic divergence between the two relationships derives in part from the polarization of the two mermaids—a temperamental and ideological contrast reflected in their manner and appearance, buttressed by age-old associations: the light-haired, obliging, impressionable Silver, rendered witless through "love," versus her self-confident, no-nonsense brunette sibling, who prizes independence and scorns age-old gendered assumptions.

Whereas Andersen moralizes, Smoczyńska politicizes her narrative along gender lines. In her coming-of-age story, the two innocent mermaids undergo a traditional initiation as they learn to smoke, drink alcohol, and realize their physical effect on men. At the same time, they share a secret, telepathic language,[16] vampiric inclinations, profound affection, and complete lack of inhibitions about baring their bodies (after all, garments hamper swimming underwater). Yet Silver ultimately perishes by romantic cliché (for example, dying for "love"), whereas Golden opts for sexual pleasure in an unorthodox experimental mode. Finding the musician Mietek irresistible, even though he informs her that he can view her only as "a fish, an animal," Silver readily sacrifices her fishtail, body, and voice via a gruesome operation to have emotional/sexual intercourse with him. All too obviously, she exemplifies the self-objectifying female willing to remake herself into what she believes a man desires, and in that sense, she is a throwback to a heteronormative hypostasis of slavish womanhood satirized above all by Angela Carter and Fay Weldon in such subversive works as, respectively, *The Bloody Chamber* (1979) and *The Life and Loves of a She-Devil* (1983).[17] Golden—whose name reflects her greater self-worth—opts for a radically different route. Unlike Silver's myopic, single-minded devotion to her "one and only," Golden's preference is for encounters of a purely physical nature with various partners, as illustrated by her sexual bout with a male nightclub guest (the German) in his car, and the intimacy she enjoys with a policewoman (Katarzyna Herman) who, after watching the sisters' frenetic Goth performance of "Czary mary" ("Abracadabra"), waylays her and takes her home for the prolonged

---

16 That language, which recalls dolphins' system of communication, belongs to what Linda Williams identifies as the horror and porn genres' inarticulateness—at least from the perspective of the "coded articulations" of human speech. See Linda Williams, "Film Bodies: Gender, Genre, and Excess," in *Film Genre Reader II*, ed. Barry Keith Grant (Austin: University of Texas Press, 1995), 143.

17 Carter's volume, a collection of stories that revise famous fairy tales, is especially pertinent to *The Lure*.

physical pleasure of both.[18] These two episodes end in vastly different ways, as discussed below.

Mermaids, of course, have a long lineage, originating in Homer's dangerous sirens and most countries' folklore. In both, eye-catching water maidens—in Slavic folklore, those who suicided by drowning when betrayed by unfaithful lovers—seduce through song and physical beauty, but prove fatal to those who succumb to their "lure."[19] Not unlike Denmark, with Copenhagen's bronze statuette of the water maiden by Edvard Eriksen, Poland adopted the legendary figure of the folkloric water spirit *syrenka* as its coat of arms and emblem of the national spirit, wielding a sword in the famous statue in the heart of Warsaw's Old Town.[20] By contrast to her Danish analogue, the Polish mermaid is a warrior, her identity signaling her readiness to defend the country and its capital—the resistance to encroachment of negative forces that Smoczyńska embodies in her fearless Golden. Silver, however, remains a clone of Andersen's pathetic, slavish mermaid. Homer's lethal sirens (only two in the *Odyssey*) and the Polish mermaid comprise the feminist forces on which *The Lure* draws to undermine Andersen's tale, yielding a highly unconventional musical.

Gender and the Genre of Horror: Vapidity vs. Vampirism

What has startled some viewers of *The Lure* is the film's unsmiling embrace of horror in a vampiric vein—normally not a facet of quality musicals, apart from the campy, gender-bending *Rocky Horror Picture Show* (1975) by

---

18 In the subtitles the translation of "Czary mary" inaccurately appears as "Holy moly."

19 On the age-old demonological persona of the mermaid/rusalka/undine from Homer to modern verbal and visual texts, see Helena Goscilo, "Watery Maidens: Rusalki as Sirens and Slippery Signs," in *Poetics, Self, Place: Essays in Honor of Anna Lisa Crone*, ed. Catherine O'Neil, Nicole Boudreau, and Sarah Krive (Bloomington: Slavica, 2007), 50–70.

20 Based on the various legends circulating about the Polish mermaid, the film *Warszawska syrena* (The Warsaw mermaid, 1956) by Tadeusz Makarczyński, conceived primarily for children, casts her as the symbolic triumph of good over evil in a narrative combining two romantic couples. Copenhagen's original mermaid now has a contentious near-twin. Reportedly, "The mermaid that has watched over the harbor in the village of Asaa, in the north of Denmark, since 2016 is not an exact replica of the landmark in Denmark's capital. But for the heirs of Edvard Eriksen, the artist who sculpted the Copenhagen statue, the Asaa mermaid bears too close a resemblance. They have initiated legal proceedings, demanding not just financial compensation, but that the sculpture in Asaa be torn down as well" (See Lisa Abend, "Denmark Now Has Two Little Mermaids. The Famous One Is Suing," *The New York Times*, August 19, 2021, https://www.nytimes.com/2021/08/17/arts/design/little-mermaid-denmark-dispute.html).

Jim Sharman,[21] which sets out to parody the genre, whereas *The Lure* relies on it to challenge the gender disposition of its Danish source. As Steve Neale, leaning on the theories of Yuri Tynianov, argues, horror as a genre not only has heterogeneous origins but also has evolved appreciably over decades.[22] In such films as the British Hammer *Dracula* series with Christopher Lee (1958–1972), the American *Friday the 13th, Halloween,* and *Nightmare on Elm Street* cycles, horror typically manifests as the relentless, luridly bloody terror to which a male aggressor or psychopath subjects primarily women. Various critics straitjacketed by a numbing fidelity to Freud ascribe men's homicidal brutality in horror movies to a displaced fear of castration—a theory that cannot cope adequately with screen scenarios in which female killers are the source of horror, including *Alien* (1979), where an alien creature fulfills the role of murderer (killing both sexes) in the interests of its species' relentless drive to reproduce. More productive and more pertinent to *The Lure* is the consistent emphasis on the female body in the genre as theorized by Carol J. Clover, Barbara Creed, and especially Linda Williams.

Clover in her discussion of pornography and horror as occupants of low niches in the conventional hierarchy of genres refers to such films, which dwell on the sensational, as "body genres"—a taxonomy singularly apposite for *The Lure,* since the female body, occasionally in choreographic numbers, is squarely at its very center throughout.[23] Equally relevant to Smoczyńska's film is Williams's shrewd observation that "pornography is today more often deemed excessive for its violence than for its sex, while horror films are excessive in their displacement of sex into violence."[24] *The Lure* teems with violence but shortchanges direct representation of sex. As much may be seen in the opening of *The Lure,* where the credit sequence opens with the intriguing animation of two identical silhouetted mermaids flying in the stratosphere around a spire against the background of a

---

21 Though initially panned by critics, the parodic film boasts a huge following and in 2005 was officially preserved in the United States National Film Registry by the Library of Congress. *Phantom of the Opera* (2004) and Tim Burton's *Sweeney Todd: Demon Barber of Fleet Street* (2007) are tamer, more recent examples of the genre, both indebted to their stage sources, while *Alleluia! The Devil's Carnival* (2016) is an exercise in "cheap thrills," and to take seriously the horror of *Little Shop of Horrors* (1986) is impossible because the film is a musical comedy, adapted from the stage version of the genre (1982)—in its turn, an adaptation of a Roger Corman film!

22 Steve Neale, "Genre," in *Film Genre Reader II*, ed. Barry Keith Grant (Austin: University of Texas Press, 1995), 149–183.

23 Carol J. Clover, "Her Body, Himself: Gender in the Slasher Film," in *Dread of Difference: Gender and the Horror Film*, ed. Barry Keith Grant (Austin: University of Texas Press, 1996). Clover's article originally appeared in *Representations* 20 (Fall 1987): 187–228.

24 Linda Williams, "Film Bodies: Gender, Genre, and Excess," 140.

full moon (associated with magic and fantasy), followed by fireworks (fig. 4.1).[25] In a downward shift from sky to sea, the ensuing ominous visuals by Aleksandra Waliszewska individualize the two anonymous mermaids, with skulls bobbing in water alongside them, as well as a mermaid pulling a swimmer underwater, true to her folkloric praxis. Instead of poeticizing mermaids, these preliminary images evoke their deadly powers and augur nothing positive even before the lyrics of the mermaids' first song introduce the violence that will eventuate. According to Waliszewska, her art inspired *The Lure*, and the knowing viewer familiar with her artwork—replete with existential horror—anticipates some of the film's vividly grisly moments.[26]

Figure 4.1. Mermaids projected against the magical moon in Aleksandra Waliszewska's original rendition. *Córki dancingu* (The Lure), 2015, dir. Agnieszka Smoczyńska.

25 For a sampling of Waliszewska's artwork, see "Aleksandra Waliszewska," Artsy, https://www.artsy.net/artist/aleksandra-waliszewska. For an interview with her, see Aleksandra Waliszewska, "I'd Like to Have a Goat Someday: An Interview with Aleksandra Waliszewska," by Filip Lech, Culture.pl, July 30, 2020, https://culture.pl/en/article/id-like-to-have-a-goat-someday-an-interview-with-aleksandra-waliszewska?utm_source=getresponse&utm_medium=email&utm_campaign=10092020en&utm_content=art4_title. For a perceptive commentary in Polish on her art, see Anka Herbut, "To nie powinno się zdarzyć," *Dwutygodnik* 135 (June 2014), https://www.dwutygodnik.com/artykul/5272-to-nie-powinno-sie-zdarzyc.html.

26 Waliszewska's message in a private correspondence via email, March 29, 2021. During the interviews that comprise the supplements on the film's DVD, Smoczyńska confirms Waliszewska's inspirational role and her part in designing the mermaids' enormous, heavy fishtails. For an analysis of Waliszewska's work, see Helena Goscilo, "Art-Horror Lite and Full Throttle: The Arresting Originality of Ewa Juszkiewicz and Aleksandra Waliszewska," in *Contemporary Slavic Horror across Media: Cursed Zones*, ed. Agnieszka Jezyk and Lev Nikulin (Manchester: University of Manchester Press, 2023).

As the credits cede to a brief prologue, we see two men and a woman amusing themselves on a dark nocturnal beach. The youngest member of the trio (Mietek) strums his guitar and, gradually joined by a female voice, sings of "Beata z Albatrosa" ("Beata from the Albatross"), casually introducing the themes of youth, loss, and sadness that the film will elaborate. In response, two nubile young females abruptly surface in the water and softly sing in response, "Help us come ashore, don't be afraid, we won't eat you."[27] Why two naked females should find it necessary to reassure men that they will not harm them becomes elucidated only later, in a strategy of delayed clarification that operates repeatedly in the film. Seductive and seemingly harmless, the beguiling pair receive the aid they seek from the youth and the older man at his side (Andrzej Konopka, Smoczyńska's husband), who obligingly pull them out of the water as the camera shifts to an inebriated middle-aged blonde (Kinga Preis), the third of the onshore trio, who utters a bloodcurdling scream. What horror has elicited that response we learn yet again only later, once the film contextualizes it after the film's title appears on the screen.

That context is Adria, a historically famous but here a slightly seamy nightclub 'for adults' in Soviet-dominated 1980s Warsaw (see chapter 1), whose manager (Zygmunt Malanowicz [1938–2021]) finally understands why the club smells of fish when he enters the dressing room of his musical trio, Figi i Daktyle (Figs and Dates)—the singer Krysia, her percussionist husband, and Mietek, their bassist son.[28] In a segment that reduces Silver and Golden to the classic scenario of female bodies under male inspection, the drummer demonstrates to the proprietor not only their lack of vaginas ("smooth, like Barbie"), but also how water poured on the two transforms them into mermaids—moreover, with preternaturally huge fishtails (fig. 4.2). The sleazy proprietor promptly hires them, in a sequence that belongs to what traditionally has been labeled the backstage aspect of musicals featuring staged songs and dance. Publicly, the female body at the nightclub is the object of obsessive fascination when Silver and Golden join Krysia's performance of songs, and especially when they appear as tuneful sirens in a giant water-filled

27 Here, as elsewhere, when the English subtitles do not translate the original Polish precisely, I provide my versions of verbal texts and song lyrics.

28 Whether Mietek is their biological offspring is never clarified, and Krysia's maternal attitude toward the two mermaids renders likely his status as simply a young fellow musician who also happens to live with the couple, as Golden and Silver do, once they begin performing at the nightclub.

champagne coupe—a spectacle that tropes consumerism, brings the audience to its feet, and becomes the city's sensation (fig. 4.3).

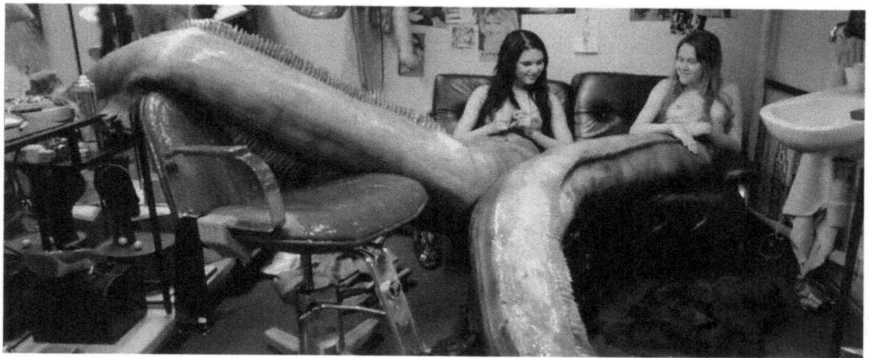

Figure 4.2. Smoczyńska endows Złota/Golden (Magdalena Olszańska) and Srebrna/Silver (Marta Mazurek) with fishtails so grotesquely enormous as to de-poeticize the standard romantic depiction of mermaids.

Figure 4.3. An enraptured audience greets the mermaids' performance at the nightclub Adria with a standing ovation.

As excitement at their appearances escalates, what starts at the opening of the Adria sequence as the rhythmic body movements of the club's personnel and clientele in tune with the performers' songs ends in a wild bacchanalia of gyrating and uncontrolled bodies that fill the screen—a frenzy repeated when they sing their Goth number and toward the end when Tryton/Triton (Marcin Kowalczyk), his metal band, and Golden take the stage. Bodily self-expression takes over not only the singers but also the club's audience, making it impossible to differentiate between the two, which characterizes the finale of many musicals, such as Emile Ardolino's feisty *Dirty Dancing* (1987).[29] What Richard Dyer calls the genre's "non-representational signs" of "colour, texture, movement, rhythm, melody, camerawork" that operate on the level of emotions come into play in full force.[30] It is as though the mermaid's cynosural bodies have infected all those frequenting the nightclub as they succumb to the pounding beat and rebellious potential of "dark magic" and a punk musical number. And since the action is set in a period following the Polish regime's imposition of martial law (1981–1983), the chaotic mass celebration could be interpreted as a protest against conservative values, which the film unmistakably mounts in the spheres of gender and family politics.

The Body Sexed and Visualized

> "Taught from infancy that beauty is woman's sceptre, the mind shapes itself to the body, and roaming round its gilt cage, only seeks to adorn its prison."
>
> —Mary Wollstonecraft

Dyer's indefatigably quoted and reprinted landmark article about the musical as entertainment aptly underscores the pleasure of watching colorfully clad bodies in motion, and not only the controlled choreography of movies built around the formidable dancing skills of Fred Astaire, Cyd Charisse, Gene Kelly, and Ginger Rogers, even though Smoczyńska replaces the emotion-based utopia that Dyer and virtually all anglophone commentators view as inhering in the genre with dystopia, most notably displayed at film's end—also at the painful conclusion of *Zimna wojna* (Cold War), analyzed in chapter 3. The inviting physicality of *The Lure* is relentless: it ranges from Krysia's wriggling as she sings and the suggestive undulations and striptease of the in-house dancer Boskie Futro/Divine Fur

---

29 *Dirty Dancing*, which I consider a musical, divides specialists in the genre. In the same volume, editor Steve Cohan refers to it as a *bona fide* film musical (Cohan, *Hollywood Musicals: The Film Reader*, 2), while the contributor Martin Rubin explicitly distinguishes it from the genre as merely one of the films "with musical performances in them." Rubin's argument rests on the fact that the musical numbers "all can be rationalized on the level of the narrative as professional stage performances or prerehearsed routines." (Martin Rubin, "Busby Berkeley and the Backstage Musical," in *Hollywood Musicals: The Film Reader*, ed. Steven Cohan [London and New York: Routledge, 2002], 57.)

30 Richard Dyer, "Entertainment and Utopia," *Movie* 24 (Spring 1977): 38; reprinted in *Genre: The Musical*, ed. Rick Altman (London: Routledge, 1980), 175–189.

(Magdalena Cielecka)[31] in Miss Muffet's "Bananowy song" ("Banana song") (fig. 4.4) to the ludicrous fight of Krysia's family, with pillows and various objects, which leaves their apartment in shambles and the three dead, until they are magically resuscitated by Divine Fur. Everyone dances in the club, just as most of the celebrants do at Mietek's wedding party on the moored ship, including the groom's father, who repeats the peculiar solo number he suddenly improvises earlier in the apartment shared by all five performers. Indisputably the sustained emphasis on body movement in sync with music largely accounts for the vibrant energy that *The Lure* emanates. Moreover, the female body as a site of pleasure accounts for an extraordinary sequence of the polymorphously perverse, in which Krysia, in the midst of intercourse with her husband, fantasizes about having a fishtail while her breasts are sucked by both Silver and Golden—a scenario immediately following Golden's mutually satisfying encounter with the lesbian policewoman (fig. 4.5). The film, in other words, pays its dues to queer encounters and desires via the liberated body as part of its rejection of conventions and taboos: Krysia's fantasy, the lesbian policewoman, and two gay men parked at night to kiss and fondle each other. And, unlike Polish musical comedies of the thirties (chapter one), the original German *Viktor und Viktoria* (directed by Reinhold Schünzel, 1933), and its American clone by Blake Edwards in 1982, *The Lure* makes no effort to restore heteronormative gender order.[32]

Figure 4.4. Adria's in-house dancer Boskie Futro/Divine Fur (Magdalena Cielecka) performs her standard striptease to the music of the "Banana Song."

31 Cielecka's notable early role is that of the nun in Barbara Sass's *Pokuszenie* (Temptation, 1995).
32 Jim Hillier and Douglas Pye, *100 Film Musicals: BFI Screen Guides* (London: Palgrave Macmillan/BFI, 2011), 238.

Figure 4.5. During sexual intercourse with her husband (Andrzej Konopka) Krysia (Kinga Preis) dreams of being suckled by the two mermaid sisters.

Yet, given the film's mélange of genres, the body has a darker side. Both mermaids' bodies are shamelessly exploited in a photo session with a German photographer, engineered to capitalize on their fame, where their partial nakedness and "bunny ears" evoke Hugh Hefner's Playboy Club (1960–1990), in which pneumatically breasted young women wore precisely such ears and little else while serv(ic)ing male customers (fig. 4.6). Moreover, the piscine odor, the disturbingly gory operation Silver undergoes, and the blood from her stitches that revolts Mietek as they start having intercourse beg for what Creed has identified as the role of the female in horror films according to Julia Kristeva's theory of abjection. As Creed maintains, abjection "does not 'respect borders, positions, rules,'" and allies itself with what "'disturbs borders, positions, order.'"[33] Following Kristeva, she links abjection to maternity, but in *The Lure* this violation of borders and order characterizes the young mermaids, whose very bodies straddle the categories of human and animal. They belong to what Noel Carroll has called the "interstitial," the categorically impure, which confounds our cognitive principles, eliciting both fear and revulsion.[34] Silver's choices identify her as the female mired in blood, malodor, and animalism that Kristeva equates with abjection, the materiality of death.[35] Starting out as an object-body of intrigued

---

33 Barbara Creed, "Horror and the Monstrous-Feminine: An Imaginary Abjection," in *Dread of Difference: Gender and the Horror Film*, ed. Barry Keith Grant (Austin: University of Texas Press, 1996), 36.

34 Noel Carroll, *The Philosophy of Horror, or, The Paradoxes of the Heart* (New York: Routledge, 1990), 38.

35 Julia Kristeva, *Powers of Horror: An Essay on Abjection*, trans. Leon S. Roudiez (New York: Columbia University Press, 1982).

desire, she undergoes voluntary maiming, bleeds onto Mietek as if "polluting" him with her menstrual flow, relies on a wheelchair for mobility, and finally moves only on crutches. Her dissolution at film's end into seafoam may seem like the equivalent of transcendence—the ineffable apotheosis that presumably rewards a woman prepared to surrender life for the sake of a beloved male, as in Andersen's scenario. Smoczyńska, however, unambiguously repudiates that viewpoint, presenting Silver's physical disfigurement and eventual evaporation from the loving perspective of Golden, who responds to the loss of her sister with violence and despair, literally jumping at Mietek's throat and tearing it out before disconsolately vanishing into the water that is her natural domain.

Figure 4.6. The photo shoot of the sisters (un)dressed as Bunnies.

The body central to the genres of cinematic horror and the musical is thematized along gender lines in *The Lure,* dramatizing, through Silver, women's readiness to subject it to excruciating operations in the interests of stimulating male desire—popular nowadays in breast and lip-filler augmentation, change of nose, removal of fat by liposuction, elimination of wrinkles, and other, potentially life-threatening, procedures for the sake of physical appeal.[36] Eagerness to undergo such a self-destructive strategy is what distinguishes Silver from Golden, and the film shoots her operation graphically, with an overhead camera, unflinchingly showing blood spurt onto her face as her lower body is cut off and

36 Adriana Prodeus pointedly states, "... to, co gubi kobietę, to wpajane jej przekonanie o własnej niedoskonałości, to podsycana przez kulturę niezgoda na siebie, to mężczyzna, który nie pozwala jej się spełnić" ("... what dooms a woman is the conviction inculcated in her about her imperfection, it's the culturally fanned self-conflict, it's the man who doesn't allow her self-fulfillment") (Adriana Prodeus, "Córki Dancingu," *Kino* 12 (2015): 67, http://kino.org.pl//index.php?option=com_content&task=view&id=2376&Itemid=1556).

replaced with a woman's standard physical parts, sewn onto her torso (fig. 4.7).[37] Although, in an example of what Martin Rubin identifies as the genre's requisite "impossibility,"[38] she sings softly throughout this grueling, fantastic procedure,[39] including a few grotesque words about bitter chocolate ("Łóżko" ["The bed"]), Smoczyńska takes care to present it as a horrific assault on vulnerable flesh, in a "gross display" within "a system of excess" that, Williams justly maintains, inheres in the genre.[40] In other words, *The Lure* is a triple body outing, for the body functions centrally on the levels of genre, gender, and theme.

Figure 4.7. Overhead shot of Silver's bloody, excruciating operation so as to lose her fishtail and acquire human legs.

Whereas Silver's love entails self-mutilation and rejection, Golden adopts what traditionally has been a quintessentially masculine prerogative: she chooses her sexual partners and disposes of them according to her will. Although in one

---

37 The young woman lying beside Silver who wishes to exchange her traditional woman's body into a seductive fishtailed one, presumably has succumbed to the romantic image of the mermaid. The surgeon who obligingly performs the exchange is, of course, male.

38 For Rubin, a prime requisite for the screen musical is the impossibility of having characters with no musical training (according to the diegesis) suddenly break into song. Impossibility, however, is fundamental to the genres of fairy tales and horror, let alone the existence of mermaids and the very notion of an operation such as Silver's, by comparison with which the impossibility of anyone's miraculous knowledge of a song's lyrics pales. (Rubin, "Busby Berkeley and the Backstage Musical," 57–58). The very premise of Smoczyńska's *Lure* embraces impossibility, rendering Rubin's argument irrelevant.

39 In that respect, the depiction of the operation recalls Bob Fosse's *All That Jazz* (1979), in which a colorful production number accompanies Joe Gideon's (Roy Schneider) open-heart surgery, which fails to save his life.

40 Williams, "Film Bodies: Gender, Genre, and Excess," 142.

sequence we see both mermaids emerge at night from the water into which Mietek and the drummer have thrown them and feast on the body parts of a homosexual couple parked nearby, that is the sole occasion on which Silver surrenders to her vampiric drives. Not so Golden, as illustrated by her first encounter with a male customer from the club's bar, when his parked car as a stereotypical haven for sexual intimacy away from prying eyes begins to throb with ominous noises before we see Golden emerge from the vehicle and slither on her fishtail toward water, the man's heart in her bloody mouth, boldly literalizing the worn metaphor of stealing someone's heart—all to the accompaniment of the Wrońskie sisters' rendition of "Zagryzienie niemca" ("Biting the German to death"). Later, after the percussionist kisses Golden's hand in apology for having tried to kill her and Silver, she bites off part of his thumb (biting the hand that feeds her?). Glimpses of the sisters' pointed vampiric teeth are relatively rare, and the final sequence, which has Golden leap onto Mietek and rip out his throat, briefly reveals her fangs but dwells on her bloodstained lips as she jumps into the Vistula/Wisła, presumably abandoning land and its inhabitants forever. The final underwater shot of tranquil, leisurely flow suggests that her natural environment is more benign than the terrestrial experiences that occasioned the irretrievable loss of her beloved companion. Earlier evidence of her inseparability from her sister are her longing perusal of sea images on a screen; her despondent solo, "Już dawno nie byłam tak samotna" ("I've not been this lonely for a long time"), when she senses that she is losing Silver to Mietek; and her refusal to sing without her sister, who, in a metaphorical sacrifice of her voice that feminists have long deplored, becomes mute after her operation. By contrast, Silver, despite the loving farewell kiss she gives Golden before approaching Mietek one last time, essentially betrays that bond when she succumbs self-obliviously to a heteronormative cliché. In doing so, she ignores not only Golden's urging, but also the advice of the experienced performer Tryton/Triton—likewise originally an aquatic creature, now assimilated on land, who, tellingly, is the sole male portrayed positively in the film.

All too clearly, Altman's notion that gender difference or, as he phrases it, "sexual differentiation," is fundamental to musicals acquires a specific, evaluative coloration in *The Lure*, where men do not come off well and become the sole victims of the mermaids' vampirism.[41] After her sexual bout with the lesbian policewoman, Golden makes no effort to kill her (fig. 4.8). One

41 Altman, *The American Film Musical*, 16–27.

could argue that the pistol that the policewoman holds to her head is an effective deterrent, but in the context of the film's treatment of gender and the ease with which Silver at one point throws Golden across the room, that weapon sooner functions as a traditional symbol of male sexuality, witnessing a sexual gratification from which it is debarred. Certainly, Golden from the start establishes her status as the exclusive owner of her body: when the coarse owner of the nightclub gives all the performers a "legs up" for good luck, the others acquiesce to the ritual, but she wards off his intrusive hands, warning, "Don't touch me!"[42] Later she brushes off an older man's attempt at an assignation by dismissively murmuring, "I love you" before quickly moving away.[43] Silver may be indentured to a hopeless love, but Golden has no intention of subordinating herself to any man. Her loyalty is to herself and her sister, and she watches over her sibling, early noticing ominous signs of "fatal attraction" (for instance, Silver lying prone on the floor of the Sezam department store as if dead before Mietek picks her up) and striving to save her weaker sibling without impinging on her selfhood. Nothing could be further removed from Andersen's notion of a self-immolating gendered ideal. It is therefore all the more startling that in a generally appreciative review Magda Mielke pronounced the contrast between the two sisters as diabolical darkness (Golden) versus "sweetness and light" (Silver), with the former evil, killing for pleasure, but the latter "guided by noble ideals" ("kieruje się szlachetnymi ideałami")—a retrograde viewpoint that allies her with Andersen's 1837 text and betrays incomprehension of Smoczyńska's immeasurably more enlightened gender politics.[44]

---

42 The English translation is interpretive and correct. Her words in the original Polish, "Nie chcę," elliptically mean "I don't want [to be touched]."

43 Here, again, Mazierska's carelessness causes her to miss the film's pointed contrast between women's willingness to be viewed as cynosural bodies (Miss Muffet, Krysia, Silver) and the alternative embodied in Golden. Mazierska claims that Smoczyńska "follows in the footsteps . . . patriarchal, objectifying cinema"—an unfounded opinion that completely ignores Golden's role in the film and those moments when female bodies arouse same-sex desire, as in Krysia's dream and the policewoman's pursuit of Golden. (Mazierska, *Polish Popular Music on Screen*, 135).

44 Magda Mielke, "Córki Dancingu—Córki Baśni," Cinerama, January 8, 2017, http://mfcinerama.pl/poliz-kino-corki-basni/.

Figure 4.8. The lesbian policewoman (Katarzyna Herman) (left) and Golden (right) find shared sexual pleasure.

The more profound though less conspicuous horror in *The Lure* comprises not any genre's conventions, but immemorial gender politics, whereby women are marginalized and deemed expendable.[45] Such is the insight of various folktales, most shockingly and overtly the French "Bluebeard," revised by numerous writers, notably Carter in "The Bloody Chamber" (1979).[46] In less lurid form, *The Lure* shows how for no visible reason one morning the drummer, who in anger temporarily kills both mermaids, later abandons the family, leaving his marriage ring on a side table. His ostensibly inoffensive son, Mietek, makes romantic overtures to Silver, has no qualms about telling her that she will always seem an animal to him even as he kisses her, gazes soulfully at her, brings her flowers after her operation, and begins having sexual intercourse with her. Yet it takes little for him to transfer his romantic interest, for he marries her substitute, Nancy (Katarzyna Sawczuk), with a speed rendered shockingly rapid by nicely calculated editing (fig. 4.9). His smiling, passive demeanor cannot disguise the nastiness of his conduct, which, like his father's abrupt departure from the family, exposes the inequities of age-old male privilege that Andersen's myopic fairy tale unproblematically takes for granted. In sum, Smoczyńska's full-length debut, which subjects Andersen's euphemistically lyricized fairy tale to a boldly visceral rectification, leaves no doubts about her feminist credentials.

---

45 As much was noticed by Fischer in his Playlist article "'The Lure' Is a Delirious, Kaleidoscopic Cannibal Mermaid Musical."

46 Perhaps the most compromised screen adaptation is Krzysztof Zanussi's German/Swiss TV film (1983) of Max Frisch's revision in his last novel (1982), both titled *Blaubart* (Blackbeard).

Figure 4.9. Celebration of the wedding between Mietek (Jakub Gierszał) and Nancy (Katarzyna Sawczuk).

From Siren Song to the Genre of Musical

An original and captivating means of building on Andersen's bare-bones plot, of course, is the amplification of the mermaid's fabled siren song into the genre of musical. As Smoczyńska accurately noted in an interview, "In Poland, there's no tradition of musicals"[47]—or of horror and vampire movies, for that matter. Obviously, her inspiration came from American musicals—a thriving genre during the studio system from the thirties to the fifties, recently (and more pertinently here) revived in a vastly different mode. Smoczyńska has little interest in the Golden Age of Hollywood musicals, specifically citing as her creative stimulus the late Bob Fosse's *Cabaret* (1972) and *All That Jazz* (1979), as well as Lars von Trier's unprecedentedly dark *Dancer in the Dark* (2000), along with videos of the eclectically inclined Icelandic singer Björk, who stars in von Trier's musical melodrama.[48] In fact, the harrowing sequence of Silver's operation recalls an

---

47 Esther Zuckerman, "Agnieszka Smoczyńska Wants to 'Kill Disney' with Her Mermaid Horror Musical *The Lure*," AV Club, February 8, 2017, https://film.avclub.com/agnieszka-smoczynska-wants-to-kill-disney-with-her-me-1798257482. The genre of horror is no less alien to Polish film, with the notable exception of Jacek Koprowicz's unusual *Medium* (1985). Smoczyńska's assertion that "there's no tradition with genre," however, is exaggerated, for Polish cinema teems with historical sagas, war films, romances, comedies, and screen adaptations of literary works.

48 As one commentator notes, "Fosse's signature style," which was "sexually charged . . . influenced everything from Michael Jackson to today's musicals" (Kat Eschner, "Choreographer Bob Fosse Is the Forgotten Author of Modern Musicals," *Smithsonian Magazine*, June 23, 2017, https://www.smithsonianmag.com/smart-news/choreographer-bob-fosse-forgotten-author-modern-musicals-180963746/).

analogous procedure in *All That Jazz*, which ends in death. For the actual music Smoczyńska turned to Ballady i Romanse, comprising the two Wrońskie sisters, with Zuzanna/Zuzia writing the lyrics, while Barbara/Basia composes the music. Their mother, like Smoczyńska's, was employed in dancing restaurants during the socialist period, an experience that enabled all three women to draw on childhood memories for their work on *Córki dancingu*, the film's original Polish title, literally translated as *Daughters of Dancing*. And dancing to disco was the rage during Poland's eighties, as certified by an eloquent albeit unobtrusive detail of the *mise en scène*: the poster in Adria's dressing room of John Badham's *Saturday Night Fever* (1977), "the most critically and commercially successful movie to feature 1970s disco music" (fig. 4.10).[49]

Figure 4.10. Adria's sleazy manager (Zygmunt Malanowicz) mesmerized by the sororial mermaids, with a poster of *Saturday Night Fever* on the wall of the dressing room as a generic and temporal marker.

One of the most striking features of the film's music, however, is its diversity, elucidated by the director's original guiding concept, which she implemented from the very start. Smoczyńska claimed, "I wanted to create the whole movie around a score, as a composition. I really could see the whole movie after we made the sound. The sound design is crucial for this. It helps you to go from the musical to the horror, from the horror to the psychological drama, to comedy,

49 Hillier and Pye, *100 Film Musicals: BFI Screen Guides*, 196. The film boosted John Travolta's film career, leading to his starring role in Randal Kleiser's unprecedentedly lucrative hit, *Grease* (1978), of which the conclusion, with a car taking off for the skies, recalls the ending of the Stalin-era musical comedy by Grigorii Aleksandrov, *Svetlyi put'* (The radiant path, 1940). For an excellent monograph on Aleksandrov's musicals see Rimgalia Salys, *The Musical Comedy Films of Grigorii Aleksandrov: Laughing Matters* (Bristol: Intellect, 2009).

and it must be very, very gentle, and it must impose the way you have to watch it."[50] In the same interview, she confided, "Every character had to have a song. We need a song for Silver and the bass player, a love song. We need a song for Golden, which reveals that she's wild and she wants something different. And we need a song for *The Lure* as a band. I wrote the emotional arc for the songwriter. Emotionally, I knew where the story had to begin and end."

In fact, music in *The Lure* assumes various forms and fulfills at least five different but interrelated functions. First of all, in practical terms, it comprises the numbers sung by Krysia (the cover of disco queen Donna Summer's "I Feel Love") and later by all three females in the nightclub as they sing "Byłaś serca biciem" ("You were my heart's beat")—a rather ironic choice in light of the mermaids' fondness of hearts for their meals.[51] This category stands apart from the others and belongs to the performative aspect of musicals, which simultaneously addresses an on-screen audience and viewers, and characterizes what Louis Giannetti has called "realistic musicals," which *The Lure* in its entirety decidedly is not.[52] Just as in conventional Hollywood musicals, however, *The Lure* does organize these performances in such a way as to have the three women face not only the diegetic audience but also the extradiegetic moviegoer (fig. 4.11).[53]

Figure 4.11. The genre's classic frontal shot of performers that folds cinema's viewers into the diegetic audience.

50 Kat Eschner, "Choreographer Bob Fosse Is the Forgotten Author of Modern Musicals."

51 The mermaids' ability to sing this number with Krysia manifestly instances Rubin's concept of impossibility.

52 Louis Giannetti, *Understanding Movies* (Upper Saddle River: Prentice Hall, 1999), 218–219.

53 Cohan, *Hollywood Musicals: The Film Reader*, 13.

Next, the unique bravura number, "Przyszłam do miasta" ("I came to the city"), executed by the singing and dancing female trio in the huge Sezam department store, where they select and buy various outfits, may be seen to advance the plot, but in fact simply exists as an excellent exercise in choreography reminiscent of classic Hollywood fare. It aids in confirming *The Lure*'s status as a bona fide musical drawing on genre traditions while surpassing them, for the three major female personae energetically participate in the sequence, whereas a Busby Berkeley spectacle would have reduced the maximally choreographed all-female dancers (never the film's leads) into an anonymous, pseudo-mechanical mass structure with scant connection to the plot.[54] And the name of the store—Sesame in English—reinforces the folkloric basis of the film's narrative, for the store is the repository of sartorial riches formerly unknown to the two mermaids, where money substitutes for Ali Baba's magic words, "Open, Sesame!" (fig. 4.12).[55] Similarly, the sisters' Goth rendition of "Czary mary" ("Abracadabra") functions as a magical aphrodisiac for the audience, especially the entranced policewoman, with whom Golden subsequently shares the duet "Porucznik MO" ("Policewoman"), which contains the policewoman's ironic, allusive promise to take Golden to Disneyland (fig. 4.13).

Figure 4.12. Long queues in front of stores, such as the one here waiting for Sezam/Sesame to open, were part of everyday life under socialism.

54 Rubin, "Busby Berkeley and the Backstage Musical," 60.

55 For the international folkloric reliance on this motif, see D. L. Ashliman, "Open Sesame!," last modified January 27, 2022, https://www.pitt.edu/~dash/type0676.html.

Figure 4.13. The Goth number performed by the sisters drives the audience to paroxysms of delight.

Third, as is fundamental for the genre, music expresses the sentiments of the film's personae—singly, in duets, and collectively, with all vocals performed by the cast. "Miej mnie w swojej opiece" ("Keep me in your care"), the duet sung by Silver and Mietek, captures a tender moment between the two, fated to become irrelevant history by film's end. A more unusual duet, by the sisters, takes place during Silver's operation ("The bed"), where she gently gives voice to her condition ("Do łóżka przykuta" / "Forged to the bed"), lying in ice on the operating table "like the catch of the day,"[56] while a psychologically divided Golden sits "at home," opposed to the procedure and urging a change of mind, yet vocally harmonizing with her sibling. And one of the most complex usages occurs in the extended sequence at the wedding celebrations on board, where the theme of loss, reprising Golden's earlier solo, has most of the major characters take turns singing "Mnie tak smutno" ("I'm so sad") and "Wszystkim tak smuto jak cholera" ("Everyone's as sad as fuck-all"), as if at a proleptic wake for the two deaths that will eventuate. At this stage, Silver has lost not only her true identity but also her voice, mobility, and her male ideal; Krysia has lost her husband; the drummer has lost his family; Golden senses that she will lose her sister; and Silver is about to lose her life, as is Mietek, turning his bride into an instant widow. Ironically, the refrain of "I'm so sad," which reprises part of Golden's earlier solo, circulates among the individuals and groups on an occasion normally characterized by a festive mood, and some unindividualized guests, in fact, drink and laugh raucously.

56 Lovell, "*The Lure*: One is Silver and the Other Golden."

This sequence offers a different perspective on what Altman, Feuer, and others have emphasized as the union of on-screen personae and their bond with audiences, for in *The Lure* the lyrics transmitted among groups in the wedding party function predictively, signaling the loss of two lives and Golden's pain at irrevocably losing her beloved life-companion, Silver. Nothing reassuring marks these losses, and the music associated with them, far from assuming the form of a rousing collective finale, is understated and melancholy, making the rounds instead of swelling into a triumphant chorus. During what is supposed to be a celebration of anticipated conjugal happiness, the common musical motif is the heterogeneous wedding guests' profession of dejection, not joy. Moreover, they stand alone or in small clusters instead of fusing in a true collective of shared values, as in musical choruses. To an extent, the music here serves as muted, prophetic mourning, capturing disappointments and auguring the fatal violence with which the film concludes.

Fourth, in addition to the personae within the diegesis, the Wrońskie duo, not unlike the chorus in Greek tragedy, diegetically and extradiegetically sing to comment on plot developments (for an analogous phenomenon, see chapter two) and the psychological states of those enacting the drama of conflicting passions. Their "Daj mi tę noc" ("Give me this night") not only evokes the expectations of the bride and Mietek as groom, but also references the last hours of Silver's terrestrial life, which she hopes to prolong for a last dance with her adored but weak and indifferent false prince.[57]

Fifth, as Smoczyńska's own comments indicate, music additionally serves as a transition between starkly contrasting sequences; and in several cases it foreshadows subsequent events. The mermaid-sisters' brief introductory number is a case in point, for with time the viewer and the human individuals within the narrative discover why they *should* fear the mermaids. Those commentators who criticized the film for its "fragmentation" (Mazierska, for instance, essentially dismissed *The Lure* as "shallow, unbelievable, and incoherent"[58]) failed to understand how music functions as modulation between sequences that, indeed, are thematically connected though varying significantly in mood.[59] In short, the

---

57 For the origins of these 1980s Polish songs, see Mazierska, *Polish Popular Music on Screen*, 135–137, whose comments focus briefly on half a dozen of the film's songs.

58 Ibid., 137.

59 Shot in approximately a month and around ninety minutes in length, the film cannot fully develop each sequence, nor does it need to, for the music enables the narrative to move between sections that contrast in tone but manage to produce what Lovell nicely sums up as "a meditation on innocence, violence, family dynamics, sexual exploitation, and feminine nature" (Lovell, "The Lure: One is Silver and the Other Golden"), all in a feminist vein.

"integrative organization" of the film's music—its singing and dancing at Adria together with the various characters' songs outside the entertainment venue *vis-à-vis* the narrative—partially recalls earlier Hollywood classics that established the standards of the genre even as Smoczyńska fundamentally redefines and capsizes them.[60]

The Lure's conclusion is, arguably, the major aspect in which the film deviates from the conventions of traditional Hollywood musicals and reveals the inapplicability—or obsolescence for today's moviemaking—of sundry American film scholars' repeatedly quoted and somewhat formulaic thesis that the genre's insistence on reconciliation of conflicts, however forced, guarantees its inevitable happy ending. Poles' habit of irony questioned such an unambiguously affirmative ending even in the sixties, exampled by Stanisław Bareja's *Małżeństwo z rozsądku* (A marriage of convenience, 1967), as did some notable Hollywood musicals (see the Introduction in this volume). As Giannetti points out, Fosse's *Cabaret* (1972) and Martin Scorsese's *New York, New York* (1977), two of the genre's most famous instances, do not follow the "boy gets girl" template at film's end.[61] Even the earlier Judy Garland vehicle directed by George Cukor, *A Star is Born* (1954)—unanimously hailed as one of the best Hollywood musicals—ends with the "boy" committing suicide. *The Lure* goes dramatically further by concluding on a tragic note of universal loss and killing both "girl" and "boy," the latter in bloody, savage slaughter that may be read as vigilante justice. Such a "solution" is normally alien to the genre, though death appears at the finish of at least two adaptations that demand its presence owing to their hypotexts: Leonard Bernstein's operatic *West Side Story* (1961), based on Shakespeare's *Romeo and Juliet,* and Norman Jewison/Tim Rice's Bible-indebted rock opera, *Jesus Christ Superstar* (1970).[62] And von Trier's melodramatic *Dancer in the Dark* is unique in executing its murderous female protagonist at its climax. Elimination, not reconciliation, likewise reigns in *The Lure,* these landmark musicals, Paweł Pawlikowski's *Cold War* (chapter three), and Kirill Serebrennikov's biopic *Leto,* though later, thus behind the scenes (chapter eight). Moreover, if, as Bruce Kawin contends, both horror and science fiction "open our sense of the possible," that sense remains in effect, for Golden's continued fantastic existence, in

---

60 See Cook and Bernink, *The Cinema Book,* 210.

61 Giannetti, *Understanding Movies,* 222.

62 In his exhaustive and occasionally exhausting study of film musicals, Altman includes *Jesus Christ Superstar* as an instance of the genre, ignoring the one uncontestable distinction between the musical and opera: the absence of spoken dialogue in the latter. *Jesus Christ Superstar* is indisputably a stunning, original rock opera. See Altman, *The American Film Musical,* 268.

addition to the disintegration of the musicians' family, defies the "restoration of the status quo,"[63] expanding the parameters of possibility.

Conclusion: The Rich Promise of Hybrids

Altman, not unreasonably, defines genres as "*ideological constructs masquerading as neutral categories.*"[64] While that strategic legerdemain may hold true for many instances of Hollywood fare, Smoczyńska blatantly hybridizes the genre of the film musical and makes no effort to camouflage her ideological stance. Genres, as Neale has insisted, "do not consist only of films: they consist also, and equally, of specific systems of expectation and hypothesis that spectators bring with them to the cinema and that interact with films themselves during the course of the viewing process."[65] Accordingly, audiences who attended *The Lure* knowing only that it was a musical doubtless responded diversely—some with shock, others with startled delight, and yet others with bewilderment—but surely even they realized that the film contravenes expectations based on Hollywood classics of the genre, however uncomprehending they may have been of the director's agenda. Although (re)viewers of *The Lure* may have been familiar with the increasing incursion of melodrama into American musicals of the 1950s, the synthesis of horror and musical, with a touch of vampirism, far surpasses the melodramatic aspects of that decade's musicals and is hardly a widespread phenomenon even today. While a few viewers and critics may still cling tenaciously to the old musical paradigm that flourished in a bygone era, Smoczyńska audaciously reformulated the genre, partly by combining her musical with the two unlikely, ostensibly incompatible genres of horror and folktale adaptation and, more importantly, by framing the entire film in a feminist polemic with one of culture's most revered sacred cows. Her fresh approach to somewhat tired material and a largely formulaic genre instances Polish directors' ability to couch new perspectives in entertaining and simultaneously thought-provoking screen narratives, evidenced also in such award-winning films as Małgorzata Szumowska's *Ciało* (Body, 2015) and Pawlikowski's two recent black-and-white screen offerings. Although the likelihood that *The Lure* will unleash a series of comparably *sui generis* Polish musicals is, at best, remote, its audacious originality leads one

63 Bruce F. Kawin, "Children of the Light," in *Film Genre Reader II*, ed. Barry Keith Grant (Austin: University of Texas Press, 1995), 319.

64 Altman, *The American Film Musical*, 5, emphasis in the original—H. G.

65 Steve Neale, "Questions of Genre," *Screen* 31, no. 1 (1990): 46.

to anticipate the director's next screen venture, which relies on David Bowie's music, with considerable impatience.

Bibliography

Abend, Lisa. "Denmark Now Has Two Little Mermaids. The Famous One Is Suing." *New York Times*. August 19, 2021. https://www.nytimes.com/2021/08/17/arts/design/little-mermaid-denmark-dispute.html.

Altman, Rick. *The American Film Musical*. Bloomington: Indiana University Press, 1989.

Ashliman, D. L. "Open Sesame!" 2013. Last modified January 27, 2022. https://www.pitt.edu/~dash/type0676.html.

Carroll, Noel. *The Philosophy of Horror, or The Paradoxes of the Heart*. New York: Routledge, 1990.

Clover, Carol J. "Her Body, Himself: Gender in the Slasher Film." In *Dread of Difference: Gender and the Horror Film*, edited by Barry Keith Grant, 66–113. Austin: University of Texas Press, 1996.

Cohan, Steve, ed. *Hollywood Musicals: The Film Reader*. London and New York: Routledge, 2002.

Cook, Pam, and Mieke Bernink. *The Cinema Book*. London: BFI, 1999.

Creed, Barbara. "Horror and the Monstrous-Feminine: An Imaginary Abjection." In *Dread of Difference: Gender and the Horror Film*, edited by Barry Keith Grant, 35–65. Austin: University of Texas Press, 1996.

Dyer, Richard. "Entertainment and Utopia." *Movie* 24 (Spring 1977): 36–43. Reprinted in *Genre: The Musical*, edited by Rick Altman, 175–189. London: Routledge, 1980.

Eschner, Kat. "Choreographer Bob Fosse Is the Forgotten Author of Modern Musicals." *Smithsonian Magazine*, June 23, 2017. https://www.smithsonianmag.com/smart-news/choreographer-bob-fosse-forgotten-author-modern-musicals-180963746/.

Feuer, Jane. *The Hollywood Musical*. Bloomington: Indiana University Press, 1993.

Fischer, Russ. "'The Lure' Is A Delirious, Kaleidoscopic Cannibal Mermaid Musical." Playlist, February 1, 2017. https://theplaylist.net/lure-delirious-kaleidoscopic-cannibal-mermaid-musical-review-20170201/.

Fraser, Lucy. *The Pleasures of Metamorphosis: Japanese and English Fairy Tale Transformations of "The Little Mermaid."* Detroit: Wayne State University Press, 2017.

Giannetti, Louis. *Understanding Movies*. Upper Saddle River: Prentice Hall, 1999.

Goscilo, Helena. "Watery Maidens: Rusalki as Sirens and Slippery Signs." In *Poetics, Self, Place: Essays in Honor of Anna Lisa Crone*, edited by Catherine O'Neil, Nicole Boudreau, and Sarah Krive, 50–70. Bloomington: Slavica, 2007.

———. "The Danish Little Mermaid vs. the Russian Rusalka: Screen Choices." In *Hans Christian Andersen in Russia*, edited by Mads Sohl Jessen, Marina Balina, Ben Hellman, and Johs. Norregaard Frandsen, 319–349. Odense: University Press of Southern Denmark, 2020.

———. "Art-Horror Lite and Full Throttle: The Arresting Originality of Ewa Juszkiewicz and Aleksandra Waliszewska." In *Contemporary Slavic Horror across Media: Cursed Zones*, edited by Agnieszka Jezyk and Lev Nikulin. Manchester: University of Manchester Press, 2023.

Henderson, Odie. "Polish Mermaid Musical 'The Lure' Gets Joyously Nasty." Village Voice, January 31, 2017. https://www.villagevoice.com/2017/01/31/polish-mermaid-musical-the-lure-gets-joyously-nasty/.

Herbut, Anka. "To nie powinno się zdarzyć." *Dwutygodnik* 135 (June 2014). https://www.dwutygodnik.com/artykul/5272-to-nie-powinno-sie-zdarzyc.html.

Hillier, Jim, and Douglas Pye. *100 Film Musicals: BFI Screen Guides*. London: Palgrave Macmillan/BFI, 2011.

Hutcheon, Linda. *A Theory of Adaptation*. New York and London: Routledge, 2006.

Kawin, Bruce F. "Children of the Light." In *Film Genre Reader II*, edited by Barry Keith Grant, 308–329. Austin: University of Texas Press, 1995.

Kristeva, Julia. *Powers of Horror: An Essay on Abjection*. Translated by Leon S. Roudiez. New York: Columbia University Press, 1982.

Lodge, Guy. "The Seaweed is Always Grislier in Agnieszka Smoczyńska's Unbalanced but Enticing Vampire-Mermaid Musical Fable." Variety, March 7, 2016. https://variety.com/2016/film/festivals/the-lure-review-1201722757/.

Lovell, Angela. "The Lure: One is Silver and the Other Golden." Criterion Collection, October 10, 2017. https://www.criterion.com/current/posts/5030-the-lure-one-is-silver-and-the-other-Golden.

Mazierska, Ewa. *Polish Popular Music on Screen*. London: Palgrave Macmillan, 2020.

Mielke, Magda. "Córki Dancingu—Córki Baśni." Cinerama, January 8, 2017. http://mfcinerama.pl/poliz-kino-corki-basni/.

Neale, Steve. "Genre." In *Film Genre Reader II*, edited by Barry Keith Grant, 159–183. Austin: University of Texas Press, 1995.

———. *Genre and Hollywood*. London and New York: Routledge, 2000.

———. "Questions of Genre." *Screen* 31, no. 1 (1990): 45–66.

Prodeus, Adriana. "Córki Dancingu." *Kino* 12 (2015): 67. http://kino.org.pl//index.php?option=com_content&task=view&id=2376&Itemid=1556.

Rubin, Martin. "Busby Berkeley and the Backstage Musical." In *Hollywood Musicals: The Film Reader*, edited by Steven Cohan, 53–64. London and New York: Routledge, 2002.

Salys, Rimgaila. *The Musical Comedy Films of Grigorii Aleksandrov: Laughing Matters*. Bristol: Intellect, 2009.

Schatz, Thomas. *Hollywood Genres: Formulas, Filmmaking, and the Studio System*. New York: Random House, 1981.

Williams, Linda. "Film Bodies: Gender, Genre, and Excess." In *Film Genre Reader II*, edited by Barry Keith Grant, 140–158. Austin: University of Texas Press, 1995.

Zipes, Jack. *The Enchanted Screen: The Unknown History of Fairy-Tale Films*. New York and London: Routledge, 2011.

Zuckerman, Esther. "Agnieszka Smoczyńska Wants to 'Kill Disney' with Her Mermaid Horror Musical *The Lure*." AV Club, February 8, 2017. https://film.avclub.com/agnieszka-smoczynska-wants-to-kill-disney-with-her-me-1798257482.

Part Two

RUSSIAN FILM MUSICALS

CHAPTER 5

Perplexing Popularity: Ivan Pyr′ev's Kolkhoz Musical Comedy Films

Rimgaila Salys

> "He served not so much power as the film. He created his own world, believed in it, immersed himself in it, and recreated it."
>
> —Aleksandr Mitta[1]

In writing about Ivan Pyr′ev (1901–1968), the low-hanging fruit for scholars has been ideological conformism in the musical comedy films, while journalists and popular authors have feasted on the director's legendary rages and vindictiveness, his love affairs, harassment of actresses, and battles with cinema administrators. Instead, without defending Pyr′ev's politics, I want to make sense of the popularity of his rural comedies with audiences during High Stalinism when the director released four kolkhoz musicals: *Bogataia nevesta* (The rich bride, 1937), *Traktoristy* (Tractor drivers, 1939), *Svinarka i pastukh* (The swineherdess and the shepherd, 1941), and *Kubanskie kazaki* (Cossacks of the Kuban′, 1949). This section is followed by a discussion of *The Rich Bride* and *Cossacks*, the first and last of the kolkhoz musicals, focusing on the constants that assured their popularity during the Stalin era.

Views on the films and their director oscillated wildly over the years, largely for political reasons. In the first year of distribution the kolkhoz comedies garnered from approximately 34.2 to 40.6 million viewers[2] and contemporaries

---

1 Aleksandr Mitta, "Pyr′ev segodnia," *Kinovedcheskie zapiski* 53 (2001): 13.

2 Aleksandr Fedorov, *Tysiacha i odin samyi kassovyi sovetskii fil′m: mneniia kinokritikov i zritelei* (Moscow: Informatsiia dlia vsekh, 2021), 44, http://www.mediagram.ru/library/.

attest to the popularity of the films during the 1930s–1940s. Scriptwriter and author Evgenii Gabrilovich recalled:

> From the mid-thirties on, Pyr'ev and his musical comedies resounded throughout the country. . . . His popularity was extraordinary. With my own eyes I saw how crowds followed him and the constant leading actress of his films on the beach of the Riga seashore, where he was vacationing. The fans moved at a reverent distance and only an occasional moan of faithfulness and rapture could be heard from the crowd.[3]

When *Swineherdess* was shown to Mosfil'm people in Alma-Ata, it elicited "tears of emotion and gratitude."[4] Whether screened for professionals or for soldiers, the film served as a reminder of a peaceful prewar era. *Swineherdess* was released in 4,000 prints and still circulated on screens in the mid-1960s.[5] Even in Alma-Ata evacuation during World War II, Marina Ladynina (1908–2003), the star of the musicals and Pyr'ev's wife, was besieged by fans who gathered every morning to await her appearance on the balcony of her apartment.[6] In 1943, Ladynina wrote Pyr'ev from Alma-Ata that she had taken their son to see *The Rich Bride*, which was showing in a local theatre and commented on the audience reaction: despite the poor-quality print and unintelligible Ukrainian dubbing, "I was surprised that they sit and don't leave . . . and they laughed wildly during Ded's whole chase after Kovyn'ko. They want comedy no matter what."[7] *Cossacks* ranked second nationally in 1950 with 40.6 million viewers in its first year of distribution.[8] Isaak Dunaevskii noted that his song, "Kakim ty byl" ("As

---

3 E. Gabrilovich et al., "Zametki na poliakh," in *Ivan Pyr'ev v zhizni i na ekrane*, ed. G. Mar'iamov (Moscow: Kinotsentr, 1994), 218. For context, the popular trophy films *Devushka moei mechty* (The woman of my dreams, directed by G. Jacoby, 1944), released in Russia in 1947, had 15.7 million in ticket sales, and the four Tarzan films (1932–1939), released in 1952, sold between 38.6 and 42.9 million tickets (S. Kudriavtsev, "Zarubezhnye fil'my v sovetskom prokate," https://kinanet.livejournal.com/13882.html). The intangible for the Pyr'ev films is, of course, the extent of official support in distribution.

4 Maia Turovskaia, "I. A. Pyr'ev i ego muzykal'nye komedii," *Kinovedcheskie zapiski* 1 (1988): 137.

5 Ivan Pyr'ev, *Izbrannye proizvedeniia v dvukh tomakh* (Moscow: Iskusstvo, 1978), 1:114.

6 Liana Polukhina, *Marina Ladynina i Ivan Pyr'ev* (Moscow: Eksmo-Algoritm, 2004), 66.

7 March 28, 1943 letter, Ladynina archive.

8 Sergei Zemlianukhin and Miroslava Segida, *Domashniaia sinemateka. Otechestvennoe kino, 1918–1996* (Moscow: Dubl'-D, 1996), 219.

you once were"), from *Cossacks* had become popular throughout the country in two weeks and so clichéd in six months that he could no longer use it in concerts.[9]

Under late Stalinism an ossified Socialist Realism was defined as a literal depiction of life, and films were viewed through this lens.[10] Although Khrushchev had regularly screened *Cossacks* for audiences during his visits to kolkhozes, after his 1956 speech at the Twentieth Party Congress in which, as part of his truth-telling regarding Stalin, he attacked films that "lacquered the state of affairs in agriculture," *Cossacks* disappeared from view until Brezhnev brought back a destalinized version in 1968.[11] The Thaw brought a focus on the individual and everyday realism—very distant from collectivist utopian musicals with a state message. Sergei Solov'ev remembers that, when he entered VGIK in 1962, his generation viewed Pyr'ev as some sort of dinosaur, a blend of crocodilian monster and amusing lover boy, whose films they could never be persuaded to see.[12] During perestroika, with its drive to unmask the hypocrisy of the Soviet era, the Pyr'ev films were still read as reality and also attacked as blatant falsifications of grim rural life.[13] By the mid-1990s time had done its work: critics began to see Pyr'ev within the context and limitations of the Stalin era, rejecting his communist principles, but also writing about his invention of a native musical comedy genre, his striving to console the people with his films through the years of war and post-war deprivation, his leadership of Mosfil'm through post-Stalin era reconstruction, as well as his multi-year struggle to establish the Union of Cinematographers.

---

9 Isaak Dunaevskii, *Kogda dusha gorit tvorchestvom: Pis'ma k Raise Rys'kinoi* (Astana: Elorda, 2000), 129.

10 Turovskaia, "I. A. Pyr'ev i ego muzyka'nye komedii," 142.

11 To my knowledge, currently available DVDs of the kolkhoz musicals use the destalinized versions of the films, except for *Svinarka i pastukh* (Panorama, 2003), and one scene in the most recent *Cossacks* DVD in which Voron stands in front of a small portrait of Stalin. In *The Rich Bride* and *Tractor Drivers* even the name of the "Stalinets" tractor has been scrubbed from the front of the machines. The original version of *Cossacks* appears to have been destroyed at the time of its redaction.

12 Sergei Solov'ev et al., "Pyr'ev segodnia," *Kinovedcheskie zapiski* 53 (2001): 6.

13 In her article on Pyr'ev's comedies, Maia Turovskaia notes that it was impossible to publish on the films during the 1970s and, again, during perestroika because the study would have entailed a scholarly discussion of the style of the Stalin era, which would have been impossible under Socialist Realism and later in the politicized environment of perestroika (Turovskaia, "I. A. Pyr'ev i ego muzykal'nye komedii," 116).

Beginnings

Pyr'ev came to musical film after several false starts. He learned the film trade as an assistant to Iurii Tarich during the 1920s and began writing scripts toward the end of the decade. In 1929 he directed the comedy *Postoronniaia zhenshchina* (An alien woman) and in 1930 the social satire *Gosudarstvennyi chinovnik* (The civil servant), which fell victim to the heated debates about the relevance of satire in a socialist society. Having learned a hard lesson, Pyr'ev never made another satirical film and returned to comedy only with *The Rich Bride*. In 1931 he contracted to film *Derevnia posledniaia* (The last village), which dealt with the founding of the first kolkhozes and the struggle against kulak opposition. Arriving to film on location in the Saratov region, he and the film crew were shocked to see the reality of collectivization. To avoid making the film without provoking the Soiuzkino administration, Pyr'ev began complaining about financial problems and the poor organization of the filming process. In the end he was fired "for opposing the interests of the film to the interests of the state."[14] With his next two films, the dramas *Konveier smerti* (The conveyor of death, 1933) and *Partiinyi bilet* (The party card, 1936), Pyr'ev finally made the career choice to throw in his lot with the regime. Six years after *The Last Village* he was to take up the kolkhoz theme in a completely different register.

Despite the Kremlin's stamp of approval for *The Party Card*, the quarrelsome director had been fired from Mosfil'm and forbidden to work in the profession for two years. However, Pavel Nechesa, the savvy head of the Kiev *kinofabrika*, hired the unemployed Pyr'ev who was in search of a film genre to call his own, approved him to film Evgenii Pomeshchikov's diploma screenplay about a kolkhoz shock worker, and provided a chauffeured car for a three-week research trip around the country. Along the way, Pyr'ev fell in love with the Ukrainian countryside and its musical culture and decided to turn the screenplay into a musical film.

Igor' Savchenko's lively *Garmon'* (The accordion, 1934) was the first kolkhoz musical comedy film, but the director never continued in the genre. Pyr'ev's eternal rival, Grigorii Aleksandrov, had been exposed to Hollywood films during his American stay in 1932, and had already made the urban musicals *Veselye rebiata* (Jolly fellows, 1934) and *Tsirk* (Circus, 1936). Pyr'ev had never even travelled outside the Soviet Union. In typical fashion, he set about reinventing the genre on his own by trial and error:

---

14 E. V. Ogneva, *Ivan Pyr'ev* (Voronezh: Izdat-Print, 2016), 61–62.

> Everything was difficult. Nothing went right. He fretted. Hypnotized by his persistence, without complaining, for hours, the woman pianist banged away at some Ukrainian song (for a sample) that usually did not fit into the footage. The *mise-en-scènes* developed in the director's script were rejected. He didn't want to consult with anyone: the head of a studio section was escorted out. Comprehending the new [field] was complicated by complete musical ignorance and the strict deadlines set by him for himself.[15]

In time, Pyr'ev arrived at the integrated musical film, using music to develop character and narrative, as well as the overall aural-visual composition, especially rhythmic montage. Without reading music, he was always able to explain to the conductor how he wanted the orchestra to play.[16] Dunaevskii, the premier songsmith of the Stalin era, wrote the music for *The Rich Bride,* but was not permitted to work on the next two Pyr'ev films by the cinema administration.[17] The music for *Tractor Drivers* and *Swineherdess,* composed by the Pokrass Brothers and Tikhon Khrennikov respectively, is less impressive. As the campaign against cosmopolitans gathered steam after 1946, directors such as Aleksandrov dropped Dunaevskii; however, Pyr'ev then commissioned him to compose the music for *Cossacks.* Finally, the musical was a good fit for Pyr'ev because it typically operates with shallow psychological characterization due to genre constraints. The director was never interested in drama that dove deeply into mental processes and his late-career adaptations of *The Idiot* (1958) and *The Brothers Karamazov* (1968) largely elide deeper religious-philosophical concerns.

The Right Time and Place

First, I want to consider the broader societal reasons facilitating the popularity of Pyr'ev's musicals. During the 1930s–1940s Russia was still an agrarian country. In 1939, the rural population comprised approximately 115 million of the

15 E. Pomeshchikov, "Rozhdenie zhanra," in *Ivan Pyr'ev v zhizni i na ekrane,* ed. G. Mar'iamov (Moscow: Kinotsentr, 1994), 86.

16 Marina Ladynina, "V poiskakh putei," in *Ivan Pyr'ev v zhizni i na ekrane,* ed. G. Mar'iamov (Moscow: Kinotsentr, 1994), 114.

17 *Stenogramma. Doklad Dunaevskogo v Muzykal'nom nauchno-issledovatel'skom institute o muzyke v kino,* May 7, 1937, RGALI, f. 2062/1/332. Given Dunaevskii's popularity and significant earnings on film music, this was probably an effort to spread the wealth among other composers.

total population of 167.3 million.[18] In addition, former peasants travelled to the cities for work during industrialization, beginning with the First Five Year Plan in 1928, and later urban workers were only one generation removed from the countryside. In the kolkhoz comedies rural agricultural workers (field workers, tractor drivers, combine operators) were able to see idealized versions of themselves, while urban workers could experience the pleasures of nostalgia (doubtless also idealized) for the wide-open spaces and natural beauty of the steppes, cultivated fields, and what remained of traditional village cultures. *The Rich Bride* and *Tractor Drivers* are set in the Ukrainian steppes and *Cossacks* in the Kuban′, while *Swineherdess* plays out in the Russian North near Vologda and the South, in the mountains of Dagestan, with only an intersection at the Moscow All-Union Agricultural Exhibition.[19] Rather than Aleksandrov's centripetal drive toward Moscow in *Jolly Fellows* and *Volga-Volga* (1938), Pyr′ev preferred to locate his films on the periphery and many of his characters speak Russian inflected with languages of the margins, whether Ukrainian-Russian, Southern Russian dialect, Georgian, Armenian, or Dagestani.

As Richard Dyer argues, "to be effective, the utopian sensibility has to take off from the real experiences of the audience."[20] Even in idealized depiction, Pyr′ev insisted on a simple version of the Stanislavsky method based on experiencing the role. Actors were expected to know and physically perform everything typical of their provincial heroes: plow, scythe, mow, ride a motorcycle or a horse, and drive a tractor. His reasoning was also practical: these skills allowed the director unlimited possibilities in staging complex sequences.[21] Pyr′ev also insisted on an accuracy of representation in agricultural work, which must have pleased and impressed his country audiences. Evgenii Pomeshchikov, the scriptwriter for *The Rich Bride,* grew up in the town of Iuzovka (now Donetsk) and as a city boy once made an ignorant agricultural error, causing Pyr′ev to explode with invectives:

---

18 See the chapters in R. W. Davies et al., eds., *The Economic Transformation of the Soviet Union, 1913–1945* (Cambridge, UK: Cambridge University Press, 1994): J. D. Barber and R. W. Davies, "Employment and Industrial Labour," 115; and S. G. Wheatcroft and R. W. Davies, "Population," 273.

19 Synopses of *Tractor Drivers* and *Swineherdess* can be found on Wikipedia.

20 Richard Dyer, *Only Entertainment* (London: Taylor & Francis Group, 2002), 27.

21 Undated notes, Ladynina archive.

> Fool! Hack! You don't know life. They bind behind the tractor not in a straight line, but in a circle! . . . If the women run after a moving tractor, after the reaper, when will they have time to bind?! . . . They ridiculed the film crew all over the village!

And he took the agronomist-consultant's fee out of the scriptwriter's pay.[22]

Py'ev also benefitted indirectly from the 1936 campaign against Formalism in the arts, specifically the *Pravda* attacks on Shostakovich's modernist opera, *Ledi Makbet Mtsenskogo uezda* (Lady Macbeth of the Mtsensk district) and his ballet, *Svetlyi ruchei* (The limpid stream). In the opera Shostakovich had repudiated the "classical principles" of simplicity, accessibility, realism, and the natural sound of the word in favor of leftist *Meierkhol'dovshchina* ("Meyerkholdism").[23] *The Limpid Stream*, whose plot was akin to the contemporaneous scenario of *The Rich Bride*, celebrated bringing in the harvest and the traditional harvest feast at a kolkhoz in the Kuban'. The *Pravda* editorial criticized the Shostakovich ballet as Formalist, ignorant of kolkhoz life and people, and contemptuous of the folk songs and dances of the Kuban'.[24] In theory, then, the cinema authorities would now be open to Pyr'ev's proposals.

In *Revolution on My Mind*, using the evidence of diaries kept by urban and rural citizens of different classes, Jochen Hellbeck argues that Western historians, because of their point of view on the Communist state, have primarily emphasized anti-Soviet resistance in their writing about Soviet citizens. Instead, diary evidence shows that many individuals "sought to realize themselves as historical subjects defined by their active adherence to a revolutionary common cause." The great number of self-educated diarists from the lower classes suggests that the appeal to get involved in the Soviet project extended far beyond the Party and the intelligentsia. Acting on their own, individuals creatively wove themselves into a loose matrix of subjectivization produced by the system.[25] It was important to participate in an historic era, to transform oneself, and write oneself into it. The implication of Hellbeck's work is that by the 1930s it was difficult for ordinary citizens to imagine alternatives to the Soviet project. Soviet values were broadly popular and the closed nature of society and state-controlled media made alternative points of view largely inaccessible. Hellbeck's

---

22 Pomeshchikov, "Rozhdenie zhanra," 87.

23 "Sumbur vmesto muzyki," *Pravda*, January 28, 1936, 3.

24 "Baletnaia fal'sh'," *Pravda*, February 6, 1936, 3.

25 Jochen Hellbeck, *Revolution on My Mind. Writing a Diary under Stalin* (Cambridge: Harvard University Press, 2006), 5, 64, 52.

work is highly influential, but also controversial: social historians point to workers' strikes in the early thirties in rural factories;[26] it is difficult to generalize on the basis of a limited number of diaries, and one can question the existence of truly private diaries in the Stalin era. Nevertheless, without overstating the case, it is conceivable that the pressure on identity formation by the Soviet state also made some part of the population more receptive to the kolkhoz musicals. As far as Pyr'ev and his actors were concerned, Ladynina remembers their sincere enthusiasm for the Stakhanovites of agriculture during work on *Tractor Drivers,* when the film studio walls were hung with the portraits of Pasha Angelina, Pasha Kovardak, and others. Her judgment on Pyr'ev: "He believed in what he glorified."[27]

With the success of the First Five-Year Plan, a closely managed press told the population that a new socialist order of economic power and plenty had arrived. Reportage now stressed a joyous celebration of Soviet accomplishments that reached its performative apex during the 1930s. In 1933, the Central Committee called a meeting of directors and scriptwriters under the slogan "Smekh—rodnoi brat sily" ("Laughter is the blood brother of strength"), intended to push the film industry toward producing sound comedies.[28] The press implanted happiness with a musical accompaniment in the consciousness of readers: under the heading "Nynche zhit' veselo!" ("Life is fun now!") *Komsomol'skaia pravda* printed a large photo of a smiling Komsomol boy playing his accordion.[29] Stalin's "Zhit' stalo veselee" ("Life has become more fun") declaration at the 1935 Stakhanovites' congress spurred the cinema authorities to develop musical comedy film as an appropriate correlate to the newly created image of Soviet success.

A Familiar Utopia

> ". . . in him also lived Vania, a village boy, the son of a rural accordion player, akin to Esenin."
>
> —Iosif Manevich[30]

---

26 Jeffrey J. Rossman, *Worker Resistance under Stalin: Class and Revolution on the Shop Floor* (Cambridge: Harvard University Press, 2005).

27 Undated notes, Ladynina archive.

28 G. V. Aleksandrov, *Epokha i kino* (Moscow: Izdatel'stvo politicheskoi literatury, 1976), 163.

29 "Nynche zhit' veselo," *Komsomol'skaia pravda,* November 15, 1933, 3.

30 Iosif Manevich, *Za ekranom* (Moscow: Novoe izdatel'stvo, 2006), 286.

Pyr'ev made films for the people, not for film critics, so that his cinema is neither esoteric nor refined and should be judged as an artefact of popular culture. The specific reasons for the popularity of the kolkhoz musicals are many and varied: topicality, a utopian discourse of happiness, familiar narratives and characters sedimented in the collective unconscious, well-known folkloric material, the attractive screen persona of Marina Ladynina, simple humor, dynamic cinematography, and accessible songs.

Pyr'ev possessed the gift of contemporaneity, always bringing the issues and emotions of the day to mass audiences. *The Rich Bride* depicts *udarniki* (shock workers) of agriculture who save the harvest during the difficult early years of kolkhozes in Ukraine. *Tractor Drivers* addresses the need for more technically qualified Stakhanovites of agriculture like Pasha Kovardak, who consulted on the film and was the model for the heroine.[31] *Tractor Drivers* also has a strongly military tone, touching upon the successful operation against the Japanese at Khasan Lake in August 1938 and calling for preparedness in the coming war against Germany. *Swineherdess,* released in 1941, advertised the All-Union Agricultural Exhibition, propounded the unity of Soviet peoples, and elicited nostalgia for the Northern Russian and Caucasus home regions that viewers hoped to see again after the war.[32] Finally, *Cossacks* takes up the question of personal life in a collective society and post-war recovery.

Pyr'ev was a man of action, but also a dreamer who believed that, no matter the obstacles, justice and good would triumph in life.[33] The path to victory lay through the Communist system; however, he was not a blind follower. The director rejected justifications for the arrests of cinema workers during the purges[34] and his inner conflict regarding the continuing failures of Soviet agriculture is evident in a letter written during the filming of the melodrama *Nash obshchii drug* (Our mutual friend, 1961):

---

31 Pyr'ev, *Izbrannye proizvedeniia v dvukh tomakh,* 1:85.

32 Johann Strauss II's *Der Zigeunerbaron* (The gypsy baron, 1885) with its positive figuration of Hungarians and Roma demonstrated how the operetta had similarly served the process of integrating empire (Richard Traubner, *Operetta: A Theatrical History* [New York: Routledge, 2003], 111).

33 Ladynina, "V poiskakh putei," 106.

34 Valerii Fomin, "Zhizn' ne slozhilas', no udalas' . . .," *Rodina* 2 (February 2007): 94. Arkadii Dobrovol'skii, the co-author of "Poliushko-pole," the original scenario for *Tractor Drivers,* was arrested in 1937 and spent twenty-one years in the camps. Ladynina sent him food parcels during this time. Upon his release, on his way home to Ukraine through Moscow, he came to her apartment and went down on his knees in the doorway, to her surprise and embarrassment (Marina Ladynina, interview by R. Salys, 1998).

> You can't show the whole truth of how collective farmers live and work . . . So it's necessary to find some middle ground between "glorification, poeticization" and the truth. But where is this middle? How do you stay on it? And how do you make the film interesting for the viewer and acceptable on Staraia ploshchad'?[35]

As a utopian discourse of happiness, the musical was a natural choice of genre for Pyr'ev. Dyer defines the Western musical similarly as offering "the image of 'something better' to escape into, or something we want deeply that our day-to-day lives don't provide. Alternatives, hopes, wishes—these are the stuff of utopia, the sense that things could be better, that something other than what is can be imagined and maybe realized."[36] Gleb Panfilov expresses the same thought about Pyr'ev's musicals: "He recreated life as the people wanted it to be, and this was his discovery."[37]

Pyr'ev was born into an impoverished Siberian peasant family in the Altai region and knew rural life only too well. After a violent confrontation with an alcoholic stepfather, armed with only a grade school education, he left the family, travelling all over Siberia to local fairs with his Tatar employers, then worked in Tomsk at various odd jobs before joining the army in 1915 as an underage volunteer.[38] Although well acquainted with the life of the people, their hardships, joys and sorrows, he openly acknowledged that he strove to poeticize them in his films, to show their lives as they should be, without denying other directors' right to "show life as it is."[39] In the same way Pyr'ev romanticized landscape, mainly in the opening scenes of the musicals, since spatial expansion (the wide, open steppe, seemingly boundless cultivated fields, large birch forests), accompanied by the temporal expansion of song, denotes a form of happiness.

In addressing the Western musical, Dyer outlines five categories of utopian sensibility that are equally applicable to the Pyr'ev films: abundance, energy (work as play), intensity (the excitement and drama of living), transparency

---

35 G. Mar'iamov, "Boitsovskii kharakter," in *Ivan Pyr'ev v zhizni i na ekrane*, ed. G. Mar'iamov (Moscow: Kinotsentr, 1994), 188–189. The Central Committee offices of the Party were located on Staraia ploshchad' Street.

36 Dyer, *Only Entertainment*, 20.

37 G. Panfilov, "Pyr'ev segodnia," *Kinovedcheskie zapiski* 53 (2001): 14.

38 Ogneva, *Ivan Pyr'ev*, 18.

39 Pyr'ev, *Izbrannye proizvedeniia v dvukh tomakh*, 1:114.

(open, honest relationships), and community (shared interests, collective activity).[40] He views these categories as utopian solutions to social inadequacies and tensions, which, as we will see, can also be applied *mutatis mutandis* to the world of kolkhoz musicals, even if the problems remain unspoken: material scarcity, alienated labor, the monotony and predictability of agricultural work, manipulation through power relations or deceit, and selfish individualism. Furthermore, in the Western musical solutions to problems are provided internally, engineered by the capitalist system.[41] The same dynamic operates in the kolkhoz films: any shortcomings are resolved by the socialist system and within the world of the film.

Pyr'ev apparently did not see any Hollywood musicals until c. 1940 when Julien Duvivier's *The Great Waltz* (1938) was released in the Soviet Union as a trophy film, but he was mad about operetta for most of his adult life and would run to see each new production in Moscow.[42] The director Vladimir Naumov, who was a childhood friend of Pyr'ev's son, Erik, remembers how Pyr'ev would almost force the two boys to attend performances: "Ivan Aleksandrovich had several passions. One such passion was the operetta. He simply adored it and would drag Erik and me to the same performances several times."[43] Both Dunaevskii and Khrennikov (the composer for *Swineherdess*) wrote operettas and Pyr'ev used Moscow operetta stars such as Vladimir Volodin and Elena Savitskaia in *Cossacks*.

The operetta is a form of musical that integrates songs and musical sequences with dialogue to dramatize a story, sometimes retaining the vocal forms of grand opera, but always relying on more accessible melodies. Songs develop character or advance the plot, which can be comic, romantic or a combination of both.[44] Vaudeville, the older genre from which operetta partly evolved, possessed

---

40 Dyer, *Only Entertainment*, 26.

41 Ibid., 27.

42 Marina Ladynina, interview by R. Salys, 1998.

43 V. Naumov, "'Obryvki' i 'konchiki' vospominanii," in *Ivan Pyr'ev v zhizni i na ekrane*, ed. G. Mar'iamov (Moscow: Kinotsentr, 1994), 160.

44 John Kenrick, *Musical Theatre: A History* (London: Bloomsbury, 2017), 21. Operettas often featured dancing, which is largely absent from the kolkhoz musicals, presumably due to lack of resources, except for simple folk dances in *The Rich Bride* and the extended waltz scenes popularized by the Viennese operetta and *The Great Waltz* and used in *The Rich Bride* and *Cossacks*. Not all the singers of the Moscow Operetta had operatic range. Vladimir Volodin (Mudretsov in *Cossacks*) with his distinctively scratchy voice and gift for comedy was an audience favorite.

similar structural components but relied more on dialogue and non-operatic singing. (Unlike the American use of the term, Russian *vodevil'* denotes a comedic play with songs and dances, not a burlesque or variety show.) In the second half of the nineteenth century in Russia the vaudeville, as a permeable popular culture genre, underwent transformation with hybrid self-definitions becoming common: "vaudeville-operetta," "drama-vaudeville," "vaudeville with choruses and dances," "farce-vaudeville," and so on. During the same period vaudeville and operetta moved much closer, using similar plots and character types, with both shifting to an emphasis on entertainment.[45]

During the Soviet era operettas, with their entertaining plots, music and dance, continued to be performed widely. Permanent operetta theatres were maintained in Moscow, Leningrad, and in smaller cities, such as Rostov, Irkutsk, Novosibirsk, Saratov, and Krasnoiarsk. Accusations of Western influence were either countered with the dubious claim that the operetta was a satirical genre, which parodied the nineteenth-century bourgeoisie,[46] or mitigated by putting on productions with the original foreign music and strategically rewritten librettos. Ladynina made her singing debut c. 1926 in what was probably an amateur operetta staged in the Siberian town of Achinsk.[47] In the Soviet era, then, operetta narratives and tropes were familiar to inhabitants of towns outside the two capitals.

The genre was most influential in Pyr'ev's preference for accessible, lively music and familiar narratives. While eschewing the operetta's vocal fireworks, Pyr'ev adopted its mixed musical-dialogue structure, as well as its most common invariant plot, descended from Commedia dell'arte, for all the kolkhoz musicals: two lovers (*inamorati*) face obstacles of various kinds that are overcome, usually with the help of secondary characters, and lead to marriage.[48]

---

45 M. Iu. Planida,"Vodevil' v otechestvennoi muzykal'noi kul'ture (konets XVIII–nachalo XXI veka): transformatsiia zhanra" (PhD diss., Rostovskaia gosudarstvennaia konservatoriia im. S. Rakhmaninova, Rostov, 2019), 9, 41.

46 Louise McReynolds, *Russia at Play: Leisure Activities at the End of the Tsarist Era* (Ithaca: Cornell University Press, 2003), 296.

47 Marina Ladynina, *Moi tvorcheskii put'* (Moscow: Goskinoizdat, 1949), 9.

48 For a survey of Commedia dell'arte in Russian culture, see Ol'ga Simonova-Partan, *Vagabonding Masks: The Italian Commedia dell'arte in the Russian Artistic Imagination* (Boston: Academic Studies Press, 2017). Evgenii Dobrenko and Natalia Jonsson-Skradol's *State Laughter: Stalinism, Populism, and Origins of Soviet Culture* (Oxford: Oxford University Press, 2022) includes an extensive study of Commedia dell'arte in kolkhoz theatrical comedies, which sometimes supplied plots for cinema.

Beginning in the mid-eighteenth century, Italian troupes participated in *narodnye gulianiia* (folk festivals) in large Russian cities. From there the Commedia dell'arte migrated to provincial *balagany* (popular plays staged in wooden structures at fairs), so that by the Soviet era the *inamorati* plot and attendant characters had long been familiar to country audiences.[49] The kolkhoz musicals also incorporate vaudeville-operetta stock characters (two lovers, schemer, rival, father figure) and selected tropes: a focus on contemporary life, a short time frame, fast-paced action, exaggerated situations (hiding in a cupboard or under a table, lengthy chases), slapstick humor, unexpected events (disasters, confusion, misunderstandings), retardation of action via the preceding, an excess of emotion, humorous, rapid-fire dialogue, unexpected social interactions in public locations, and the inevitable happy ending.[50]

In each kolkhoz film Pyr'ev adopted to differing degrees a descendant of the *inamorati*, the nineteenth-century bourgeois operetta-vaudeville plot of the eligible and rich young woman pursued by a fortune-hunting suitor, while the true lover is hindered by an obstacle to their marriage, such as deceit, misunderstanding, or sometimes an elder. The "rich bride" theme is transferred to the Soviet context in which *trudodni* (work days) or Stakhanovite status comprise the heroine's wealth. While not ignoring the labor status of the sincere suitor, the rich bride always chooses love above all as the basis of true happiness, just as in the operetta. In *Tractor Drivers* Mar'iana Bazhan prefers Klim, the true lover, over many money-grubbing suitors (fig. 5.1), including Nazar, the false suitor of her own devising. In *Swineherdess* Glasha is pursued and tricked by the fortune-hunting village dandy Kuz'ma, while Musaib, the true lover, temporarily loses touch with her. Pyr'ev explained that *Swineherdess* would especially resemble an operetta in that the lyrical sections were written in verse, and prose dialogues would move into song and back.[51] Strange to say, it turns out that a foreign, urban, commercial genre with bourgeois roots underlies Pyr'ev's native, rural, socialist musicals.

---

49 A. F. Nekrylova, *Russkie narodnye gorodskie prazdniki, uveseleniia i zrelishcha. Konets XVIII–nachalo XX veka* (Leningrad: Iskusstvo, 1988), 162.

50 Planida, "Vodevil' v otechestvennoi muzykal'noi kul'ture," 63; Jennifer Terni, "A Genre for Early Mass Culture: French Vaudeville and the City, 1830–1848," *Theatre Journal* 58, no. 2 (May 2006): 234, 237.

51 Ogneva, *Ivan Pyr'ev*, 121.

Figure 5.1. Mar'ianka and a mercenary suitor, *Tractor Drivers.*

The 1935–1936 cultural revolution that replaced Leninist-Trotskyite internationalism with Stalinist national Bolshevism emphasized *narodnost'*—the creative powers of the folk, the artistic merits of the national epics, as well as Russia's glorious historical past, and the years 1937–1941 saw a renaissance in folkloristics.[52] Pyr'ev may well have seen *Sorochinskaia iarmarka* (The fair at Sorochintsi, directed by A. Riabov, 1936) and *Svad'ba v Malinovke* (The wedding in Malinovka, directed by B. Aleksandrov, 1936), the two folk operettas staged in 1937 by the Moscow Operetta Theatre under the new initiative.[53]

The kolkhoz comedy films attracted viewers by presenting folklife and lore, customs and rituals—all eliciting the pleasure of recognition. Provincial fairs and *balagany* were living memories from Pyr'ev's childhood. He chose to show the most familiar folklife artifacts that audiences would immediately recognize, those no less stereotypical—or no more kitschy by today's standards—than the

---

52 L. Maksimenkov, *Sumbur vmesto muzyki. Stalinskaia kul'turnaia revoliutsiia, 1936–1938* (Moscow: Iuridicheskaia kniga, 1997), 213; Frank Miller, *Folklore for Stalin. Russian Folklore and Pseudofolklore of the Stalin Era* (Armonk: M. E. Sharpe, 1990), 10.

53 The regime was also adept at playing the compensatory folklore card during times of crisis, such as the purges and postwar food shortages.

material culture and settings of American folk musicals of the era, such as *The Little Colonel* (1935) or *State Fair* (1945). The kolkhoz musicals display Ukrainian whitewashed huts with thatched roofs and northern Russian wooden houses, as well as traditional dress, whether embroidered blouses or the Dagestani shepherd's shaggy hat. Speech is sprinkled with Ukrainian in *The Rich Bride*: *divchina* ("young woman"), *bisova dusha* ("devilish soul"), as well as *surzhik*, a mix of Ukrainian and Russian in *Cossacks*: *bohatyi urozhai* ("abundant harvest"), *sho* (a variant of *chto*—what), *Divis', kumon'ka, iaka smelost'!* ("Look, dearie, what daring!"), and has accented Russian in the case of non-Slavs (*Tractor Drivers* and *Swineherdess*). There are familiar village types such as an elderly nightwatchman, a wise grandmother, hefty female cooks, and gossipy keepers of domestic fowl. There are familiar rituals—the weeping bride comforted by village girlfriends (fig. 5.2) or Voron's Cossack threat to kidnap a wife, and recognizable pastimes: folksongs and *chastushki*, folk dances, folkloric verbal battles of the sexes, a sleighride in the forest with tinkling harness bells, fortune telling with cards, snacking on sunflower seeds.[54] The characters of

Figure 5.2. Grieving before marriage, *The Swineherdess and the Shepherd.*

54 The *chastushka* is a humorous or satiric folk poem consisting of rhymed four-line stanzas with high beat frequency and often accompanied by a balalaika or accordion.

Swineherdess often speak in simple rhymes, thereby enhancing the folkloric flavor of the film. Pyr'ev included *chastushki* in every kolkhoz musical, not only as iconic examples of folk culture but also as a cinematic device: their comic content typically underscored or furthered aspects of the narrative.[55]

With her ethereal blonde looks and infectious laugh, Marina Ladynina fit perfectly into this country world. The actress grew up in the Siberian village of Nazarovo in a poor peasant family. She graduated from GITIS (State Institute of Theatre Arts) and was working at the Moscow Art Theatre when Pyr'ev changed her life forever by casting her as the lead in *The Rich Bride.* At GITIS, when students were required to depict figures from famous paintings, she was assigned Vasnetsov's *Alenushka* (1881), the lyrical image of a young peasant woman that Ladynina tried to convey in the kolkhoz comedies, especially *The Rich Bride* and *Swineherdess.*[56] As the star of the musicals, she portrayed the modern agricultural worker who was technologically up to date, but at the same time appealed to audiences by her natural appearance, gentle singing and speaking voice, and refined manners, all in peasant clothing. In contrast, even though Liubov' Orlova played peasant workers in *Volga-Volga* and *Svetlyi put'* (The radiant path), her heavy makeup, over-bleached hair, and hard-edged voice marked her as a Westernized film star, making Ladynina seem all the more Russian.

There is no question that laughter is a powerful tool for encouraging identification with those around us, yet another contributing factor to the popularity of the kolkhoz comedies. Three of the Pyr'ev films carry the subtitle "musical comedy" and one simply "comedy"—the mutilated *Tractor Drivers.*[57]

---

55 A few recognizable fairy tale motifs are scattered throughout the Pyr'ev films: for example, In *Tractor Drivers* Klim arrives in a randomly chosen part of the Ukrainian countryside, comes to a crossroads where he must choose a direction, and later answers in Ukrainian *shchastia shukaiu* ("I'm searching for my happiness/fate") when asked why he has come to the kolkhoz. He is given a task to fulfill by an elder (reforming the lazy Nazar), completing the task successfully wins him the hand of the Stakhanovite princess, Mar'iana Bazhan, and the film ends with a bountiful marriage feast. Like fairy tales, the kolkhoz musicals leave history for an idealized world of abundance, love, social equality, and pacified nature.

56 Marina Ladynina, interview by R. Salys, 1998.

57 Semen Dukel'skii, the head of the film industry in 1938–1939, insisted on 600 meters of cuts to *Tractor Drivers,* apparently because of its over-the-top comedy scenes. Pyr'ev refused and kept refusing until, in the director's brief absence from Moscow, Dukel'skii had the cuts made and copies of the film printed. Pyr'ev was despondent because his favorite comic episodes with Petr Aleinikov and Boris Andreev had been removed. When the film was first shown at Dom kino, the director did not attend. Pyr'ev was not mentioned in the first review of *Tractor Drivers,* in accordance with his wishes. It was only after the enthusiastic public reception of the film that the director acknowledged it as his own. E. Gal'perin, "Dalekoe i blizkoe," in

The Rich Bride, the earliest of the musicals, employs considerable physical humor: Marinka rains blows on the devious Kovyn'ko, while chases provide vaudevillesque slapstick comedy. The films all rely on verbal humor: witty exchanges (in *Cossacks* Andrei and Mudretsov joust in rhymed comic couplets), satiric *chastushki,* habitually repeated phrases, a peasant's drawling speech (Fedia in *Cossacks).* There are parodic urban *zhestokie romansy* ("cruel romances") in *The Rich Bride* and *Swineherdess,* but no irony to be seen anywhere in the films. In *Tractor Drivers,* Petr Aleinikov displays the transgressive hooligan humor that made him so popular with Soviet audiences (fig. 5.3), followed by Nikolai Kriuchkov (Kuz'ma) as a self-important, lazy village dandy in *Swineherdess* and smart-mouth Yurii Liubimov (Andrei) in *Cossacks.*

Figure 5.3. Savka challenges Klim, *Tractor Drivers.*

Pyr'ev's cinematography is simple and straightforward in the sense that he preferred continuity editing with occasional cross-cutting for contrast, and there are few special effects (*Tractor Drivers* and *Swineherdess* use rear projection) and

---

Ivan Pyr'ev v zhizni i na ekrane, ed. G. Mar'iamov (Moscow: Kinotsentr, 1994), 97–98; Pyr'ev, *Izbrannye proizvedeniia v dvukh tomakh,* 1:107–109.

no video dissolves. Consistent with the musical's lack of psychological depth and Pyr'ev's own preferences, the films have very few close-ups, instead working with medium and long shots in which he conveys a general picture, whether of a group or an expansive landscape. In *The Rich Bride, Tractor Drivers,* and *Cossacks* Pyr'ev pays special attention to location shots of the steppe and cultivated fields in order to bring open space into the film. He likes to film human beings in the steppe because they are visible from great distances, but still part of a larger landscape (fig. 5.4).[58] While Aleksandrov structured his musicals around Orlova, who was often filmed in close-up, Pyr'ev saw Ladynina, the female lead, as part of the larger canvas of the frame. There are no close-ups in *Cossacks,* for example, only medium shots, emphasizing both the actors and the surroundings, giving them equal presence on the screen, yet close enough to show body language and reactions in conversation. As Peresvetova sings "As You Once Were," which concerns her past with Voron, we are shown a real river along whose banks she travels, which is also the symbolic river of time.

Figure 5.4. Landscape with workers, *Cossacks of the Kuban'.*

58 Pyr'ev, *Izbrannye proizvedeniia v dvukh tomakh,* 1:100–101.

The driving energy of Pyr′ev's cinematography doubtless contributed to the popularity of the kolkhoz films with audiences. Memoirists have noted the director's passionate temperament and inexhaustible energy, which probably elicited both his love for the fast-paced peripeties of musical comedy and his cinematic dynamism. In *Cossacks,* for example, dynamism is created through a repeating visual alternation as we are shown the plethora of goods at the fair: the camera first pans right across ceramics with standing customers; this alternates with a stationary camera and moving crowds of customers; then the camera pans left across different consumer wares, heightening the sense of movement. Perhaps most striking are Pyr′ev's shots of harvesting, as in the prologue to *Cossacks,* his love of rapid montage in which editing is coordinated with visuals and music.

In writing on *The Conveyor of Death* in 1933, Bela Balash put his finger on the pluses and minuses of Pyr′ev's method: ". . . Pyr′ev's best qualities lead him down the path of the greatest mistakes. It is his extraordinary cinematic fantasy and his fiery cinematic rhythm, his barbarian talent. Where the rhythm is not burdened with knowledge and culture, there he has the greatest surge."[59] Pyr′ev had also worked in Meyerhold's theatre for a time, which may have cemented his taste for excess. His emotional, romantic mindset and wildly dynamic style both gave life to the musicals but also led to blatant exaggerations. In *Tractor Drivers,* Klim's hopak is speeded up comically as he outdances the lazy tractor drivers, but the rapid-fire documentary footage of Soviet tanks included in the film now appears ridiculous.

In writing about song, Dyer notes that it is often apprehended as something almost magical, with a direct line to feeling: "Song, like all art, is at the intersection between individual feeling and the socially and historically specific shared forms available to express that feeling."[60] Music and song were similarly crucial to the kolkhoz comedies because they played on the emotions of audiences and therefore "helped to weaken any intellectual resistance they may have had to the message of the film."[61] As popular culture artifacts, the comedies were designed for viewers with limited musical training. In his film work Dunaevskii always aimed to write songs that corresponded to the folk melos:

---

59 Bela Balash, "Varvarskii talent," *Kino* 55 (1933): 2.

60 Richard Dyer, *In the Space of a Song* (London and New York: Routledge, 2012), 2.

61 Richard Taylor, "The Stalinist Musical: Socialist Realism and Revolutionary Romanticism," in *A Companion to Russian Cinema*, ed. Birgit Beumers (Chichester: John Wiley & Sons, Inc., 2016), 147.

> Our masses do not perceive any melodies that do not correspond to the national sound perception to which their ears are accustomed. . . . Why does the broad population *here* not sing the wonderful American and English blues songs and foxtrots? Because they're not ours! Their entire architectonics, rhythmics, intervals are foreign to our ears![62]

Dunaevskii was so successful with "Oi, tsvetet kalina" ("Oh, the guelder rose is blooming") from *Cossacks* that it soon acquired the *renommée* of a folk song. Although the Pokrass Brothers' "Tri tankista" ("Three tankers") from *Tractor Drivers* was adopted by the military, neither the other songs in the film nor those of Khrennikov for *Swineherdess* remained in popular memory because they lacked the qualities outlined by Dunaevskii.

The kolkhoz musicals employ three categories of songs: true Ukrainian folk songs (more in *The Rich Bride* and *Tractor Drivers*); lyrical love songs composed to resemble folk melodies, as well as satirical *chastushki*; and mass songs in march rhythm, expressing a love of homeland and agricultural labor or a defensive stance against coming war. As Pyr'ev gained experience integrating music with narrative, the number of composed songs in each musical gradually increased and the later musicals, *Swineherdess* and *Cossacks*, open with instrumental overtures rather than songs.[63] The treatment of songs within films is traditional—mainly diegetic with either diegetic or extra-diegetic instrumental accompaniment.

Mass songs were particularly well-suited to the kolkhoz musicals because, with their energetic rhythms and hortatory language, they embodied the Soviet era's view of agricultural work as pleasure. According to Marx, socialist labor was no longer alienated, instead becoming free and creative, and "creative labor" developed into one of the main ideological topoi of the Soviet era. While labor during the twenties was cast as a difficult and heroic feat, by the mid-thirties it was regularly conceptualized in artistic works as pleasure (fig. 5.5). The emotional charge of melody, song, and comedic laughter was presented not only as relaxation after the workday, but also as the affective motivator to labor.[64] Exploiting their broad popularity, song and comedic laughter were framed as both the expression of individual emotion and a source of social energy.

---

62 March 20, 1935 letter, Dunaevskii family archive.

63 *Tractor Drivers* has fewer songs because it was so severely cut before release.

64 Ili'a Kalinin, "'Nam smekh i stroit' i zhit' pomogaet': politekonomiia smekha i sovetskaia muzykal'naia komediia (1930-e gody)," *Russian Literature* 80 (2013): 125–130.

Figure 5.5. The joy of work: Glasha, *The Swineherdess and the Shepherd.*

The paradigm of work coded as pleasure, as transmitted in the kolkhoz musical, overlaps with the discourse of the American folk musical. The activities of people going about their everyday business are transformed with the help of rhythm and song into joyful entertainment: in *Summer Stock* (1950) Judy Garland's driving a new tractor from town to her farm turns into a happy song. Rick Altman's definition of the American folk musical is largely applicable to the kolkhoz comedies. In both, the union of the couple parallels the making of a stable community, but the folk musical is never solely about the couple in love because they are always representative of the entire community. In the kolkhoz musicals, too, the couples are model representatives of the collective: Marinka and Zgara in *The Rich Bride,* Mar'iana and Klim in *Tractor Drivers,* Glasha and Musaib in *Swineherdess,* and Dasha and Nikolai in *Cossacks.* The making of the couple further parallels the civilizing of the land, whether this means successfully bringing in the harvest or bringing order to chaos.[65] The chaos may be a natural calamity (the storm threatening the harvest in *The Rich Bride*) or even a human disaster—for example, the disruptively lazy brigade members in *Tractor*

65 Altman, *The American Film Musical,* 310.

Drivers whom the culture hero Klim Iarko brings to order. However, while the American folk musical turns on nostalgia for a mythic communal past, the kolkhoz musicals seek to create a mythic communal future.

Like the utopian Vincente Minnelli musicals such as *Meet Me in St. Louis*, the kolkhoz genre is energized by affirming the group, but also by acknowledging the real need for self-expression, by maintaining the tension between self and society. The individual ultimately finds a place in society through both acculturation and individuation.[66] During High Stalinism cinematic heroes performed feats of labor and struggled with enemies (*Chapaev*, 1934, *Shchors*, 1939), but such endeavors often supplanted or attenuated an onscreen personal life. Pyr'ev's musicals were widely popular because they openly returned personal life to the medium and, in fact, we will see that the kolkhoz films become increasingly concerned with the needs of the individual.

Two Rich Brides and a Screwball

The Rich Bride

Shock worker Marinka Lukash and the best local tractor driver, Pavlo Zgara, are working in a Ukrainian kolkhoz during harvest time. They love each other but Alesha Kovyn'ko, the kolkhoz bookkeeper, has designs on Marinka and drives a wedge between the lovers by falsifying Marinka's work day count to make her appear lazy to Pavlo. Marinka is insulted by Pavlo's suspicions and breaks with him. Her women's brigade supports her and initiates a mowing competition with Pavlo, which he loses. Later, when a rainstorm threatens, Kovyn'ko brings Pavlo and his tractor to help the women save the harvest. Kovyn'ko confesses his machinations to Marinka and the lovers are reunited at the kolkhoz harvest festival.

Pyr'ev borrowed the title of Aleksandr Ostrovskii's well known comedy, *Bogatye nevesty* (The rich brides, 1876), for his film because both take up the social issue of calculated marriage for gain in their respective eras. The fortune-hunting bookkeeper Kovyn'ko has set his sights on Marinka, the rich Soviet bride with 400 workdays, 200 poods of bread,[67] 3,000 rubles, chickens, a cow, as well as good looks, all of which he has meticulously calculated (fig. 5.6). When she is rewarded with a trip to Moscow or a seaside resort, he dreams of accompanying her as the "beloved husband," a parasitical male. Satirical targets in Soviet

---

66 J. P. Telotte, "Self and Society: Vincente Minnelli and Musical Formula," *Journal of Popular Film & Television* 9, no. 4 (1982): 181–182.

67 A pood is an obsolete unit of weight equivalent to 36.11 pounds.

comedies of the 1930s were a delicate matter because ministries would object when their sailors, policemen, army officers, fishermen and the like were seen as ridiculous, but bean-counting accountants had always been fair game. Later in the film parallel editing underscores the contrast between characters: the main love scene between Marinka and Zgara (disinterested affection) is cross-cut with Kovyn'ko's sighing over Marinka's assets (mercenary courtship).

Figure 5.6. Kovyn'ko and Marinka, *The Rich Bride.*

Kovyn'ko is the central comic character of the film, as conveyed through verbal and slapstick humor. He constantly natters about his plans, driving the barber to drown him out by trumpet playing. He sings *chastushki* satirizing Zgara and a "cruel romance" to Marinka that only makes her laugh but runs away from any perceived threat. Although Kovyn'ko separates Marinka and Zgara by manipulating numbers (his forte), he is not a true villain, in agreement with the laws of the genre, but instead warns the kolkhoz workers of the approaching storm, gets Zgara's help in finishing the mowing, and confesses his "intrigue" to Marinka.

Following the operetta-vaudeville paradigm, Marinka chooses true love over a host of obstacles. She is supported by the barber who declares: "Liubov' est'—vysshaia mechta" ("Love is—the loftiest dream"), and he is the secondary character who facilitates the lovers' union. Two elders put up economic obstacles. Ded, Marinka's grandfather, comes upon the couple kissing and questions Zgara about his profession. Palaga, the women's brigade leader, asks questions that reveal Marinka's personal rather than ideological choice of mate:

> "Is he a Stakhanovite? A shock worker?"
> "I don't know."
> "Maybe he's a slacker?"
> "Who knows . . . It doesn't concern the brigade."

In fact, it is the brigade's pressure on her to check Zgara's labor status that gives Kovyn'ko an opportunity to continue his tricks. The same scene with Palaga also underscores personal life in a way that is missing from the other musicals and most Stalin-era films: while the women's brigade is having lunch in the fields, the mothers among them nurse their babies (we hear *poel* ["he's eaten"]), and then hand them back to a nanny in a field nursery on wheels (fig. 5.7). In the kolkhoz films the main characters have no biological parents, only non-authoritative grandparents in *The Rich Bride* and *Swineherdess* and a controlling former guardian in *Cossacks*. In Western musicals the parentless young are typically left free to act; here the heroines also follow their hearts. Only in *The Rich Bride*, the first

Figure 5.7. The field nursery, *The Rich Bride.*

kolkhoz musical, does the heroine silently look to Palaga, the state surrogate, for approval at the end of the film.

The lyrics for the three songs in *The Rich Bride* were written by Vasilii Lebedev-Kumach, who had rocketed to fame the previous year with "Pesnia o rodine" ("Song of the motherland") for Aleksandrov's *Circus*. The lyrics in the two mass songs, "Idem, idem, veselye podrugi" ("Let's go, let's go, merry girlfriends") and "Oi vy koni" ("Oh, you horses") include three of Lebedev-Kumach's invariant motifs, also typical of the era: defense of the homeland ("No one will ever walk in our republics"), the open path to advancement for all, and abundance ("All roads in the world are open to us . . . Flowers grow and children rejoice, and grains are sprouting in the rich fields!"). "Pro liubov'" ("About love"), the one love song in *The Rich Bride*, is sung together by the couple just before the culminating kiss, and then separately by each when languishing apart—a rudimentary double-focus narrative. *Swineherdess* follows the same pattern in "Pesnia o Moskve" ("Song about Moscow"), which is elaborated fully as Glasha and Musaib first sing in a duet, then twice individually during their separation, and again as a couple at the end of the film. Onscreen kissing is still allowed in 1937 as Ded hunts out couples in the bushes and Marinka raises her arm to her forehead when kissed by Zgara in a private gesture of ecstasy (fig. 5.8)

Figure 5.8. After the kiss: Marinka and Pavlo, *The Rich Bride*.

that later is displaced into state ecstasy when the heroine of Aleksandrov's *The Radiant Path* makes the same gesture while receiving a Kremlin award. After Stalin voiced disapproval of the kissing in *Volga-Volga* (1938), onscreen smooching disappeared from Soviet films, including Pyr'ev's last two musicals.[68]

Agricultural work is figured both visually and aurally as significant and pleasurable in the film. Under the opening titles wheat fields rippling in the wind are filmed with rapid tracking, accompanied by the energetic "Oh, You Horses," which continues in a slower, more expansive tempo as Zgara and his helper come into view and the latter makes gestures affirming both the majesty of the land and his reaction of overwhelming joy. In the same way, the two harvesting scenes of the film are elevated by dynamic montage and Dunaevskii's symphonic accompaniment. The competition with Zgara especially foregrounds the women's ecstasy of labor. The significance of agricultural work is also enhanced by the male brigade leader's comparing the harvest to a military operation in the face of coming war and the tractors to cavalry horses: "What is a harvest? A harvest is a tactical strike!"; "Boys, to your horses!" Men and women each have a mass song referencing the joy of work: "Oh, you horses, you steel horses, / Battle comrades-tractors, / Hum more merrily my dears"; "Let's go, let's go, merry girlfriends! . . . Come on girls, come on beauties! Let the country sing about us! . . . Let the new day overtake yesterday with its cheerful, joyful work!" Although women remain conventionally coded as agricultural workers in *The Rich Bride*, as represented in Mukhina's *Worker and Farm Laborer* (1937), mechanized and manual labor are still defined as equals and the women's song proposes parity between the sexes: "Bloom, land, where a free woman walks in the same ranks as a man." Laughing, teasing, shouting abuse, and singing, the women are allotted more screen time than the men. In the folkloric competition between male and female, between the women and Zgara, the feisty women (complete with flag planted for battle and comic marching to a drumbeat), take over the mowing when his tractor breaks down, thereby winning the labor contest (fig. 5.9). Later, Zgara mows for the women, enabling them to gather and tie up sheaves before a rainstorm—a genre-driven happy resolution to the battle of the sexes.

---

68 *Stenogramma soveshchaniia v TsK VKP(b) pod predsedatel'stvom A. A. Zhdanova po voprosam khudozhestvennogo kinematografa*, May 14, 1941, RTsKhIDNI, f. 77/1/919.

Figure 5.9. The women save the day, *The Rich Bride*.

The Rich Bride is the most vaudevillesque of the kolkhoz comedies, loaded with familiar comic tropes. In his role as night watchman, Ded roots out couples from the bushes with comic Ukrainian *tikaite* ("run along") and a smirking *vinovat* ("sorry"). With his pasted-on Chaplin mustache, genteel pretensions, off-key singing and jumping about, Kovyn'ko is just plain silly. Physical comedy abounds: Marinka howls over Zgara's supposed contempt for her labor prowess (fig. 5.10), the angry barber chases Kovyn'ko in and out of the cupboard in which he tries to hide, and Ded pursues him through the village with a shotgun. When threatened, Kovyn'ko pretends bravado: "U menia kharakter!" ("I have a temper!"—comically repeated throughout the film). When he confesses his machinations to Marinka, she is ecstatic, while he weeps (comic incongruity), and her joyful kissing and hugging of Kovyn'ko causes a misunderstanding with Zgara, who misinterprets what he sees through the window, thereby postponing the couple's reunion (comic retardation). The kolkhoz awards ceremony is deftly cross-cut with Ded chasing Kovyn'ko with a shotgun and other comic scenes—a disrespectful mix of the ideological with slapstick that became impossible in the later musicals. Dunaevskii explained that it was his idea to conclude the film with an extended waltz sequence, thereby avoiding the usual bravura finale.[69]

69 *Stenogramma. Doklad.*

Figure 5.10. Howling over the insult, *The Rich Bride.*

Cossacks of the Kuban'

Released in 1950, *Cossacks* became the most popular of the kolkhoz comedies thanks to Nikolai Pogodin's witty screenplay, Dunaevskii's music, song lyrics by Isakovskii and Vol'pin, and Pyr'ev's dynamic color cinematography.[70] Filmed thirteen years after *The Rich Bride, Cossacks* was a more sophisticated vehicle, not only technologically (it used Agfa color film taken from Germany during the war), but also as an integrated musical that was aware of the Hollywood comedy tradition.

---

70 Pogodin was best known for the dramas *Aristokraty* (The aristocrats, 1934) and his Lenin trilogy (1937–1958), but also wrote comic plays and filmscripts. The distant source of *Cossacks* is Pogodin's mediocre 1938 play, *Dzhiokonda*. Many of Isakovskii's simple but heartfelt poems were set to music, including "Katiusha" and "Vragi sozhgli rodnuiu khatu" ("The enemy burned his hut"). Vol'pin wrote comic plays and satiric verse, eventually working for *Krokodil*. After the war he co-authored many filmscripts with Nikolai Erdman.

On the way to the autumn fair in the Kuban', Galina Peresvetova, the chairwoman of the kolkhoz "Zavety Il'icha" (Il'ich's precepts), unexpectedly encounters an old flame, Gordei Voron, now the chair of "Krasnyi partizan" (Red partisan), stirring up memories in both of them. At the same time, Dasha Shelest, a heroine of socialist labor from Voron's kolkhoz, also unexpectedly encounters Nikolai Kovylev, a horse breeder from Peresvetova's collective farm, whom Dasha had previously met on a train. At the fair Peresvetova enrages Voron by lowering produce prices, which he and the other male chairs had kept high for three years, by supporting Dasha's planned marriage to Nikolai, which Voron regards as robbery of a prized worker, and by undermining his male dignity in various comic ways. Two horseraces bring the conflict to a head: Nikolai wins his race, earning Voron's permission to marry Dasha, but the couple then foils Voron's plan to have them live at his kolkhoz. To assuage his pride, Peresvetova allows Voron to win their harness race, his one victory in the battle of the sexes, but is disgusted by his renewed anger at Dasha's marriage, for which he blames her, breaks with him, and leaves for home. Koren', the local Party official, and Voron's friend Dergach convince Voron of Peresvetova's longstanding affection for him. He rides after her and the couple is reconciled.

Soviet agriculture was in ruins at the end of the war: "Total grain production was less than 50% of that in 1940. 25% of all tractors, 19% of all combines and 78% of all trucks had been lost. In addition, the number of horses, which in 1940 had been only 58% of that in 1928, was halved again by 1945."[71] Stalin's prewar policy of squeezing the peasantry in order to fund industrialization had not changed. Finally, in 1946 a drought led to a poor harvest, followed by famine in 1947.[72] Pyr'ev later recalled that both he and Pogodin were well aware of the problems with Soviet agriculture at the time and did not set out to make a realistic film about the life of the peasantry.[73] Instead, *Cossacks* was inspired by the director's disappointment after visiting a counterfeit fair organized by a local *raitorg* (district trade center), intended to attract people from nearby kolkhozes in order to sell them stale goods. He recalled the bustling, prosperous Siberian fairs he had visited as an adolescent

71 Stefan Hedlund, *Crisis in Soviet Agriculture* (London: Routledge, 2019), 67.

72 Michael Ellman, "The 1947 Soviet Famine and the Entitlement Approach to Famines," *Cambridge Journal of Economics* 24, no. 5 (September 2000): 603–630.

73 Pyr'ev, *Izbrannye proizvedeniia v dvukh tomakh*, 1:131.

working for Tatar manufacturers: "A fair is first of all a spectacle, a colorful, bright, inviting spectacle. Besides trade, there were always carousels, a circus, and *balagany* at fairs."[74] And this is the kind of fair—with a carousel, a circus, colorful posters advertising the acts, a movie theatre, and stalls overflowing with goods—that he staged in the film. Consequently, in the difficult time of post-war reconstruction, agricultural workers were entertained by a colorful spectacle very different from their lived reality.[75] Although the outdoor scenes in the fields and at the hippodrome were shot at "Kuban'," one of the few truly prosperous sovkhozes in the country,[76] Pyr'ev freely admitted that there were no fairs at the time in the Kuban' region, but he wasn't bothered by that fact—he expected there would be eventually.[77] Not surprisingly, the title of the completed film was *Veselaia iarmarka* (The jolly fair), but Stalin changed it to *Kubanskie kazaki*, possibly intending to throw a bone to a group traditionally hostile to the regime.

While both *The Rich Bride* and *Tractor Drivers* are concerned throughout with overcoming difficulties pertaining to agricultural work, *Cossacks* finishes with harvest activities from raking through piling up mountains of grain to loaded trucks departing the fields, all in the prologue. This is the only labor we will see until the last minutes of the film because success in the fields is no longer the point. The day dawns under the introductory titles and work begins with the "Urozhai" ("Harvest") song. While allowing for technological advances, harvesting is filmed much as in *The Rich Bride*: longshots of the cultivated steppe both with and without workers, a tracking shot along a field of standing wheat, images of wheat rippling in the wind, men on tractors and scything, women with rakes. Once again, both song and image convey the joy of work (fig. 5.11). After trucks haul away sacks of grain, the music softens, we see fields with stubble, ducks and cattle picking up loose grain—harvesting is done.

---

74 "Iarmarka—eto prezhde vsego zrelishche, i zrelishche krasochnoe, iarkoe, zazyvaiushchee. Pomimo torgovli na iarmarkakh vsegda byli karuseli, tsirk, balagany" (Pyr'ev, *Izbrannye proizvedeniia v dvukh tomakh*, 1:129).

75 The Rodgers and Hammerstein musical *State Fair* (1945) also reflected the need for normality at the end of the war, accomplished by resurrecting the American agrarian myth.

76 L. Okhrimenko, interview by R. Salys, 1998.

77 Pyr'ev, *Izbrannye proizvedeniia v dvukh tomakh*, 1:178.

Figure 5.11. Harvest song: Vasia and friends, *Cossacks of the Kuban'*.

The Rich Bride and *Tractor Drivers* advocated for collectivization, the Stakhanovite movement, and preparations for war in mass song. However, the more trying the time for the country, as during World War II and post-war reconstruction, the more later kolkhoz musicals moved away from ideology toward personal fulfillment, making them all the more attractive to audiences. *Swineherdess* primarily depicts traditional rural life in northern Russia and the Caucasus. There are no mass songs, only a mention of the capital city as meeting place for the lovers in the lyrical "Song about Moscow," and a coda on war added to the same song at the conclusion of the film.[78] In *Cossacks*, mass song and ideology exist on the margins, at the beginning and end of the film; the middle is an extended, festive celebration. The entrance arch of the Kuban' fair, inscribed "Osenniaia iarmarka" ("Autumn fair") (fig. 5.12) faces inward, enclosing participants in enchanted space where anything can happen.[79] Like *Swineherdess*, *Cossacks* uses the "unex-

---

78 *Swineherdess* was Pyr'ev's favorite, mainly because he considered it his first "Russian national film" ("natsional'no russkaia kartina"), which determined his future artistic direction (Pyr'ev, *Izbrannye proizvedeniia v dvukh tomakh*, 1:112).

79 On claustrophobic space in Pyr'ev's kolkhoz films, see E. Dobrenko, "Iazyk prostranstva, szhatogo do tochki, ili estetika sotsial'noi klaustrofobii," *Iskusstvo kino* 9 (1996): 108–117.

pected encounter" motif of vaudeville-operetta, as future lovers meet away from home in a holiday idyll.

Figure 5.12. The autumn fair, *Cossacks of the Kuban'*.

Dasha Shelest, a heroine of socialist labor, is the "rich bride" of *Cossacks* who chooses the true love of Nikolai Kovylev over Vasia Tuzov, a financially interested suitor from her own collective farm. At one point, Gordei Voron, her kolkhoz chair, even bribes Vasia by promising to pay all expenses connected to his pursuit of Dasha, including a set of fancy new clothes. Nikolai's friend, Andrei, the *svat* (matchmaker), as he identifies himself in an early episode, is the reimagined trickster-helper of Commedia dell'arte who aids the lovers in overcoming obstacles to their marriage. In order to locate Dasha among the crowds at the fair, he devises a ruse that also outwits Vasia, the false suitor: over the loudspeaker comes the announcement that two of Dasha's acquaintances await her at the entrance to the movie theatre. Andrei then makes Vasia pay him for two tickets for the women and leaves him ticketless while the foursome goes to the movies. What made the trick even more comic for audiences is that the episode parodied a *stiliaga*'s purchase of scarce goods from a black marketeer: Vasia has dressed up in a plaid *stiliaga* jacket and cap with a fashionably short tie, while Andrei, playing a shady character with his collar turned up and a *kubanka* (Cossack hat) pulled down to his eyes, sells him the movie tickets at an exorbitant price (fig. 5.13).[80] The "matchmaker" later tries to persuade Peresvetova to let Nikolai marry Dasha, then tells him of Voron's secret pact with Dasha, motivating him to win the race, and finally, with a triumphant smirk, invites Voron and company to the wedding feast at Peresvetova's kolkhoz.

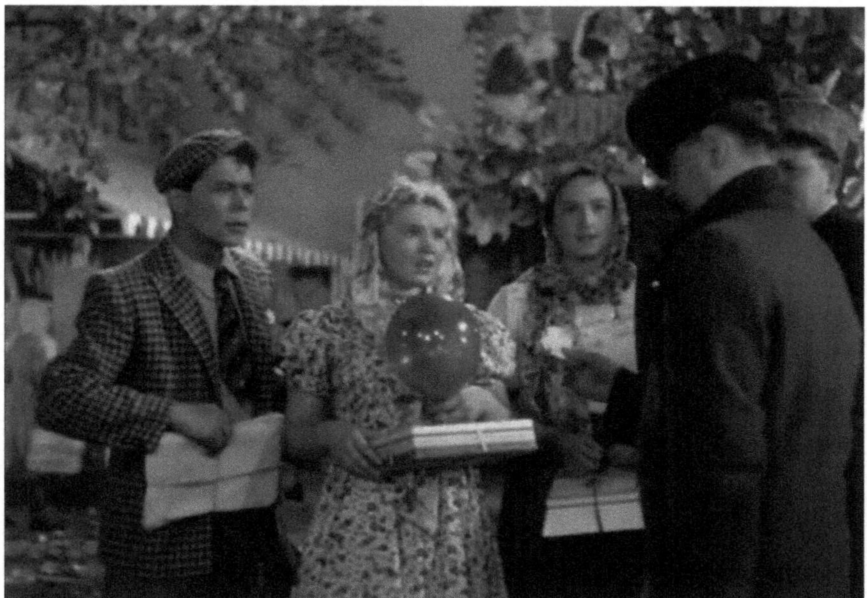

Figure 5.13. Andrei offers Vasia movie tickets, *Cossacks of the Kuban'*.

Love, not ideology, is constituted as the basis of happiness. As Nikolai searches for Dasha at the fair, Andrei directs his gaze to the grandstand, where she stands with other celebrities. As he exclaims, "I see her," the camera instead shows us Koren', the regional party official, beginning his speech. Ignoring

---

80 Comedy directors were especially attuned to the latest developments in Soviet life that had comic potential. The first known use of the term *stiliaga* occurred in D. G. Beliaev's satirical piece of the same name in the March 1949 issue of *Krokodil* (D. G. Beliaev, "Stiliagi," *Krokodil* 7 (March 1949), http://beliy.ru/work/stilyagifilm/-id=356.htm). *Cossacks* was shot during the summer and fall of 1949 and released in February 1950. Given the nationwide distribution and popularity of *Krokodil*, as well as the rampant speculation after the war, audiences watching the film in 1950 and subsequent years would have recognized the types portrayed in the episode.

Koren′ completely, the two young Cossacks instead move closer to the grandstand to get a better view of Dasha. Peresvetova also advocates for the lovers to Voron: "They're in love." When Voron calls the planned marriage a "political matter" ("Eto delo politicheskoe") because Dasha is being "stolen" from his kolkhoz, Peresvetova responds: "Eto delo ikh lichnoe" ("It's their personal matter"). Koren′, the wise official, sorts things out: he rebuts Voron's territoriality with a reference to a unified Soviet state, but then also turns to the personal by convincing him of Peresvetova's affection.

Pogodin increased the comedic charge of *Cossacks* by structuring the narrative around two couples instead of a single romantic pair, as in the three preceding kolkhoz films. Musicals often include a comic secondary pair along with the primary lyric couple.[81] *Cossacks* reverses the pattern: Dasha and Nikolai make a rather saccharine young romantic couple, as demonstrated in their conversation during the talent show. Dasha has a modest appearance, always with a smoothly combed-back, plain hairdo, which contrasts starkly with the rolls of curled bangs à la Marika Rökk in *Devushka moei mechty* worn by the girlfriends flanking her on either side during the talent show. The romantic couple becomes secondary as the temperamental elders, Peresvetova and Voron, go at each other in classic screwball comedy fashion. Nevertheless, Nikolai's steeplechase victory and Peresvetova's intentional loss of the harness race are both central to the resolution of the narrative.

In musical and romantic comedy films, the male and female have contrasting personalities and represent opposing social values but must compromise in order to reach a happy outcome in the relationship. (*The Sound of Music* is an American example.) Screwball comedy, the transgressive stepchild of romantic comedy, shares its basic plotline but accomplishes the happy ending through a verbal and sometimes physical (slapstick) battle of the sexes upon which sexual attraction has been displaced.[82] Romance typically depends not just on affection, but also on isolation from the claims of everyday life,[83] as is the case in *State Fair* and *Devushka moei mechty*.[84] The holiday atmosphere of

81 At the time of filming, Ladynina was forty-one, still a star but no longer an ingenue, which may have influenced the structure of the scenario. *Tractor Drivers* has a rudimentary secondary comic couple in Kirill Petrovich and Markovna, but the line is not developed.

82 Cele Otnes and Elizabeth Peck, *Cinderella Dreams: The Allure of the Lavish Wedding* (Berkeley: University of California Press, 2003), 168.

83 David R. Shumway, "Screwball Comedies: Constructing Romance, Mystifying Marriage," in *Film Genre Reader*, ed. Barry Keith Grant (Austin: University of Texas Press, 2012), 4:471.

84 Pogodin and Pyr′ev would have seen the popular *Devushka moei mechty*, released for public screening in 1947.

the Kuban' fair provides just such an environment for Peresvetova and Voron. The screwball couple's conflict is never externally motivated; they themselves create the obstacles in their relationship. Our pair are etymological opposites: "Light" (*svet*) forms Peresvetova's name, while Voron's surname derives from the (black) raven and their verbal jousting continues throughout the film:

> "Don't you recognize me?"
> "How can I not recognize you, Gordei Gordeich? I can recognize you a mile away."
> "Am I really so noticeable?"
> "Your mustache is noticeable . . . Cossacks mostly don't wear mustaches nowadays."
> "Well, what does it matter to me? I'm a bachelor, a free Cossack. If I feel like it, I'll grow a beard too."
> "Grow braids if you like, Gordei Gordeich!"[85]

And later:

> "I'll steal you away, I swear, I'll steal you!"
> "I can't hear you."
> "I'll put you on a horse and take you away to my kolkhoz."
> "Why to yours? I have my own."

Their repartee finally culminates in the concrete competition of the harness race.

The woman is the dominant figure in screwball comedies and often humiliates the male.[86] The screwball heroine knows her true feelings about the male, even before battle is joined, and admits them at some point. In an early scene

---

85 I reproduce here the dialogue in transliteration:

> "Ne uznaete?"
> "Kak ia mogu Vas ne uznat', Gordei Gordeich? Da Vas za verstu uznaesh'."
> "Neuzheli ia takoi zametnyi?"
> "Usy u Vas zametnye . . . A teper' i kazaki bez usov bol'she khodiat."
> "Nu a mne-to chto? Ia chelovek kholostoi, kazak vol'nyi. Zakhochu—i borodu otpushchu."
> "Otpuskaite khot' kosy, Gordei Gordeich!"

86 Wes D. Gehring, *Romantic vs. Screwball Comedy. Charting the Difference* (Lanham: Scarecrow Press, 2008), 2.

of Howard Hawks's *Bringing Up Baby* (1938), Susan tells a secondary character that she intends to marry David, only he doesn't know it yet. Peresvetova's "As You Once Were" makes her feelings clear from the beginning ("My soul is open / Open to you alone") and she admits her love publicly to Dergach and Koren'. Voron simply appears to become increasingly oblivious to his true feelings as the battle escalates: "Oi, baba! Oi, zmeia!" ("What a broad! What a viper!").

Gordei Gordeevich is an old-school type stuck in the traditional ways both physically and intellectually. He still wears a Cossack mustache, which amuses Peresvetova, and at times uses old-fashioned expressions: "Vovek pochtenie" ("My respects forever"), "Serdtse moe opiat' podaet trevozhnye zvonki" ("My heart is ringing alarm bells again"). The Voron character is modeled on Vasilii Chapaev from the 1934 film in which the similarly impulsive, blustering, comically choleric, poorly educated, mustachioed hero sings the Cossack song "Chernyi voron." Gordei Gordeevich loves to brag about his own kolkhoz, which he regards as his personal fiefdom. After the race he still carries a horsewhip when imposing his will regarding where Dasha and Nikolai will live, yet another revenge move against Peresvetova. He does not understand change: "Situatsiiu ne ponial" ("I/you didn't understand the situation") becomes a comic refrain in the film.

The strong woman in screwball comedies threatens the masculinity of her partner (fig. 5.14) and, in *Cossacks,* the power of patriarchy. For three years Voron has been the leader of an all-male group of kolkhoz chairs who engage in the price fixing of produce at the fair.[87] Just as he proposes raising prices, Peresvetova challenges this patriarchy by announcing a twenty-five percent reduction as a modern strategy to earn more through selling more. In Voron's world, women are commodified, and not far removed from kolkhoz produce, which is demonstrated early on when Andrei and the other single men meet Mudretsov (Voron's manager) and his women kolkhoz workers on the way

87 More prosperous kolkhozes that produced grain and produce above the compulsory government quotas were able to sell them profitably at fairs or on the black market (Moshe Lewin, *The Making of the Soviet System* [New York: Pantheon Books, 1985], 172–173). At the beginning of the film, when Andrei jokingly calls himself an "agent" for the purchase of marriageable young women, the real-world reference is to agents who bought up large quantities of foodstuffs needed by other kolkhozes or urban enterprises.

to the fair. Mudretsov warns the men away from a truck loaded with young women and watermelons with a double entendre for viewers: "Grazhdane, podal'she ot produkta! Ruki k tovaru ne protiagivat'!" ("Citizens, stay away from the product! No reaching out for the goods!," fig. 5.15). Voron introduces Dasha and her team to another kolkhoz chair as "our capital" and his reaction to her marriage plans is similarly economic, eliciting her angry response:

> "But I'm getting married, Uncle Gordei."
> "This isn't a marriage, it's robbery! Robbery! I'd just like to know, what did this Peresvetova buy you with?"
> "What do you mean 'bought'? Aren't you ashamed, Uncle? Am I some sort of thing or what?"

Figure 5.14. Screwball couple: Voron and Peresvetova, *Cossacks of the Kuban'*.

Figure 5.15. Stay away from the product! *Cossacks of the Kuban'.*

Voron's objections to the marriage, like his impulsive lowering of produce prices at the fair and hasty purchase of a piano for his kolkhoz, are only proxies in the screwball war with Peresvetova.

Peresvetova's dominance is concretely manifest when the two *ptichnitsy* (poultry women), who always know the truth, observe her accidentally slipping a horse collar on Voron's neck: "Avdot'ia, there's a reason why she collared him." Other screwball comedies similarly concretize "getting the man" via physical comedy: in *Bringing up Baby* Susan throws a butterfly net over David's head and laughs. In the end the rules of the genre dictate that the male and female compromise. Peresvetova thoroughly enjoys pulling ahead of Voron during the harness race (fig. 5.16) but holds back when she realizes that a loss will destroy his already fragile self-esteem. Voron recognizes the value of culture as he takes comfort in Hamlet's speech about "the slings and arrows of outrageous fortune" and the lyrical, but also funny "O, nimfa!" ("O nymph!"), and at the end swallows his pride to ride after Peresvetova.[88]

---

88 Parodying the classics as a way to elevate popular culture was a staple of 1930s Hollywood comedy, in, for example, *Roman Scandals* (directed by F. Tuttle, 1933) and *Champagne Waltz* (directed by A. E. Sutherland, 1937), released in the Soviet Union as trophy films in 1940 and 1942.

Figure 5.16. The harness race: Peresvetova and Voron, *Cossacks of the Kuban'*.

In the kolkhoz musicals, it appears that the heroines have made it up the career ladder from agricultural shock worker Marinka Lukash in *The Rich Bride* to skilled tractor driver-Stakhanovite and brigade leader Mar'iana Bazhan in *Tractor Drivers* to Peresvetova, a modern kolkhoz chair who is electrifying her collective farm. Nevertheless, gender relations in the films remain fully traditional. Klim Iarko meets Mar'iana Bazhan in stock romantic fashion by rescuing and bringing her home after a motorcycle accident. Glasha Novikova accedes to Kuz'ma's pressure to marry because in her village she is expected to marry *someone*. Dasha Shelest readily agrees to move to her new husband's kolkhoz. Peresvetova allows Voron to win the harness race, but the question of who will give up an important position to move to a spouse's kolkhoz remains outside the boundaries of the film.

Cossacks uses both physical comedy and comic dialogue, much of it based on folklore. Andrei and Mudretsov almost come to blows as they argue over the women, and Mudretsov loses his straw hat not once but twice (a well-worn comic device) as he runs after his truck. Voron struggles to remove the horse collar slipped on by Peresvetova; Vasia hobbles along with a despairing expression after losing the steeplechase. The piano salesman almost falls off his bench while playing "like Gilel's," comic because he also immediately switches to popular music. The Jewish salesman is afflicted with constant sneezing, a parody that could pass only during the ongoing campaign against cosmopolitans. Comic incongruity plays out as Fedia the weightlifter cannot fight when called upon to help because, as he explains, his arms are full of packages. The main verbal miscommunication of *Cossacks* is the screwball dialogue (too lengthy to include here) between Voron and Peresvetova over Dasha and Nikolai's wedding, which he initially misinterprets as his own with Peresvetova, only leading to continuing hostilities.

Popular folk culture pervades the film, adding color, humor, and movement. Male Cossack clothing is recognizable but generalized without reference to a specific region. Peresvetova and the poultry women often dress in red peasant chic when they are central to an episode, exploiting the fact that *Cossacks* was one of the first postwar color films (fig. 5.17). In agreeing to the marriage, Voron tells Nikolai to send matchmakers, implying that the folk custom is still being observed in the Kuban', if only as a formality. Flirtatious male-female repartee between Andrei and the women sets the tone for the film:

> "So, who are you?"
> "We're lonely, single people, we drive, we walk about, we're looking for something we haven't lost."[89]

Figure 5.17. Performance of the poultry women, *Cossacks of the Kuban'*.

---

89 The last phrase is a folk saying. See "Pro poisk," no. 7, Dettext, https://dettext.com/poslovicy-i-pogovorki/pro-poisk/.

The same back and forth occurs as Dasha and Liuba try to shake Vasia and Fedia at the fair.

A diegetic show within the film show is not unusual in folk musicals (as in the 1945 *State Fair* and *Summer Stock*) because it highlights the talents of their stars, often showcasing them in a more familiar urban vehicle. However, Pyr'ev was less interested in foregrounding the talents of his actors than in presenting visual and verbal folk culture at a high level. In *Cossacks* professional folk dancers perform two of three acts—the women's "Oh, the Guelder Rose Is Blooming" and the Cossack sword dance, with the film's actors participating at convenient points; only the poultry women with Ded perform their own *chastushki* and dances.

The poultry women (*ptichnitsy*) and truthtellers Khristoforovna and Nikanorovna (fig. 5.17) are interesting secondary characters for a number of reasons: They embody the older ways of the folk, travelling to the fair with oxen and crates of live geese, singing through the night; they speak in familiar proverbs, perform transgressive *chastushki,* and dance simply but well. At the beginning of the film, the women comment on Peresvetova's widowhood with ready proverbs:

> "A widow's lot is a bitter lot, my dear."
> "God forbid—to be widowed and to burn."
> "Oh, my dear, better to burn seven times than to be widowed once."[90]

In their satirical *chastushki* the *ptichnitsy* reject out-of-date fabrics being sold at the fair, recap past events (Voron's attempt to raise prices; the horse collar incident), and reiterate female dominance, always in repartee with Ded: "Today women are at the wheel, Nikanorovna." "We're reaching the Kremlin, Khristoforovna." The extended *chastushka* on the Peresvetova-Voron romance also furthers the narrative by publicly offending Voron's male pride, thereby motivating the continuation of the screwball battle.

---

90 Below I give the dialogue in transliteration:

> "Vdov'e delo—gor'koe delo, kuma."
> "Ne dai bozhe—vdovet' da goret'." [Both proverbs are from V. Dal', "Poslovitsy russkogo naroda," Vdahl.ru, accessed August 1, 2022, https://vdahl.ru/. See *muzh-zhena* section.]
> "Ekh, kuma, luchshe sem' raz sgoret', chem odin vdovet'" [Ukrainian proverb, see *Poslovitsy i pogovorki*, http://www.poslovitsy-pogovorki.com/p/28219.php.]

Ideology in both song and dialogue (Koren″s speech opening the fair and his instruction of Voron at the close—the obligatory leading role of the Party) frames the beginning and end of *Cossacks*, but the film proper is concerned with personal matters, as underscored by the two lyrical songs, "As You Once Were" and "Guelder Rose." "Harvest," the introductory song, praises Kuban′ workers and grain production, and also plays instrumentally later as the camera pans across the plethora of goods at the fair (the result of the harvest in music rather than words). However, the song does something more interesting by introducing the main characters (as yet unnamed) as they sing phrases that define each of them. Vasia and the Cossacks want all the young women to be "both pretty and smart"; Dasha and friends respond with a wish "that young Cossacks would love them more passionately." "Not a grain will be lost" defines Voron's penny-pinching manager Mudretsov. The older generation differs from the young people in disinterested commitment: for Peresvetova, "we were not attracted by awards," for Voron, "we grew our bread for the honor of the labor."[91] The pragmatic Mudretsov then intervenes: "if we're given an award for this [labor]," and Dasha's group continues, "we won't say no, it's not necessary"; Andrei and Nikolai add, "we'll answer that it is." The energetic "Harvest" song then slows and becomes quieter, transitioning into the melancholy folk song "Uzh ty pole moe" ("You are my field"), sung by the poultry women.

The closing ideological song, "Ne za temi dal′nimi moriami" ("Not beyond those distant seas"), first sung by the reconciled Peresvetova and Voron, is a mass song in most of its stereotypical language: for example, "Our happiness walks beside us. We don't need to look for it," but the melody is lyrical, referencing the subdued happiness of those, like Peresvetova and Voron, who managed to survive the war. The genre ending concludes as the couple drives off down the country road, but they are immediately (and unrealistically) followed by a tractor, the transition to a second, public ending. Ladynina later commented that audiences applauded the final reconciliation of Peresvetova and Voron because it was both the narrative and emotional finale of the film. "This is where it should have ended. And then, who needed to finish the film with countless tractors and a long song about the Soviet land"[92] As "Not beyond those distant seas" continues, the plowing scenes with Dasha, Liuba and real kolkhoz workers are also

91 Ladynina's rising into the frame from the bottom edge here is borrowed from Orlova's identical movement at the conclusion of *Spring*.

92 Undated notes, Ladynina archive.

relatively subdued. Stepping out of the diegesis, the entire cast then arrives to wave good-bye to us, suturing us into the film through friendly, direct address, followed by the usual bravura symphonic close.

By 1949, Dunaevskii had extensive experience composing for film, so that his musical arrangement for *Cossacks* is more nuanced than that of *The Rich Bride*. Dunaevskii explained that he worked by first composing a central song and then doing the musical arrangement of the film using the central song as a point of departure. Instrumental phrases from the song then recur not as the leitmotif of a character (common in musicals), but as a comment on the character's *situation*.[93] "As You Once Were," the central song of *Cossacks*, tells the entire story of Peresvetova's past with Voron, which is never explained in the dialogues. In their youth Peresvetova had married someone else: "even if I could not unite my fate with yours," for which he has always blamed her: "Why did you want to blame me again for your losses?" Her husband was apparently killed early on in the war, but Peresvetova did not forget Voron and waited for him to return: "I waited for you the whole war." She had reconciled herself to his rejection until their chance meeting on the way to the fair: "Why have you disturbed my peace?" but is again ready to love: "Look, look, my soul is open, open to you alone." Peresvetova's slow, reflective tempo now speeds up as the song shifts to the lively kolkhoz women who continue it with the same "my soul is open," since Dasha is about to encounter Nikolai. From this point on, instrumental phrases from "As you once were" define Peresvetova and Voron's situations: the continuing misunderstandings when she confesses her love before Dergach and in the following scene as Voron despairs of her love; during their competition in the race; when she rejects Voron for his stubbornness regarding Dasha's marriage and leaves for home, since he has not changed: "As you once were, so you remain"; when Voron rides after her at the end, finally disproving the words of the song. "As you once were" soon became popular beyond movie theatres because it expressed the suffering and losses of so many women during the war. Its subdued melody and lyrics conveyed resignation, melancholy, as well as hope.

The second lyric song, "Guelder Rose," is more limited in significance, but also became widely popular. Dasha and girlfriends perform it at the talent show, telling her unspoken love for Nikolai:

---

93 *Stenogramma. Doklad.*

To my misfortune, I fell in love with a fellow.
I can't open up,
I can't find the words.

. . .

But a girl's love
Grows stronger every day.

. . .

My dear, good one,
Guess for yourself!

Their love scene follows. With its repetitive melody and simple lyrics, "Guelder Rose" is the best example in the musicals of Dunaevskii's gift for composing in the style of the folksong and, in fact, it has been widely performed as such up to the present.

A Cinema for the Folk

By the end of the 1920s it had become obvious that the avantgarde cinema that had dominated the scene during the decade had left theatres empty. Boris Shumiatskii, appointed as head of the industry in 1930, set out to develop a socialist equivalent of Hollywood film that would embed ideology in entertainment, making the pill go down easily, while generating sorely needed revenues. The goal was "a cinema for the millions" (the title of Shumiatskii's 1935 book) and the model film was *Chapaev*.[94] While losing its world-class status with the downgrading of avantgarde film, Soviet cinema acquired an enthusiastic domestic audience. Instead of demanding deep thought and reflection, it offered emotional engagement, and its unpretentious stories acquired the status of mythologems.[95] As a cinema for the masses, the kolkhoz comedies took up issues of the day while entertaining and energizing audiences with humor, dynamic cinematography, and accessible songs carried out of the movie theatre. Viewers experienced the pleasure of recognition from familiar folk culture to

94 Richard Taylor, "Soviet Cinema as Popular Culture: Or the Extraordinary Adventures of Mr. Nepman in the Land of the Silver Screen," *Revolutionary Russia* 1 (1988): 45–46.

95 Maia Turovskaia, "Gollivud v Moskve, ili sovetskoe i amerikanskoe kino 30-kh–40-kh godov," *Kinovedcheskie zapiski* 97 (2010): 54.

well-known characters, and the comedies addressed the personal needs of the individual through tales of romance. With time the films moved from an emphasis on ideology, such as the Stakhanovism of agriculture and defense (preparations for the coming war) in *The Rich Bride* and *Tractor Drivers* to the largely national and personal in *Swineherdess* and *Cossacks*. But the vaudeville-operetta romantic plot and comic devices that had been at the heart of the musicals from the very beginning invariably guaranteed their success with cinemagoers less interested in education and government policy than in entertainment and escape into utopian worlds.

Bibliography

Aleksandrov, G. V. *Epokha i kino*. Moscow: Izdatel'stvo politicheskoi literatury, 1976.

Altman, Rick. *The American Film Musical*. Bloomington: Indiana University Press, 1989.

Balash, Bela. "Varvarskii talant." *Kino* 55 (1933): 2.

"Baletnaia fal'sh'." *Pravda*. February 6, 1936, 3.

Barber, J. D., and R. W. Davies. "Employment and Industrial Labour." In *The Economic Transformation of the Soviet Union, 1913–1945*, edited by R. W. Davies et al., 81–105. Cambridge: Cambridge University Press, 1994.

Davies, R. W., et al., eds. *The Economic Transformation of the Soviet Union, 1913–1945*. Cambridge: Cambridge University Press, 1994.

Dobrenko, E. "Iazyk prostranstva, szhatogo do tochki, ili estetika sotsial'noi klaustrofobii." *Iskusstvo kino* 9 (1996): 108–117.

Dunaevskii, Isaak. *Kogda dusha gorit tvorchestvom: pis'ma k Raise Rys'kinoi*. Astana: Elorda, 2000.

Dyer, Richard. *Only Entertainment*. London: Taylor & Francis Group, 2002.

———. *In the Space of a Song*. London and New York: Routledge, 2012.

Ellman, Michael. "The 1947 Soviet Famine and the Entitlement Approach to Famines." *Cambridge Journal of Economics* 24, no. 5 (September 2000): 603–630.

Fedorov, Aleksandr. *Tysiacha i odin samyi kassovyi sovetskii fil'm: mneniia kinokritikov i zritelei*. Moscow: Informatsiia dlia vsekh, 2021. http://www.mediagram.ru/library.

Fomin, Valerii. "Zhizn' ne slozhilas', no udalas'. . . ." *Rodina* 2 (February 2007): 91–99.

Gabrilovich, E., et al. "Zametki na poliakh." In *Ivan Pyr'ev v zhizni i na ekrane*, edited by G. Mar'iamov, 218–225. Moscow: Kinotsentr, 1994.

Gal'perin, A. "Dalekoe i blizkoe." In *Ivan Pyr'ev v zhizni i na ekrane*, edited by G. Mar'iamov, 89–98. Moscow: Kinotsentr, 1994.

Gehring, Wes D. *Romantic vs. Screwball Comedy. Charting the Difference*. Lanham: Scarecrow Press, 2008.

Hedlund, Stefan. *Crisis in Soviet Agriculture*. London: Routledge, 2019.

Hellbeck, Jochen. *Revolution on My Mind. Writing a Diary under Stalin*. Cambridge: Harvard University Press, 2006.

Kalinin, Il'ia. "'Nam smekh i stroit' i zhit' pomogaet': politekonomiia smekha i sovetskaia muzykal'naia komediia (1930-e gody)." *Russian Literature* 80 (2013): 119–140.

Kenrick, John. *Musical Theatre: A History*. London: Bloomsbury, 2017.

Kudriavtsev, S. "Zarubezhnye fil'my v sovetskom prokate." https://kinanet.livejournal.com/13882.html.

Ladynina, Marina. Interview by R. Salys, 1998.

———. *Moi tvorcheskii put'*. Moscow: Goskinoizdat, 1949.

———.V poiskakh putei." In *Ivan Pyr'ev v zhizni i na ekrane,* edited by G. Mar'iamov, 106–116. Moscow: Kinotsentr, 1994.

Lewin, Moshe. *The Making of the Soviet System*. New York: Pantheon Books, 1985.

Maksimenkov, L. *Sumbur vmesto muzyki. Stalinskaia kul'turnaia revoliutsiia, 1936–1938*. Moscow: Iuridicheskaia kniga, 1997.

Manevich, Iosif. *Za ekranom*. Moscow: Novoe izdatel'stvo, 2006.

Mar'iamov, G., ed. *Ivan Pyr'ev v zhizni i na ekrane: stranitsy vospominanii*. Moscow: Kinotsentr, 1994.

———. "Boitsovskii kharakter." In *Ivan Pyr'ev v zhizni i na ekrane,* edited by G. Mar'iamov, 182–196. Moscow: Kinotsentr, 1994.

McReynolds, Louise. *Russia at Play: Leisure Activities at the End of the Tsarist Era*. Ithaca: Cornell University Press, 2003.

Miller, Frank. *Folklore for Stalin. Russian Folklore and Pseudofolklore of the Stalin Era*. Armonk: M. E. Sharpe, 1990.

Mitta, Aleksandr. "Pyr'ev segodnia." *Kinovedcheskie zapiski* 53 (2001): 13.

Naumov, V. "'Obryvki' i 'konchiki' vospominanii." In *Ivan Pyr'ev v zhizni i na ekrane,* edited by G. Mar'iamov, 159–177. Moscow: Kinotsentr, 1994.

Nekrylova, A. F. *Russkie narodnye gorodskie prazdniki, uveseleniia i zrelishcha. Konets XVIII–nachalo XX veka*. Leningrad: Iskusstvo, 1988.

"Nynche zhit' veselo." Illustration. *Komsomol'skaia pravda,* November 15, 1933, 3.

Ogneva, E. V. *Ivan Pyr'ev*. Voronezh: Izdat-Print, 2016.

Okhrimenko, L. Interview by R. Salys, 1998.

Otnes, Cele, and Elizabeth Peck. *Cinderella Dreams: The Allure of the Lavish Wedding*. Berkeley: University of California Press, 2003.

Panfilov, G. "Pyr'ev segodnia." *Kinovedcheskie zapiski* 53 (2001): 14.

Planida, Mariia Iur'evna. "Vodevil' v otechestvennoi muzykal'noi kul'ture (konets XVIII–nachalo XXI veka): transformatsiia zhanra." PhD diss., Rostovskaia gosudarstvennaia konservatoriia im. S. Rakhmaninova, Rostov, 2019.

Planida, M. Iu., and T. S. Rudichenko. "Vodevil' v Rossii: adaptatsiia i zhanrovye transformatsii." *Iuzhno-Rossiiskii muzykal'nyi al'manakh* 3 (2019): 71–76.

Polukhina, Liana. *Marina Ladynina i Ivan Pyr'ev*. Moscow: Eksmo-Algoritm, 2004.

Pomeshchikov, E. "Rozhdenie zhanra." In *Ivan Pyr'ev v zhizni i na ekrane,* edited by G. Mar'iamov, 82–88. Moscow: Kinotsentr, 1994.

Pyr'ev, Ivan. *Izbrannye proizvedeniia v dvukh tomakh,* vol. 1. Moscow: Iskusstvo, 1978.

Rossman, Jeffrey J. *Worker Resistance under Stalin: Class and Revolution on the Shop Floor*. Cambridge: Harvard University Press, 2005.

Shumiatskii, Boris. *Kinematografiia millionov*. Moscow: Kinofotoizdat, 1935.

Shumway, David R. "Screwball Comedies: Constructing Romance, Mystifying Marriage." In *Film Genre Reader,* edited by Barry Keith Grant, vol. 4, 463–483. Austin: University of Texas Press, 2012.

Solov'ev, Sergei, et al. "Pyr'ev segodnia." *Kinovedcheskie zapiski* 53 (2001): 4–14.

"Sumbur vmesto muzyki." *Pravda*. January 28, 1936, 3.

Taylor, Richard. "Soviet Cinema as Popular Culture: Or the Extraordinary Adventures of Mr. Nepman in the Land of the Silver Screen." *Revolutionary Russia* 1 (1988): 36–56.

———. "Singing on the Steppes for Stalin: Ivan Pyr'ev and the Kolkhoz Musical in Soviet Cinema." *Slavic Review* 58, no. 1 (Spring 1999): 143–159.

———. "The Stalinist Musical: Socialist Realism and Revolutionary Romanticism." In *A Companion to Russian Cinema*, edited by Birgit Beumers, 139–157. Chichester: John Wiley & Sons, Inc., 2016.

Telotte, J. P. "Self and Society: Vincente Minnelli and Musical Formula." *Journal of Popular Film & Television* 9, no. 4 (1982): 181–193.

Terni, Jennifer. "A Genre for Early Mass Culture: French Vaudeville and the City, 1830–1848." *Theatre Journal* 58, no. 2 (May 2006): 221–248.

Traubner, Richard. *Operetta. A Theatrical History.* Revised ed . New York: Routledge, 2003.

Turovskaia, Maia. "I. A. Pyr'ev i ego muzykal'nye komedii." *Kinovedcheskie zapiski* 1 (1988): 111–146.

———. "Gollivud v Moskve, ili sovetskoe i amerikanskoe kino 30-kh–40-kh godov." *Kinovedcheskie zapiski* 97 (2010): 51–63.

Wheatcroft, S. G., and R. W. Davies. "Population." In *The Economic Transformation of the Soviet Union, 1913–1945*, edited by R. W. Davies et al., 57–80, 273–276. Cambridge: Cambridge University Press, 1994.

Zemlianukhin, Sergei, and Miroslava Segida. *Domashniaia sinemateka. Otechestvennoe kino, 1918–1996.* Moscow: Dubl'-D, 1996.

Archival Sources

Dunaevskii letter to G. Aleksandrov. March 20, 1935. Dunaevskii family archive (uncatalogued). Moscow.

Marina Ladynina archive. Moscow. Ladynina's uncatalogued papers were in her possession until her death in 2003. The present whereabouts of the archive are unknown to me.

Stenogramma. Doklad Dunaevskogo v Muzykal'nom nauchno-issledovatel'skom institute o muzyke v kino. May 7, 1937. RGALI. F. 2062/1/332.

Stenogramma soveshchaniia v TsK VKP(b) pod predsedatel'stvom A. A. Zhdanova po voprosam khudozhestvennogo kinematografa. May 14, 1941. RTsKhIDNI. F. 77/1/919.

CHAPTER 6

The Thaw as Carnival: Soviet Musical Comedy after Stalin

Lilya Kaganovsky

This chapter examines El′dar Riazanov's first musical comedy film, *Karnaval′naia noch′* (Carnival night 1956) as "carnivalesque" in the Bakhtinian sense—that is, a mode that overturns structures that underpin a social order through humor and chaos.[1] Coming on the heels of the 20th Party Congress and the beginning of de-Stalinization, directed by a young new director (Riazanov) and starring an unknown actress (Liudmila Gurchenko), this 1956 musical comedy strove to find its own individual voice, plot, look, and sound in direct opposition to the Stalinist musical film that preceded it. A "remake," as Alexander Prokhorov and Elena Prokhorova have suggested, of Grigorii Aleksandrov's 1938 *Volga-Volga*,[2] *Carnival Night* stages its resistance to old forms of authoritarianism and utopian togetherness typical of the musical through masquerade and carnival: by destabilizing categories like gender and heterosexual romance, subverting standard musical numbers, and openly mocking the voice of state power and its "acousmatic" reach (fig. 6.1).[3]

---

1 I am not the first, of course, to tie Riazanov's carnival to Bakhtin's; see Evgeny Dobrenko, "Soviet Comedy Film; or, the Carnival of Authority," *Discourse* 17, no 3 (Spring 1995): 49–57.

2 Alexander Prokhorov and Elena Prokhorova, *Film and Television Genres of the Late Soviet Era* (New York: Bloomsbury, 2017), 117.

3 As Michel Chion has defined it, the *acousmêtre* is a disembodied voice whose "sourcelessness" suggests "the paranoid and often obsessional panoptic fantasy . . . of total mastery of space by vision" (Michel Chion, *The Voice in Cinema*, trans. Claudia Gorbman [New York: Columbia University Press, 1999], 24). As I have argued elsewhere, sound technology was often figured as an *acousmêtre* in early Soviet sound films, bypassing the human subject in

Figure 6.1. Broadcasting technology as carnivalesque (*Carnival Night*, 1956).

In its tongue-in-cheek undermining of hierarchy and authority, *Carnival Night* may very well have been an anomaly: a "sincere" musical comedy that anticipated and helped to usher in the openness, youthfulness, and optimism of the early Thaw (1956–1964).[4] The power of music and laughter is called upon to undo the power of authoritarian rule—and suddenly, after twenty years of "singing in the steppes for Stalin," we find ourselves beyond the need for a unified

favor of a voice that spoke both from within and from *beyond* the film. See Lilya Kaganovsky, *Voice of Technology: Soviet Cinema's Transition to Sound, 1928–1935* (Bloomington: Indiana University Press, 2018).

4 In his era-defining article, "Ob iskrennosti v literature" ("About sincerity in literature"), published in the literary journal *Novyi mir* in December 1953, Vladimir Pomerantsev argued that Stalinist literature's greatest sin was its "insincerity" and "lacquering of reality" (Vladimir Pomerantsev, "Ob iskrennosti v literature," *Novyi mir* 12 [December 1953]: 218–245). Pomerantsev called instead for "confessional prose" that rejected clichéd language, plots, and characters (see Denis Kozlov and Eleonory Gilburd, eds., *The Thaw: Soviet Society and Culture during the 1950s and 1960s* [Toronto: University of Toronto Press, 2013], 50; see also Anne E. Gorsuch and Diane P. Koenker, *The Socialist Sixties: Crossing Borders in the Second World* [Bloomington: Indiana University Press, 2013]; Marko Dumančić, *Men Out of Focus: The Soviet Masculinity Crisis in the Long Sixties* [Toronto: University of Toronto Press, 2021]).

voice, no longer singing in concert or marching in unison.[5] The film may well have been ahead of its time. Despite its enormous popularity with Soviet audiences, neither Riazanov nor Gurchenko was quite able to replicate its success in their next features: Riazanov's next film, *Devushka bez adresa* (A girl without an address, 1957), was a romantic comedy with roots still firmly planted in Socialist Realism, while his only true musical, *Gusarskaia ballada* (Hussar ballad, 1962), while charming, was a costume drama visually and musically out of step with the modernity and New Wave sensibility of the 1960s.[6] Indeed, following the release of the 1966 *Beregis' avtomobilia* (Beware of the car), Riazanov became a director mainly associated with Soviet comedy rather than musical film as such, though his films always included individual musical numbers. Similarly, Gurchenko's next role in *Devushka s gitaroi* (A girl with a guitar, 1958), written specifically for her, did not bring her the kind of accolades audiences might have expected, while her refusal to cooperate with the KGB during the 1957 International Youth Festival made her the target of a smear campaign that derailed her career for nearly a decade.[7] It was therefore not until 1982 that the two would work together again, in *Vokzal na dvoikh* (Railway station for two).

Nevertheless, *Carnival Night* survives as an example of what a Soviet, non-Stalinist musical comedy could be and do—a film referenced again and again in popular culture. In 1969, Igor' Il'inskii reprised his role from the film in a spin-off, *Staryi znakomyi* (An old friend); in 1996, Evgenii Ginzburg created a concert film for television called *Carnival night 2*; and in 2007, marking the fiftieth anniversary of the film's release, Riazanov directed *Carnival Night 2; or Fifty Years Since*, starring Gurchenko and Vladimir Zel'din. But perhaps the most

---

5 Richard Taylor, "Singing on the Steppes for Stalin: Ivan Pyr'ev and the Kolkhoz Musical in Soviet Cinema," *Slavic Review* 58, no. 1 (Spring 1999).

6 Among other things, the film was based on Aleksandr Gladkov's 1941 play, *Davnym-davno* (A long time ago), which was based on Nadezhda Durova's memoirs of her adventures during the Napoleonic wars. Disguised as a man, Durova became a decorated soldier in the Russian cavalry and the first known female officer in the Russian military. Her memoirs, *Zapiski kavalerist-devitsy* (The cavalry maiden), were published in 1836.

7 On Riazanov, see David MacFadyen, *The Sad Comedy of Èl'dar Riazanov: An Introduction to Russia's Most Popular Filmmaker* (Quebec City: McGill-Queen's University Press, 2003); Alexander Prokhorov, "Cinema of Attractions versus Narrative Cinema: Leonid Gaidai's Comedies and El'dar Riazanov's Satires of the 1960s," *Slavic Review* 62, no. 3 (Fall 2003): 455–472; and Michele Leigh, "A Laughing Matter: El'dar Riazanov and the Subversion of Soviet Gender in Russian Comedy," in *Women in Soviet Film: The Thaw and Post-Thaw Periods*, ed. Marina Rojavin and Tim Harte (New York: Routledge, 2018), 112–133; as well as Riazanov's own memoirs, *Eti neser'eznye, neser'eznye fil'my* (These unserious, unserious films), published in 1977. On Gurchenko, see Rimgalia Salys, "Liudmila Gurchenko: Stardom in the Late Soviet Era," in *Women in Soviet Film: The Thaw and Post-Thaw Periods*, ed. Marina Rojavin and Tim Harte (New York: Routledge, 2018), 28–48.

compelling tribute to the production of *Carnival Night* comes from the 2013 television serial *Ottepel'* (The thaw, directed by Petr Todorovskii), in which a young and inexperienced film director takes over the production of a musical film, *Devushka i brigadir* (A girl and a foreman), and attempts to break out of the confines imposed on the genre by the conventions of Stalinist cinema.

Stalinist Culture and the Imposition of the Voice

Riazanov (1927–2015) represents what might be called the "second generation" of Soviet filmmakers—those who came of age after the war, were educated at the All-Russian State Institute of Cinematography (VGIK), and were taught by the early masters of Soviet cinema. A student of Grigorii Kozintsev, Riazanov attended Sergei Eisenstein's lectures on cinema, graduating from VGIK in 1950. His first job was at the Central Studio for Documentary Film (TsSDF), where he shot and edited newsreels (*kinozhurnaly*), including *Pioneriia* (1931–1987; aimed at Soviet youth and initially created and edited by Arsha Ovanesova), *Soviet Sport* (since 1924), and *Novosti dnia* (News of the day, 1944–1983).[8] He joined Mosfil'm in 1955, where his first feature film was the wide-screen musical film-review *Schastlivaia iunost'* (Happy youth, 1955, co-directed with Sergei Gurov, and released in regular format as *Vesennie golosa* [Spring voices]). That effort was followed by the path-breaking *Carnival Night,* which Riazanov was urged to direct by none other than Ivan Pyr'ev—the director of the Mosfil'm studios (1954–1957), who had made his career directing "tractor musicals," and was, at that time, the most influential man in the Soviet motion picture industry (see chapter five). Riazanov's *Carnival Night* broke all the rules of the Soviet musical film comedy previously established by Pyr'ev and Aleksandrov, undoing the conventions of the Stalin-era tradition.

Like Marlen Khutsiev's *Vesna na Zarechnoi ulitse* (Spring on Zarechnaia Street, 1956) and Mikhail Kalatozov and Sergei Urusevskii's *Letiat zhuravli* (The cranes are flying, 1957), *Carnival Night* was a harbinger of the new cultural freedoms of the Thaw, the release—among other things—from the imposition of ideology being spoken directly from the screen. In *Carnival Night* sound technology, and specifically, broadcasting technology, briefly reverses the hierarchy between the state and its citizens, between the single authoritative voice and the masses. And while Riazanov did not stay with the musical genre, he continued to make what

---

8 *News of the Day* grew out of *Sovkinozhurnal* (1925–1931) and *Soiuzkinozhurnal* (1931–1944).

became known as the "sad comedies" of the 1960s, 1970s, and 1980s, which focused on the ordinary lives of Soviet citizens, caught up in the absurdities of Soviet everyday life (for the Polish analogue, see chapter two). He remains one of the most beloved of Soviet film directors, a "larger than life" figure and "the king of Russian comedy," whose sad films advocated, as David MacFadyen has put it, "cheer in a cheerless land."[9]

We might begin by looking at Riazanov's first feature film, co-directed with Gurov and written by Boris Laskin.[10] Focusing on the miracles of new Soviet technology—a television set that acts as both receiver and transmitter—*Happy Youth* and its later incarnation, *Spring Voices* (hereafter I will refer to both versions of the film as *Happy Youth*), showcased new developments in Soviet cinema through a range of musical numbers shot in wide-screen format.[11] The opening sequence takes us inside a student workshop in Moscow, where young inventors work on various technological and mechanical projects, including radio-controlled vehicles and different kinds of radio-receivers. It seems important to the overall message of the film that the first receiver—the radio—short-circuits, and the students turn eagerly toward an experimental television set that, unlike a regular TV, responds to written or even spoken requests from viewers and can show you "anything you want" (including yourself, a boy you are interested in, and even events from the past, as if literally every aspect of Soviet life has been recorded and can be broadcast at any time). As we learn later in the film, the initials PTPV on the television set stand for "ordinary television, plus imagination" (*prostoi televizor plius voobrazhenie*). We are then treated to an hour of musical programming filmed at the Bolshoi Theater, which, when broadcast in its original wide-screen format, would have given the film viewer the impression of total immersion.

Happy Youth therefore acts as an advertisement for the new visual technology both inside and outside the film: the new Soviet wide-screen technology on the

---

9 MacFadyen, *The Sad Comedy of Èl'dar Riazanov*, 6.

10 Sergei Gurov was a documentary filmmaker and editor; Boris Laskin was a prolific screenwriter, poet, and humorist, whose lyrics included "Tri tankista" ("Three tankmen drivers") and "Marsh tankistov" ("March of the tankmen drivers"), both written for Pyr'ev's 1939 film *Traktoristy* (Tractor drivers). He was the screenwriter for *Carnival Night* (together with Vladimir Poliakov) and author of its comic fable number, "Medved' na balu" ("The bear at the ball").

11 On Soviet wide-screen technology, see Nikolai Mayorov (as Nikolai Maiorov), "Khronika sovetskogo shirokogo ekrana," *Tekhnika i tekhnologii kino* 3 (2009), https://web.archive.org/web/20160305054022/http://ttk.625-net.ru/files/605/531/h_69ffbffaaae86a6e32b3f7de417eeb85; and his "A First in Cinema . . . Stereoscopic Films in Russia and the Soviet Union," *Studies in Russian and Soviet Cinema* 6, no. 2 (2012): 217–239.

one hand, and the (imaginary) interactive television on the other. After rejecting the radio transmitter, the young inventors interact with the television set, asking it questions and receiving answers, requesting specific programs, and the like. If we were to stretch the ideological implications of this conceit, we might say that after years of audio and oral dominance—loudspeakers on Soviet streets, a one-channel radio set in every home, the coming of sound to cinema—there is a choice being made here in favor of the visual image, as well as a desire for two-way communication: this new television responds to viewers' requests, showing them what they want rather than what they are allowed (or supposed) to see. Even the film's second title, *Spring Voices,* used for its non-wide-screen release, underscores the multiplicity of voices that might now be allowed to sound from the imaginary television set and, like Khutsiev's 1956 film, makes reference to the Thaw's most operative metaphor of spring and rebirth.

The larger context for this attention to broadcasting and reception is the history of Soviet radio, along with the introduction of sound and Socialist Realism to Soviet cinema in the early 1930s, both of which produced a certain kind of dominance of the voice over the visual image.[12] As Stephen Lovell has noted, in Russia, from the early 1920s onwards, "the spoken word received new kinds of amplification," both literally (in the form of the loudspeakers that were set up in public places in urban areas) and metaphorically (in the form of broadcasting). Radio offered a way of "projecting the voice of authority into every workplace and communal flat in the USSR" and of showing Soviet people exactly how to "speak Bolshevik."[13] Starting on May 1, 1921, loudspeakers that looked like gramophone pipes were erected in town squares and began to deliver the contents of various officially approved newspaper articles. This became the privileged way that the radio entered Soviet life. A megaphone at the top of a high pole (and its more intimate counterpart—the radio speaker on the wall of a room, hanging from the ceiling), delivering to the consciousness of its audience the State's directives, simply by its position made the official word sacred. The

---

12 See Sabine Hänsgen (as Sabina Hensgen), "'Audio-Vision': O teorii i praktike rannego sovetskogo zvukovogo kino na grani 1930-kh godov," in *Sovetskaia vlast' i media*, ed. Hans Günther (as Hans Giunter) and Sabine Hänsgen (St. Petersburg: Akademicheskii proekt, 2006), 350–364; Iurii Murashov, "Elektrifitsirovannoe slovo. Radio v sovetskoi literature i kul'ture 1920–30-kh godov," in the same volume; Oksana Bulgakowa (as Oksana Bulgakova), *Golos kak kul'turnyi fenomen* (Moscow: Novoe Literaturnoe Obozrenie, 2015); Stephen Lovell, *Russia in the Microphone Age: A History of Soviet Radio, 1919–1970* (Oxford: Oxford University Press, 2015); and Kaganovsky, *Voice of Technology: Soviet Cinema's Transition to Sound, 1928–1935*.

13 Stephen Lovell, "Broadcasting Bolshevik: The Radio Voice of Soviet Culture, 1920s–1950s," *Journal of Contemporary History* 48, no. 1 (2013): 80.

concept of a "voiceover" was literalized, materialized in the form of an intrusive address, accessible to everyone.

Moreover, there was a direct technological as well as ideological link between Soviet radio technology and the new technology of sound film (developed in the Soviet Union around 1927–1928),[14] which in its own way also helped to bring the voice of state power to Soviet screens. Early Soviet sound cinema, with its preference for showing us the sources of sound, such as radio receivers, loudspeakers, and gramophone pipes, borrowed its visual iconography from the new culture of radio-listening (see, for example, the radio-listener in the opening shots of Dziga Vertov's first sound film, *Entuziazm: Simfoniia Donbassa* (Enthusiasm: Symphony of the Donbass, 1930). But more than that, there was a fundamental technical connection between the two media: they used the same *tonfilm* technology to record and reproduce sound, eschewing the unpredictability of live broadcasting to address the mass Soviet listener. The war had brought "the apotheosis of totalitarian broadcasting," as broadcasting was reduced to a single authoritative channel and disseminated to the vast majority of listeners by wire.[15] It is this authoritative voice—Stalin's directives spoken by Iurii Levitan—that *Carnival Night,* and perhaps even *Spring Voices,* tries to disrupt. In *Spring Voices,* we see the radio rejected as a broken and outmoded technology in favor of a new two-way communication system. The suggestion seems pretty clear: given the reality of one-way radio broadcasting, the film imagines instead a world in which audiences would be able to communicate their wishes and desires to the people in charge of the programs, and to see and hear whatever they wanted.

In the early 1950s, another technological revolution took place in film that once again altered the shape of cinematic spectacle, both image and sound. Technicolor, Cinerama, wide-screen, and 3D cinema changed the possibilities of how cinema could look, while innovations in sound technology changed how cinema could sound. What Oksana Bulgakowa has called the "second sound revolution" introduced stereo sound recorded onto magnetic tape, multi-channel

---

14 The first practical sound-on-film systems were created almost simultaneously in the Soviet Union, the United States, and Germany. Pavel Tager began his experiments with sound in Moscow in 1926, and just a few months later, in 1927, Aleksandr Shorin started his own research on synchronized sound in Leningrad. The first experimental sound-on-film program—excerpts from the 1927 film *Baby riazanskie* (Women from Riazan', directed by Ol'ga Preobrazhenskaia)—was demonstrated on October 5, 1929, in Leningrad in the Sovkino Cinema, specially equipped with Shorin's sound-on-film system. On early Soviet sound experiments, see Andrey Smirnov, *Sound in Z: Experiments in Sound and Electronic Music in Early 20th-Century Russia* (London: Koenig Books, 2013).

15 Lovell, *Russia in the Microphone Age: A History of Soviet Radio, 1919–1970,* 147.

sound, improved FM frequencies for radio, directional microphones, and new placement for both microphones (during recording) and speakers (during playback).[16] Like early sound films, Thaw films return again and again to the presence of the tape-recorder, the telephone, and the radio—technologies capable of bringing us disembodied voices, long gone or far away. Indeed, anxieties about the independent nature of the voice permeate sixties cinema, allowing us to hear voices not as "married" to bodies but independent of them. "Listen, Zhenia," Lena tells her friend on the telephone in Marlen Khutsiev's 1967 *Iiul'skii dozhd'* (July rain), "Maybe you don't actually exist? Well, maybe you're not really there. Maybe you're just a voice?"

The changes in sound technology in the 1950s coincided with de-Stalinization and the beginnings of the Khrushchev Thaw, and we can clearly trace this evolution away from the "voice of power" that characterized Soviet sound cinema of the Stalin period in both Riazanov's first musical-review film, *Spring Voices*, and his first musical comedy, *Carnival Night*.

Carnival or *Balagan*?

Riazanov's *Carnival Night* opens with a young woman sliding down a wooden ramp toward the camera, laughing, before pronouncing the stunt a great success: "Amazing!" she says, "this is how our guests will arrive to greet the New Year." The conceit of the film is a New Year's Eve carnival put on by the members of the Moscow House of Culture to ring in the New Year and to show off their artistic skills as amateur artists, dancers, and musicians. Enjoyment of the upcoming festivities is put at risk by the temporary director, Ogurtsov (played by Il'inskii), who is worried about how a carnival with masks, skits, and jokes might be perceived by those at the top and wants to ensure that all skirts are properly long, all jokes explained away, and all semblance of youth culture (such as a jazz band) "isolated" (*izolirovany*). In particular, he wants to open the carnival with a lecture—"about forty minutes or so"—on a serious topic, to give the carnival a properly uplifting feel, replace the jazz band with an orchestra from a senior citizens' home, and turn a clown act into a lesson in morality. It is easy to see that the obvious conflict of the film is between the old guard, represented by Ogurtsov, and the vibrant new youth culture—represented by Lena, Grisha, the

---

16 Oksana Bulgakowa, "Vocal Changes: Marlon Brando, Innokenty Smoktunovsky, and the Sound of the 1950s," in *Sound, Speech, Music in Soviet and Post-Soviet Cinema*, ed. Lilya Kaganovsky and Masha Salazkina (Bloomington: Indiana University Press, 2014), 146.

painter Usikov, the jazz musicians, and everyone else involved in the ruse—who figure out a way not only to put on a New Year's Eve carnival on their own terms, but to make the director its unwitting star. This is accomplished in part by the use of sound technology—specifically, broadcasting technology that, at a crucial moment, projects Ogurtsov's voice out to the entire audience, turning his denunciation into yet one more joke at his expense.

As many critics have noted, both at the time of its release and since, *Carnival Night* is a kind of remake of the 1938 *Volga-Volga,* the third musical comedy directed by Aleksandrov, starring Liubov' Orlova, with music by Isaac Dunaevskii and lyrics by Lebedev-Kumach. It was one of Stalin's all-time favorite films.[17] To quote MacFadyen, almost immediately after the film's release, the press likened *Carnival Night* to *Volga-Volga,* "despite the complete absence of either the ships from that musical classic or anything even resembling a river."[18] In *Volga-Volga,* just as in Riazanov's film, a group of amateur musicians, thwarted by the town's bureaucrat (also played by Il'inskii), sets out to perform at a talent competition in Moscow to show off their musical skills and prove that in the Soviet Union literally *anyone* belonging to any profession can be a musician, a song writer, or a performer, no formal training required.[19] One of the film's memorable lines, "to sing like that you have to study for twenty years," became shorthand for the Stalin period and its utopian aspirations to turn the whole country into a "never-ending round of singing and dancing," embodying on-screen Stalin's mantra, "life has become better, comrades, life has become more joyous."[20] As Prokhorov and Prokhorova point out, however, while the prominence of musical numbers in late-Soviet comedy signals its continuity with the 1930s and 1940s musical comedy, the role of songs in most of these

---

17 See, for example, Dobrenko, "Soviet Comedy Film; or, the Carnival of Authority"; Katerina Clark, "Grigorii Aleksandrov's *Volga-Volga,*" in *Language and Revolution: Making of Modern Political Identities,* ed. Igal Halfin (London: Frank Cass, 2002); Prokhorov and Prokhorova, *Film and Television Genres of the Late Soviet Era.* Famously, Stalin watched *Volga-Volga* numerous times and sent it to US President Roosevelt as a present in 1942. On Aleksandrov, see Rimgaila Salys, *The Musical Comedy Films of Grigorii Aleksandrov: Laughing Matters* (Bristol: Intellect, 2009).

18 MacFadyen, *The Sad Comedy of Èl'dar Riazanov,* 54.

19 As Dobrenko points out, while the characters in *Volga-Volga* are professionally marked (letter carrier, water carrier, yardman, militiaman, cook, waiter, accountant, and so forth), none of them works: "The letter carrier refuses to send telegrams; the water carrier is drunk all the time; the yardman sleeps; the militiaman doesn't protect anyone and doesn't preserve order; the cooks and waiters in the restaurant, instead of serving patrons, sing about their 'winning the many victories on the food-front'; the accountant spends his time with an amateur symphony orchestra" (Dobrenko, "Soviet Comedy Film; or, the Carnival of Authority," 50).

20 Taylor, "Singing on the Steppes for Stalin": 145.

films was radically different from their earlier counterparts: the Soviet mass song of Stalin-era productions was "loud, choral, and served as the ideological dominanta of the narrative." In contrast, "songs in the comedies of Gaidai, Riazanov, Zakharov, and many others are low key, personal and, more often than not, work in counterpoint to the narrative."[21]

Thus, the differences between the two musical comedies are perhaps as informative as their similarities. We might recall that *Volga-Volga* opens with a very deliberate musical address to the viewer (typical for Aleksandrov): "Dear viewers, we are calling your attention to the prologue"—a narrative song that introduces the film and each of its main characters in turn: "Here you see Byvalov, a gigantic bureaucrat. He's played by the actor Il'inskii." As Peter Kupfer has noted, to ensure that the messages of all his musical comedies were delivered clearly, Aleksandrov ended each of his films "by turning the main characters toward the camera to sing a culminating version of the film's theme song." But in *Volga-Volga,* Aleksandrov and Dunaevskii go further by addressing the audience directly at the very beginning of the film: "While the purpose of the final scene is to broadcast the moral message of the film as unambiguously as possible, the direct address at the beginning serves, ostensibly, to introduce the main characters." But the overall effect of this opening, as Kupfer stresses, is more significant because it soon becomes evident that the (diegetic) characters can "hear" the (non-diegetic) music: "As the singing narrator mentions their names, they turn to acknowledge the audience."[22] Each actor is framed by an iris, a stylized reference to early silent film. The choice of this framing (which creates a portrait-like image by limiting the visual field), along with their mugging for the camera and the song's direct address, signals the film's awareness of itself as a theatrical construct, a self-consciousness of itself as spectacle aimed at an audience.

From the prologue, the film opens (literally, by widening out to full frame) onto the happy couple perched on top of a haystack and, as Orlova dismisses the camera and viewer with a wave of her hand, there is a sudden sense of movement as the barge they are on pushes off from the river bank and away from the camera. The shot seems mobile, but, like most shots in the movie, is, in fact, filmed from a single vantage point with a stationary camera. Indeed, it might not be an exaggeration to say that, despite the fact that the plot of the film is about getting to Moscow (and therefore, ostensibly, about mobility),

21 Prokhorov and Prokhorova, *Film and Television Genres of the Late Soviet Era,* 114.

22 Peter Kupfer, "*Volga-Volga*: The Story of a Song," *The Journal of Musicology* 30, no. 4 (Fall 2013): 531.

the film itself is about stasis and immobility.[23] The static frontal shots are a formal way of registering that in the village of Melkovodsk ("Shallow waters"), despite twenty years of Soviet power, nothing has really changed from the "olden days": An urgent ("lightning") telegram is delivered by a slow-moving barge, the telephone connection is so bad that people have to shout out of the window, the horse-and-buggy always stops at the village pub and refuses to move again until it gets a treat, the mass-produced musical instruments are all defective, and the barge spends the first fifteen minutes of the film stuck in the middle of the river. Before anyone can reach Moscow, both the steamship and the sailboat run aground and have to be towed until the passengers are picked up by a motor ship named Joseph Stalin. This country-village backwardness is encapsulated by the character played by Il'inskii, a bureaucrat by the name of "Byvalov"—whose name means a "former person"—interested only in his own personal gain, and specifically, in being promoted and reassigned to a position in Moscow.

In contrast, Riazanov's musical comedy opens with our heroine, Lena (Gurchenko), framed within a cardboard sun on top of a slide, surrounded by fake snow and Christmas trees (fig. 6.2). A highly mobile thirty-second tracking shot follows Lena as she skillfully slides down the slope in a pencil skirt and high heels, confirming that all is going well with New Year's Eve preparations. She briefly chats with the cleaning lady, ducks behind an electrician's ladder (thereby avoiding its occupant), and hurries up the stairs, where she reminds two ballerinas of their upcoming rehearsal. A second minute-long tracking shot picks up Lena at the top of the stairs (now joined by Grisha, the electrician and love interest) and tracks back through the halls of the House of Culture, with Lena and Grisha "walking and talking" toward the camera, until Lena reaches the director's office.[24] Along the way, we learn that a "natural

---

23 Dobrenko likewise observes that "the opposition "movement/immobility" is central to the film (Dobrenko, "Soviet Comedy Film; or, the Carnival of Authority," 51). This is clearly intentional: compare this scene to the opening of Aleksandrov's first musical comedy, *Veselye rebiata* (Jolly fellows, 1934), in which a highly mobile camera tracks across fields and over streams as it follows Leonid Utesov around the countryside. Both films were shot by Vladimir Nil'sen.

24 "Walk and talk" is a storytelling technique used in filmmaking and television production in which a number of characters have a conversation while walking somewhere. In this case, the technique is used to emphasize how busy Lena is, but also to provide smooth transitions from one location to another, and to add visual interest to what might otherwise be static "talking heads" sequences. The walk and talk technique also combines exposition with a visual introduction to the major locations, in this case, the interiors of the Central Theater of the Soviet Army, where the film was shot.

disaster" has occurred—Serafim Ivanovich Ogurtsov has been appointed temporary director—and also that Grisha wants to speak "seriously" with Lena, but that she always finds a way to get out of it. This fluid opening—shot in real time (two long takes) and in a real location (as opposed to a sound stage)—is the complete reverse of the static, theatrical, pointedly antirealist opening of *Volga-Volga*, and speaks to newly transformed genre conventions, the liberated mobility of the camera, and to the youth and energy of the protagonists, all of which marks this film so clearly as a harbinger of the Thaw rather than a product of High Stalinism.[25]

Figure 6.2. Opening shot, Lena and the sun (*Carnival Night*, 1956).

25 Riazanov's cameraman was Arkadii Kol'tsatyi [Abram Naumovich Kopelevich], whose career in Soviet cinema spanned the decades from the 1920s to the 1970s. He worked closely with Fridrich Ermler, and shot, among other films, such classics as *Poruchik Kizhe* (Lieutenant Kizhe, 1934), *Velikii grazhdanin* (The great citizen, 1937), *Muzykal'naia istoriia* (Musical story, 1940), *Velikii perelom* (The great turn, 1945), and *Taras Shevchenko* (1951, with D. Demutskii).

The fluid movement of camera and characters comes to a halt inside the director's office, where we first hear Ogurtsov's voice addressing the New Year's Eve planning committee, before a reverse shot reveals him to the audience, wearing a clown mask (fig. 6.3). "Why does a Soviet citizen need to hide his face?" he asks, rhetorically, concluding: "this isn't normal" ("eto ne tipichno")—a line that will become a refrain throughout the film. Again, it is worth pointing out that Ogurtsov is an entirely different kind of bureaucrat from Byvalov. If Byvalov in *Volga-Volga* was clearly a product of bygone times, as his name suggests, Ogurtsov is the "pickled" bureaucrat of the Stalin era. He acts not out of self-interest or self-promotion, but out of a pathological fear of those at the top. Initially greeting the planning committee with the words, "Are you familiar with Comrade Telegin? A leader of the trade union and deputy of the city council?," he goes on to explain that there is both an obligation and a responsibility to spend the New Year's Eve joyously, but also, pointing meaningfully above him, in such a way that "no one could say anything about it." We must conduct our festivities at the "highest level," he says and, most importantly, "seriously" (which he mispronounces: *sur'ezno*). In response to Lena's explaining that putting on a good show is "no joke," Ogurtsov replies that he doesn't make jokes and won't let others make them either.

Figure 6.3. Ogurtsov, masked (*Carnival Night*, 1956).

Specifically, Ogurtsov wants to safeguard against what he perceives as the evening's lack of seriousness and possible amorality that risks turning a "carnival" (something organized, urban, and sophisticated) into a *balagan* (a disorganized, even chaotic mess) (fig. 6.4).[26] In this way, he is echoing not the bureaucrat Byvalov, but rather Strelka's stuffy tuba-playing accountant fiancé, Alesha, who at the beginning of *Volga-Volga* refuses to acknowledge that a mail carrier could also be a composer, subjects Strelka to a comically tuneless performance of Wagner's "Death of Isolde" on his tuba, and calls her amateur musical group a *balagan*. The opposition, then, is between the formal (sophisticated, urban, organized, classically trained) and the "folksy" (spontaneous, messy, chaotic, unstudied), which in *Volga-Volga* is resolved through a musical merging and the generic reunification of the happy couple at the end of the film. Moreover, as Kupfer argues, more than just the story of Strelka's song, *Volga-Volga* can also be understood as a parable of the development of Soviet music in the 1930s: as he puts it, Aleksandrov and Dunaevskii "not only symbolically reconstruct the growing pains of Soviet music in this period," but also suggest a successful path forward by advocating for a new musical style that merges the traditional oppositions of "high" and "low," professional and amateur, sophisticated and accessible, instrumental and vocal, foreign and domestic, and old and modern.[27] (See chapter one for discussion of a similar merger envisioned in Leon Trystan's *Piętro wyżej* [One Floor Up, 1937] in Polish film of this period.) Alesha and Strelka's winning combination of symphony and folk song joins together the "twin pillars" of Socialist Realism: *ideinost'* (proper ideological content) and *narodnost'* (nationalism). By couching the film's resolution in images of Soviet modernization, Kupfer argues, Aleksandrov and Dunaevsky align their "story of a song" with the broader modernist projects of the Soviet Union in the 1930s—"nation building, mythmaking, and citizen formation"—presenting a utopian working model of successful Soviet music that is "sophisticated yet accessible."[28]

---

26 A *balagan* is an old Russian tradition of traveling village fairs with a puppet theater, clown acts, and so forth.

27 Kupfer, "*Volga-Volga*: The Story of a Song," 537.

28 Ibid.

Figure 6.4. Carnival or *balagan*? direct address to the viewer (*Volga-Volga*, 1938, author's collection).

In *Volga-Volga*, the initial chaos of "the people's creation"—the village's clownish song and dance numbers of the first part of the film and Strelka's own incomplete, halting song about the Volga—give way to high Stalinist pageantry: a stage, a committee, formal attire, properly played instruments, and the transformation of Strelka's simple musical theme into an orchestral composition. As Anna Nisnevich notes, the Volga song, heard by turns as a solo line, in full orchestral rendition, sung *a capella*, played by a jazz band, dutifully read from notation, and "freely improvised upon," emerges as supple enough to embrace as many different styles of delivery as there are groups to perform it—"all while keeping its core, its original melody, fully intact." The little tune comes to exemplify the modern, Soviet community "by transcending any single style of composition or performance."[29] Because of its simplicity and mutability, the song easily wins the competition at the Moscow Olympiad, an "official feast," as Bakhtin would have it, which asserts "all that [is] stable, unchanging, perennial: the existing hierarchy, the existing religious, political, and moral values, norms, and prohibitions."[30] The film's finale underscores allegiance to official Soviet ideology and film as spectacle: standing on a stage and once more directly addressing the viewer, the cast members of *Volga-Volga* warn us that bureaucrats like Byvalov can be found

29 Anna Nisnevich, "Ear of the Beholder: Listening in *Muzykal'naia istoriia* (1940)," in *Sound, Speech, Music in Soviet and Post-Soviet Cinema*, ed. Lilya Kaganovsky and Masha Salazkina (Bloomington: Indiana University Press, 2014), 196.

30 Mikhail Bakhtin, *Rabelais and His World*, trans. Hélène Iswolsky (Bloomington: Indiana University Press, 1965), 9.

anywhere and that enemies may be destroyed through laughter as well as by other means. The stage itself, as Evgenii Dobrenko reminds us, is pompously decorated with Soviet slogans and the medallion-like Soviet state coat of arms, with the members of the presidium dressed in national costumes of the peoples of the Soviet republics. "What we see is a poster," writes Dobrenko, "All the action has been aimed towards the footlights, and has finally reached them."[31]

The film cast takes a bow toward the camera and raises a cardboard cut-out of the word *konets* ("the end"), while the screen fades to black horizontally from the top, imitating a descending curtain. In other words, *Volga-Volga* intentionally preserves the theatrical footlights that Bakhtin finds so alien to carnival culture. As he puts it, "carnival does not know footlights, in the sense that it does not acknowledge any distinction between actors and spectators. Footlights would destroy a carnival, as the absence of footlights would destroy a theatrical performance. It is not spectacle, it is lived (by people—they all participate)."[32] In *Volga-Volga,* the distinction between actors and spectators, spectacle and reality, is very deliberately preserved and the laughter squarely contained within the diegesis, without spilling out beyond its tightly delineated frame.[33]

In contrast to *Volga-Volga* and in the true spirit of Bakhtinian carnival, Riazanov's *Carnival Night* precisely eschews the footlights and dissolves the proscenium. There is little to no distinction in the film between actors and spectators—all are invited to participate in the New Year's Eve celebration, which serves, in Bakhtin's terms, as a "temporary liberation from the prevailing truth and from the established order," marking the suspension of "all hierarchical rank, privileges, norms, and prohibitions."[34] Comrade Telegin and his wife, despite his high rank and her corpulent figure, can jump down the slide and put on a mask, Lena can step off the stage to be joined by singing waitresses, the accountant can recite a pointed fable, the stuffy librarian can sing a beautiful romance, a serious lecturer can suddenly burst out in song and dance mincingly across the stage, and an orchestra of senior citizens can turn out to be a group of young men wearing fake beards. This is precisely the characteristic logic of carnival, of the "turnabout," a continual

---

31 Dobrenko, "Soviet Comedy Film; or, the Carnival of Authority," 51.

32 Bakhtin, *Rabelais and His World,* 7.

33 Though perhaps even here we might ask how a line like "avtora skhvatili" ("they've caught [arrested] the author") played for laughs in 1938, in the middle of the Stalinist terror and nightly arrests. Dobrenko calls this the "phenomenon of state-appropriated laughter," concluding that "Socialist Realism does not know humor, just as it does not know the carnival in the Bakhtinian sense"—"the spectator *must* laugh, since refusal to laugh is understood as a sign of dangerous dissent, a refusal to participate in authority's event." (Dobrenko, "Soviet Comedy Film; or, the Carnival of Authority," 49, 55, 56).

34 Bakhtin, *Rabelais and His World,* 10.

shifting from top to bottom, from front to rear, of numerous parodies and travesties, humiliations, profanations, comic crownings and uncrownings, a second life, a "world inside out" (*à l'envers*) that militates against "all pretense of immutability," and which demands "ever changing, playful, undefined forms."[35] Thus, for example, the heterosexual romance remains extremely chaste—compare, for example, Lena and Grisha's hesitant kiss at the end of the film, with Strelka and Alesha's passionate embrace at the beginning of *Volga-Volga*;[36] rather, as often happens in Soviet film, heterosexual romance is displaced into the homosexual register. Tellingly, there are not one, not two, but four different same-sex embraces: while Grisha is waiting for a kiss from Lena, he gets one from the male janitor instead; two male party guests, each intending to kiss the same woman, end up kissing each other; Ogurtsov gets manhandled by the magician in preparation for his number; the lecturer deeply kisses the painter who got him drunk and then develops a highly mannered way of speaking about the stars, dancing, gesticulating, and swinging his briefcase, before performing his final number off-stage: a rendition of a popular Helena Loubalová song, which he sings first in a low bass and then in a very high falsetto (Figs. 6.5a, 6.5b, 6.5c).

Figure 6.5a. The kiss: Grisha and the janitor.

35 Ibid., 11.

36 The chaste kiss, however, is also a nod to Stalinist convention, if we remember that "after Stalin voiced disapproval of the kissing in *Volga-Volga* (1938), onscreen smooching disappeared from Soviet films, including Pyr'ev's last two musicals" (see chapter five in this volume).

Figure 6.5b. The kiss: two party guests.

Figure 6.5c. The kiss: the lecturer and the painter.

Importantly, there is no return to "normal time" at the end of the film, no recourse to mass song (as in *Circus*), no ideological message spoken directly to the viewer (as in *Volga-Volga*), but simply a question left unanswered: "Will there be a new happiness?" At that point the romantic couple disappears into a sea of dancers as the camera moves back and up to an overhead shot of waltzing couples, streamers, confetti and balloons, and a big clock at the far end of the hall (as opposed to the medallion-like Soviet state coat of arms of *Volga-Volga*), showing that it is now 6:06 am, the morning of the next day. The cut to a blue screen and the words "The End" signals the film's conclusion, but not before Ogurtsov gets in a final word. "Comrades," he says, "just one minute: I want to let you all know, officially, that I take no responsibility for anything that has happened here today!" Or, as a less literal translation would have it: "I take no responsibility for this mess!"

Thus, in *Carnival Night*, something entirely different happens from the usual conventions of the genre of musical comedy in its classic Stalinist form. And, ironically, it is specifically Ogurstov's fear of the *balagan* and his insistence on taking everything "suriously" that turns the New Year's Eve festivities into a carnival in its proper, Bakhtinian sense. In fact, the festivities Lena had initially planned, with their staged musical numbers, tame comedy routines, and showcase of amateur talent (actually performed by professional dancers and musicians) would not have produced the carnival laughter necessary to undo the officialdom of Soviet culture, nor resulted in a film that "updated the syntax of Stalinist musical comedy."[37] For Bakhtin, in carnivals proper, with their long and complex pageants and processions, there was the "feast of fools" (*festa stultorum*) and the "feast of the ass"; there was the special free "Easter laughter" (*risus paschalis*), consecrated by tradition. Civic and social ceremonies and rituals took on a comic aspect as clowns and fools, constant participants in these festivals, mimicked serious rituals; comic protocol, election of a king and queen to preside at a banquet "for laughter's sake" (*roi pour rire*)—"these were sharply distinct from the serious, official, ecclesiastical, feudal, and political cult forms and ceremonials."[38] Ogurtsov's unwitting role as the butt of all the jokes, his unexpected appearances and disappearances on stage, his pompous rhetoric amplified and broadcast for everyone to hear—his playing the "festival ass," in other words—allow for the welcome escape from the

---

37 Prokhorov and Prokhorova, *Film and Television Genres of the Late Soviet Era*, 108.
38 Bakhtin, *Rabelais and His World*, 5.

"usual official way of life."[39] In *Carnival Night,* as in a true Bakhtinian carnival, the laughter is not individual, but "of all the people"; it is directed at everyone, and it is ambivalent: "gay, triumphant, mocking, deriding. It asserts and denies; buries and revives."[40] Ogurtsov himself underscores this fact in his denunciation, commenting that his descent onto the stage in a magic box suspended on a wire caused "the unhealthy laughter of the entire audience" ("nezdorovyi smekh vsego zala"), and begs the authorities to take appropriate measures against those comrades who have "very naïvely taken me for a fool" ("ochen' naivno dymaiut, chto oni nashli v moem litse duraka"). He pauses here to confirm the last sentence, which his secretary dutifully repeats, "They've taken you for a fool."

The End of the Mass Song and Finding an Individual Voice

The genre of musical comedy, as it developed together with the sound film, was meant to showcase unity, anticipating the demands of Socialist Realism that were being formulated at around the same time. In 1935, the All-Union Creative Conference on Cinema Affairs adopted the principles of Socialist Realism as set out for literature, with sound cinema now ready to furnish a form "intelligible to the millions." By 1935, Soviet cinema had produced around twenty sound films, two of which became instant classics of Socialist Realism: the civil war film *Chapaev* (directed by the Vasiliev brothers, 1934) and the musical comedy *Veselye rebiata* (Jolly fellows, directed by Aleksandrov, 1934). The shift in Soviet ideology was also underscored by the publication, likewise in 1935, of Boris Shumiatskii's *Kinematografiia millionov* (A cinema for the millions), which became a blueprint for Soviet cinema.[41] Shumiatskii regarded sound technology as what would make Socialist Realism possible in the cinema. He noted Stalin's express command that Soviet cinema develop synchronized sound, which would act as a "large, supplementary force to the artistic expression of our ideas."[42] In *Cinema for the Millions,* Shumiatskii devoted an entire chapter to *Jolly Fellows,*

---

39 Ibid., 8.

40 Ibid., 11–12.

41 An excerpt from Shumiatskii's book, translated as "A Cinema for the Millions," may be found in Richard Taylor and Ian Christie, *The Film Factory: Russian and Soviet Cinema in Documents, 1896–1939* (London: Routledge, 1988), 358–369.

42 Boris Shumiatskii, *Kinematografiia millionov. Opyt analiza* (Moscow: Kinofotoizdat, 1935), 12.

arguing that even its critics could not deny "its cheerfulness, its *joie de vivre* and its laughter." He particularly praised those early sound films—*Vstrechnyi* (Counterplan, composed by D. Shostakovich, sound operated by L. Arnshtam, 1932), *Poruchik Kizhe* (Lieutenant Kizhe, composed by S. Prokofiev, 1934), and *Ankara—serdtse Turtsii* (Ankara—heart of Turkey, sound directed by Arnshtam, composed by Osman Zeki Üngör, Erkem Zeki, and Cemal Reşit Rey, 1934)—in which sound was "tightly" linked with the visual image, in which there was no experimentation, no unnecessary sound effects, and where music was not used to create "its own sound-objects," but simply added to the visual image. He contrasted these successful uses of sound with several particularly unsuccessful examples—*Dezertir* (Deserter, directed by V. Pudovkin, composed by Iu. Shaporin, 1933), *Vosstaniie rybakov* (Revolt of the fishermen, directed by E. Piskator, composed by Vladimir Fere, N. Chemberdskii, and Ferenc Szabó, 1934), and O. Dovzhenko's *Ivan* (composed by Iu. Meitus and B. Liatoshinskii, 1932)—in which sound was disjointed from the visual image. Referencing Eisenstein, Pudovkin, and Aleksandrov's 1928 "Statement on Sound,"[43] Shumiatskii argued that sound should not be used contrapuntally, but instead, can be organized in such a way that it provides a "*realistic* image," creating a unified audio-visual field.[44]

The Stalinist musical comedy was born precisely out of this need for "light, joyous entertainment," which, according to Shumiatskii, was the "right" of all Soviet citizens. But it was also born from the introduction of sound to cinema: as Richard Barrios has argued, "as the one genre not possible in silent film, musicals were inevitable."[45] It was "[neither] theater nor cinema, but something altogether new," as René Clair commented after seeing *The Broadway Melody* (directed by Harry Beaumont, 1929).[46] In the Soviet Union, the two leading figures in the production of Soviet musical comedies were Aleksandrov and Pyr'ev. Most notably, Aleksandrov produced (in close collaboration with Dunaevskii and Lebedev-Kumach) *Jolly Fellows, Circus, Volga-Volga,* and *Svetlyi put'* (The radiant path, 1941), films that are considered the epitome of the genre to this day. They specifically reflected Stalin's cultural mandate to "turn fairy tales into reality," uniting ideology with entertainment and creating an idealized space of

43 Eisenstein, Pudovkin, and Aleksandrov's "Zaiavka (Budushchee zvukovoi fil'my)" was first published in Russian in *Zhizn' iskusstva*, August 5, 1928, and *Sovetskii ekran*, August 7, 1928. It is translated as "Statement on Sound" in Taylor and Christie, *The Film Factory*, 234–235.

44 Shumiatskii, *Kinematografiia millionov. Opyt analiza*, 222–225.

45 Richard Barrios, *A Song in the Dark: The Birth of the Musical Film* (Oxford: Oxford University Press, 2010), 59.

46 Quoted ibid., 67.

Soviet togetherness filled with singing and dancing. As Katerina Clark has written, *Volga-Volga* was the third of four musical comedies made by Aleksandrov in the 1930s "to orders from on high." In August 1932, Aleksandrov had been invited to Gorky's dacha, where Stalin, who "happened" to be visiting, spoke of the need for a new Soviet culture that would be an "upbeat, joyous art [*bodroe, zhizneradostnoe iskusstvo*], full of fun and laughter":

> In 1933 (or the fall of 1932, dates vary) the Party Central Committee called a conference of film people at which they advanced the slogans "Give Us Comedy" and "Laughter Is the Brother of Strength," and called on the country's chief film directors to produce comedies. Those assembled were told that viewers' letters were demanding comedies. Eisenstein thereupon produced a comedy script *MMM*, one of his many projects of the 1930s not to reach fruition. These developments coincided more or less with the coining of the term Socialist Realism (May 1932) and with the attempt by leading figures in Soviet culture and politics in the ensuing months to try to formulate exactly what it might mean. *Volga-Volga,* it should be noted, was described in the standard Soviet book on film comedies of that era (by R. Iurenev, 1964), as a paradigm of socialist realist comic film.[47]

Similarly, during the Stalin period, Pyr′ev was known best for his "tractor musicals" (several also scored by Dunaevskii and with lyrics by Lebedev-Kumach), which, as Taylor has put it, perfectly captured on celluloid Stalin's mantra (see chapter five).[48] It was Pyr′ev who encouraged Riazanov to make *Carnival Night,* the first post-Stalinist musical comedy, which explicitly takes on the conventions of the genre. Interestingly enough, however, Pyr′ev not only convinced Riazanov to make *Carnival Night* but was also responsible for casting both Gurchenko and Il′inskii, and insisting that Riazanov reshoot various comedic numbers.[49] As Mariia Molchanova tells it,

---

47 Clark, "Grigorii Aleksandrov's *Volga-Volga,*" 185.

48 Taylor, "Singing on the Steppes for Stalin": 145.

49 Mariia Molchanova, "*Karnaval'naia noch'*: pervaia samostoiatel'naia rabota Riazanova," Diletant. media, 2017, accessed October 12, 2021, https://diletant.media/articles/38597118/.

> Ivan Aleksandrovich [Pyr'ev] painstakingly selected music and words: the film was a musical and the experienced master understood how much the quality of the footage depended on it. Some things happened for the first time on the set; for example, the soundtrack for the songs was recorded separately. When Liudmila Markovna [Gurchenko] sang a song without the accompaniment of the orchestra, using only one earpiece, the whole film crew came to watch. For the first time, instead of pavilions for filming, Riazanov used the real interiors of the Soviet Army Theater. During the filming process, there was a lot of improvisation: this is how the lecturer Almazov (Sergei Filippov) appeared literally from real life. At that time there was a widespread fashion for paid lecturers who were invited to deliver public lectures.[50]

In this way, the "master" of Stalinist musical comedy was also partially responsible (perhaps, unwittingly) for the "mess" of its undoing.

By the late thirties, when the transition to sound was complete, the Soviet film industry really had become a cinema "intelligible to the millions," with sound seamlessly synchronized with the moving image and serving as its ideological support, with an emphasis on dialogue and song and dance numbers, and no contrapuntal or dialogic or other formalist "tricks." But the new sound technology brought with it an extradiegetic element: the "out-of-field" voice now audible from the screen. With uncanny visibility, Soviet sound cinema (re)produced not just *any* voice, but the acousmatic voice of state power—"unanchored" and "free-floating"—that addressed the viewer directly from the screen. Sound film in general and musical film in particular played a role in the creation of a "cinema for the millions" and the production of a cinema "intelligible to the masses."[51] Much of this was turned upside down by the Twentieth Party Congress and the process of de-Stalinization that began dismantling the Stalin cult and its cinematic supports. Indeed, to a degree, Khrushchev's "secret" speech created its own "carnival time," a "second life of the people," who for a brief time "entered

---

50 Ibid.

51 Following on the heels of the successful releases of *Chapaev* and *Jolly Fellows*, the 1935 All-Union Creative Conference on Cinema Affairs adopted the principles of Socialist Realism as set out for literature. But the first shift in ideology can be traced back to the 1928 All-Union Party Conference on Cinema, which first decreed that Soviet cinema "must furnish a 'form that is intelligible to the millions.'" See B. Ol'khovyi, *Puti kino. Pervoe vsesoiuznoe partiinoe soveshchanie po kinematografii* (Moscow: Teakinopechat', 1929).

the utopian realms of community, freedom, equality, and abundance."[52] As Riazanov himself noted in his memoirs, "We were making *Carnival Night* in 1956 when the Twentieth Party Congress opened up new perspectives on the development of our country. In our understanding, the figure of Ogurtsov represented everything that 'had been' [*otzhivshee*], with his morality of 'what if something happens?' and his position that it is always easier to ban something than to allow it."[53]

Through the assistance of "modern technology," the off-screen voice (of state power, of ideology, of Socialist Realist conventions) is folded back into the diegesis and made ridiculous: first, by Grisha trying to express his intimate feelings via a gramophone record that is accidently broadcast to the entire House of Culture; and second, by Ogurtsov dictating his official letter of denunciation, which is intentionally broadcast to an entire ballroom of merry guests ringing in the New Year. Making Ogurtsov the "festival ass" was, of course, a pointed move in 1956—it signaled the dismantling of a certain kind of official word and the first sign of the Thaw. Ogurtsov's posturing in front of the mirror with his hand in his vest is clearly a reference to Napoleon, and to all the other dictators recently diseased: Mussolini, Hitler, Stalin (fig. 6.6). The power of laughter is called upon to undo the power of authoritarian rule—and suddenly, after twenty years of marching in lockstep, we find ourselves beyond the need for a unified voice, no longer singing in concert or unison. Ogurtsov's final address to the viewer, "I take absolutely no responsibility for this mess!" while looking directly at the camera, is a typical comedic breaking of the fourth wall, but it also recalls all the moments in Stalinist cinema of characters speaking ideological messages directly to the viewer (fig. 6.7).[54] In this case, it also testifies to the undoing of authoritarian speech, which is exiled beyond the borders of the film itself (between the words "The End" and "The End of the Film"). As MacFadyen puts it, Ogurtsov has been displaced, and is now "off-screen and locked away, an ignored voice. His voice—outside of our sentimental busy frame—has even become nondiegetic; nobody hears it or cares to. . . ."[55]

---

52 Bakhtin, *Rabelais and His World*, 9.

53 El'dar Riazanov, *Eti neser'eznye, neser'eznye fil'my* (Moscow: Soiuz Kinematografistov, 1977), 32.

54 As in the finale of *Volga-Volga*, but also in a film like Fridrich Ermler's *Krest'iane* (The peasants, 1935) and Dovzhenko's *Aerograd* (Aerocity, 1935).

55 MacFayden, *The Sad Comedy of Èl'dar Riazanov*, 63.

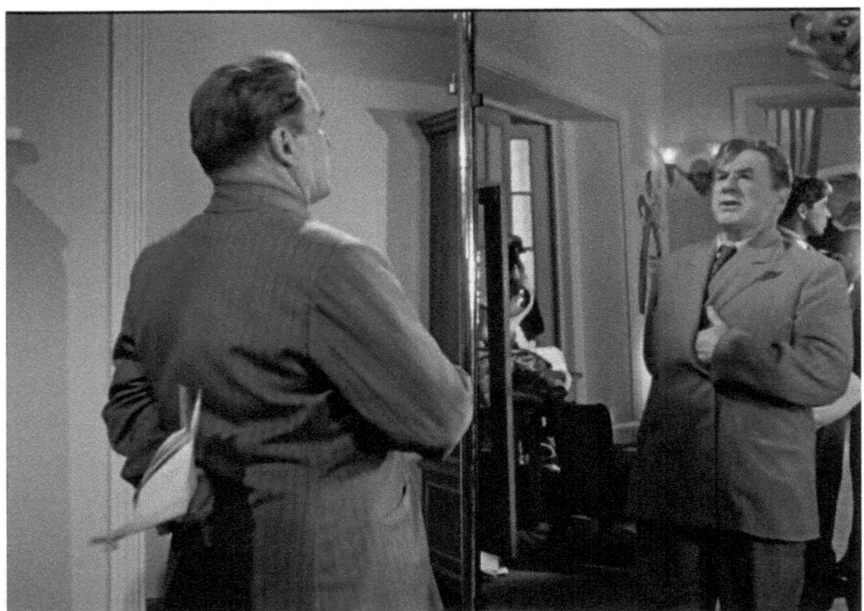

Figure 6.6. Napoleon (*Carnival Night,* 1956).

Figure 6.7. "I take absolutely no responsibility for this mess!" (*Carnival Night,* 1956).

Both Clark and Dobrenko draw our attention to the "twenty years" needed to learn how to sing, pointing out that the span marks exactly the time between the 1917 Revolution and the making of *Volga-Volga,* as well as the time between

Volga-Volga and *Carnival Night,* but I want to suggest a different temporality. For Bakhtin, the carnival feast is essentially related to time, but it also linked to moments of crisis, "of breaking points in the cycle of nature or in the life of society and man"[56]—in this case, the end of Stalinism, signaled by the Twentieth Party Congress and Khrushchev's "secret" speech. But carnival time, as Bakhtin stresses, is only a temporary liberation from the prevailing truth and from the established order[57] and Riazanov's film seems very much aware of this. The temporality of the film is marked specifically by the central song, the "five minutes" of remaining time of the old year during which you could still fix everything that had gone wrong, before the New Year strikes. As Usikov concludes in one of the film's final lines, "It is bitter, bitter, my friends, to find that we have grown a year older. But, since we are still young, there is no time to lose!" Indeed, we might think of *Carnival Night* not only as the inverse of the Stalinist musical comedy, but also as the opposite of Riazanov's sad comedies to come: an upbeat musical film that wants to believe that a new happiness might still be possible, if only for "five minutes."

Bibliography

Bakhtin, Mikhail. *Rabelais and His World.* Translated by Hélène Iswolsky. Bloomington: Indiana University Press, 1965.

Barrios, Richard. *A Song in the Dark: The Birth of the Musical Film.* Oxford: Oxford University Press, 2010.

Bulgakowa, Oksana. "Vocal Changes: Marlon Brando, Innokenty Smoktunovsky, and the Sound of the 1950s." In *Sound, Speech, Music in Soviet and Post-Soviet Cinema,* edited by Lilya Kaganovsky and Masha Salazkina, 145–162. Bloomington: Indiana University Press, 2014.

Clark, Katerina. "Grigorii Aleksandrov's *Volga-Volga.*" In *Language and Revolution: Making of Modern Political Identities,* edited by Igal Halfin, 184–199. London: Frank Cass, 2002.

Chion, Michel. *The Voice in Cinema.* Translated by Claudia Gorbman. New York: Columbia University Press, 1999.

Dobrenko, Evgeny. "Soviet Comedy Film; or, the Carnival of Authority." *Discourse* 17, no. 3 (Spring 1995): 49–57.

Dumančić, Marko. *Men Out of Focus: The Soviet Masculinity Crisis in the Long Sixties.* Toronto: University of Toronto Press, 2021.

Eizenshtein [Eisenstein], Sergei, Vsevolod Pudovkin, and Grigorii Aleksandrov, "Zaiavka (Budushchee zvukovoi fil'my)." *Zhizn' iskusstva,* August 5, 1928, and *Sovetskii ekran,* August 7, 1928.

---

56 Bakhtin, *Rabelais and His World,* 9.

57 Ibid., 10.

Gorsuch, Anne E., and Diane P. Koenker, eds. *The Socialist Sixties: Crossing Borders in the Second World*. Bloomington: Indiana University Press, 2013.

Hänsgen, Sabine [Sabina Hensgen]. "'Audio-Vision': O teorii i praktike rannego sovetskogo zvukovogo kino na grani 1930-kh godov." In *Sovetskaia vlast' i media*, edited by Hans Günther [Hans Giunter] and Sabine Hänsgen [Sabina Hensgen], 350–364. St. Petersburg: Akademicheskii proekt, 2006.

Kaganovsky, Lilya. *Voice of Technology: Soviet Cinema's Transition to Sound, 1928–1935*. Bloomington: Indiana University Press, 2018.

Kozlov, Denis, and Eleonory Gilburd, eds. *The Thaw: Soviet Society and Culture during the 1950s and 1960s*. Toronto: University of Toronto Press, 2013.

Kupfer, Peter. "*Volga-Volga*: The Story of a Song," *The Journal of Musicology* 30, no. 4 (Fall 2013): 530–576.

Leigh, Michele. "A Laughing Matter: El'dar Riazanov and the Subversion of Soviet Gender in Russian Comedy." In *Women in Soviet Film: The Thaw and Post-Thaw Periods*, edited by Marina Rojavin and Tim Harte, 112–133. New York: Routledge, 2018.

Lovell, Stephen. "Broadcasting Bolshevik: The Radio Voice of Soviet Culture, 1920s–1950s," *Journal of Contemporary History* 48, no. 1 (2013): 78–97.

———. *Russia in the Microphone Age: A History of Soviet Radio, 1919–1970*. Oxford: Oxford University Press, 2015.

MacFadyen, David. *The Sad Comedy of Èl'dar Riazanov: An Introduction to Russia's Most Popular Filmmaker*. Quebec City: McGill-Queen's University Press, 2003.

Mayorov, Nikolai [Nikolai Maiorov]. "Khronika sovetskogo shirokogo ekrana," *Tekhnika i tekhnologii kino* 3 (2009). Accessed October 12, 2021. https://web.archive.org/web/20160305054022/http://ttk.625-net.ru/files/605/531/h_69ffbffaaae86a6e32b3f7de417eeb85.

———. "A First in Cinema . . . Stereoscopic Films in Russia and the Soviet Union/" *Studies in Russian and Soviet Cinema* 6, no. 2 (2012): 217–239.

Molchanova, Mariia. "*Karnaval'naia noch'*: pervaia samostoiatel'naia rabota Riazanova." Diletant. media, 2017. Accessed October 12, 2021. https://diletant.media/articles/38597118/.

Murashov, Iurii. "Elektrifitsirovannoe slovo. Radio v sovetskoi literature i kul'ture 1920–30-kh godov." In *Sovetskaia vlast' i media*, edited by Hans Günther [Hans Giunter] and Sabine Hänsgen [Sabina Hensgen], 17–38. St. Petersburg: Akademicheskii Proekt, 2006.

Nisnevich, Anna. "Ear of the Beholder: Listening in *Muzykal'naia istoriia* (1940)." In *Sound, Speech, Music in Soviet and Post-Soviet Cinema*, edited by Lilya Kaganovsky and Masha Salazkina, 193–211. Bloomington: Indiana University Press, 2014.

Ol'khovyi, B. *Puti kino. Pervoe vsesoiuznoe partiinoe soveshchanie po kinematografii*. Moscow: Teakinopechat', 1929.

Pomerantsev, Vladimir. "Ob iskrennosti v literature." *Novyi mir* 12 (December 1953): 218–245.

Prokhorov, Alexander. "Cinema of Attractions versus Narrative Cinema: Leonid Gaidai's Comedies and El'dar Riazanov's Satires of the 1960s." *Slavic Review* 62, no. 3 (Fall 2003): 455–472.

Prokhorov, Alexander, and Elena Prokhorova. *Film and Television Genres of the Late Soviet Era*. New York: Bloomsbury, 2017.

Riazanov. El'dar. *Eti neser'eznye, neser'eznye fil'my*. Moscow: Soiuz Kinematografistov, 1977.

Salys, Rimgaila, *The Musical Comedy Films of Grigorii Aleksandrov: Laughing Matters*. Bristol: Intellect, 2009.

———. "Liudmila Gurchenko: Stardom in the Late Soviet Era." In *Women in Soviet Film: The Thaw and Post-Thaw Periods*, edited by Marina Rojavin and Tim Harte, 28–48. New York: Routledge, 2018.

Shumiatskii, Boris. *Kinematografiia millionov. Opyt analiza.* Moscow: Kinofotoizdat, 1935.

Smirnov, Andrey. *Sound in Z: Experiments in Sound and Electronic Music in Early 20th-Century Russia.* London: Koenig Books, 2013.

Taylor, Richard. "Boris Shumyatsky and the Soviet Cinema in the 1930s: Ideology as Mass Entertainment." *Historical Journal of Film, Radio and Television* 6, no. 1 (1986): 43–64.

———. "Singing on the Steppes for Stalin: Ivan Pyr'ev and the Kolkhoz Musical in Soviet Cinema." *Slavic Review* 58, no. 1 (Spring 1999): 143–159.

——— [Richard Teilor]. "K topografii utopii v stalinskom miuzikle." In *Sovetskoe bogatstvo. Stat'i o kul'ture, literature i kino*, edited by Marina Balina, Evgenii Dobrenko, and Iurii Murashov, 358–370. St. Petersburg: Akademicheskii proekt, 2002.

Taylor, Richard, and Ian Christie, eds. *The Film Factory: Russian and Soviet Cinema in Documents, 1896–1939.* London: Routledge, 1988.

CHAPTER 7

Constructing the Pop Diva: Alla Pugacheva, Sofia Rotaru, and the Celebrity Musical of the 1970s–1980s

Alexander Prokhorov and Elena Prokhorov

In the 1970s and 1980s, Alla Pugacheva and Sofia Rotaru became the two leading pop singers in the Soviet Union.[1] They competed for the status of top singer during the last two decades of the Soviet Union and played a key role in redefining the modes of pop music that dominated Soviet radio and television broadcasts as well as LP recordings. Both performers used the genre of the film musical in promoting their careers. This chapter examines two film musicals, *Zhenshchina, kotoraia poet* (The woman who sings, directed by Aleksandr Orlov, 1978 [hereafter *WWS*]) and *Dusha* (*Soul*, directed by Aleksandr Stefanovich, 1981), specifically the ways they changed Soviet conventions of the genre and, in the case of *WWS*, challenged patriarchal norms of late-Soviet society.

Rotaru was born in a Moldovan family in rural Western Ukraine and started her career in Chernivtsi. The Soviet musical industry initially cast her as an ethnic pop singer. For example, in 1965 and 1966 she appeared in short musical documentary films, *Pesni schastlivogo kraia* (Songs of a happy land, directed by

1 Aleksei Beliakov, *Alla Pugacheva. Zhizn' i udivitel'nye prikliucheniia velikoi pevitsy* (Moscow: Komsomol'skaia Pravda, 2019), 118; David MacFadyen, *Red Stars: Personality and the Soviet Popular Song, 1955–1991* (Montreal: McGill-Queen's University Press, 2001), 142; Olga Partan, "Alla: The Jester-Queen of Russian Pop Culture," *Russian Review* 3 (2007): 484; Fedor Razzakov, *Pugacheva protiv Rotaru. Velikie sopernitsy* (Moscow: Eksmo, 2011), 5.

Rostislav Sin'ko) about the good life in Soviet Western Ukraine and *Solovei iz sela Marshintsy* (The nightingale from the village of Marshintsy, directed by Rostislav Sin'ko), roughly with the same imperial idea about Western Ukraine, produced by the Ukrainian television studio Ukrtelefilm. Both films framed a young talent singing in Moldovan, with Russian voiceover explaining that Sofia Rotar', a daughter of a simple grape farmer, recently had become famous not only in Ukraine, but in Moscow as well.[2] Credits in *The Nightingale* depicted the singer's success by placing her profile next to the Kremlin tower (fig. 7.1). The early days of Rotaru's career summarized in this image, in fact, replicated the master plot of Stalin-era musicals.[3] In 1971, the film musical *Chervona ruta* (Red flower, 1971) launched Rotaru's career beyond Ukraine.[4] Even though she

Figure 7.1. Sofia Rotaru's profile in the credits of the Ukrainian documentary film *Solovei iz sela Marshintsy* (Nightingale from the village of Marshintsy), 1966, dir. Rostislav Sin'ko.

---

2 Sofia Rotar' was the second of six children, several of whom also had a stage career of their own. At times they performed with Sofia, the most successful sibling. In a way the Rotar' family may be seen as a Soviet counterpart of the (Michael) Jackson family.

3 For a discussion of Stalin-era musical genre conventions, see Rimgaila Salys's chapter in this volume (chapter five) and her monograph on Grigorii Aleksandrov (Rigmalia Salys, *The Musical Comedy Films of Grigorii Aleksandrov: Laughing Matters* [Bristol: Intellect, 2009]).

4 *Chervona ruta* is a mythological flower with magic power from a Ukrainian folk legend. The legend goes that this flower turns red on Ivan Kupalo Day, and if a girl finds the flower, she will find love. In addition to this romantic overtone, *chervona* (red in Ukrainian) possibly was music to ideological censors' ears. For more information on Ivan Kupalo's Day see Linda J. Ivanits, *Russian Folk Belief* (Armonk: M. E. Sharpe, 1989), 10–11.

remained a pop folk singer, she started touring with her own musical group, Chervona Ruta, managed by her husband, Anatolii Evdokimenko. The following year the sole Soviet state-owned record label, Melodiia, released Rotaru's solo LP record (fig. 7.2).[5]

Figure 7.2. Sofia Rotaru's first LP.

Rotaru continued performing ethnic folk pop until the late 1970s. With the growth of her all-Union popularity, she received offers from composers to perform Russian language songs, both lyrical and patriotic, which ultimately led to her status as the leading Soviet pop singer. She quickly became the favorite performer of several Politburo members, including Leonid Brezhnev himself,[6]

---

5 Razzakov, *Pugacheva protiv Rotaru. Velikie sopernitsy*, 20–21.

6 Pugacheva, on the other hand, enjoyed the support of Filipp Bobkov, the KGB general who was the head of the Fifth Directorate in charge of censorship and political surveillance over the intelligentsia and cultural affairs at large. Hence, as the leading pop singer in the police state, Pugacheva was of obvious interest to the KGB general in charge of culture. Bobkov did not try to recruit the performer; rather, he occasionally helped her with her career (Beliakov, *Alla Pugacheva. Zhizn' i udivitel'nye prikliucheniia velikoi pevitsy*, 177–178). In 1983–1984, the unruly Pugacheva, who was on tour in the German Democratic Republic, negotiated a defection with a French producer who had arranged her concert in Olympia Hall in Paris in 1982. Luckily for the KGB, they caught wind of this plan via an interpreter who also worked as a KGB agent. As a result, Pugacheva met with her "sponsor" Bobkov and somehow changed her mind (Razzakov, *Pugacheva protiv Rotaru. Velikie sopernitsy*, 139).

and in the 1970s she even started touring abroad—in 1973 in West Germany, and then performing at the Bulgarian Music Festival, Golden Orpheus. In 1974, 1977, and 1978 Rotaru represented the Soviet Union at the Sopot International Music Festival. Musical films—the short documentaries mentioned above as well as features later in her career—promoted her celebrity status. *Soul* played a pivotal role in Rotaru's career because in the course of this film's production she shed the image of an ethnic performer and started collaborating with Soviet rock musicians, aspiring to a career as an international pop singer.

In contrast, Pugacheva from the very beginning enjoyed the career of a Soviet pop singer devoid of any folk flavor.[7] Her first song, titled "Robot," was broadcast on the radio program "Good Morning!" in 1965 and dealt with a typical Thaw-era theme—humanizing an automaton. She collaborated with vocal-instrumental ensembles (VIAs), which emerged in the 1960s as a Soviet response to the rising popularity of Western rock music in the Soviet Union.[8] Many of the VIAs performed folk-pop and sang in the languages of Soviet republics: Ukrainian, Belorussian, Moldovan, Uzbek, and so on.[9] But Pugacheva sang with VIAs performing in Russian, first with Novyi elektron, then with Moskvichi, and later with Veselye rebiata.[10] Notably, in the early 1970s she also served as a vocalist for Oleg Lundstrem's big band—a jazz collective that performed American-style music after their post-World War II reimmigration from China.[11] Like Rotaru, Pugacheva saw the film musical as a vehicle to promote her celebrity status nationwide. In other words, instead of a talented singer performing numbers in a socialist realist narrative—a standard genre model from the 1930s through the 1960s—the new film musical focused exclusively on the persona of the pop diva. Both Rotaru and Pugacheva cultivated an image of the diva, who, in the words of Motti Regev, organize their celebrity status "around

---

7 Pugacheva was trained as a music teacher. For her graduation exam in 1968, she chose to stage a choral version of Isaak Dunaevskii's "Lullaby" from Grigorii Aleksandrov's musical *Tsirk* (Circus, 1936). The exam included both choral and solo parts. Though she received a good grade for the choral part, her solo performance on the exam did not go as well. She failed the test because her performance was considered too theatrical and infected with a pop music flavor, which was unacceptable for the Soviet educational system (Razzakov, *Pugacheva protiv Rotaru. Velikie sopernitsy*, 16).

8 Richard Stites, *Russian Popular Culture* (Cambridge: Cambridge University Press, 1992), 162–163.

9 For example, Chervona Ruta sang in Ukrainian, Pesniary performed in Belarusian, Norok performed in Moldovan, Yalla—in Uzbek. Of course, being "minor" brothers and sisters in the big Soviet family of nations, each of these groups also included in their repertoire songs in Russian.

10 Beliakov, *Alla Pugacheva. Zhizn' i udivitel'nye prikliucheniia velikoi pevitsy*, 79–81.

11 Ibid., 82–87.

projections of dramatized and magnified visual images of femininity, coupled with a musical repertoire that encompasses diverse pop-rock styles."[12]

Soviet Musicals in the 1970s–1980s

Since the star singer played the central role in the late socialist musical, her professional career organized the narrative.[13] Such a narrative constituted a major departure from the conventions of the Soviet film musical as it took shape under Stalin. The primary focus in the latter was on labor and social mobilization. In contrast to the Hollywood musical, where song and dance numbers were about romance and staging the show, musical numbers in Stalinist films highlighted work (see chapter five). Work at the factory or on the collective farm was joyful and brought happiness to the characters. Any romance culminating this utopian happiness was a bonus for the audience.

In contrast, musicals of the 1970s and 1980s privilege the performer's professional career and her agency, which often manifests itself in a conflict with the musical collective. Notably, the individual performer is proven correct in this confrontation with the group—a plot development tabooed during earlier Soviet periods. This career-development story motivates the choice of settings and reflects major changes in Soviet society. Specifically, films feature the locations of leisure and entertainment industries where the protagonist's professional life takes place: concert halls, recording studios, seaside resorts, and even night clubs. Factory and collective farm mobilization are no longer at the center of the genre, which instead concentrates on the individual choices of the star and her professional success. In lieu of the big Soviet family, the celebrity is

---

12 Motti Regev, *Pop-Rock Music: Aesthetic Cosmopolitanism in Late Modernity* (Hoboken: Wiley, 2013), 39. Like Madonna, almost from the very outset of her career, Pugacheva has been projecting the image of a rebellious woman on top whom you either love or hate but cannot ignore. While equally talented and successful, Rotaru in her artistic persona was somewhat more contained.

13 In addition to *The Woman Who Sings* and *Soul*, popular musicals of the late-socialist era include Aleksandr Orlov's *Udivitel'nyi mal'chik* (Amazing boy, 1970), Aleksandr Stefanovich's *Dorogoi mal'chik* (Dear boy [dear in the sense of both beloved and costly], 1974), Nikolai Koval'skii's *Tol'ko v miuzik-holle* (Only in the music hall, 1980), Tat'iana Lioznova's *Karnaval* (Carnival, 1981), Viktor Makarov and Aleksandr Polynnikov's *Beregite zhenshchin* (Take good care of women, 1981), Valerii Shulzhik's *Prezhde chem rasstat'sia* (Before parting, 1984). Mark Zakharov's films for television, such as *Dvenadtsat' stul'ev* (Twelve chairs, 1976) and *Obyknovennoe chudo* (An ordinary miracle, 1978), are a related phenomenon. All these works focus on artistic agency, frequently expressed through musical numbers.

surrounded by a professional community, and relations within this community are an indispensable part of the narrative.

The late Soviet musical brought to a wider audience those performers and musical genres that used to be invisible in cinemas. In the case of pop music performers, such as Pugacheva or Rotaru, they were usually limited to the TV screen, or sang offscreen, often uncredited. As for rock musicians, such as Mashina vremeni (Time Machine, featured for the first time in *Soul*), they could not even appear on television, let alone the big screen. Even when Pugacheva, Rotaru, and kindred singers were included in television concerts, they were just items in a bigger master plot, as, for instance, in the "Song of the Year" television concert on New Year's Day,[14] where these singers represented important ideological themes, such as the Great Patriotic War or the "family" of Soviet republics. For example, Rotaru, for whose artistic persona's folk identity was important, represented either Soviet Ukraine or Soviet Moldavia. In her turn, Pugacheva embodied the modern Soviet Russian woman and, true to the logic of the empire, was ethnically unmarked, for Russianness was a default identity.

Despite the rigid structure of these broadcast events, even in such ideologically controlled shows as the annual "Song of the Year" concert, singers like Pugacheva or Rotaru gradually stopped serving the function of mere embodiments of certain Soviet myths and acquired clout and star status. For example, both Rotaru and Pugacheva started performing several songs at the "Song of the Year" concert instead of just one, as did most other singers. The same change in the status of Rotaru and Pugacheva happened at the major Soviet-style review television show—*Goluboi ogonek* (The little blue light)—where both performers started making regular appearances in the 1970s. The show appeared on Soviet television in 1962 and was broadcast during major Soviet holidays, with the New Year show being the biggest.[15] It was a bizarre Soviet hybrid. The setting was that of a restaurant *mise en scène* built in a studio, but the guests at the tables were bona fide famous Soviet people—heroic coalminers and collective farmers wearing their state awards, cosmonauts, and other such celebrities. In the style of review theater, the entertainment ranged from classical music to folk and pop songs and from circus numbers to

---

14 Known as "Pesnia Goda," "Song of the Year" has been an annual music festival on New Year's Day since 1971. Rotaru appeared in the festival annually from 1973 till 2020, except for 2002. Pugacheva has been a major presence as well. Thus, Rotaru appeared in forty-seven televised final competitions and Pugacheva—in more than twenty.

15 The show still appears every year on New Year's Eve on Channel Russia.

standup comedy. The flow was strictly controlled by the hosts—state television anchors—who smiled on the occasion of a festive event. At first Rotaru and Pugacheva appeared with their musical numbers on *The Little Blue Light* shows, but in 1977, as an exception to the rule, Pugacheva became the first female pop singer to host the entire event. And the following year she starred in *The Woman Who Sings.*[16]

Late-socialist musicals represented the success of a singer above all through a recognition of her talent. This recognition, however, downplayed references to monetary perks—a necessary concession to Soviet ideology. At the same time, the film's diegesis was sending conflicted messages. The celebrity was surrounded by signs of material gain: private cars, usually domestic but at times foreign; fashionable outfits, including Western-style clothing, with denim jeans as the ultimate fetish (fig. 7.3); expensive Western-branded musical equipment; and, occasionally, sail boats (fig. 7.4). Travel, at times abroad, was part of celebrity characters' lifestyle. Touring was connected to money-making, which in the Soviet code of conduct was a shameful and often illegal activity. In *WWS*, for example, musicians ask the administrator about their per diem and he shames them by saying that they cannot think of anything but money. Yet, while money was an embarrassing topic, financial gain and glamour became part of the late-socialist narrative of popularity and success.

---

16 Television broadcasts of late-Soviet pop music concerts established conventions of Soviet-style televised vaudeville shows, with the *Song of the Year* broadcasts being perhaps the most famous one. In late-Soviet culture, programs mimicking cabaret-style entertainment started appearing on television as well. Notably, the most famous one masqueraded as a transplant from the Polish cabaret scene and was titled *Kabachok "13 stul'ev"* (Pub "13 chairs," 1966–1980). Visiting Poland and inspired by the Polish TV show *Kabaret Starszych Panów* (The older gentlemen's cabaret, 1958–1966), Soviet actor Aleksandr Beliavskii proposed the idea of a similar show for Soviet television. The Soviet show was set in a Polish pub, where characters (because they were Western foreigners, namely Poles) performed more risqué humorous skits written by Polish-language authors, including Julian Tuwim and Stanisław Jerzy Lec. The skits alternated with international song numbers lip-synced by the characters. Many songs were in Polish but occasionally songs could be in French and even English, such as for example, ABBA's "Money, Money, Money" or Sylvie Vartan's "L'amour au diapason." Meanwhile *Pub "13 Chairs"* lasted until 1980, when the Polish revolution put an end to the subversive show. As Oleg Khavich notes in his article, by that time any mention of Poland on Soviet TV was perceived as a call to mutiny (see his "Kabachok '13 stul'ev' i Kabaret Starszych Panów," Ukraina.ru, June 20, 2021, accessed July 15, 2021, https://ukraina.ru/exclusive/20210620/1031282547.html). For a discussion of Poland's tradition of cabaret entertainment and its impact on Polish-language film musicals, see Beth Holmgren's contribution to this volume (chapter one).

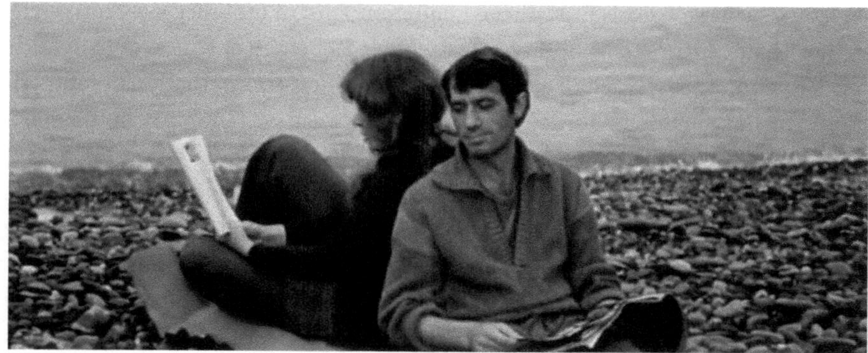

Figure 7.3. Anna Strel'tsova (Alla Pugacheva) in denim jeans, *Zhenshchina, kotoraia poet* (The woman who sings), 1978, dir. Aleksandr Orlov.

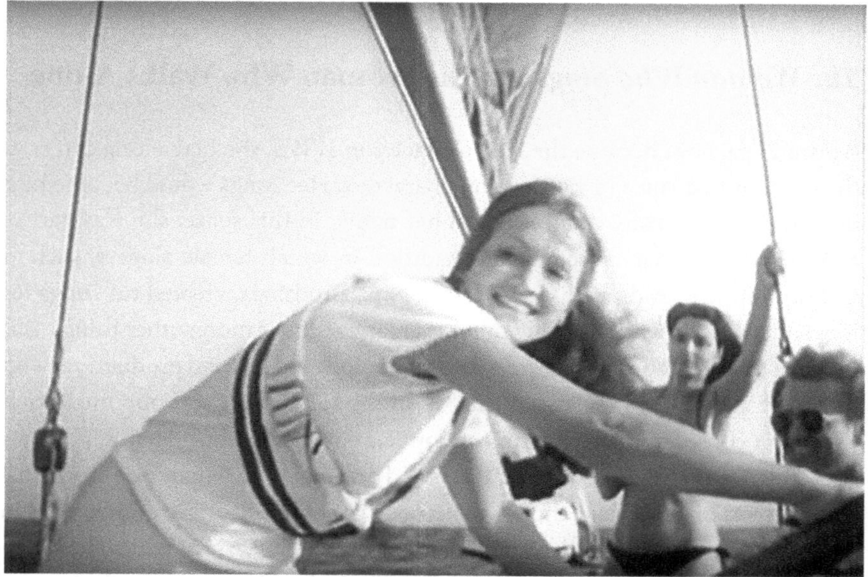

Figure 7.4. Viktoriia Svobodina (Sofia Rotaru, left) steering a yacht, *Dusha* (Soul), 1981, dir. Aleksandr Stefanovich.

A quick disclaimer here: in Stalinist musicals characters did tour as well, given that Stalinism was about modernity and a certain kind of mobility. However, the ultimate destination of both Marion Dixon in *Circus* (1936) and Tania Morozova in *Svetlyi put'* (Radiant path, 1940) was Moscow, and there was nowhere for them to go after this, other than to fly, like the lead actress in *Radiant Path,* in a convertible around the Kremlin. Professional success and a good life in late-socialist musicals introduced a different kind of mobility—a centrifugal, rather than centripetal mobility—that enabled characters to travel to seaside resorts, to the least Sovietized Baltic republics, and to international competitions west of the Soviet border. Admittedly, the westward mobility in the musical created conflicting agendas. On the one hand, it was flattering for Soviet pop musicians to win an award at a Western musical festival; on the other hand, to show Soviet singers actually in Western settings could raise unreasonable expectations on the part of the viewers about the limits of permissible mobility and freedom at large. Thus, in *Soul,* singer Viktoriia Svobodina travels to an unspecified German-speaking country, where a generic Intermusik competition takes place, evoking the Intervision Song Contest. The B-roll for the imaginary German musical festival was taken from the Sopot International Song Festival, where both Rotaru and Pugacheva participated in the mid-to-late 1970s.[17]

The Woman Who Sings, or The Woman Who Walks Alone

Before Pugacheva became the lead character in *WWS,* she had a long career as the unidentified voice of various film characters. Her songs would become hits, but the credits usually did not reveal her name. In this sense, she was part of a "venerable" patriarchal cinematic tradition in which female singers, such as Larisa Mondrus, Aida Vedishcheva, and Nina Brodskaia, created hit songs for film soundtracks, without being mentioned in credits. Among other things, this practice casts light on the hierarchy of Soviet modes of cultural production, with literature and cinema located at the top of the food chain and pop music and television considered lower forms of popular entertainment.[18] Hence, if a filmmaker, as, for example, Leonid Gaidai, relied on music by a female pop singer like Vedishcheva or Brodskaia, there was no need to credit the origin of the voice. In *Kavkazskaia plennitsa* (Kidnapping, Caucasian style, 1967), Vedishcheva performs the hit song about bears, without credit. In *Ivan Vasil'evich meniaet professiiu* (Ivan Vasil'evich: back to the future, 1973), Brodskaia sings one of the hit

---

17 It is quite telling that in 1981, Stefanovich decided not to send Svobodina to Sopot and to exclude the actual footage of the singer (Rotaru) in the competition. Without available evidence, we can only speculate that by 1981 Polish locations, especially the Baltic shore where the Solidarność revolution was ablaze, were undesirable on the Soviet screen.

18 A parallel to this phenomenon is Polish film during its socialist phase, when critics deemed comedy an inferior and insignificant genre. For a discussion of this cultural rigidity see Helena Goscilo's article on Stanisław Bareja in chapter two.

songs, "S liubov'iu vstretit'sia" ("Finding love"), but she also received no credit.[19] Such gendered marginalization was especially telling because male actors would often perform songs on screen and were recognized as both singers and actors. See, for example, Iurii Nikulin and Andrei Mironov in *Briliantovaia ruka* (The diamond arm, 1969).[20] A particularly egregious instance of patriarchal appropriation is El'dar Riazanov's use of Pugacheva's voice for four songs performed by the female lead, Barbara Brylska, in his *Ironiia sud'by* (Irony of fate, 1976).[21] Considering how central the songs are to the film and their success outside the filmic text, it is quite shocking that for a long time popular audiences remained ignorant of the actual performer's identity because the film entirely omitted Pugacheva's name from the credits.[22]

---

19 Originally the song was recorded by Rotaru, but her lower voice was a poor match for the voice of female lead Natal'ia Selezneva, who was "singing" the song in the film. For a discussion of Rotaru and Brodskaia's performance of "Finding Love" see Igor' Tsaler, "'Zvenit ianvarskaia v'iuga!' Nina Brodskaia ili Sofiia Rotaru?," Yandex Zen, October 22, 2019, https://zen.yandex.ru/media/tsaler/zvenit-ianvarskaia-viuga-nina-brodskaia-ili-sofiia-rotaru-5dacbfbb06cc4600b034c6e1.

20 What is even more egregious is that Brodskaia, Vedishcheva, and Pugacheva were professionally trained and popular singers, whereas Mironov and especially Nikulin, a circus clown, had lesser credentials as professional singers.

21 The well-known Polish actress Barbara Brylska became popular with Soviet audiences from such films as *Faraon* (Pharaoh, directed by Jerzy Kawalerowicz, 1966) and especially *Anatomia miłości* (Anatomy of love, directed by Roman Załuski, 1972). The latter was released in the Soviet Union in a censored form but still acquired a cult status as an erotic love story. As Denis Gorelov reminds us, films about guilt-free romantic relations between well-dressed people not burdened by any social or ideological agenda were practically non-existent in the Soviet Union and made *Anatomy of Love* an event, even in the abridged version (Denis Gorelov, *Igra v pustiaki, ili "Zoloto Makkeny" i eshche 97 inostrannykh fil'mov sovetskogo prokata* [Moscow: Gorodets-Fliuid, 2020], 138–139). After vetting several popular Soviet actresses, such as Liudmila Gurchenko and Svetlana Nemoliaeva, Riazanov succeeded in convincing Brylska, whom he remembered from *Anatomy of Love*, to star as Nadia Sheveleva (El'dar Riazanov, *Nepodvedennye itogi* [Moscow: Vagrius, 1995], 210–211). See also Anna Veligzhanova, "Lukashina mog sygrat' Andrei Mironov," *Komsomol'skaia pravda*, December 26, 2002, https://www.kp.ru/daily/22944/690/.

22 Notably, Pugacheva worked not only for central studios in Moscow but also for Tadzhikfil'm, where she provided the singing voice for female and male child characters: Mukadas Makhmudov's *Otvazhnyi Shirak* (Courageous Shirak, 1976) and Makhmudov and Valerii Kharchenko's *Povar i pevitsa* (The cook and the singer, 1978). She also was the musical voice for characters in Pavel Arsenov's *Korol'-olen'* (King-Stag, 1969), Orlov's *Amazing Boy* (1970), and Isaak Magiton's *Tsentrovoi iz podnebes'ia* (A center from the skies, 1975). In *Amazing Boy*, Pugacheva performed songs for multiple characters, adult females as well as children. It is worth noting here that she was lot more successful in her professional role than Mondrus, Brodskaia, and Vedishcheva. All three combined a vibrant *estrada*, radio, and television presence with virtually complete cinematic invisibility. By the 1970s, the antisemitic management of Gosteleradio, above all its chief, Sergei Lapin, forced Mondrus, Brodskaia, and Vedishcheva into emigration and ultimately oblivion in the Soviet Union.

Meanwhile, as Pugacheva's singing career was developing, she started appearing as herself on television, radio, and in international competitions. Thus, her eventual visibility and centrality in *WWS* became a logical continuation of her rise as a celebrity. The production and release of *WWS* challenged the established tradition of the Soviet film musical, because Pugacheva was a pop singer, not a film actress, and through her, other forms of cultural production—above all, pop music—acquired greater cultural legitimacy and visibility. As the female lead of a major film production that sold fifty-five million tickets in 1979, Pugacheva through her performance leveled important ideological hierarchies. For example, in *WWS* the state agenda is simply absent. Moreover, heteronormative romance goes nowhere twice. Instead of a standard plot development, the filmmaker chooses to fail both romantic relationships in order to focus on the pop diva's artistic agency; in the film she appears under the name of Anna Strel'tsova, and her true third love is her singing. Hence the working title of Orlov's film—*Third Love.*

WWS's handling of the lead character's maternity is quite unconventional for the Soviet film as well. Instead of a standard pronatalist plot, or at least showing a conflict between the woman's career and her role as a mother, the film privileges Strel'tsova's career both narratively and visually. Her child's birth and rearing happen as part of a crisis in her career. Once Anna's musical group shows up at her doorstep asking her to come back, the child issue evaporates into thin air. Occasionally we see some of the stage staff babysitting the child. The film does not mark this as bad mothering; rather, the child, along with romantic engagements, constitutes part of Anna's identity, while preference is given to the diva's talent and agency.

Another convention that *WWS* challenges is the traditional director-actress coupling in life and on screen. Soviet film directors frequently filmed their wives in lead roles: Grigorii Aleksandrov and Liubov' Orlova, Ivan Pyr'ev and Marina Ladynina, Sergei Bondarchuk and Irina Skobtseva, Vladimir Men'shov and Vera Alentova, and so on.[23] *WWS* is closer to a swinger party than to a traditional director/wife arrangement. Orlov's wife Alla Budnitskaia appeared in *WWS* in a supporting role while the couple's close friend Pugacheva performed in the lead role. Her husband filmmaker, Stefanovich, a friend of the couple, in turn was closely involved with the production. Reportedly, when Stefanovich married Pugacheva, his boss, Bondarchuk, called this a huge mistake and a downshifting move for Stefanovich: why would a director marry a pop singer (a *pevichka*)

---

23 On Pyr'ev and Ladynina, see Rimgaila Salys's chapter five in this volume.

instead of marrying a more respectable, and perhaps easier to discipline, person—that is, a film actress? In fact, the opposite happened: Pugacheva became a much bigger star than her director husband. Her rebellious nature, however, confirmed Bondarchuk's concern during the filming of *Soul*, as we discuss below.

In fact, Anna in *WWS* cherishes agency above all else: She initiates and breaks off all kinds of liaisons and relations herself. Moreover, she is unwilling to compromise her independence and share power even when she seemingly has none. In *WWS*, there are only two female characters, Anna Strel'tsova (Pugacheva) and her friend Masha (Budnitskaia). They represent the unruly woman and the good-girl trajectories of a romantic plot.[24] Anna refuses to settle down with a man and to give up her artistic career, while Masha, who initially supports Anna, ends up marrying that very same man once Anna separates from him. The musical numbers in the film mirror narrative turns and characterizations of the protagonist, in both a conventional and a creative way. As an instance of the first, Anna's personal drama finds an outlet in performance. More creatively, the "failed" number at the film's beginning foreshadows her struggle to remain herself. It is set in a music hall where Anna is simply one of the chorus girls. The director micromanages them, and midway through the rehearsal Anna walks out, refusing to be handled by the controlling director—inevitably, male.

In this respect, even if the film is not autobiographical, Anna is the pop diva's *alter ego*. Pugacheva's refusal to submit to authority, especially in what concerned her career, manifested itself in the process of casting for *WWS*. During the interviews conducted by veteran male directors of the studio Mosfil'm, Pugacheva snapped at patronizing comments by Lev Arnshtam when he criticized her style: "Who are you to teach me how to act on stage?" In response, the studio head, Nikolai Sizov, explained to Pugacheva that Arnshtam had important credentials as the renowned director of such films as *Zoia* (1944), a nationalistic melodrama about the war martyr Zoia Kosmodem'ianskaia. Pugacheva immediately shot back that this was a terrible film that, moreover had nothing to do with the current situation. Then she slammed the door. Sizov swore that she

---

24 In our use of the term "the unruly woman," we draw on Kathleen Rowe's discussion in *The Unruly Woman: Gender and the Genres of Laughter* (Austin: University of Texas Press, 1995). Evoking the works of Mikhail Bakhtin and Natalie Zeman Davis, Rowe contends that "the topos of the unruly woman . . . reverberates whenever women disrupt the norms of femininity and the social hierarchy of male over female through excess and outrageousness" (ibid., 31). The unruly "woman on top" creates disorder by attempting to dominate men. Her body is excessive, and she refuses to control her physical and sexual appetites; she is loud; she jokes, mocks men, and laughs at them.

would never appear in Mosfil'm studio productions. Later, however, he had to back off and admit that Pugacheva was obviously irreplaceable for this film.[25]

The filmmakers offer an innovative approach to the genre of the musical. On the one hand, they are aware of the conventions of the classical backstage musical as Rick Altman outlines it for us,[26] but instead of embracing the familiar production of the show/love plot parallel, they complicate the story. For example, while Pugacheva's career goes up, her romantic relations all fail, as we discuss below. On the other hand, the film mixes narrative turns of the backstage musical with the narrative devices of the celebrity biopic. Notably, the celebrity at the center of the picture was a female and very much alive—a very daring move, especially in the culture where celebrity usually meant dead male political leaders or military commanders.

In their film, Orlov and Pugacheva redefine the Soviet musical film's approach to the authenticity of performance. There is no realism in *WWS* as it was understood by socialist realist directors; instead, what we get are manufactured and performed numbers that lay bare their constructed nature. The authenticity here is in revealing the site of production, the pop diva's domain. In the number that opens the film—"A Song about Me"—the viewers meet the film director and the shooting crew and observe the cameras and even the wind machine.[27] What gives the number its authenticity is the familiar persona of a pop star, Pugacheva herself. She performs the role of a pop diva whose excess is in stark contrast to the familiar repressed and static style of the Soviet stage. Her persona is excessive in its delivery, in its visibility of female performance, and in its acknowledgement of sexuality as part of a woman's identity. For example, the opening song starts with the singer in a white dress, her red hair covered by a white scarf, singing about her being like everyone else in her pursuit of happiness. When the song shifts to a more dramatic melody and lyrics about stormy weather in her personal experience, she takes off her scarf and the wind machine fills it with air, transforming it into a sail, which flies in the air together with Pugacheva's unruly mane of red hair.

Every costume in the film becomes a plastic object to which Pugacheva gives special significance through her performance. With the help of the Soviet Union's premier fashion designer, Viacheslav Zaitsev, in the film Pugacheva developed

---

25 Razzakov, *Pugacheva protiv Rotaru. Velikie sopernitsy*, 65.

26 Altman, *The American Film Musical*, 210–234.

27 For a classic discussion of the film musical as simultaneously demystifying and remystifying the myth of entertainment and authenticity see Jane Feuer, "The Self-Reflexive Musical and the Myth of Entertainment," *Quarterly Review of Film Studies* 2, no. 3 (1977): 313–326.

her signature style—a bright, loose chiffon dress. In contrast to a tight-fitting dress, which Rotaru prefers, Pugacheva's chiffon dresses are open-ended in their interpretation. First, they exist on the threshold between an undergarment and a dress, thus foregrounding the performer's sensuality. Second, they are expressive canvases, which the performer uses to paint a variety of emotions: from soft to dramatic, to rebellious. Moreover, in the case of her famous red and black chiffon dress, it is closer to an abstract art canvas rather than just a singer's costume. In addition to stimulating desire in the viewer, it provides a range of possibilities for interpretation and engagement with the performer's act (fig. 7.5). Obviously, in the Soviet Union, the red color had associations with the official ideology. Yet, without any audience studies to back up our claim, we would like to argue that the red-haired diva in a flaming outfit singlehandedly changed the meaning and myth of the red from the revolutionary color to the color of individual stardom and sexuality. Roland Barthes would be proud of Pugacheva's agency and skill of myth-making, especially in reference to the color red.[28] Notably, with the years, Pugacheva used the loose dresses to hide her excessive weight. Her body type,

Figure 7.5. Alla Pugacheva in her famous red dress (SPUTNIK / Alamy Stock Photo).

28 Roland Barthes, "The Rhetoric of the Image," in *Image-Music-Text*, trans. Stephen Heath (New York: Hill and Wang, 1977), 33–34.

however, offered a more democratic model than Rotaru's, one with which many Soviet women could identify. The fact that she became a mega star without possessing a perfect hourglass figure was reassuring, and starkly contrasted with Rotaru's slim form, which few female viewers could even dream of emulating. In this respect, too, she fit the mold of the "unruly woman" who challenges patriarchy through excess, both verbal and physical.

Costume, setting, music, and lyrics form a symphonic relationship in Pugacheva's numbers. For example, close to the film's end Masha tells Anna that she and Anna's former boyfriend are getting married. Anna does not openly reproach her friend; instead, all her emotions and pain are sublimated into the following song. The lyrics come from William Shakespeare's "Sonnet 90," while the music is by Pugacheva herself. She wears a striking black and white outfit: a black cape with a hood, and a white blouse underneath. This color contrast highlights emotional laceration. It is not quite clear whether the pain comes from the separation from her male lover or the betrayal by her female friend. For the dramatic setting the filmmaker chose the ruins of a Gothic bridge in the Marfino estate near Moscow. The authenticity of emotions clashes with the staged setting. At the same time, this setting is as far removed from the Soviet present as it can be. The artistic genius of the protagonist thus transforms the break-up into a creative act.

While Pugacheva challenges the limits of the permissible via her performance and costume, the camera often censors the diva via framing: the viewers rarely see the full figure of the singer, which limits the potential sensuality of her numbers. Pugacheva is often filmed from the waist up. In numbers shot on location the singer becomes part of a picturesque setting, which works well with the theatrical style of her performance but decenters her somewhat as the lead singer. In the "Sonnet 90" number, the waist-up effect is created by her lower body hidden behind an architectural detail. This approach to visualizing the performer is especially striking when compared to Polish television footage of her performances in Sopot 79, which is shot in longer takes alternating close ups with long takes of Pugacheva moving freely around the stage, sitting down at the edge of the stage at times and revealing a part of her leg (fig. 7.6). Clearly, Polish television and cinema allowed for more eroticism and freedom than puritanical Soviet cinema.[29]

---

29 Notably, in 2014, Stefanovich directed a mini-series about Pugacheva, *Kurazh* (Drive, 2014). Among other things, the series depicts Pugacheva's performance in Sopot coinciding with the Solidarity-led uprising on Poland's Baltic shore. The series portrays Pugacheva, Stefanovich, and their crew as naïve Soviets uninformed about the ongoing revolution and blind to the events unfolding around them. For example, the van in which they are traveling from Warsaw to Gdansk and Sopot is used by their Polish colleagues as a cover for transporting weapons for the protesters. Not surprisingly for a series funded by Russia's Channel One and released

Figure 7.6. Alla Pugacheva at the Sopot International Music Festival.

The making of *WWS* was also marked by a scandal around song authorship and revenues from the lucrative business of song composing. Pugacheva complained to Stefanovich about earning eight rubles a concert, though her concerts often filled entire stadiums. Stefanovich told her that song performance is not where cash is; you have to write music or lyrics to collect royalties. After this, Pugacheva wrote several songs to be included in the film. Aleksandr Zatsepin and Leonid Derbenev, who were commissioned to write songs for the film, were outraged that the director included several songs by another author without their knowledge. They threatened to prevent the film from being released. Pugacheva and Stefanovich found a solution, creating a story about a sick young composer who asked them to include his songs in the film. His name was Boris Gorbonos and, according to Stefanovich, he was paralyzed and could not visit the studio. The name, in fact, was a registered pen name of Pugacheva's in the Soviet All-Union Agency on Copyright (VAAP). Eventually, the Mosfil'm leadership agreed to keep the songs and release the film. Zatsepin and Derbenev, however, never worked with Pugacheva again.[30]

---

at the beginning of Russia's war against Ukraine, a character calls Pugacheva's performance at the festival amidst the revolution "a feast in the time of a plague."

30 Beliakov, *Alla Pugacheva. Zhizn' i udivitel'nye prikliucheniia velikoi pevitsy*, 123–124.

Besides Pugacheva's creative voracity, this incident is symbolic of the late Soviet cultural industry in two other ways. First, even in the Soviet Union the commercial priorities were studio executives' paramount concern. Filmmakers tried to profit from their labor, and the studio wanted to ensure that they did not shelve a film that could be a box office success. Second, this controversy exposed the gender dynamics in the Soviet musical and film industry. Namely, a female performer who challenged male authors' monopoly on cultural production and financial power could not win without resorting to wiles. When Pugacheva tried to get revenues from her authorship, she had to pretend to be specifically a *male* composer. As a performer, a person with lower cultural authority, she could not openly under her real name claim to be a legitimate author. Worried that Gorbonos might turn out to be a dissident or an underground artist, Sizov as studio chief demanded a confirmation of Gorbonos's identity, and Stefanovich asked the makeup artists at the studio to disguise Pugacheva as a male composer (mustache and all), sitting at a piano with Pugacheva's photo in front of him (fig. 7.7).[31]

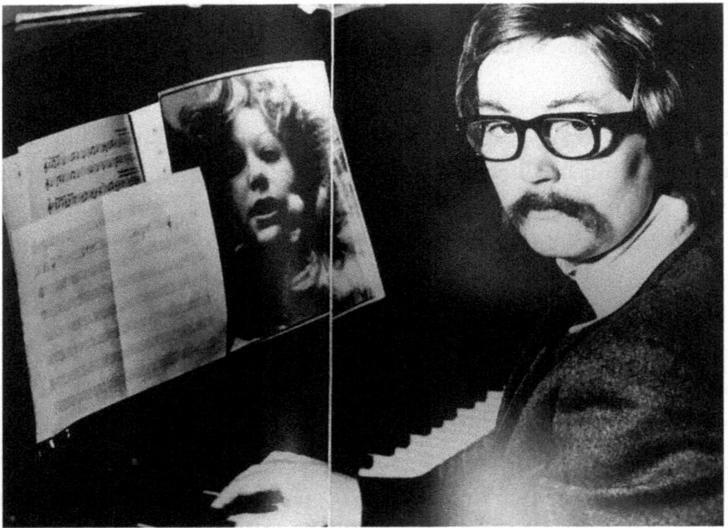

Figure 7.7. Alla Pugacheva posing as Boris Gorbonos.

31 Cited from B. M. Pokrovskii, ed., *Alla Pugacheva glazami druzei i nedrugov. Kniga pervaia* (Moscow: Tsentrpoligraf, 1997), 160–161. See also Razzakov, *Pugacheva protiv Rotaru. Velikie sopernitsy*, 66–67. In his book about Soviet pop music after Stalin, David MacFadyen notes that in her interview to an Estonian newspaper, Pugacheva eventually confessed that Boris Gorbonos was her *nom de plume*—the one she had to adopt, perhaps, to avoid "prejudices against a female composer" (MacFadyen, *Red Stars: Personality and the Soviet Popular Song, 1955–1991*, 251).

Both the viewers' responses and critics' comments about the film were largely positive. Viewers voted Pugacheva actress of the year in 1979 (*Sovetskii ekran* 10 [1980]) and bought fifty-five million tickets to the film. Critics compared the film with American and European melodramas but admitted that there were no Soviet analogues to what Orlov had produced. Meanwhile, nobody compared the film to socialist realist film musicals or reproached the film for ideological weaknesses. Instead, one critic noted that Pugacheva was exuberant in her performance, thus defying the promise to be like everyone else, the line from her famous opening song: "She is by no means an ordinary person."[32] Obviously, from the point of view of audiences in 1978, this fantasy of a glamorous life was not a flaw. In fact, it is the aura of celebrity that brought viewers to movie theaters in the first place.

Soul: Mentoring the Pop-Rock Diva

After the success of *WWS*, Stefanovich and Pugacheva proposed to produce another musical loosely based on her biography, with Stefanovich himself as the director. Because of huge revenues from *WWS*, Mosfil'm gave a lot of creative freedom to the filmmaker, and there was no casting for the lead role: the film was tailored to Pugacheva's persona. An unexpected turn of events derailed all the plans: a conflict between Pugacheva and the film crew resulted in the crew refusing to work with the singer. The studio bosses threatened to close the production and ban Stefanovich from the profession unless he saved the funds already spent on the film.

Most accounts of the fallout, above all Stefanovich's, blame the singer for her arrogance and rudeness. Meanwhile, we would like to suggest here that there might be another side to the story. Stefanovich wanted full control of the production and there were at least two contenders. First, Pugacheva herself, who was at the zenith of her popularity and felt confident enough to challenge anyone about creative matters. Notably the conflict originally was about Pugacheva's costume: she insisted on wearing what she liked, and the film costume designer and the director wanted to follow their own ideas. Having won a difficult struggle over authorship of songs in her previous film, Pugacheva felt that she could have greater artistic control over the second film. The conflict eventually became physical, with the singer famously tearing apart the costume designer's coat and

32 V. Ivanova, "Davaite govorit' spokoino," *Sovetskii ekran* 22 (1979): 5.

smashing the windshield of her director-husband's car. The studio executives chose to agree with Stefanovich's suggestion to replace the unruly Pugacheva with her main competitor in the industry—Rotaru, and the more obedient star played the lead role of Viktoriia Svobodina—the film's lead character (fig. 7.8). Ironically, the protagonist's surname invokes freedom in Russian. Why Rotaru would wish to follow in Pugacheva's footsteps is a separate question. Perhaps she agreed because playing the lead role in a Mosfil'm production was a major step up for the singer, since her previous musical film—*Gde ty, liubov'?* (Where are you, love? directed by Valeriu Gagiu, 1981) was produced by the provincial Moldova Film.

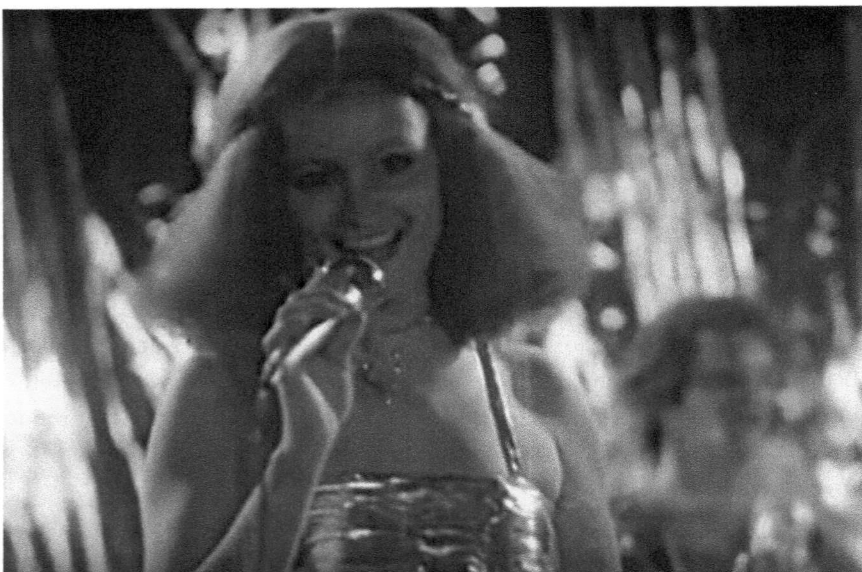

Figure 7.8. Sofia Rotaru as Viktoriia Svobodina, *Dusha* (Soul, 1981, dir. Aleksandr Stefanovich).

Once Stefanovich reestablished his control over his star, he had to deal with yet one more issue. He invited Rolan Bykov—a prominent actor and director—to play the role of Svobodina's concert administrator, Albert. Being a director himself, Bykov constantly felt the urge to interfere with the shooting. Stefanovich recollects finding an ingenious solution. Rotaru was insecure about her acting skills because she was not a professional actress and Stefanovich asked Bykov to mentor her. Thus, everyone got what he and she wanted, and the lead female star could boast of multiple male advisors.

In the updated version of the celebrity vehicle, Stefanovich decided to invite the rock group the Time Machine—at the time, a risky gesture, for it brought a semi-official band into a Mosfil'm production. According to the plot, Viktoriia undergoes a major creative crisis: she is losing her voice and feels stuck in her artistic persona. The search for new ideas leads to a serendipitous encounter. At the recording studio, Viktoriia meets the lead singer with the Romantic name of Vadim (played by Mikhail Boiarskii), who takes her to a nightclub outside of Moscow and explains to her that he and his nameless group (played by the Time Machine) are not allowed to sing inside the Moscow beltway.[33]

Some time later, Albert, realizing that Viktoriia's singing days are over and that she needs a new star vehicle, independently comes up with the idea to send Viktoriia to an international competition in Germany with a new and hip group—Vadim's band. After a series of misunderstandings, Viktoriia proves that she can sing in a new youthful rock style and, despite her ailing vocal cords, decides to go to Germany. Though at the risk of losing her voice completely, she helps to launch the career of the new group. As Albert had explained to her earlier, show business is for the young. Albert's words are especially obnoxious because age seems not to be a problem for the males, but in the case of the female star, her professional lifespan is short even without failing vocal cords.

Viktoriia realizes that her major narrative function is to sacrifice herself for young males. In Germany, she loses her voice on stage and walks off after telling Vadim: "I'm done. Full speed ahead, guys!" ("Vse! Vpered, rebiata!"). On the surface, this dispiriting ending echoes the last sequence of *WWS*: performance is portrayed as an experience that takes all of your life energy. In *WWS*, we see a montage sequence of Anna's final performance in the film and her exhaustion in front of a mirror in a dressing room. Yet the very last frame of the film is the shot from behind Anna as she faces the audience in her famous red dress, her arms outstretched like the wings of a bird about to take off (fig. 7.9).

---

33 It is worth noting that the name of Time Machine is never mentioned in the film and only appears in the final credits, where only the most patient viewers would see it. Soviet and Russian cultural and political administrators seem to be afflicted with a superstitious fear of naming certain individuals and groups. Apparently, the name Time Machine struck terror in their bureaucratic hearts, just as politicians these days are afraid to pronounce Aleksei Navalny's name in a similar fashion, referring to him as the Berlin patient or the blogger.

Figure 7.9. Alla Pugacheva as Anna Streltsova, *Zhenshchina, kotoraia poet* (The woman who sings), 1978, dir. Aleksandr Orlov.

In contrast, *Soul* ends with Viktoriia leaving the stage and walking into the light: her career is over, but her sacrifice was not in vain—a quite traditional gender role for the female lead. Her extreme close up on the TV screen (fig. 7.10) is intercut with four men looking at her suffering. Three of them are Vadim, Albert, and her former husband Sergei. The fourth male onlooker is the TV producer, played by Stefanovich himself. His assistant tells him that Viktoriia seems to be in trouble, to which the "compassionate" producer responds in a business-like manner: "Just in case, prepare to interrupt the broadcast for technical reasons." If Hollywood directors, as Laura Mulvey contended, objectify women via a sexualizing gaze, the late Soviet males (possibly out of sheer impotence) simply

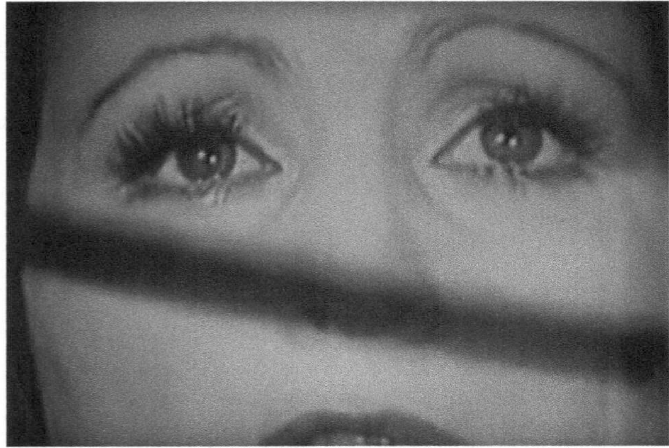

Figure 7.10. Viktoria Svobodina's (Sofia Rotaru) televised drama, *Dusha* (Soul), 1981, dir. Aleksandr Stefanovich.

bury the poor female celebrity at the film's end.[34] They prove expendable, but the show must go on.

To be fair, the representation of Time Machine, while revolutionary for Soviet cinema of the time, is also not kind to the semi-banned group. The band's appearance in a major Mosfil'm production was a huge breakthrough for the performers and for rock music as a genre of pop to be performed in a Soviet film musical. At the same time, studio executives tried to contain the subversive potential of the songs and the visual presence of the unofficial rock musicians. Out of the ten songs in the film, seven were authored by Time Machine, but only one of them was performed solely by the group, and extra diegetically, at that. The other songs were performed by Rotaru and Boiarskii, with the band as accompaniment. Rotaru and Boiarskii were not part of youth rock culture and were, in fact, fully integrated into Soviet pop music and cinema. Their performance of the Time Machine pieces worked to defuse the explosive potential of the unruly rockers. In addition, censors demanded changes in the most subversive lines of several songs. For example, in the song "Kogo ty khotel udivit'?" ("Whom did you want to surprise?") censors wanted the line "All the rebels will end up in prison" ("No vsekh buntarei ozhidaet tiur'ma") changed to "But all the rebels lack intelligence" ("No vsem buntariam ne khvataet uma"). And in the song "Campfire," censors altered "God watches over me" ("Bog khranit menia") to "Destiny watches over me" ("Sud'ba khranit menia").[35]

While those changes were noticeable only to the most hardcore fans of the group, the reassignment of the songs to Rotaru and Boiarskii radically changed the meaning of the songs, making them pop entertainment with slightly edgier overtones. The song "Za tekh, kto v more!" ("To those at sea!") is a typical Andrei Makarevich parable about storm and change as a necessary part of life, for stagnant waters cause insanity: "It's much harder not to lose your mind from boredom and to survive absolute calm." When Rotaru and Boiarskii perform this song, it transforms from a social commentary into a meaningless pop tune accompanying two performers' burgeoning romance. The performers are dressed in shiny sparkling overalls and jump/fly upwards. Moreover, Makarevich and Kutikov, the two lead musicians of Time Machine, serve the role of chorus boys and jump upwards together with them. While there is no doubt that the fans celebrated the appearance of their idols on the big screen, the film fully integrated

---

34 The late Soviet director pushes the Hollywood male gaze to its murderous logical conclusion. For the classic discussion of the Hollywood part of the story, see Laura Mulvey, "Visual Pleasure and Narrative Cinema," *Screen* 16, no. 3 (1975): 6–18.

35 Razzakov, *Pugacheva protiv Rotaru. Velikie sopernitsy*, 107.

the rock musicians into the Soviet pop music scene and expertly emptied their songs of any subversive commentary. The way the sequence was recorded was an apt metaphor for what was done to Time Machine: The musicians simply jumped on a trampoline, but for the final edit, the downward part of their movement was cut out, and the viewers enjoyed only the montage sequence of their optimistic upward mobility.

Reviewers were not too kind to *Soul,* with the notable exception of the formidable Neia Zorkaia. She cites the titles of two reviews, "Fal'shivaia dusha" ("Fake soul") and "Poteriali dushu" ("Soul-less"), and, in contrast, lauds the film's creators for introducing rock music to general audiences, as well as their expert use of widescreen and camerawork. The problem with the film, according to Zorkaia, is in the embarrassment of narrative lines that the scriptwriter offered to the filmmaker: (1) the female lead's illness, (2) her creative crisis, (3) the conflict between the individual artist and the collective, and (4) the burden of popularity and fame. Despite all these shortcomings, Zorkaia concludes on a positive note, praising the film for its innovative sound and expert use of the visual form.[36] Within the context of Soviet film criticism and ideological censorship, Zorkaia is incredibly clever here, for she finds purported fault with several issues but simultaneously normalizes the use of rock music in mainstream Soviet cinema.

Both *WWS* and *Soul* were pivotal for the two divas' careers and for the industry, for they experimented with a new type of screen musical, built entirely around the persona of the pop-rock diva. The films focus on their performative images of femininity coupled with various pop-rock styles. In the conflict between the individual and the collective, both films assert the individual talent of the diva as the prime value. The fact that both of these groundbreaking films focus on a female star perhaps achieved something that the filmmakers, all men, did not quite expect. They empowered female performers and made them visible and more legitimate than they had ever been. Certainly, Pugacheva and Rotaru became unstoppable after adding a major cinematic appearance to their pop music careers.[37] The Soviet pop-diva musicals introduced the new

---

36 Neia Zorkaia, "Kazhdyi, pravo, imeet pravo," *Sovetskii ekran* 23 (1982): 13.

37 In 1985, Pugacheva capitalized on the success of *The Woman Who Sings* with another musical film, *Prishla i govoriu* (I've come to speak up, directed by Naum Ardashnikov, 1985). Soviet film critics branded the star vehicle tasteless while the audiences voted it one of the best films of the year. For example, in his article for *Pravda,* Valerii Kichin laments the filmmaker's obsession with Pugacheva's celebrity lifestyle and its materialist perks, such as her Mercedes car and her bourgeois kitchen, with its built-in bar counter. He poses a very loaded question: "In what kingdom does this fairy tale take place? ("V kakom korolevstve siia skazka proiskhodit?").

phenomenon of a mega-star—part of Hollywood's studio system—to late-Soviet culture.

Both films became a watershed between the traditional Soviet film musical and the celebrity-driven vehicle that came to dominate late and post-Soviet media culture. Their time of release is significant as well. By the early and mid-1980s the Soviet Union had joined the rest of the world in the media revolution combined with political and economic changes triggered by Mikhail Gorbachev. Both *WWS* and *Soul* functioned within the framework of what Henry Jenkins calls "transmedia storytelling."[38] The celebrity film musical became part of a network of texts, such as television programs, radio broadcasts, live concerts, LPs, audio and video tapes, poster art, and so on—all of them creating a complete entertainment experience revolving around the pop-diva personas. In contrast to Orlova or Ladynina, whose celebrity image during an earlier era was tightly controlled by the film director and the Soviet state—the sole *de facto* producer—the late Soviet pop diva exercised an unusual degree of agency, which eventually led to unprecedented financial power and entrepreneurship. The coda to the story of the two stars is their place in the economic transformation from the state-run culture industry into market-driven entertainment.

In the late 1980s, both Pugacheva and Rotaru developed a network of media ventures. For example, in 1988 Pugacheva established Theater of Song, soon followed by a private company bearing the star's iconic first name—Alla. These ventures organized musical festivals, concert tours, released recordings and produced merchandise, including t-shirs, calendars, and even the perfume Alla.[39] The same year, Rotaru signed a contract with the company Muzyka to organize

---

See Valerii Kichin, "Mersedes, akkordeon i chechetka," *Pravda*, December 14, 1985, 3. The editors of the bimonthly *Smena* echoed the *Pravda* journalist in expressing their concern that the makers of *I've Come to Speak Up* abandoned the good old tradition of socialist realist musicals and chose to emulate Western models. In order to present such a critical perspective as *vox populi*, the editors published a letter by a vigilant engineer-viewer, Igor' Bodnaruk, titled "False Note" ("Fal'shivaia nota," reproduced in *Alla Pugacheva glazami druzei i nedrugov. Kniga pervaia*, ed. B. M. Pokrovskii [Moscow: Tsentrpoligraf, 1997], 387–390). The engineer allegedly was upset that Pugacheva did not follow tasteful models, such as *Veselye rebiata* (Jolly fellows, directed by Grigorii Aleksandrov, 1934), and instead imitated Western musicals, such as *ABBA* (directed by Lasse Hallström, 1977) and *Disco Dancer* (directed by Babbar Subhash, 1982 (ibid., 387–388). Notably, *Disco Dancer* was by no means a Western film, but an Indian musical that became one of the top-grossing films of the early 1980s in the Soviet Union. Meanwhile, for most of the viewers the diva's appearance trumped any flaws in the film. This chasm between official reception and popular acclaim (now in the open) was a sign of changes to come.

38 Henry Jenkins, *Converge Culture: Where Old and New Media Collide* (New York: New York University Press, 2006), 20–21.

39 Beliakov, *Alla Pugacheva. Zhizn' i udivitel'nye prikliucheniia velikoi pevitsy*, 262.

nationwide tours for a set of pop and rock groups controlled directly or indirectly by the pop diva herself.[40] Clearly, there were quite a few business ventures that took their root at this time, but few of them had women at their helm and were successful, especially in the media and music industries. Finally, both pop divas crossed Soviet borders in several other significant ways. They started recording their albums abroad, keeping their earnings in international banks, and touring worldwide.[41] In fact, on February 28, 1988, Pugacheva became the first major Soviet pop singer to tour Israel—three years before diplomatic relations between Israel and the Soviet Union were even re-established.

In an old Soviet joke, an encyclopedia entry mentions Brezhnev as a minor politician in the era of Pugacheva.[42] While today's young generation barely remembers the late General Secretary of the Soviet Union, Pugacheva and Rotaru continue appearing on post-Soviet television channels and, even more importantly, on streaming services. Maybe the current Russian president will similarly go down in history as a minor politician in the era of Pugacheva, Rotaru . . . and perhaps Pussy Riot.

Bibliography

Altman, Rick. *The American Film Musical.* Bloomington: Indiana University Press, 1987.

Barthes, Roland. "The Rhetoric of the Image." In his *Image-Music-Text,* translated by Stephen Heath, 32–51. New York: Hill and Wang, 1977.

Beliakov, Aleksei. *Alla Pugacheva. Zhizn' i udivitel'nye prikliucheniia velikoi pevitsy.* Moscow: Komsomol'skaia Pravda, 2019.

Bodnaruk, Igor'. "Fal'shivaia nota." In *Alla Pugacheva glazami druzei i nedrugov. Kniga pervaia,* edited by B. M. Pokrovskii, 387–390. Moscow: Tsentrpoligraf, 1997.

Feuer, Jane. "The Self-Reflexive Musical and the Myth of Entertainment." *Quarterly Review of Film Studies* 2, no. 3 (1977): 313–326.

Gorelov, Denis. *Igra v pustiaki, ili "Zoloto Makkeny" i eshche 97 inostrannykh fil'mov sovetskogo prokata.* Moscow: Gorodets-Fliuid, 2020.

Ivanits, Linda J. *Russian Folk Belief.* Armonk: M. E. Sharpe, 1989.

Ivanova, V. "Davaite govorit' spokoino." *Sovetskii ekran* 22 (1979): 4–5.

Jenkins, Henry. *Converge Culture: Where Old and New Media Collide.* New York: New York University Press, 2006.

Khavich, Oleg. "*Kabachok '13 stul'ev'* i *Kabaret Starszych Panów.*" Ukraina.ru, June 20, 2021. Accessed July 15, 2021. https://ukraina.ru/exclusive/20210620/1031282547.html.

---

40 Razzakov, *Pugacheva protiv Rotaru. Velikie sopernitsy,* 169, 175.

41 Ibid., 185.

42 Partan, "Alla: The Jester-Queen of Russian Pop Culture": 484.

Kichin, Valerii. "Mersedes, akkordeon i chechetka." *Pravda*, December 14, 1985, 3.

MacFadyen, David. *Red Stars: Personality and the Soviet Popular Song, 1955–1991*. Montreal: McGill-Queen's University Press, 2001.

Mulvey, Laura. "Visual Pleasure and Narrative Cinema." *Screen* 16, no. 3 (1975): 6–18.

Partan, Olga. "Alla: The Jester-Queen of Russian Pop Culture." *Russian Review* 3 (2007): 483–500.

Pokrovskii, B. M., ed. *Alla Pugacheva glazami druzei i nedrugov. Kniga pervaia*. Moscow: Tsentrpoligraf, 1997.

Razzakov, Fedor. *Pugacheva protiv Rotaru. Velikie sopernitsy*. Moscow: Eksmo, 2011.

Regev, Motti. *Pop-Rock Music: Aesthetic Cosmopolitanism in Late Modernity*. Hoboken: Wiley, 2013.

Riazanov, El'dar. *Nepodvedennye itogi*. Moscow: Vagrius, 1995.

Rowe, Kathleen. *The Unruly Woman: Gender and the Genres of Laughter*. Austin: University of Texas Press, 1995.

Salys, Rimgaila. *The Musical Comedy Films of Grigorii Aleksandrov: Laughing Matters*. Bristol: Intellect, 2009.

Stefanovich, Aleksandr. *Kurazh: dokumental'nyi roman o shou-biznese vremen SSSR*. Moscow: Ripol klassik, 2014.

Stites, Richard. *Russian popular culture*. Cambridge: Cambridge University Press, 1992.

Tsaler, Igor'. "'Zvenit ianvarskaia v'iuga!' Nina Brodskaia ili Sofiia Rotaru?" *Yandex Zen*, October 22, 2019. Accessed July16, 2021. https://zen.yandex.ru/media/tsaler/zvenit-ianvarskaia-viuga-nina-brodskaia-ili-sofiia-rotaru-5dacbfbb06cc4600b034c6e1.

Veligzhanova, Anna. "Lukashina mog sygrat' Andrei Mironov." *Komsomol'skaia pravda*, December 26, 2002. Accessed September 3, 2021. https://www.kp.ru/daily/22944/690/.

Zorkaia, Neia. "Kazhdyi, pravo, imeet pravo." *Sovetskii ekran* 23 (1982): 12–13.

CHAPTER 8

Postmodernity, Freedom, and Authenticity in Kirill Serebrennikov's *Leto* (2018)

Justin Wilmes

In summer of 1981, a young Viktor Tsoi is introduced to Mike Naumenko of Zoopark and the Leningrad rock scene. Immediately recognizing the talent of the nineteen-year-old Tsoi at a party on the beach, Naumenko begins to mentor him and champion his music. While a poignant friendship and musical dialogue emerge between the two songwriters, a romantic connection between Tsoi and Natasha, Naumenko's wife, quickly becomes evident. The three spend the summer among a close-knit company of Leningrad rockers, feeling their way through this love triangle, their musical collaboration, and aesthetic polemics. Directed by one of Russia's most experimental and transgressive directors about a beloved cultural icon, it is no surprise that Kirill Serebrennikov's *Leto* (Summer), which tackles this scenario, was met with such anticipation and scrutiny, and became, arguably, the country's biggest cinematic event of 2018.[1] *Leto* was nominated for a record-breaking twelve Nika Awards (sometimes referred to as the "Russian Oscars"), and was selected to compete at the 2018 Cannes International Film Festival, where it took home the award for Best Soundtrack. The film was widely acclaimed by Russian critics and viewers, though it had a sharply divided

1 Throughout this chapter I use the film title *Leto*, the Russian word for "summer," as the filmmakers chose to retain the Russian title rather than translate it in international distribution.

reception by the icons of the Russian rock movement, who raised questions about its historical authenticity.[2]

Part postmodern backstage musical, part historical biopic, *Leto* challenges simple categorization, and from this uncomfortable marriage of genres stemmed much of the debate around the film. Given its array of realist features, including naturalistic black and white cinematography, quotidian scenes from the lives of its subjects, and musical performances that are mostly diegetically embedded in the narrative—it is understandable that many viewed and evaluated the film through the lens of a realist, historical biopic, and overlooked its structure as a film musical. Upon closer examination, *Leto* is in fact meticulously structured as a musical, not merely a film about music. Its twenty distinct musical numbers, which comprise over half of the film, fall into two distinct categories: diegetic rock performances by the musicians and fantasy numbers that clearly enter a performative, supradiegetic space. However, in contrast to classical approaches to the musical, *Leto*'s engagement with the genre is markedly postmodern, laying bare its own artifice and devices, slipping into free fantasy, but frequently informing the viewer through its narrator, Skeptic, "This never happened." This chapter examines *Leto*'s engagement with the film musical genre and considers how its form explores two salient tropes in the Leningrad rock movement: the sociopolitical position of those who wished, as anthropologist Aleksei Yurchak describes, to live *vne* ("outside") of the ideological coordinates of this system; and the problem of derivation and authenticity in a society that idolized foreign cultural expression.

Genre Trouble: Postmodern Musical Meets Historical Biopic

While popular among film critics and viewers, *Leto* was met with scathing criticism by some of the Russian rock community, including key members of the movement and close friends of Tsoi and Naumenko, such as musician Boris Grebenshchikov, Kino co-founder Aleksei Rybin, and Andrei Tropillo, studio producer for much of the Leningrad rock movement (all three of whom are referenced in the film). Based loosely on the memoirs of Natasha Naumenko, the script was written by Michael and Lily Idov and later heavily revised and

---

2 Prominent Russian film critic Anton Dolin opined that *Leto* is "Kirill Serebrennikov's best film" (Anton Dolin, "Leto, Fokstrot, Krasotka na vsiu golovu," YouTube, 2018, https://www.youtube.com/watch?v=UfCqmbAXWsA). The film has a composite rating of 7.4/10 on KinoPoisk, making it one of the highest-rated films by Russian viewers in the past decade.

reworked by Kirill Serebrennikov in collaboration with the Idovs. Many contemporaries of Tsoi and Naumenko disputed Natasha's recollections of the romantic tensions among the three—which ultimately became a central focus of the film—claiming that they were greatly exaggerated, if they existed at all. After reading the initial script, Boris Grebenshchikov remarked: "The script is a lie from start to finish. We lived differently. This script is nothing but Moscow hipsters who don't know how to do anything except f**k at others' expense. The script was written by someone from another planet . . . I think I'm right, as I lived through that time."[3] Aleksei Rybin, co-founder of Kino, also panned the initial script and asked that his name be removed from the film. Tropillo spoke out vehemently against the film in a YouTube address.[4] Leading Tsoi biographer and historian Vitaly Kalgin took a more evenhanded view of *Leto*, describing it as "nice" and "not a bad film," but emphasizing that it was primarily a composite portrait of 1980s Russian rock culture, which had little to do with the historical biography of Tsoi.[5] It is worth noting that criticism of historical veracity is a staple of the reception of such musical biopics. The film about Russia's other most famous rock (bard) musician, *Vysotskii. Spasibo, chto zhivoi* (Vysotsky. Thank you for being alive, directed by Petr Buslov, 2011), was met with similarly scathing criticism from contemporaries and family members of Vladimir Vysotsky. And a second attempt at a biopic about Tsoi, the 2020 film *Tsoi* (directed by Aleksei Uchitel'), was almost universally panned, and ridiculed for its loose treatment of history.[6]

While some resistance to cinematic depictions of Tsoi from the guardians of Russian rock history may be inevitable, the polarized assessment of *Leto* also

---

3 "Stsenarii—lozh' ot nachala do kontsa. My zhili po-drugomu. V ego stsenarii moskovskie khipstery, kotorye krome kak tra***t'sia za chuzhoi schet, bol'she nichego ne umeiut. Stsenarii pisal chelovek s drugoi planety. . . . Mne kazhetsia, ia prav, potomu chto ia v to vremia zhil." Sergei Kagermazov, "Grebenshchikov raskritikoval fil'm Serebrennikova o Tsoe," MR7.ru, February 15, 2018, https://mr-7.ru/articles/177055/.

4 "Mnenie Andreia Tropillo. Kirill Serebrennikov. Fil'm 'Leto.' Viktor Tsoi," YouTube, September 16, 2017, accessed August 20, 2021, https://www.youtube.com/watch?v=QzO8OMPbpqs.

5 "I can't say that I didn't like the film. The film, of course, isn't bad. But I didn't like it as a film about Tsoi. Because it's not about Tsoi at all. It's the story of young musicians, and if you were to give them other names, nothing would change." Andrei Berezhnoi, "Zhenshchiny v fil'me 'Leto' krutiat Tsoem kak khotiat," *Natsiia*, June 13, 2018, https://nationmagazine.ru/events/zhenshchiny-v-filme-leto-krutyat-neprobivaemym-tsoem-kak-khotyat-/.

6 See "Aleksei Uchitel' otvetil na pretenzii syna Tsoia," RIA Novosti, November 18, 2020, accessed August 20, 2021, https://ria.ru/20201118/uchitel-1585141702.html; and "Marina Vladi osudila sozdatelei fil'ma 'Vysotskii. Spasibo, chto zhivoi,'" *Izvestiia*, December 22, 2011, accessed August 20, 2021, https://iz.ru/news/510509. In the Western context, recent musical biopics *Bohemian Rhapsody* (2018) about Freddie Mercury of Queen and *Rocketman* (2019) about Elton John, were subjected to similar historical critiques.

certainly stems from its hybrid genre and the very different, often diametrically opposed, goals of the musical and historical biography. Many underscored that historical accuracy was simply not the objective of the film. Rather, as is typical of the musical genre, it was an attempt to capture the mood and atmosphere, the "music, love, and freedom" of this time period, as prominent music critic Mikhail Kozyrev argued.[7] Some contemporaries of Tsoi and participants in the Russian rock movement gave the film high praise. Artemy Troitsky, organizer of Naumenko and Tsoi's first concerts, writes: "If you judge it as a genre film, it's completely wonderful. Joyful, romantic, sentimental, everything as it should be. If one looks at it through the lens of the 'biopic,' then, of course, *Leto* doesn't fly, since the degree of veracity is relatively small."[8]

Characteristically for its director, *Leto* anticipates such historical objections, laying bare its own artifice and employing a range of postmodernist devices. As critic Rita Safariants observes, "*Summer* is positioned as a provocation to the staunch policing of historical authenticity surrounding the mythology of late-Soviet underground rock music."[9] Among the film's many postmodernist features, most notable is the quasi-narrator, Skeptic (Aleksandr Kuznetsov), whose name, among other things, gestures to the skepticism of contemporary critics and viewers, and who appears before and after *Leto*'s more fantastical, performative moments, frequently quipping: "This never happened" (fig. 8.1).[10] Similarly, when Tsoi, played by Korean-German actor Teo Yoo, first appears on screen on the beach, Skeptic remarks wryly to the camera: "Doesn't look like him!"[11] Dressed all in black, with an anachronistic haircut and glasses, Skeptic seems to

---

7 Alia Ponomareva, "Svobodnoe 'Leto' arestovannogo Serebrennikova: pervye reaktsii na fil'm," Radio Svoboda, June 6, 2018, https://www.svoboda.org/a/29274929.html. Scriptwriter Michael Idov similarly emphasized that his interest in writing the script was not historical veracity, but that it is a film about "youth, love, and figuring things out" (Michael Idov, "Audiences and Online Reception: Before and after COVID: A Conversation with Michael Idov," Zoom conversation hosted by the Ohio State University, November 18, 2020.

8 Artemii Troitskii, "Leta ne budet," Ekho Moskvy, June 12, 2018, https://echo.msk.ru/blog/troitskiy/2220134-echo.

9 Rita Safariants, "*Summer* (*Leto*, 2018)," *KinoKultura* 61 (2018), http://www.kinokultura.com/2018/61r-leto_RS.shtml.

10 All filmgrabs in this chapter are from *Leto* (Summer 2018), directed by Kirill Serebrennikov.

11 The casting of Teo Yoo as Tsoi sparked its own series of praise and criticism. Many remarked that Yoo bears a striking resemblance to Tsoi, while others claimed the opposite. Moreover, Yoo, who does not speak Russian but meticulously memorized his Russian lines, was dubbed over by Russian actor and musician Denis Kliaver. I would argue that this imparted a certain emotional distance and felicitous, ephemeral quality to Tsoi, which worked well for the character. See Aleksandra Zerkaleva, "'Konechno, ne pokhozh.' Interv'iu chetyrekh Tsoev," *Kore Saram: Zapiski o koreitsakh*, June 26, 2018, https://koryo-saram.ru/konechno-ne-pohozh-intervyu-chetyreh-tsoev/.

be a tongue-in-cheek nod to precisely the contemporary Moscow "hipster" that Leningrad rockers like Grebenshchikov lambasted for their outsider take on the period.

Figure 8.1. Skeptic informs the viewer, "This never happened."[12]

While in part a realistic backstage musical—or one about a performer in which the musical numbers are naturally embedded in the story rather than supradiegetic—it also slips frequently into performative numbers that are situated as the free fantasy of the storytellers, about what might have been, but explicitly was not. While *Leto*'s slippage between realist and performative spaces is less clear-cut than that of many musicals, adding fuel to the fire of debates about authenticity, it nonetheless is a film musical much more than a biopic, structured primarily by its musical numbers and observing many of the conventions of the genre.[13] Typically of the genre, the musical numbers reinforce the events and themes of the story while also creating a meta-diegetic plane of meaning. For instance, *Leto* is roughly bookended by the songs "Leto" ("Summer")—Naumenko's anthem to carefree summer life, which he sings on the beach—and the Kino song "Konchitsia leto" ("Summer's ending"), which plays emphatically

12 All film stills in this chapter are from *Leto* 2018, dir. Kirill Serebrennikov.

13 As some have observed, to whatever extent *Leto* is a biopic, it is much more about Naumenko than Tsoi. Tsoi's biographer Kalgin remarked: "In general I'm surprised: Why do people consider *Leto* a film about Tsoi? He's in the background there, nothing more. His character, though distorted, isn't fully explored. *Leto* is a film about Mike Naumenko and his wife" (Berezhnoi, "Zhenshchiny v fil′me 'Leto' krutiat Tsoem kak khotiat").

as the closing credits roll. This deliberate framing with two songs is but one of many musical elements that structure the story, and contributes to its diegetic and meta-diegetic discourses, evoking an array of meanings: the nostalgia and longing for a fleeting, carefree moment of youth that inevitably drew to a close; the end of an optimistic and heady period in Russian rock history that would be curtailed by harsher censorship and personal tragedy; and the end of Tsoi, Naumenko, and Natasha's close relationship.[14] Thus, through its title, the juxtaposition of these 'theme songs,' the film trailer (which features Naumenko's song "Leto"), and so on, "summer" becomes an extended, multivalent trope in the film.

Throughout the film the musical performances by Zoopark and Kino, while realistic and almost entirely diegetic, are not arbitrarily placed, but are situated such that each reflects in some way on the events of the story, adding layers of meaning through their lyrics and thematic content. After self-sacrificially leaving Tsoi and Natasha alone for a night so that they may determine their feelings, Naumenko returns home around sunrise as the Zoopark song "6 utra" ("6 in the morning") plays on the soundtrack. Beyond its superficial connection to the early morning setting, there is a more subtle and meaningful connection between the song and the diegesis as well. Naumenko sings on the track, "I love them all / Well, almost all / And I just want everyone to be happy," underscoring the high-minded and benevolent nature of Naumenko as a character and the platonic relationship binding the three.

Though there are many such musical bridges in the film, connecting the music to the physical space via bricolage, or connecting broader themes in the story to the song lyrics, perhaps the most poignant is Tsoi's performance of "Derevo" ("Tree") in the film's final scene. Having drifted apart from Naumenko musically and distanced himself from the couple out of respect for their relationship, Tsoi sings one of his most melancholy, serious, and philosophical songs in this scene. Obsessed with whether Naumenko will come to the concert, when Tsoi finally sees him in the crowd he interrupts his band and begins a solo performance of "Tree" as though he were singing it directly to Naumenko. He sings "I know my tree won't live but a week. / I know my tree is doomed to perish in this city. / But I spend all my time with it. / I'm fed up with everything else. / It

14 Artemy Troitsky underscores this meaning of the film in his review: "The relatively carefree 'summer' (1981–1982) of Tsoi and his friends didn't last long: autumn and winter came. The persecution of rock, 'blacklists,' the arrest of musicians, police roundups at concerts. That was already 1983–1984. And it got even more fierce. We were, as the British inventors of boxing put it, 'saved by the bell.' If M. S. Gorbachev's saving bell hadn't sounded in 1985, everything would have turned out differently" (Troitskii, "Leta ne budet").

seems to be my home. / It seems to be my friend. / I planted a tree. / I planted a tree. . . ."[15] Naumenko looks on intently, his expression pregnant with emotion, before abruptly leaving the hall "to smoke." A tear rolls down Natasha's cheek as she smiles broadly and the audience breaks into rapturous applause (fig. 8.2).

Figure 8.2. Naumenko and Natasha watch Tsoi's performance of "Tree."

Here again Tsoi's song operates on multiple levels of signification. Most overtly, like the tree that "won't last a week and is doomed in this city," captions flash on the screen reminding the audience that both Tsoi ("1962–1990") and Naumenko ("1955–1991") died young, at the ages of twenty-eight and thirty-six, respectively. The Leningrad rock movement and the fervor of newfound freedom on the eve of perestroika, too, would be a fleeting moment in Russian cultural history. Less obvious, but perhaps more poignant in the scene, is the metaphor of lovingly, painstakingly cultivating a tree: "But I spend all my time with it. / I am fed up with everything else. / It seems to be my home. / It seems to be my friend"—which appears to describe both their friendship and the worldview Tsoi and Naumenko shared vis-à-vis music. As the film underscores, unlike much of the Leningrad rock movement (and global rock music in general), which was largely derivative and imitative, both songwriters took a serious, philosophical approach to their songwriting, and strove for something original, even transcendent, in their music. The final scene underscores this

15 "Ia znaiu—moe derevo ne prozhivet i nedeli. / Ia znaiu—moe derevo v etom gorode obrecheno. / No ia vse svoe vremia provozhu riadom s nim. / Mne vse drugie dela nadoeli. / Mne kazhetsia, chto eto moi dom. / Mne kazhetsia, chto eto moi drug. / Ia posadil derevo. / Ia posadil derevo."

unique bond between Tsoi and Naumenko, which could not be tarnished even by their romantic tensions or musical disagreements.[16]

In addition to the diegetic performances of Kino and Zoopark, *Leto* consists of four non-diegetic numbers that comprise the film's purely fantastical and most flamboyant scenes. As Rick Altman observes in his seminal study of the film musical, one of the most salient features of the genre is the way in which it moves between diegetic action, to diegetic music, to supradiegetic performance, often by means of an audio dissolve.[17] In classical film musicals, a range of other devices for facilitating this transition between realist diegesis and supradiegetic performance are employed, such as the musical bridge or bricolage.[18] However, in contrast to conventions of the classical film musical, in Serebrennikov's *Leto* the numbers are explicitly framed as the free fantasy of the characters and/or the postmodern narrator, Skeptic, who looks directly into the camera and informs the viewer with a wink that the events never occurred. Notably, all four of the supradiegetic numbers are Western songs—covers of The Talking Heads' "Psycho Killer," Iggy Pop's "Passenger," Lou Reed's "Perfect Day," and David Bowie's "All the Young Dudes"—sung in thickly accented English by the characters and choralized by the "grey masses" and bystanders of mainstream Soviet society. Skeptic introduces these songs by speaking their lyrics, translated into Russian, directly to the camera (a detail that might be overlooked by viewers not familiar with the songs). Rather than slipping gradually between the diegetic track into supradiegetic performance through the intermediary of music, as is typical in more traditional film musicals, what musicologist Guido Heldt calls "the leveling of representational levels" occurs in *Leto* through a self-conscious narrator.[19] Yet again, Serebrennikov chooses to lay bare the film's artifice, replacing the more unobtrusive audio dissolve with this direct address by its narrator.

In one such number, Tsoi, Naumenko, and company are riding on a suburban train when a member of the group is accosted by an ideologically conservative passenger: "The government gave you an education ... So that you would build a home, start a family, plant your own roots. But you just shout! Bastards! You

---

16 If we extend the metaphor of the tree further, Naumenko and Zoopark established the "roots" of a strain of Leningrad rock music that Tsoi and Kino would culminate into a flourishing "tree" as arguably the most iconic band in Russian rock music history.

17 Altman, *The American Film Musical*, 62–73.

18 For a good discussion of the structural devices of the film musical such as audio dissolves, bricolage and others, see Thomas Schatz, *Hollywood Genres: Formulas, Filmmaking, and the Studio System* (Philadelphia: Temple University Press, 1981); Altman, *The American Film Musical*; and Feuer, *The Hollywood Musical*.

19 Guido Heldt, *Music and Levels of Narration in Film* (Bristol: Intellect, 2013), 137.

sing the songs of our ideological enemy!"[20] One of the more audacious members of the group, nicknamed "Punk" (Aleksandr Gorchilin), is punched in the face and then detained by an off-duty KGB officer. As Punk's face is smeared in blood, Skeptic turns to the camera and speaks the opening lines of "Psycho Killer" by The Talking Heads: "I can't seem to face up to the facts, / I'm tense and nervous and I can't relax. / I can't sleep because my bed's on fire. / Don't touch me, I'm a real live wire." In a moment of exuberance and unbridled mayhem, the group breaks into rioting, song and dance, karate kicking and playfully throwing tomatoes at their oppressors (fig. 8.3). The gender-bending Punk grabs one of the conservative male attackers and plants a kiss on him, recalling Banksy's sexually transgressive work "Kissing Coppers" (2004) and the Russian work "Era miloserdiia" ("The era of mercy," 2004) by Sinie Nosy that it inspired. The scene, moreover, pays homage to the 1988 cult film *Igla* (The needle, directed by Rashid Nugmanov), which stars Tsoi in the lead role and includes scenes of Tsoi as larger-than-life action hero, using martial arts against a band of criminals.

Figure 8.3. Fantasy revolt on the train to the tune of The Talking Heads' "Psycho Killer."

20 This is another of the film's postmodern ironies and embedded jokes. The conservative patriot is played by Aleksandr Bashirov, whose reputation as an alcoholic and cult actor, as well as his previous performances in the rock films *Igla* (1988) and *Assa* (1987), impart a range of metacinematic associations to the scene.

The fantastical numbers of *Leto* celebrate their own exuberance and haptic enjoyment for its own sake. As Heldt observes:

> What musical numbers show off is first and foremost themselves: their own inventiveness, virtuosity, joyful abundance of extrovert skill (in singing, dancing, but also in film-making). That this usually takes place in supradiegetic space, beyond the confines of a "realistic" storyworld, may be only partially due to the fact that their virtuosity would be difficult to do in the storyworld.[21]

Moreover, the performance of "Psycho Killer" is an example of the musical number as a culmination and venting of emotion. As Heath Laing argues, "The integrated number comes at a point in the musical narrative when the need for emotional expression has reached a particularly high point. Often this is an expression of feeling that can no longer be contained by the character(s), or an emotion which must be acknowledged and shared in order to progress in the narrative."[22] However, in Serebrennikov's self-conscious framing, these fantasy scenes fulfill an important additional function. When the song ends, the camera quickly cuts back to the original scene and we see the group of musicians sitting in silence with downcast expressions as Punk is escorted away by the police. This juxtaposition of fantasy with what actually occurs underscores the gulf between the characters' desires and the stifling realities of late-Soviet life.

Per Altman, another defining feature of the film musical is a dual-focus narrative that ultimately ends in resolution.[23] Here, too, Serebrennikov's film

---

21 Heldt, *Music and Levels of Narration in Film*, 138.

22 Heather Laing, "Emotion by Numbers: Music, Song and the Musical," in *Musicals: Hollywood and Beyond*, ed. Bill Marshall and Robynn Stilwell (Bristol: Intellect, 2000), 5–13.

23 "Society is defined by a fundamental paradox: both terms of the oppositions on which it is built (order/liberty, progress/stability, work/entertainment, and so forth) are seen as desirable, yet the terms are perceived as mutually exclusive. Every society possesses texts which obscure this paradox, prevent it from appearing threatening, and thus assure the society's stability. The musical is one of the most important types of text to serve this function in American society. By reconciling terms previously seen as mutually exclusive, the musical succeeds in reducing an unsatisfactory paradox to a more workable configuration, a concordance of opposites. Traditionally, this is the function which society assigns to myth." Altman, *The American Film Musical*, 27.

engages the genre in postmodern fashion and attempts to straddle the difficult line between conventions of the musical and the historical biopic. Indeed, as in the classical musical formula, *Leto* is built on a series of dualities, explored through both the romantic and the musical rivalry—albeit relatively friendly and benevolent—between Naumenko and Tsoi: established rock aesthetics (largely inspired by classic rock artists) and new and emerging rock aesthetics (such as New Wave); irony and deconstructive songwriting impulses versus simplicity and sincerity, and others. However, the film's most important duality is not at all personified by the opposition of Naumenko and Tsoi—namely, the opposition of freedom and oppression/cultural stagnation—but is explored as an opposition of the protagonists collectively against their environment. I would argue that, through the characters' escapist flights of fancy and fantastical musical numbers, the contradictions of freedom and oppression in Soviet life are resolved for the viewer in a similar manner to that described by Altman: ". . . preventing them from appearing threatening . . . and reducing an unsatisfactory paradox to a more workable configuration, a concordance of opposites."[24]

Leto subverts the conventional ending of the "show musical"—a musical in which the uniting of a couple corresponds to the success of a show or performance.[25] Like several other recent film musicals, such as the celebrated Irish musical *Once* (directed by John Carney, 2007) and American *La La Land* (directed by Damien Chazelle, 2016), the ending of *Leto* is melancholy and anti-climactic: Tsoi and Natasha take the high road and do not consummate their romantic desires, while Naumenko and Tsoi drift apart musically. This subversion of the fairytale ending reflects the film's pretensions to realism and historical fidelity, and again points to the hybrid nature of its genre.[26] Nonetheless, the film's finale—Tsoi's performance of "Tree" onstage, with Naumenko and Natasha in the audience, discussed above—can be viewed as a variation of the show musical in which narrative tensions

24 Ibid., 27.

25 Ibid., 126–127.

26 In interview, Serebrennikov gestured to the conscious avoidance of the traditional fairytale ending: "I did everything I could to not turn the film into a fairy tale" (Afanas'eva, "Interv'iu na udalenke: Kirill Serebrennikov"). Similarly, scriptwriter Michael Idov remarked in discussion that he did not want to write a typical musical with an ending that is triumphant and happy, given the tragic ending of the lives of Tsoi and Naumenko (Idov, "Audiences and Online Reception").

are sublimated and partially resolved in the form of Tsoi's exceptional music.

Having discussed some key structural elements of *Leto*—its tensions between historical biopic and musical fantasy; its (often postmodern) engagement with the structure and conventions of the film musical, and others—let us consider how the film's narrative and musical form explore its two key preoccupations: the attempt to carve out individual freedom and live "outside" of a stifling socio-political environment; and the complex question of imitation and authenticity in this period and cultural milieu.

Living *Vne*: A Dialogue Between 1981 and 2018

> I was thinking of writing a song, not about anyone or anything, completely devoid of any meaning . . . The absence of meaning in a song is, in my opinion, a virtue.
>
> —Mike Naumenko, *Leto* (2018)

> The television man is crazy, saying we're juvenile delinquent wrecks, / But man, I need a TV when I've got T. Rex.
>
> —David Bowie, "All the Young Dudes" (1972)

In one of *Leto*'s more memorable and politically suggestive scenes, Naumenko, Tsoi, and their band members meet with the administrators of the Leningrad Rock Club to get approval for Tsoi's debut concert. The censor (subtly performed by Iuliia Aug) is somewhat taken aback as she reads Tsoi's "crude" lyrics aloud: "I'm a good-for-nothing, ohh, ohh / I'm a good-for-nothing, mama, mama" ("Ia bezdel'nik, ooo, ooo / Ia bezdel'nik, ooo, mama, mama"). One of the band's promoters intervenes, cleverly invoking a range of late-Soviet clichés, and insists that each of Tsoi's songs is in fact a parody and critique of various social problems: "social parasitism" (*tuneiadstvo*), "sexual promiscuity," and "teenage alcoholism." Ironically, Tsoi's songs are clearly exemplars, rather than critiques, of these very phenomena—a fact that the censor seems to be aware of, which she indicates with a knowing smile. The stifling ideological environment of the *zastoi* (Stagnation) period of the Soviet Union appears elsewhere in the film primarily as a muted backdrop against which Tsoi and the others live their lives, such as the larger-than-life mural of Leonid Brezhnev (fig. 8.4), but here they are brought to the forefront.

Figure 8.4. The backdrop of Soviet ideology in *Leto.*

Such markers of Brezhnevian *zastoi* clearly evoke and are in dialogue with the authoritarian turn, censorship, and political repression of "late Putinism" (roughly 2012 to the present), a period that in recent years has often been referred to as a "new Stagnation" (*novyi zastoi*).[27] The political dimensions of

27 For uses of the term *novyi zastoi*, see Sergei Guriev, "Novyi zastoi Rossii," *Project Syndicate*, November 14, 2013; Andrei Sharogradskii, "Dobro pozhalovat' v zastoi," Radio Svoboda, September 5, 2017, accessed August 20, 2021, https://www.svoboda.org/a/28717385.html;

Leto took on even greater significance when Serebrennikov was arrested midway through its production, on charges that were widely viewed as politically motivated, and was forced to complete the film while under house arrest in 2017.[28] And yet, as numerous critics pointed out, the political discourse of the film is strikingly understated and non-confrontational.[29]

Another example of the exploration of freedom and constraint is found in the film's cinematography, as camera operator Vladislav Opel'iants methodically uses open- and closed-form shots to further underscore this opposition throughout the film. The apotheosis of cinematographic liberation occurs in the early scene on the beach in which the group drinks, plays music, and dances naked around the fire. Here the open space and absence of a frame, the summer sun and fresh air, convey a haptic sense of freedom reflecting the inner freedom of the characters. By contrast, many later scenes—such as the scene of ideological oppression in the suburban train and even the intimate *kvartirnik* (apartment concert)—are shot with tight, close framing and evoke the limitations imposed on the characters' freedom (fig. 8.5).

Nonetheless, while it may be tempting to reduce Serebrennikov's film to an oblique allegory about Putin-era authoritarianism, I would argue that *Leto*, like the 1980s subculture it portrays, is an example of artistic expression attempting to exist "outside" of these ideological strictures altogether. In his influential study of late Soviet culture, Yurchak problematizes characterizations of the culture of the period into reductive binaries of official/dissident, conformist/non-conformist, and so forth, instead emphasizing the paradoxes and complex interplay between official and unofficial culture. Among other arguments, Yurchak describes the prominent subjective mode and practice of living *vne* (outside) of the dominant discourse. He focuses on "urban cultural milieus of the 1960s and 1970s, whose members thought of themselves as living in a reality 'different' from the 'ordinary' Soviet world. These communities of archeologists, theoretical physicists, literature lovers, mountain climbers, rock musicians, and

---

Dmitrii Prokof'ev, "Esh' bednykh," *Novaia gazeta*, May 4, 2021m https://novayagazeta.ru/articles/2021/05/04/esh-bednykh.

28 The political fate of the director became further tied to the semiotics of the film at its premiere at the Cannes International Film Festival in 2018. When Serebrennikov was banned from travel due to his legal proceedings, his cast appeared on the red carpet at Cannes carrying a sign reading "Kirill Serebrennikov," underscoring their support for the director and the injustice of the accusations against him.

29 See, for example, Dolin, "Leto, Fokstrot, Krasotka na vsiu golovu" and Safariants, "*Summer* (*Leto*, 2018)."

Figure 8.5. Open and closed framing is used throughout the film.

so on, created a kind of 'deterritorialized' reality that did not fit the binary categories of either support of or opposition to the state."[30]

This insightful reading of a "deterritorialized" existence of many in late Soviet society sheds light on the songwriting, aesthetics and *zhiznetvorchestvo* (poetic lifestyles) of Leningrad rock musicians like Tsoi and Naumenko. Rather than standing in direct or explicit opposition to the state, Tsoi, Naumenko and many others epitomized a "dropping out" from Soviet life that recalls the *vnutrenniaia immigratsiia* (internal immigration) of many writers and intellectuals of the period. Glorifying work as boiler-room attendants, singing about drinking, parties, and other quotidian and personal themes, Kino and Zoopark's discographies largely reflect, not an explicit critique of official culture, but a stubborn

30 Alexei Yurchak, *Everything Was Forever, until It Was No More* (Princeton: Princeton University Press, 2013).

assertion of a "third space" and dogged resistance to logocentrism of any kind, whether official or dissident.[31] Indeed, Tsoi and others' embrace of the image of the *bezdel'nik* ("idler" or "good-for-nothing") is an ironic reappropriation of the Soviet labeling of their social milieu as such. This ironic engagement with Soviet semiotics and attempt to find a "third way" also echoes the aesthetics of Soviet neo-conceptualist artists in the 1970–1980s, such as Dmitry Prigov.

In one of its fantasy numbers, Skeptic introduces a cover of David Bowie's "All the Young Dudes," quoting its refrain: "What the hell do I need your TV for when I've got T. Rex?" While a nod to the universal experience of alienated youth, the placement of this song in the narrative also evokes the pervasive ideology of Soviet television and the so-called "zombification" through television propaganda in the Putin era. In a scene shortly before this musical number, Naumenko bets one of his friends a beer that the first words on the television will be "100,000 tons" or "Leonid Il'ich," evoking the television propaganda of both eras.

Leto thoughtfully explores this subjective position of living *vne*. In the opening scene, having just finished his song "Drian'" ("Scum")—which riles up its young audience with its vulgar refrain, "Ty drian'!" ("You're scum!")—the artist Isha exclaims: "Mike, that was f**king awesome! It was so crude and awful, such disgusting and ugly rhymes. '*Drian'*' is a hit!" Later in the film, in the clearest articulation of this philosophical commitment and approach to songwriting, Naumenko tells "Bob" (Grebenshchikov): "I was thinking of writing a song not about anyone or anything, completely devoid of any meaning . . . The absence of meaning in a song is, in my opinion, a virtue." These small asides are not arbitrary dialogue, but act as signposts throughout the film, pointing to its broader philosophical and aesthetic reflections. While the position of consciously dropping out, deliberate slackerism, and aesthetic transgression can be traced through an array of counter-culture movements in global history—such as the Beat Movement of the 1950s–1960s and the punk movement in the 1970–1980s—this ethos took on its own resonance and localized meanings in the Soviet context.

---

31 In the film, Naumenko expresses ambivalence toward his own apolitical position. In one fantasy scene, ostensibly manifesting Naumenko's guilt and self-doubt, Skeptic berates him for his political disengagement: "Greetings, Dylan, greetings, Lou Reed! Only Dylan f**king sang about Vietnam! Dylan sang about a falsely accused black boxer! And what do you sing about, Mike? What is your rock'n'roll about? What is this song about? It's the song of a satisfied, benevolent guy who simply doesn't give a shit what sort of monstrous country he lives in . . ."

While Tsoi and Kino are often viewed retrospectively as political icons and remembered for songs like "Khochu peremen" ("I want change"), which became an anthem of perestroika, their broader discography, and indeed much of 1980s Russian rock, belies that characterization. To their credit, the filmmakers resisted the massive temptation to turn *Leto* into a political anthem of their own. Rather, Serebrennikov's film is a counter-history of sorts, which reclaims Tsoi and Leningrad rock from retrospective politicization and historical reductivism, and instead explores the paradoxical position of living *vne*, or of creating one's own world of relative freedom within a stifling political environment. As Troitsky wrote in his review of the film: "*Leto* presents a clear uplifting message. In short: How to remain free people and live in an unfree country."[32] The film's soundtrack reflects precisely this sensibility, featuring none of Kino's politically charged songs, only several offbeat and less common tracks—all the more beloved by dedicated fans for this reason—such as "Bezdel'nik" ("I'm a good-for-nothing, mama, mama"); "Moi druz'ia" ("My friends go through life at a march / And stop only at beer kiosks"); "Vremia est', a deneg net" ("I have time, but no money"), and "Vos'miklassnitsa" ("Eighth-grade girlfriend").[33] The director's comments about the film reflect a conscious desire to eschew a socio-political emphasis. Looking back on *Leto* in a 2020 interview, Serebrennikov reflected:

> [In] *Leto* we told the story of very young people who love, carouse, compose music, and live a wonderfully happy life. No one had yet drunk himself to death, no one had yet succumbed to the temptations of fame, no one had died. They're all still young, it's the very beginning of the 1980s. For them this life was wonderful, the happiest time, and so that flare of happiness and charm is in the film. I didn't want to make a dark story. I don't really like the Soviet Union, but it would be false to tell about these people in a socially critical light. I wanted to tell the story of love and being in love with music, creation, and freedom. To show that these people were free despite all of the hell in the *sovok* [Soviet mentality] that surrounded them.[34]

---

32 Troitskii, "Leta ne budet."

33 This is also a relatively faithful observance of chronology. Most of the songs featured in the film come from Kino's first album, *45*, the recording of which in summer of 1981 is the subject of the narrative.

34 Afanas'eva, "Interv'iu na udalenke: Kirill Serebrennikov."

In short, *Leto*'s dialogue with contemporary Russian society consists not only of its portrayal of ideological *zastoi* and looming censorship, but also the subjective mode of attempting to live outside of those parameters, to carve out one's own world of meaning and freedom despite sociopolitical realities. As one review of the film pointed out, Serebrennikov himself has attempted to do just that through his work at Gogol Center: "[Serebrennikov's] Gogol Center embraces a similar cosmopolitanism, gathering around itself a group of young people who wants to break away from *sovok* and follow the scent of freedom, among other things, through the tortuous paths of art."[35] Despite the director's controversial reputation and legal troubles, his body of work reflects the primacy of transgressive aesthetics over transgressive ideology, which resonates with the lives and art of Tsoi, Naumenko, and the 1980s Russian rock movement.

On Derivation, Reification, and the Imaginary West

> "What will Americans see in my songs after the Beatles, the Stones, the Doors, Led Zeppelin, the Clash, Joy Division, Bowie, Dylan, T. Rex, even Blondie?"
>
> —Mike Naumenko, *Leto* (2018)

Through both its narrative and its soundtrack, *Leto* constructs an intercultural dialogue and complex discourse on authenticity and imitation. Let us consider a final supradiegetic (fantasy) number and how it functions structurally and thematically within the film. Tsoi and Natasha board a tram together on their way to bring Naumenko a birthday present. In a moment of situational bricolage, the grey Soviet passengers on the tram break into a choralized version of "Passenger" by Iggy Pop. As in the other fantasy scenes, colorful illustrations are scrawled on the frame as Tsoi surfs the roof of the tram (fig. 8.6). The absurdity and humor of Soviet *babushki* singing Iggy Pop's rock ballad in thickly accented Russian provides its own sort of postmodern performance, underscoring its irony and artifice yet again, but also expressing the inner exuberance of Tsoi and Natasha when together, and allowing the characters to break free temporarily from their drab reality in a moment of fantasy. Furthermore, in this and virtually

35 Anzhelika Artiukh and Denis Solov'ev-Fridmanm, "Eto sladkoe slovo 'svoboda,'" ArtTerritory, June 14, 2018, https://arterritory.com/ru/ekran_-scena/recenzii/22085-eto_sladkoe_slovo_svoboda/.

all the English-language numbers, a moment of genuine intercultural dialogue unfolds. Like the lyrical hero in Iggy Pop's "Passenger," Tsoi and Natasha are passengers on a metaphorical "journey of life." From the pent-up frustrations and alienation of youth in "Psycho Killer" and "All the Young Dudes" to the existential reflection of life's journey in "Passenger," each of these moments of homage to global rock history are a nod to universal human experiences of youth, freedom, and creativity, which resonated with Tsoi, Naumenko, and other Soviet youth in their own way. At the same time, the featured songs in the film are not anchored in a historical period or cultural context, spanning approximately fifteen years and coming from American, British, and Russian rock. The songs are performed and presented self-consciously as simulacra, copies of copies, drawing attention to what Jacques Derrida described as the free play of signifiers in postmodernist artworks.

Figure 8.6. Tsoi surfs the roof of the tram during Iggy Pop's "Passenger."

Another dimension of the film's intercultural and musical dialogue is the tremendous influence that American and British rock idols exerted on Naumenko, Tsoi, and other Russian rock musicians. In several scenes, the two discuss their primary influences, such as Lou Reed, The Velvet Underground, T. Rex, Blondie, and Bob Dylan. Naumenko and Tsoi chat about an early album of The Velvet Underground and the two express their admiration for its deliberate lo-fi recording quality. Tsoi remarks, "I like that it's, like, not recorded very well," and Naumenko responds, "Exactly!" Throughout the film one detects various "deconstructive" aesthetic influences from Western rock musicians on the songwriting of Tsoi and Naumenko, ranging from gestures of transgressive, personal liberation to a conscious primitivism. Their discussions of Western idols, moreover, become proxies for their own aesthetic polemics and tensions within

Russian rock. Naumenko greatly admires Lou Reed's songwriting, but Tsoi finds him "cynical" and "arrogant" at times (a view that Natasha, significantly, shares with Tsoi). Ostensibly, this debate gestures to the tension in the songwriting of Kino and Zoopark between deconstructive impulses of nonsense, absurdity, and irony, on the one hand, and of sincerity and earnest sentiments, on the other, which Tsoi embraced more than many of his contemporaries.[36]

Indeed, the film's complex discourse on derivation and originality reveals an acute sense of identity crisis and anxiety of influence within the Russian rock movement, which is a microcosm of late-Soviet culture writ large. In another scene, Tsoi and his band work on the song "Moe nastroenie" ("My mood"), and the guitarist Lenia suggests playing the song in the style of the Sex Pistols. Tsoi objects: "You're always trying to change my songs. Maybe we could try to simply sing them?" Lenia says, "But they're sort of . . . childish or something," to which Tsoi responds, "And is that bad?" Tsoi's *sui generis* songwriting—at times naively sentimental, even childlike—was one of the unique features that allowed Kino to stand out from the rest of the movement.[37] As Dolin remarked, "[*Leto*] is also a story about the derivative quality [*vtorichnost'*] of Russian rock vis-à-vis the West. About copying, the impossibility of finding its own path. And the drama of a person who does find his own path, as Viktor Tsoi managed to do."[38]

In this regard, *Leto* is part of a broader reevaluation of the late-Soviet period in recent Russian cinema and is arguably in dialogue with films such as *Ischeznuvshaia imperiia* (Vanished empire, directed by Karen Shakhnazarov, 2008) and *Stiliagi* (Hipsters, directed by Valery Todorovsky, 2008), which revisit the paradoxes of late-Soviet youth culture, much of which was expressed in the borrowed aesthetics and cultural codes of the West. *Hipsters*—the other most significant film musical in post-Soviet Russia—depicts the *stiliagi* subculture in the Soviet Union of the 1950–1960s. The protagonists of *Hipsters* create their own vivid world of wild jazz parties, garish zoot suits, and take American

---

36 In another scene, Tsoi and Naumenko disagree about the growing influence of New Wave, which Tsoi likes and of which Naumenko disapproves. Kino would go on to embrace New Wave aesthetics (synthesizers, rhythms, make-up and dress) and would be one of their defining features, which the film briefly shows in its conclusion.

37 The juxtaposition of Tsoi's intimate, earnest songwriting and Naumenko's embrace of a more conventional rock persona (glamour, deconstructive and ironic gestures, and so forth) is further emphasized in another scene. After their small apartment concert, they are each asked what their ideal concert would be. Naumenko lists a series of glamorous spectacles and effects, while Tsoi remarks that his ideal is something akin to this small *kvartirnik*, or in a little tavern, because he likes to be able to look his audience in the eye.

38 Dolin, "Leto, Fokstrot, Krasotka na vsiu golovu."

nicknames, only to ultimately learn that the Western world they have been dreaming of does not exist. As Freddy tells Mels when he returns from America in the film's finale: "There are no *stiliagi* there!" Similarly, *Vanished Empire*—not a musical but a drama centered on similar paradoxes of late socialism—is a nostalgic portrait of teenagers in 1970s Moscow in which three friends start a rock band named "Red Trousers," have romantic adventures, and buy illicit Western records and jeans on the black market. In the film's finale, in a flash-forward decades later, the protagonists Sergei and Stepan run into each other at an airport and reminisce. Significantly, in this moment of nostalgia for their ephemeral, lost youth in the 1970s, the only memory the two friends share is of their friend Kostia's stylish car—a Czech Tatra—that is, yet another foreign, hard-to-come-by luxury item from the period.[39] A similar paradox emerges in *Leto*. Its nostalgic retrospective on youth and freedom, the Leningrad rock movement, and the metaphorical summer of 1981 is a longing for a time in which its participants themselves were longing for a different life. In essence, a dream about a dream.

In his aforementioned monograph, Yurchak reflects on such cultural formations in late-Soviet society, arguing that what he calls the "Imaginary West" was part and parcel of living outside (*vne*) in a deterritorialized reality. In one part of the study that examines "the cultural and discursive phenomenon" that he calls the Imaginary West, Yurchak identifies it as "a local cultural construct and imaginary that was based on the forms of knowledge and aesthetics associated with the 'West,' but not necessarily referring to any 'real' West, and that also contributed to 'deterritorializing' the world of everyday socialism from within."[40] In *Leto*, the "Imaginary West" constitutes both an escape from and de-territorialization of unappealing Soviet realities, but also a source of anxiety of influence for its musician protagonists. Notably, Naumenko translates numerous lyrics of Western bands, copying them down in dozens of notebooks, a subtle detail that underscores this theme. When his friends encourage him to sing in English and market his music to the West, he responds, "What

39 Lilya Kaganovsky examines similar themes of originality and imitation vis-à-vis the West in the film *Stiliagi*, writing: "Not only was the entire style [of the *stiliagi*]—clothing and hairstyles, musical tastes, moral values—'borrowed' from the West, but by the time the latest fashions made it to the Soviet Union . . . by the time trophy films, new jazz records, and fashion magazines showed up in the Soviet Union, they were already out of date. The *stilyagi* copied, in other words, a style that was already passé. Todorovsky's film takes up precisely this problem of originality and imitation." Lilya Kaganovsky, "Russian Rock on Soviet Bones," in *Sound, Speech, Music in Soviet and Post-Soviet Cinema*, ed. Lilya Kaganovsky and Masha Salazkina (Bloomington: Indiana University Press, 2013), 261.

40 Yurchak, *Everything Was Forever, until It Was No More*, 34.

will Americans hear in my songs that is new after the Beatles, the Stones, the Doors, Led Zeppelin, the Clash, Joy Division, Bowie, Bolan, Dylan, T. Rex, even Blondie?"

However, recent Russian cinema's discourse on late Soviet imitation does not simply criticize the latter but raises complex questions about the nature of authenticity and meaning in the postmodern age. In *Hipsters*, when Freddy informs Mels that "*stiliagi* don't exist" in the West, Mels responds emphatically: "But we do!" After Naumenko's self-deprecating remark about the insignificance of Russian rock compared to its Western idols, his friend responds: "Yes, but we have you! Vitia [Tsoi]! Bob [Grebenshchikov]!" Such scenes reflect on the derivative aspects of the Leningrad rock movement, but also on how the floating signifiers of global rock culture became moored and reified in this specific place and time, creating their own very real, vital movements in the specific cultural context of late socialism. These moments, moreover, reflect the paradoxes of authenticity and questions about the possibility of originality more broadly in postmodernity—a period marked by global flows of culture, ubiquitous media and spectacle, and the mechanical reproduction of art—which are not unique to Russian culture (on both deterritorialization and authenticity in the Polish context, see chapter three). Such complex questions have been explored in a range of works dealing with philosophy and aesthetic theory, such as Walter Benjamin's "Art in the Age of Mechanical Reproduction" (1935), Guy Debord's *The Society of the Spectacle* (1967), and Jean Baudrillard's *Simulacra and Simulation* (1981).

Leto's complex discourse on authenticity and imitation is explored not only thematically—namely, as a source of debate between the characters, but also on the level of form. In addition to postmodern elements previously discussed—such as the self-conscious narrator Skeptic, whimsical sketches scrawled on the frame, meta-cinematic references, and others—a *mise en abyme* recurs in *Leto* as a friend of the band shoots a documentary of Kino and Zoopark. The scratchy home video at times fills the frame, creating an aura of authenticity, while at others is simply embedded within it, drawing attention to the film's constructed nature. Finally, in a postmodern scene *par excellence*, just after Naumenko has declared the relative insignificance of Russian rock music compared to the West, he stands in the corridor staring at records on the wall, superimposing himself and his friends onto the album covers of the Who, the Beatles, Blondie, Pink Floyd, and others (fig. 8.7). The scene evokes not only the Leningrad musicians' anxiety of influence, but visualizes a palimpsest quality of global rock music, and postmodern cultural production.

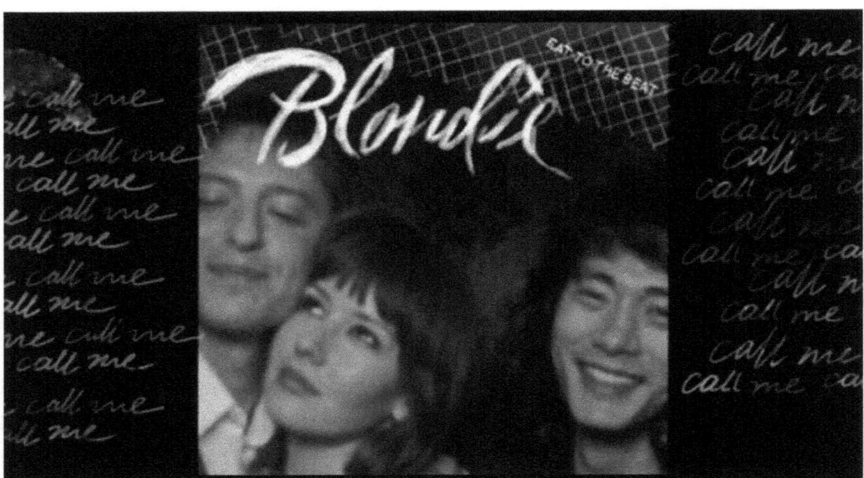

Figure 8.7. Naumenko imagines his friends on the covers of Western rock albums.

Significantly, Serebrennikov's embrace of postmodernist aesthetics is not merely subversive and deconstructive. On the contrary, despite its reflexive framing, *Leto* is heartfelt and full of sentiment—echoed by its dedication before the closing credits, "To those we love"—earnestly exploring the thrill of youth and romance, and the personal lives of Tsoi and the Naumenkos. At the same time, its narrator Skeptic and various meta-cinematic ironies lay bare the film's artifice and point to the impossibility of "authentic" representation. We can view Serebrennikov's framing and directorial style as a reflection of the cultural idiom of postmodernity—its formal pastiche, acute anxiety of influence, and hyper awareness of audience—or what Frederic Jameson calls the pattern of the "mode of production" of postmodernity, but without its usual intonation.[41] In this way, Serebrennikov's *Leto* attempts to straddle the line between postmodernist aesthetics and sincerity. Thus, as Tsoi and Naumenko wrestle in the narrative with their own complex questions about imitation, originality, earnest sentiment, and ironic distance, Serebrennikov himself explores similar questions through *Leto*'s complex meta-cinematic discourse, attempting to reconcile "authentic" representation with playful, postmodern irony; the conventions of the theatrical musical with the realist biopic; and so on. One of the film's true achievements lies in such parallelism and echoes between its various planes of signification—between narrative, soundtrack, genre elements, and even the artistic reflections

41 See Frederic Jameson, "The Aesthetics of Singularity," *New Left Review* 92 (2015): 101–103.

of its protagonists and Serebrennikov himself—allowing *Leto* to balance emotional resonance and reflexivity, and to cohere as both text and hypertext.

Bibliography

Afanas'eva, Elena. "Interv'iu na udalenke: Kirill Serebrennikov." YouTube, April 17, 2020. Accessed August 20, 2021. https://www.youtube.com/watch?v=vJyx3-O3oVI.

"Aleksei Uchitel' otvetil na pretenzii syna Tsoia." RIA Novosti, November 18, 2020. Accessed August 20, 2021. https://ria.ru/20201118/uchitel-1585141702.html.

Altman, Rick. *The American Film Musical.* Bloomington: Indiana University Press, 1987.

Artiukh, Anzhelika, and Denis Solov'ev-Fridman. "Eto sladkoe slovo 'svoboda.'" ArtTerritory, June 14, 2018. Accessed August 20, 2021. https://arterritory.com/ru/ekran_-scena/recenzii/22085-eto_sladkoe_slovo_svoboda/.

Berezhnoi, Andrei. "Zhenshchiny v fil'me 'Leto' krutiat Tsoem kak khotiat." *Natsiia,* June 13, 2018. Accessed August 20, 2021. https://nationmagazine.ru/events/zhenshchiny-v-filme-leto-krutyat-neprobivaemym-tsoem-kak-khotyat-/.

Dolin, Anton. "Leto, Fokstrot, Krasotka na vsiu golovu." YouTube, 2018. Accessed August 20, 2021. https://www.youtube.com/watch?v=UfCqmbAXWsA.

———. "*Leto* Kirilla Serebrennikova: kollektivnyi son o minuvshei epokhe." *Meduza,* May 10, 2018. Accessed August 20, 2021. https://meduza.io/feature/2018/05/10/leto-kirilla-serebrennikova-kollektivnyy-son-o-minuvshey-epohe.

Feuer, Jane. *The Hollywood Musical.* Bloomington: Indiana University Press, 1993.

Guriev, Sergei. "Novyi zastoi Rossii." *Project Syndicate,* November 14, 2013.

Heldt, Guido. *Music and Levels of Narration in Film.* Bristol: Intellect, 2013.

Idov, Michael. "Audiences and Online Reception: Before and after COVID. A Conversation with Michael Idov." Zoom conversation hosted by the Ohio State University, November 18, 2020.

Jameson, Fredric. "The Aesthetics of Singularity." *New Left Review* 92 (2015).

Kaganovsky, Lilya. "Russian Rock on Soviet Bones." In *Sound, Speech, Music in Soviet and Post-Soviet Cinema,* edited by Lilya Kaganovsky and Masha Salazkina, 252–272. Bloomington: Indiana University Press, 2013.

Kagermazov, Sergei. "Grebenshchikov raskritikoval fil'm Serebrennikova o Tsoe." MR7.ru, February 15, 2018. Accessed August 20, 2021. https://mr-7.ru/articles/177055/.

Laing, Heather. "Emotion by Numbers: Music, Song and the Musical." In *Musicals: Hollywood and Beyond,* edited by Bill Marshall and Robynn Stilwell, 5–13. Bristol: Intellect, 2000.

"Marina Vladi osudila sozdatelei fil'ma 'Vysotskii. Spasibo, chto zhivoi.'" *Izvestiia,* December 22, 2011. Accessed August 20, 2021. https://iz.ru/news/510509.

"Mnenie Andreia Tropillo. Kirill Serebrennikov. Fil'm 'Leto.' Viktor Tsoi." YouTube, September 16, 2017. Accessed August 20, 2021. https://www.youtube.com/watch?v=QzO8OMPbpqs.

Ponomareva, Alia. "Svobodnoe 'Leto' arestovannogo Serebrennikova: pervye reaktsii na fil'm." Radio Svoboda, June 6, 2018. Accessed August 20, 2021. https://www.svoboda.org/a/29274929.html.

Prokof'ev, Dmitrii. "Esh' bednykh." *Novaia gazeta,* May 4, 2021. Accessed August 20, 2021. https://novayagazeta.ru/articles/2021/05/04/esh-bednykh.

Safariants, Rita. "*Summer* (*Leto*, 2018)." *KinoKultura* 61 (2018). Accessed August 20, 2021. http://www.kinokultura.com/2018/61r-leto_RS.shtml.

Schatz, Thomas. *Hollywood Genres: Formulas, Filmmaking, and the Studio System*. Philadelphia: Temple University Press, 1981.

Sharogradskii, Andrei. "Dobro pozhalovat' v zastoi." Radio Svoboda, September 5, 2017. Accessed August 20, 2021. https://www.svoboda.org/a/28717385.html.

Surganova, Elizaveta, and Tat'iana Shorokhova. "Stsenaristy 'Leto': 'Etot fil'm ne ob uzhasakh sovetskoi sistemy.'" KinoPoisk, June 7, 2018. Accessed August 20, 2021. https://www.kinopoisk.ru/media/article/3192645/.

Troitskii, Artemii. "Leta ne budet." Ekho Moskvy, June 12, 2018. Accessed August 20, 2021. https://echo.msk.ru/blog/troitskiy/2220134-echo.

Yurchak, Alexei. *Everything Was Forever, until It Was No More*. Princeton: Princeton University Press, 2013.

Zerkaleva, Aleksandra. "'Konechno, ne pokhozh.' Interv'iu chetyrekh Tsoev." *Kore Saram: Zapiski o koreitsakh*, June 26, 2018. Accessed August. 20, 2021. https://koryo-saram.ru/konechno-ne-pohozh-intervyu-chetyreh-tsoev/.

Filmography

Polish

Bareja, Stanisław, dir. *A Marriage of Convenience* (*Małżeństwo z rozsądku*, 1967).
Fethke Jan & Konrad Tom, dirs. *Forgotten Melody* (*Zapomniana melodia*, 1938).
Krawicz, Mieczysław, dir. *Paweł and Gaweł* (*Paweł i Gaweł*, 1938).
———. *Robert and Bertrand* (*Robert i Bertrand*, 1938).
Pawlikowski, Paweł, dir. *Cold War* (*Zimna wojna*, 2018).
Smoczyńska, Agnieszka, dir. *The Lure* (*Córki dancingu*, 2015).
Trystan, Leon, dir. *One Floor Up* (*Piętro wyżej*, 1937).
Waszyński, Michał, dir. *What My Husband Is up to at Night* (*Co mój mąż robi w nocy*, 1934).

Russian

Aleksandrov, Grigorii, dir. *Volga-Volga* (1938).
Orlov, Aleksandr, dir. *The Woman Who Sings* (*Zhenshchina, kotoraia poet*, 1978).
Pyr'ev, Ivan, dir. *The Rich Bride* (*Bogataia nevesta*, 1937).
———, dir. *Tractor Drivers* (*Traktoristy*, 1939).
———, dir. *The Swineherdess and the Shepherd* (*Svinarka i pastukh*, 1944).
———, dir. *Cossacks of the Kuban'* (*Kubanskie kazaki*, 1949).
Riazanov, El'dar, dir. *Carnival Night* (*Karnaval'naia noch'*, 1956).
Riazanov, El'dar and Sergei Gurov, dir. *Spring Voices* (*Vesennie golosa*; original release: *Happy Youth* [*Schastlivaia iunost'*], 1955).
Serebrennikov, Kirill, dir. *Leto* [*Summer*] (*Leto*, 2018).
Shakhnazarov, Karen, dir. *Vanished Empire* (*Ischeznuvshaia imperiia*, 2008).
Stefanovich, Aleksandr, dir. *Soul* (*Dusha*, 1981).
Todorovsky, Valery, dir. *Hipsters* (*Stiliagi*, 2008).

Index

Accordion, The (Garmon'), 21, 176
ABBA, 254n16, 271n37
About Little Red Riding Hood (Pro krasnuiu shapochku), 28
Adria, The, nightclub, 44, 48–49, 150–51, 153, 161, 166
Adventure at Marienstadt, An (Przygoda na Mariensztacie), 16–17, 130–31
Adventure with a Song, An (Przygoda z piosenką), 16
Aerocity (Aerograd), 243n54
Afterimages (Powidoki), 109
After the Rain on Thursday (Posle dozhdichka v chetverg), 28
Aksenchuk, Ivan, 144
Aladdin, 6
Aleinikov, Petr, 188n57, 189
Aleksandrov, Grigorii, 9n29, 19, 22–24, 26–27, 31, 122, 161n49, 176–78, 190, 197–98, 220, 223, 228–29, 230n23, 233, 239–41, 251n7, 258
Alentova, Vera, 258
Alhambra, fictional entertainment club, 44–50, 55, 68
Ali Baba, 163
Alien, 148
Alien Woman, An (Postoronniaia zhenshchina), 176
Alla, company, 271
Alleluia! The Devil's Carnival, 148n21
All-Russian State Institute of Cinematography, The (VGIK), 175, 223
All That Jazz, 4, 156n39, 160–61
All-Union Agency on Copyright (VAAP), 263
All-Union Agricultural Exhibition (VDNKh), 23, 178, 181
All-Union Creative Conference on Cinema Affairs, 239, 242n51
All-Union Party Conference on Cinema, 242n51
Alma-Ata, 174
Alone (Odna), 20
Altman, Richard (Rick), 2, 5, 7–8, 18, 22, 41, 61, 117–19, 145, 165, 166n62, 167, 260, 281, 283–84
Amazing Boy (Udivitel'nyi mal'chik), 252n13, 257n22
American in Paris, An, 3, 99
Anatomy of Love (Anatomia miłości), 257n21
Anders' Army. *See* General Władysław Anders' Army
Andersen, Hans Christian, 142–47, 155, 158–60
Andreev, Boris, 188n57
Andrews, Julie, 3, 9
Andrzejewska, Jadwiga, 43, 52, 58, 78
Angelina, Pasha, 180
Ankara—Heart of Turkey (Ankara—serdtse Turtsii), 240
Annabella (Charpentier, Suzanne Georgette), 42
Annette, 6n22
Antonia, 9
Ardashnikov, Naum, 270n37
Ardolino, Emile, 152
Aria Diva, 141
Armatys, Leszek, 53
Arnold, Gina, 134
Arnshtam, Lev, 240, 259

Arsenov, Pavel, 257n22
Asaa, village, 147n20
Ashes and Diamonds (Popiół i diament), 16
Assa, 282n20
Association of Polish Stage Artists (ZASP), 15
Astaire, Fred, 2, 95, 152
As You Like It, 2
Attenborough, Richard, 10
Aug, Iuliia, 285
Austin, Thomas, 7n25

backstage musical, 44, 260, 275, 278
Bacon, Lloyd, 1
Badham, John, 5, 161
Bagiński, Adolf (pseud. Dymsza), 11, 12n38, 13–15, 40, 42–43, 45, 68–73, 75, 77–78
Bakhtin, Mikhail, 27n96, 83, 125, 220, 234–35, 238–39, 245, 259n24
Balash, Bela, 191
Ballady i Romanse, band, 161
Banksy, street artist, 282
Barber of Warsaw, The, cabaret (Cyrulik Warszawski), 68, 70
Barbican, 88, 98
Barefoot Contessa, The, 12n41
Bareja, Stanisław, 14, 16–18, 82–89, 91–96, 97n41, 99n45, 100–102, 104, 106–13, 130–31, 166
BAREJADA festival, 85
Barnet, Boris, 21
Barrios, Richard, 240
Barthes, Roland, 261
Bashirov, Aleksandr, 282n20
Baudrillard, Jean, 295
Beatles, The, rock group, 295
Beaumont, Harry, 240
Beauty and the Beast, 6
Bee Gees, 5
Before Parting (Prezhde chem rasstat'sia), 252n13
Beliavskii, Aleksandr, 254n16
Benjamin, Walter, 126, 295
Bennett, Bruce, 122
Benny Goodman Story, The, 29
Berkeley, Busby, 2, 78, 106, 163
Berlin, 4, 66, 131
Bernstein, Leonard, 89, 106, 166
Beware of the Car (Beregis' avtomobilia), 222
Bible, 166
Bielicka, Hanka, 91
Big Beat, The (Mocne uderzenie), 16–18
Bilyk, Roman, 31n106
biopic, 6, 14, 28–29, 31, 166, 260, 275–78, 284–85, 296
Birkholc, Robert, 71
Björk, Guðmundsdóttir, Icelandic singer, 160
Blackbeard (Blaubart), 159n46
Black Pearl (Czarna perla), 13
Blok-Muza-Film, studio, 12
Blondie, rock group, 292, 295
Bloody Chamber, The, 146, 159
Blue Angel, The, 68
Blum, Leon, 47
Bobkov, Filipp, 250n6
Bobrowska, Alicja, 91, 110
Bodnaruk, Igor', 271n37
Bodo, 14
Bodo, Eugeniusz. *See* Junod, Bohdan Eugène
Body, The (Ciało), 167
Bogue, Ronald, 124–25
Bohème, La (Puccini), 6n21
Bohemian Rhapsody, 276n6
Boiarskii, Mikhail, 32n108, 267, 269
Bolan, Marc, 295
Bolshoi Theater, The, 23, 224
Bolek and Lolek (Bolek i Lolek), 12
Bolesławski, Ryszard, 10
Bolesto, Robert, 141
Bondarchuk, Sergei, 258–59

Bonusiak, Edward, 111n64
Borodino, 27
Bortniczak, Stefania, 121n15
Bow, Clara, 42
Bowie, David, 142, 168, 281, 289, 295
Boyer, Jean, 9
Boyle, Danny, 117
Boym, Svetlana, 119, 138
Braunek, Małgorzata, 99n46
Breton, André, 103
Brezhnev, Leonid, 26, 28, 175, 250, 272, 285, 289
Bringing Up Baby, 208, 210
Brodskaia, Nina, 256, 257nn19–20, 257n22
Broadway Melody, The, 240
Brothers Karamazov, The, 177
Brylska, Barbara, 257
Buczkowski, Leonard, 16–17, 130
Budnitskaia, Alla, 258–59
Bykov, Rolan, 266
Bukówiec Górny, 120n14, 121n15
Bulgakowa, Oksana, 226
Bulgarian Music Festival, Golden Orpheus, 251
Buratino's Adventures (Prikliucheniia Buratino), 28
Burszta, Józef, 122n17
Burton, Tim, 148n21
Buslov, Petr, 276
Byron, George Gordon, poet, 98
By the Bluest of Seas (U samogo sinego moria), 21

Cabaret, 4, 160, 166
Cage aux folles, La, 84
Cannes International Film Festival, 4, 31n106, 116, 274, 287n28
Carax, Leos, 6n22
Carnegie Hall, the, 133n43
Carney, John, 284
Carnival, The (Karnaval), 28, 252n13
Carnival Night, The (Karnaval'naia noch'), 26–27, 220–23, 224n10, 226–28, 231–32, 235, 238–39, 241, 243–45
Carnival Night 2 or Fifty Years Since, 222
Carousel, 3
Carroll, Beth, 118
Carroll, Noel, 154
Carter, Angela, 146, 159
Carter, Rubin, 289n31
Casino de Paris, 60
Catch-22, 84
Cavalry Maiden, The (Zapiski kavalerist-devitsy), 26, 222n6
Cavell, Stanley, 17
Caucasus, the, 181, 203
Cękalski, Eugeniusz, 44
Center from the Skies, A (Tsentrovoi iz podnebes'ia), 257n22
Central Studio for Documentary Film, The (TsSDF), 223
Central Theater of the Soviet Army, The, 230n24, 242
Chabówka, 121n15
Champagne Waltz, 210n88
Channel Russia, 253n15
Channel One, 262n29
Chapaev, 194, 208, 216, 239, 242
Chaplin, Charlie, 8, 83–84, 96n39, 199
Charell, Erik, 9
Charisse, Cyd, 2, 152
Charleston, dance, 86, 95–96
Chazelle, Damien, 6, 119, 284
Chemberdskii, Nikolay, 240
Chernivtsi, 248
Chervona Ruta, musical group, 250, 251n9
Chevalier, Maurice, 9
Chicago, 6
Chief Council of the Film Industry, 69
China, 251
Chion, Michel, 220n3
Chopin, Frédéric, 23

choreography, 2, 4, 18, 98, 104, 106n57, 152, 163
Chrzanowski, Przemysław, 130–31n40
Churikova, Inna, 32
Chyła, Tadeusz, 89
Cielecka, Magdalena, 153
Cine-City, 25
Circus, The (Tsirk), 9n29, 22–23, 31, 176, 197, 238, 240, 251n7, 255
Civil Servant, The (Gosudarstvennyi chinovnik), 176
Clair, René, 112, 240
Clark, Katerina, 241, 244
Clash, The, rock group, 295
classical music, 23–24, 44, 61, 66, 69, 130, 253
Clover, Carol Jeanne, 148
Cobain, Kurt, 32n107
Coen Brothers, 117
Cohan, Steven, 145n15, 152n29
Cold War, 18, 31, 118, 134
Cold War, The (Zimna wojna), 18–19, 116–22, 124–25, 127, 130–31, 133nn42–43, 134–39, 152, 166
Columbia, studio, 13
Commander's Cross of the Order of Polonia Restituta, The, 85
Commedia dell'arte, 184–85, 204
Committee for Social Self-Defense, The (KOR), 112
Communism, 28, 85, 119, 128, 131, 138
Connell, John, 134
Conrich, Ian, 123
Conveyor of Death, The (Konveier smerti), 176, 191
Cook and the Singer, The (Povar i pevitsa), 257n22
Copenhagen, 147
Coquatrix, Bruno, 133n43
Corman, Roger, 5, 148n21
Cossacks of the Kuban' (Kubanskie kazaki), 23–26, 173, 200–217
Counterplan (Vstrechnyi), 240
Courageous Shirak (Otvazhnyi Shirak), 257n22
Cranes Are Flying, The (Letiat zhuravli), 223
Creed, Barbara, 148, 154
Crimea, 25
Criterion Collection, the, 141, 143,
Crosland, Alan, 1
Cukor, George, 166
Curtiz, Michael, 30
Czyżewska, Elżbieta, 91, 94, 95n38, 101

Dagestan, 178, 187
dance, 2–5, 11, 14, 18, 26n93, 30–31, 40–41, 44, 48–50, 53–56, 71–72, 77, 95–96, 105–6, 128–29, 130n40, 131, 150, 165, 184, 213, 234–35, 242, 252, 282
Dancer in the Dark, The, 160, 166
Darnton, John, 89
Davies, Valentine, 30
da Vinci, Leonardo, 103n55
Davis, Natalie Zeman, 259n24
Davydov, Aleksandr, 28
DC Comics, Inc., 98
Dean, Basil, 9
Dear Boy (Dorogoi mal'chik), 252n13
Death of Isolde (Wagner), 233
Debord, Guy, 295
Deleuze, Gilles, 124
Deluge, The (Potop), 99n44
Demarczyk, Ewa, 133n43
Demoiselles de Rochefort, Les, 9
Demutskii, Daniil, 231n25
Demy, Jacques, 6, 9, 125
Denmark, 147
Deranged, 142
Derbenev, Leonid, 263
Dereza, 28
Derrida, Jacques, 292
Deserter (Dezertir), 240

Diamond Arm, The (Briliantovaia ruka), 257
Dietrich, Marlene, 68
Dirty Dancing, The, 152
disco, 5, 19, 161–62
Disco Dancer, The, 271n37
Disneyland, 163
Dobrenko, Evgeny, 27n96, 228n19, 230n23, 235, 244
Dobrovol'skii, Arkadii, 181n34
Dolin, Anton, 275n2, 293
Dom kino, 188n57
Donetsk, 178
Donnelly, Kevin J., 118
Doors, The, rock group, 295
Double Life of Veronique, The (Podwójne życie Weroniki), 116
Dovzhenko, Oleksandr, 240, 243n54
Dracula (Hammer film series), 148
Dread (Strachy), 44
Dreigroschenoper, Die, 9
Drive (Kurazh), 262n29
Dubrovnik, 131–32
Dukel'skii, Semen, 188n57
Dunaevskii, Isaak, 22, 25, 174, 177, 183, 191–92, 198–200, 215–16, 228–29, 233, 240–41, 251n7
Durova, Nadezhda, 26, 222n6
Duvivier, Julien, 183
Dvořák, Antonín, 65
Dybbuk, The (Dybuk), 12
Dyer, Richard, 7, 18, 108, 152, 178, 182, 191
Dylan, Bob, 289n31, 292, 295
Dymsza, Adolf. *See* Bagiński, Adolf
Dzigan, Efim, 28n99
Dziworski, Bogdan, 127n38

Eastern Bloc, 92, 105, 131
Eastern Trade Fairs (Lwów), 69
Edwards, Blake, 9, 153
Eisenstein, Sergei, 19–20, 22, 83, 223, 240–41
Eisler, Jerzy, 85n14
Ekk, Nikolai, 20
El Cid, 12n41
Eliade, Mircea, 93
England, 9
entertainment, 1, 3–4, 7, 11–12, 14, 16, 21, 31, 39, 44–45, 48–49, 55–56, 59–60, 66, 79, 83–84, 108, 152, 166, 184, 193, 216–17, 240, 252–53, 254n16, 256, 260n27, 269, 271, 283n23
Enthusiasm: Symphony of the Donbass (Entuziazm: Simfoniia Donbassa), 226
Erdman, Nikolai, 200n70
Eriksen, Edvard, 147
Ermler, Fridrich, 231n25, 243n54
Europe, 8–10, 17, 41n5, 55, 105, 116–18, 132–34
Evdokimenko, Anatolii, 250
Evergreen, 9
Everyone Is Free to Love (Każdemu wolno kochać), 42
Everything Is Rhythm, 10

Faintsimmer, Aleksandr, 27
Fair at Sorochintsi, The (Sorochinskaia iarmarka), 186
Fairbanks, Douglas, 9, 83
Fantasia Film Festival, the, 141
Falk, Feliks, 112
Fall of the Roman Empire, The, 12n41
Feniks, studio, 12
Fere, Vladimir, 240
Fertner, Antoni, 51, 71
Fethke, Jan, 43–44, 52–54, 57–58, 69–70
Feuer, Jane, 2, 5, 7, 18, 44, 49n25, 64, 145, 165
Fijewski, Tadeusz, 76
Filippov, Sergei, 242
Film Comment, blog, 133n42
First Five-Year Plan, 24, 178, 180

Fischer, Russ, 159n45
Fitzgerald, Francis Scott, 92n32
Flashdance, 8
Flying down to Rio, 2
folk culture, 24, 122, 130, 138, 188, 212–13, 216
folk(lore) festival, 121n15, 125n32, 185, 194, 238
folk music, 120, 121n15, 123, 126–27, 130–31, 134
Fołtyn, Maria, 141
Forgotten Melody (Zapomniana melodia), 15–16, 44, 45n18, 51–59, 68, 71, 78
Fortuna, Piotr, 16, 92n31, 93, 99, 100n48, 106, 111n64
42nd Street, 2
Footlight Parade, 2
Fosse, Bob, 4, 6, 19, 156n39, 160, 166
Fox, studio. *See* Twentieth-Century Fox
France, 9, 131
Fraser, Lucy, 143n10, 145n14
Fredro, Aleksander, 69, 71
Freud, Sigmund, 13n45, 148
Friday the 13th, 148
Friedmann, Stefan, 99n46
Frisch, Max, 159n46

Gabrilovich, Evgenii, 174
Gagiu, Valeriu, 266
Gaidai, Leonid, 229, 256
Garbo, Greta, 8
Gardan, Juliusz, 13, 61
Garland, Judy, 2, 166, 193
Garmash, Sergei, 31
Gay Divorcée, The, 2
Gdansk, 262n29
General Władysław Anders' Army, 12–13, 79
genre, 1–11, 14, 16–19, 21–22, 24, 26–28, 30–33, 39–42, 44, 49, 64, 77–78, 82–83, 85, 88, 90, 96, 98, 100, 105, 106n57, 107, 108n60, 112, 117–19, 130, 138, 141–43, 146n16, 147–48, 152, 154–56, 159–60, 162–64, 166–67, 175–77, 182–85, 194–95, 198, 210, 214, 223, 231, 238–41, 248, 251–53, 256n18, 260, 269, 275, 277–78, 281, 284, 296
genre conventions, 2, 7, 12, 17, 19, 27, 41, 53, 65, 68, 77–78, 88, 101, 104–105, 117, 138–39, 153, 159, 166, 223, 231, 236n36, 238, 241, 243, 248, 249n3, 252, 254n16, 258, 260, 278, 281, 284–85, 296
genre film, 42, 65, 68, 277
genre's syntax, 24, 119
Germany, 9–10, 15, 40, 181, 200, 226n14, 250n6, 251, 267
Giannetti, Louis, 2, 162, 166
Gibson, Christopher, 134
Gierasieński, Romuald, 47–48, 51
Gierszał, Jakub, 146, 160
Gietz, German Heinz, 135
Gilbert, John, 8
Ginzburg, Evgenii, 222
Girl Can't Help It, The, 3
Girl with a Guitar, A (Devushka s gitaroi), 27, 222
Girl without an Address, A (Devushka bez adresa), 222
GITIS (State Institute of Theatre Arts), 188
Gladkov, Aleksandr, 26–27, 222n6
Glenn Miller Story, The, 29
Godard, Jean-Luc, 119
Godina, Karpo Ačimović, 133n42
Goethe, Johann Wolfgang von, 109
Gogol Center, theater, 291
Gold, Artur, 44, 49, 79
Gold Diggers of 1933, 106n57
Gold, Henryk, 44
Golden Duck Award, 85
Golden Orpheus. *See* Bulgarian Music Festival

Gorbachev, Mikhail, 28–29, 271, 279n14
Gorbonos, Boris (Pugacheva, Alla), 263–64
Gorchilin, Aleksandr, 282
Gorczyńska, Maria, 46–47
Gorelov, Denis, 257n21
Gosteleradio, 257n22
Goulding, Alfred John, 10
Grease, 5, 8, 161n49
Great Dictator, The, 84
Great Caruso, The 29
Great Citizen, The (Velikii grazhdanin), 231n25
Great Depression, 1, 5, 23
Great Terror (*ezhovshchina*), 22
Great Turn, The (Velikii perelom), 231n25
Great Waltz, The, 183
Grebenshchikov, Boris, 275–76, 278, 289, 295
Greco, Juliette, 133n43
Green, Joseph, 39n1, 49n23
Gromadzka, Wiesława, 121n15
Grossówna, Helena, 11, 13, 15, 45, 51, 57–58, 60–61, 63, 68–78
Guattari, Pierre-Félix, 124
Gurchenko, Liudmila, 27, 220, 222, 230, 241–42, 257n21
Gurov, Sergei, 223–24
Győri, Zsolt, 119
Gypsy Baron, The, 181

Halka, 141
Hallo, Fred the Beard, or The Final Performance of the King of Safebreakers (Hallo Szpicbródka czyli ostatni występ króla kasiarzy), 16
Hairspray, 6n19
Halloween, 148
Hallström, Lasse, 271n37
Hamilton, 6
Hamlet, Prince of Denmark, The Tragedy of, 103n53, 210
Hammer Film Productions, Ltd., 148
Hammerstein, Oscar Greeley Clendenning, II, 202n75
happy ending, 3–5, 7, 18, 33, 45, 50, 104, 131, 139, 144, 166, 185, 206
Happy Guys, The (Veselye rebiata). See Jolly fellows, The
Happy Youth (Schastlivaia iunost'), 223–24
Hawks, Howard, 208
Hefner, Hugh Marston, 154
Heldt, Guido, 281, 283
Helen Morgan Story, The, 30
Hellbeck, Jochen, 179
Heller, Joseph, 84
Hemar, Marian, 16
Hendrix, Jimmi, 32n107
Hercules, 6
Herman, Katarzyna, 146, 159
Hertz, Aleksander, 12
Herzog, Amy, 123–25
High Stalinism, 173, 194, 231
Hipsters (Stiliagi), 22, 28, 30–31, 293, 295
His Majesty, the Shop Clerk (Jego ekscelencja subject), 21
Hitchcock, Alfred, 14n51, 113
Hitler, Adolf, 84, 243
Hoffman, Jerzy, 99n44, 112
Holland, Agnieszka, 112
Hollywood, 1, 3–7, 9–10, 12–19, 22, 25, 26n93, 30, 33, 40–41, 48, 49n25, 53, 78, 99, 104–105, 107–108, 119–20, 142, 144–45, 152n29, 160, 162–63, 166–67, 176, 183, 200, 210, 216, 252, 268, 269n34, 270
Holocaust, 79
Homer, poet, 147
Howard, Ron, 145
Humoresque (Dvořák), 65
Hussar Ballad, A (Gusarskaia ballada), 26, 222
Hutcheon, Linda, 142

Iakovlev, Iurii, 27n94
Iakovleva, Elena, 32
Iankovskii, Oleg, 31
Ida, 18
Idiot, The, 177
Idov, Lily, 275–76
Idov, Michael, 275–76, 277n7, 284n26
Iggy Pop, singer, 281, 291–92
Il est charmant, 9
Il'inskii, Igor', 222, 227–30, 241
integrated musical, 2, 119, 177, 200
Intergirl, The, 32
International Film Festival Fantasporto, the, 142n1
International Youth Festival, 222
Intervision Song Contest, 256
Iron Curtain, 116, 118, 132
Irony of Fate, The (Ironiia sud'by), 27, 32, 257
Isakovskii, Mikhail, 200
Is Lucyna a Girl? (Czy Lucyna to dziewczyna?), 13, 14n50, 61
Israel, 135, 272
It'll Be Better (Będzie lepiej), 12
It's Always Fair Weather, 3
Iuzovskii, Mikhail, 28
Ivan, 240
Ivan Vasil'evich: Back to the Future (Ivan Vasil'evich meniaet professiiu), 256
I've Come to Speak up (Prishla i govoriu), 270–71n37

Jackson, Michael, 160n48, 249n2
Jacobson, Hymie, 49
Jacoby, Georg, 174n3
Jagielski, Sebastian, 66
Jahoda, Mieczysław, 16
Jailhouse Rock, The, 3
James, Henry, 92n32
Jameson, Frederic, 296
Járosy, Fryderyk, 16, 45–46, 50
Jazzmen. See *We're from Jazz*
Jazz Singer, The, 1, 9
Jenkins, Henry, 271,
Jesus Christ Superstar, 166
Jewison, Norman, 166
John, Sir Elton Hercules, 276n6
Jolly Fair, The (Veselaia iarmarka). See *Cossacks of the Kuban' (Kubanskie kazaki)*
Jolly Fellows, The (Veselye rebiata), 22–23, 29, 122, 176, 178, 230n23, 239–40, 242n51, 270–71n37
Jolson, Al, 1
Jopek, Anna Maria, 132n41
Joplin, Janis, 32n107
Joy Division, rock group, 295
Julski, Cezary, 109
July Rain (Iiul'skii dozhd'), 227
Junod, Bohdan Eugène (pseud. Bodo, Eugeniusz), 11, 13–16, 40, 43, 45, 59–62, 64–73, 77–79
Junod, Theodore, 59

Kaczyński, Lech Aleksander, former President of Poland, 85
Kaganovsky, Lilya, 294n39
Kalatozov, Mikhail, 223
Kalgin, Vitaly, 276, 278n13
Kamenskaia, 32
Kamień Duży, 121n15
Kapela Manugi band, the, 121n15
Karabasz, Kazimierz, 127
Kawalerowicz, Jerzy, 257n21
Kawin, Bruce F., 166
Kazanskii, Gennadii, 28
Kazimierz Dolny, 121n15, 125
Kelly, Gene, 2, 99, 152
Kennedy, John, 4
Kennedy, Robert, 4
KGB, The, 222, 250n6, 282
Khachaturian, Aram, 25
Kharchenko, Valerii, 257n22
Khasan, Lake, 181

Khavich, Oleg, 254n16
Khrennikov, Tikhon, 25, 27, 177, 183, 192
Khrushchev, Nikita, 26, 175, 227, 242, 245
Khutsiev, Marlen, 223, 225, 227
Kichelewski Audrey, 126n33, 134
Kichin, Valerii, 270n37
Kiciński, Tomasz, 120n14
Kidnapping, Caucasian Style (Kavkazskaia plennitsa), 256
Kiepura, Jan, 68
Kieślowski, Krzysztof, 112, 116
Kiev, 176
King, Martin Luther, Jr., 4
King-Stag (Korol'-olen'). 257n22
Kino, film magazine, 20, 47
Kino, group, 31, 275–76, 278–79, 281, 288, 290, 293, 295
KinoPoisk, web portal, 275n2
Kiss Me Kate, 4
Klee, Paul, 103
Kleiser, Randal, 161n49
Klejsa, Konrad, 82n1, 85, 111
Kliaver, Denis, 277n11
Kmon, Gabriela, 121n15, 125n32
Knife in the Water (Nóż w wodzie), 17, 132
Kobiela, Bogumił, 91, 110–11
Kołbielszczyzna, 130n40
kolkhoz comedy, 21, 186
kolkhoz musical, 173, 176, 188, 193, 197
Kol'tsatyi, Arkadii (Kopelevich, Abram Naumovich), 231n25
Kolyma, 27
Komeda, Krzysztof, 17–18, 132
Komsomol'skaia Pravda, The, 180
Konarski, Feliks, 16
Kongress tanzt, Der, 9
Konopka, Andrzej, 150, 154
Koprowicz, Jacek, 160n47
Korczyna, 125n32
Kosmodem'ianskaia, Zoia, 259
Koval'skii, Nikolai, 252n13
Kovardak, Pasha, 180–81
Kowalczyk, Marcin, 151
Kozintsev, Grigorii, 20, 223
Kozyrev, Mikhail, 277
Kraków, 10
Krawicz, Mieczysław, 13, 40, 42, 45, 69, 73–76
Kremlin, 21, 23, 176, 198, 213, 249, 255
Kressyn, Miriam, 49
Kristeva, Julia, 154
Kriuchkov, Nikolai, 189
Krokodil, magazine, 200n70, 205n80
Kroll, Anatolii, 28
Krosno, 121n15, 125n32
Krukowski, Kazimierz, 47–49, 51
Kryzhovnikov, Zhora, 32
Kuban' region, 178–79, 201–3, 207, 212, 214
Kultura, publishing house, 112
Kulturarbeiter, 15, 26, 103
Kupfer, Peter, 229, 233
Kutikov, Aleksandr, 269
Kutz, Kazimierz, 85
Kurz, Iwona, 116
Kuznetsov, Aleksandr, 277
Kwaśniewska, Wiesława, 94
Kwieks's Gypsy ensemble, The, 77

Lady Macbeth of the Mtsensk District (Ledi Makbet Mtsenskogo uezda), opera, 179
Ladynina, Marina, 174, 180–81, 184, 188, 190, 206n81, 214, 258, 271
Laing, Heather, 283
La La Land, 6, 119, 142, 284
Lane, Anthony, 6n22, 17
Lang, Fritz, 9
Lapin, Sergei, 257n22
Laskin, Boris, 224
Last Village, The (Derevnia posledniaia), 176

Łazuka, Bohdan, 91, 94
Lebedev-Kumach, Vasilii, 22, 24, 197, 228, 240–41
Lec, Stanisław Jerzy, 254n16
Led Zeppelin, rock group, 295
Lee, Christopher, 148
Legally Blonde, 6n19
Lehár, Franz, 2n5
Leningrad, 184, 226n14,
Leningrad Rock, 31, 274–75, 278, 280, 281n16, 285, 288, 290, 294–95
Lenin, Vladimir, 123
Leo-Film, studio, 12
Lepin, Anatolii, 27
LeRoy, Mervyn, 106n57
Leto (Summer, The), 31, 166, 274–78, 281, 283–87, 289–91, 293–97
Letters to Santa 3, 4 (Listy do M. 3, 4), 85n16
Levitan, Iurii, 226
Liatoshinskii, Boris, 240
Library of Congress, 148n21
Lieutenant Kizhe (Poruchik Kizhe), 231n25, 240
Life and Loves of a She-Devil, The, 146
Limpid stream, The (Svetlyi ruchei), 179
Lion King, The, 6n19
Lioznova, Tat'iana, 28, 252n13
Liszt, Franz, 23
Little blue light, The, TV show *(Goluboi ogonek)*, 253–54
Little Colonel, The, 187
Little Mermaid, The, 144–45
Little Shop of Horrors, The, 5, 148n21
Liubimov, Yurii, 189
Łódź, 10–11, 39n1, 59–60, 82n1
Long Time Ago, A (Davnym-davno), 26, 222n6
Look up and Laugh, 9
Loubalová, Helena, 236
Lovell, Angela, 143, 165n59
Lovell, Stephen, 225
Love Me or Leave Me, 3
Love Parade, The, 9
Lubelski, Tadeusz, 40, 44
Lubitsch, Ernst, 2n5, 3, 9, 17, 105
Luhrmann, Baz, 6
Lumière, Auguste and Louis, 112
Lundstrem, Oleg, 251
Lungin, Pavel, 29
Lure, The (Córki dancingu), 19, 141–43, 145, 146n17, 147–49, 152–57, 159, 161–63, 165–67

McDonald, Jeanette, 9
MacFadyen, David, 224, 228, 243, 264n31
Machulski, Juliusz, 84, 85n16
Madonna, Louise Ciccone, 252n12
Magiton, Isaak, 257n22
Majerczyk-Bobak, Katarzyna, 121n15
Majewski, Jerzy S., 48
Makarczyński, Tadeusz, 147n20
Makarevich, Andrei, 269
Makarov, Viktor, 252n13
Makhmudov, Mukadas, 257n22
Malanowicz, Zygmunt, 150, 161
Malcolm X, 4
Mamele, 39n1
Mankiewiczówna, Tola, 46–47
Mann, Anthony, 12n41, 29
Man of Marble, The (Człowiek z marmuru), 136
Man/Woman Wanted (Poszukiwany, poszukiwana), 14, 88n21, 105n56
Marciniak, Katarzyna, 122
Marfino, estate, 262
Marriage of Convenience, A (Małżeństwo z rozsądku), 16–18, 82–84, 86–87, 91, 100–101, 104–106, 108–109, 111–13, 166
Marshall, Rob, 6
Marvel Comics, 98
Mary Poppins, 3

Marx, Karl, 192
Matter to Settle, A (Sprawa do załatwienia), 15
Matuszkiewicz, Jerzy, 88
Mazierska, Ewa, 89n23, 111, 117, 119, 121, 122n17, 143n7, 158n43, 185
Mazowsze ensemble, the, 126, 130, 132n41
Mazurek, Marta, 146, 151
Medium, 160n47
Meet Me in St. Louis, 2, 194
Meitus, Iulii, 240
Melikian, Anna, 144
Melodiia, record label, 250
Melodies of the Veriiskii Quarter (Melodii Veriiskogo kvartala), 26n93
Men'shov, Vladimir, 28, 258
Mercanton, Louis, 9
Mercury, Freddie, 276n6
Merry Widow, 2n5, 9
Messman, Vladimir, 20
Metro-Goldwyn-Mayer (MGM), 2, 13
Metropolis, 9
Meyerhold, Vsevolod, 179, 191
Middle East, 13, 79
Mielke, Magda, 158
Milian, Jerzy, 18
Minkov, Mark, 28
Minnelli, Vincente, 2, 194
Minotaur, 109
Minsk, 30
Mironov, Andrei, 257
Mishmash or a Mess-Up, A (Miszmasz czyli Kogel Mogel), 85n16
MMM, 241
Modzelewski, Eugeniusz, 10
Molchanova, Mariia, 241
Moldavia, 253
Molinaro, Édouard, 84
Mondrus, Larisa, 256, 257n22
Moniuszko, Stanisław, 141
Moore, Colleen, 42
Morrison, Jim, 32n107
Morskie Oko (revue theater in Warsaw), 59–60
Morstin, Agnieszka, 116
Moscow, 28, 79, 178, 181n34, 183–84, 188n57, 194, 197, 203, 224, 226n14, 227, 228–30, 234, 249, 255, 257n22, 262, 267, 276, 278, 294
Moscow Doesn't Believe in Tears (Moskva slezam ne verit), 28
Moscow Art Theatre, 188
Moscow Operetta Theatre, 183, 186
Mosfil'm, studio, 174–76, 223, 259–60, 263, 265–67, 269
Moskvichi, VIA, 251
Moulin Rouge!, 6
Mukhina, Vera, 198
Mulvey, Laura, 102n51, 268
Munk, Andrzej, 112
Murav'eva, Irina, 28
Musical Story (Muzykal'naia istoriia), 231n25
Music Man, The, 3
Mussolini, Benito, 243
Muzyka, company, 271
My Fair Lady, 3

Nagiev, Dmitrii, 32n108
Napoleon, Bonaparte, I, 243–44
Napoleonic War, 26, 222n6
Naumenko, Mike, 31–32, 274–81, 284–85, 288–89, 291–96
Naumenko, Natasha, 31, 274–76, 278n13, 279–80, 284, 291
Naumov, Vladimir, 183
Navalny, Aleksei, 267n33
Nazi, 4, 15, 44, 79
Neale, Steve, 7n25, 8, 108n60, 148, 167
Nechaev, Aleksei, 28
Nechaev, Leonid, 28
Nechesa, Pavel, 176
Needle, The (Igla), 282

Negri, Pola, 10
Nemoliaeva, Svetlana, 257n21
Nestroy, Jan, 69
Neufeld, Max, 9
News of the Day, newsreel (*Novosti dnia*), 223
New Wave, music, 222, 284, 293n36
New Year Adventures of Masha and Vitia, The (*Novogodnie prikliucheniia Mashi i Viti*), 27
New York City, 4, 66
New York Times, The, 89
New York, New York, 4, 166
Ney, Nora, 16
Nichols, Mike, 84
Niewiera, Elwira, 12n42
Nightingale from the Village of Marshintsy, The (*Solovei iz sela Marshintsy*), 249
Nightmare on Elm Street, 148
Nijinsky, Vaclav, 70
Nika, award, 31n106, 274
Nikulin, Iurii, 257
Nil'sen, Vladimir, 23, 25, 26n92, 230n23
Ninotchka, 3, 105
Nisnevich, Anna, 234
Niżyńska, Bronisława, 15, 70
Norðfjörð, Björn, 119
Norok, group, 251n9
Novyi electron, VIA, 251
Novyi mir, journal, 221n4
Nowicki, Piotr, 10
Nowina-Przybylski, Jan, 39n1, 40
Nugmanov, Rashid, 282

Odyssey, 147
Oh! What a Lovely War, 10
Oklahoma, 3
Olbrychski, Daniel, 85n18, 91, 95, 99–102, 111
Older Gentlemen's Cabaret, The, TV show (*Kabaret Starszych Panów*), 254n16
Old Friend, An (*Staryi znakomyi*), 222
Olszańska, Magdalena, 146, 151
Olympia Hall, 250n6
Once, 284
One Floor Up (*Piętro wyżej*), 13–14, 45, 59–63, 65, 67–69, 71, 73, 78, 233
One Hour with You, 9
Only in the Music Hall (*Tol'ko v miuzik-holle*), 252n13
On the Town, 99
Opel'iants, Vladislav, 287
Opoczno, 121n15
Ordinary Miracle, An (*Obyknovennoe chudo*), 252n13
Ordonówna, Hanka, 16
Orlov, Aleksandr, 248, 252n13, 255, 257n22, 258, 260, 265, 268
Orlova, Liubov', 22–23, 28, 188, 190, 214n91, 228–29, 258, 271
Orwid, Józef, 61–62, 71
Oscar, award, 4, 17–18, 28, 116, 144, 274
Osiecka, Agnieszka, 89
Ostrowska, Ela, 82n1
Ostrovskii, Aleksandr, 194
Otello, 12n41
Our Mutual Friend (*Nash obshchii drug*), 181
Ovanesova, Arsha, 223
Oz, Frank, 5

Pabst, Georg Wilhelm, 9
Pajama Game, The, 4
Palme d'Or, award. *See* Cannes International Film Festival
Pan Dodek, 15
Papa Is Getting Married (*Papa się żeni*), 44
Paris, 3, 6, 60, 70, 112, 116n2, 118, 132, 133n43, 134, 250n6
Paris Olympia Music Hall, the, 133n43
Party Card, The (*Partiinyi bilet*), 176
Party Central Committee, the, 180, 182n35, 241
Passendorfer, Jerzy, 16–17

Paweł and Gaweł (Paweł i Gaweł), 13, 14n50, 15, 45, 69–78
Pawlicki, Maciej, 84
Pawlikowski, Paweł, 18–19, 116–20, 121n15, 125, 127–28, 131, 134, 136–37, 166–67
Peasants, The (Krest'iane), 243n54
Pesniary, group, 251n9
Petersburski, Jerzy, 43–44, 46, 48–49
Phantom of the Opera, The, 148n21
Pharaoh (Faraon), 257n21
Piaf, Edith, 133n43
Piecyk, Ryszard, 121n15
Pink Floyd, rock group, 295
Pioneriia, newsreel, 223
Pirate, The, 2
Piskator, Erwin, 240
Planet of Singles, The (Planeta Singli), 85n16
Playboy Club, the, 154
Płotnicki, Bolesław, 91, 110
Pogodin, Nikolai, 200–201, 206,
Pogorzelska, Zula, 40, 42–43, 46, 68, 70
Pokora, Wojciech, 105
Pokrass Brothers, 177, 192
Poland, 5, 8, 10–12, 15–16, 18–19, 23, 30, 39n1, 40–41, 44, 49, 54–55, 68, 78–79, 84–85, 89–90, 92–93, 95, 96n39, 104–105, 108–109, 111–12, 116, 118, 122–23, 126–28, 130–32, 133nn42–43, 134–35, 137–38, 141, 147, 160–61, 254n16, 262n29
Polański, Roman, 17, 132
Poliakov, Vladimir, 224n10
Polish People's Republic, The (PRL), 16, 82, 85n14
Politics (*Polityka*), 85n16
Polynnikov, Aleksandr, 252n13
Pomerantsev, Vladimir, 221n4
Pomeshchikov, Evgenii, 176, 178
Poznań, 15, 59
Pravda, newspaper, 179, 270n37, 271
Preis, Kinga, 150, 154
Prigov, Dmitry, 289
Prince and the Dybbuk, The (Książę i dybuk), 12n42
Preminger, Otto, 14n51
Prends la route, 9
Presley, Elvis, 3n10
Preobrazhenskaia, Ol'ga, 226n14
Prodeus, Adriana, 155n36
Prokhorov, Alexander and Elena, 27n96, 220, 228, 248
Prokofiev, Sergei, 25, 240
propaganda, 17, 21, 24, 89, 111, 123, 138, 289
Pub "13 chairs," TV show (*Kabachok "13 stul'ev")*, 254n16
Puccini, Giacomo, 6n21
Pudovkin, Vsevolod, 19–20, 240
Pugacheva, Alla, 29, 248, 250n6, 251, 252n12, 253–66, 268, 270–72
Purimshpiler, Der, 39n1, 49n23
Pussy Riot, art group, 272
Putin, Vladimir, 286–87, 289
Pyr'ev, Ivan, 22–27, 84, 173–86, 188–92, 194, 198, 200–202, 203nn78–79, 206n84, 213, 223, 236n36, 240–42, 258

Qui Pro Quo, cabaret, 13–15, 53, 59–60
Queen, group, 276n6

Radiant Path, The (Svetlyi put'), 22–23, 161n49, 188, 198, 240, 255
Radio Corporation of America (RCA, studio), 1
Railway Station for Two, A (Vokzal na dvoikh), 222
Rajewski, Wojciech, 103
reconciliation, 24, 31–32, 50, 65, 68, 104, 145, 166, 214
Red Boogie, The, 133n42
Red Flower, The (Chervona ruta), 249

Reed, Lou (Lewis Allan), 281, 289n31, 292–93
Regev, Motti, 251
Reinart, Emile, 10
Replewicz, Maciej, 86
Revolt of the Fishermen (Vosstaniie rybakov), 240
Rex-Film, studio, 12
Rey, Cemal Reşit, 240
Riazanov, El'dar, 26–27, 32, 220, 222–24, 227–30, 231n25, 235, 241–43, 245, 257
Rice, Tim, 166
Richardson, Tony (Cecil Antonio), 31
Rich Brides, The (Bogatye nevesty), book, 194
Rich Bride, The (Bogataia nevesta), 24–25, 173–74, 175n11, 176–79, 181, 183n44, 187–90, 192–200, 202–3, 211, 215, 217
Riga, 174
Rivals (Rywale), 60
Road to Life (Putevka v zhizn'), 20
Robert and Bertrand (Robert i Bertrand), 13, 15, 45, 69–72
Rock around the Clock, 3
Rocketman, 276n6
Rocky Horror Picture Show, The, 4, 10, 147
Rodgers, Richard Charles, 202n75
Rogers, Ginger, 2, 95, 152
Rökk, Marika, 206
Rolling Stones, The, rock group, 295
Roman Holiday, 12n41
Romeo and Juliet, 106, 166
Romanówna, Janina, 91
Roman Scandals, 210n88
Romanticism, 93, 138
Roosevelt, Franklin, 228n17
Rosner, Eddie, 27
Rosołowski, Piotr, 12n42
Rotaru, Sofia, 29, 248–51, 252n12, 253–56, 257n19, 261–62, 266, 268–72
Rouge et Le Noir, Le, 103n53
Rowe, Kathleen, 259n24
Rózewicz, Stanisław, 82
Różycki Bazaar, the market, 91, 101, 105
Rubin, Martin, 152n29, 156, 162n51
Rusalka, 144
Rusalochka, 144
Russia, 5, 8, 9n29, 29–32, 93, 174n3, 177–78, 184, 203, 225, 293
Russian Oscar. *See* Nika, award
Russ, Joanna, 143n10
Ruszkowski, Wojciech, 46
Rybin, Aleksei, 275–76
Rydzewska, Joanna, 117
Rydet, Zofia, 127n38
Ryder, Aleksander, 10
Rzeszewski, Janusz, 16

Sądek, Napoleon, 43, 69–70
Safariants, Rita, 277
Salys, Rimgaila, 84
Saratov, 176, 184
Sass, Barbara, 153n31
Saturday Night Fever, 5, 31, 161
Savchenko, Igor', 21, 176
Saville, Victor, 9
Savitskaia, Elena, 183
Sawczuk, Katarzyna, 159–60
Schatz, Thomas, 41n5, 130
Schlechter, Emanuel, 43, 45–46, 48, 61, 68–70, 79
Schneider, Roy, 156n39
School of Musical Education and Theatrical Dance, 53
Schuchardt, Tomasz, 14
Schünzel, Reinhold, 9, 153
Scorsese, Martin, 4, 166
Selezneva, Natal'ia, 257n19
Sempoliński, Ludwik, 60, 62
Serebrennikov, Kirill, 31, 166, 274, 276, 281, 283, 284n26, 287, 290–91, 296–97

Sex Pistols, rock group, 293
Sezam, department store, 158, 163
Seven Brides for Seven Brothers, 3
Shakespeare, William, 103n53, 106, 166, 262
Shakhnazarov, Karen, 28–29, 293
Shall We Dance, 95
Shaporin, Iurii, 240
Sharman, Jim, 4, 148
Shchors, 194
Shel'menko the Orderly (Shel'menko-denshchik), 26n93
Shengelaia, Georgii, 26n93
Shklovsky, Viktor, 20
Shorin, Aleksandr, 226n14
Shostakovich, Dmitrii, 20, 25, 179, 240
Shub, Esfir', 20
Shulzhik, Valerii, 252n13
Shumiatskii, Boris, 20, 25, 216, 239–40
Sutherland, Albert Edward, 210n88
Sfinks, studio, 12
Silk Stockings, 3
Singing Fool, The, 1, 9–10
Singin' in the Rain, 3, 99
Sinie Nosy, art-group, 282
Sin'ko, Rostislav, 249
Sizov, Nikolai, 259, 264
Skarbek-Malczewski, Jan, 10
Skobtseva, Irina, 258
Skolimowski, Jerzy, 17
Skoneczny, Czesław, 63
Smena, magazine, 271n37
Smith, Imogen Sara, 133n42
Smoczyńska, Agnieszka, 19, 30, 141–42, 144–48, 149n26, 150–52, 155–56, 158–61, 165–67
Snow White and the Seven Dwarfs, 6, 145n12
Socialist Realism, 21, 100, 105, 108–109, 130, 175, 222, 225, 233, 235n33, 239, 241, 242n51
Soiuzkino, 176
Soiuzkinozhurnal, newsreel, 223n8
Solidarność, 112, 256n17, 262n29
Solov'ev, Sergei, 175
Some Like It Hot, 14, 112n66
song and dance, 2, 14, 18, 26n93, 105, 234–35, 242, 252, 282
Songs of a Happy Land (Pesni schastlivogo kraia), 248
"Song of the Year," annual TV concert ("Pesnia Goda"), 253, 254n16
Songster of Warsaw, The (Pieśniarz Warszawy), 12–13, 61
Sopot International Music Festival, 251, 256, 262–63
Sorokin, Vladimir, 28
Soul (Dusha), 248, 251, 252n13, 253, 255–56, 259, 265–66, 268, 270–71
Sound of Music, The, 3, 206,
soundtrack, 5, 31n106, 44, 64, 127, 242, 274, 279, 290–91, 296
Soviet Army Theater. *See* Central Theater of the Soviet Army
Sovetskii ekran, magazine, 240n43, 265
Soviet labor camp, 14, 16, 19, 59, 79, 181n34
Soviet regime, 16, 18, 21, 22n79, 90
Soviet Sport, newsreel, 223
Soviet Union, 9n29, 18–19, 20n69, 21–23, 25, 28–29, 79, 83, 87, 178, 183, 210n88, 226, 228, 233, 240, 248, 251, 257nn21–22, 260–61, 264, 271–72, 285, 290, 293, 294n39
Sovkinozhurnal, newsreel, 223n8
Sovremennik orchestra, The, 28
Spider-Man, 6n19
Splash, The, 145
Spring, The (Vesna), 26, 214n91
Spring on Zarechnaia street (Vesna na Zarechnoi ulitse), 223, 225
Spring Voices (Vesennie golosa), 223–27
St. Petersburg, 53
Stagnation (*zastoi*), 28–29, 285–86

Stakhanovites, 17, 180–81, 185, 188n57, 196, 203, 211, 216
Stalin, Joseph, 19, 21–26, 30, 132, 161n49, 173, 175, 177, 180, 186, 194, 196, 198, 201–202, 220–23, 226–32, 234, 235n33, 236n36, 238–43, 245, 249, 252, 255, 264n31
Stanislavsky, Konstantin, 178
Star Is Born, A, 166
Starski, Ludwik, 17, 43, 45, 53, 55–56, 61, 69, 73, 76
State Fair, 187, 202n75, 206, 213
Stendhal, Marie-Henri Beyle, 103n53
Stefanovich, Aleksandr, 248, 252n13, 255, 256n17, 258, 262n29, 263–68
Stępowski, Jarema, 92
Strauss, Johann, II, 181n32
Strictly Ballroom, 6n20
Subhash, Babbar, 270n37
Summer, Donna, 162
Summer Stock, The, 193, 213
Sundance Film Festival, the, 141, 142n1
Sundance Institute, the, 142
Sunday Musicians, The (Muzykanci), 127
Sutton, Martin, 64
Sweeney Todd: Demon Barber of Fleet Street, 148n21
Swineherdess and the Shepherd, The (Svinarka i pastukh), 24–25, 173–74, 175n11, 177–78, 181, 183, 185, 187–89, 192–93, 196–97, 203, 217
Swing Time, 2
Sygietyński, Tadeusz, 126
Syrena Theater, the, 15
Szabó, Ferenc, 240
Szaro, Henryk, 60
Sztaba, Zygmunt, 135
Szumowska, Małgorzata, 167
Szymanowski, Karol, 13n47

Tadzhikfil'm, studio, 257n22
Tager, Pavel, 226n14
Take Good Care of Women (Beregite zhenshchin), 252n13
Talking Heads, The, rock band, 281–82
Tarantino, Quentin, 117
Taras Shevchenko, 231n25
Tarich, Iurii, 176
Tarnowski, Tadeusz, 121n15
Tarzan films, 83, 174n3
Taxi Blues, 29
Taylor, Richard, 21, 24n86, 241
Tea Jazz Orchestra, 13
Teddy Bear, (Miś), 109, 111
technology, 9, 20, 72, 220n3, 221, 223–24, 226–28, 239, 242–43
Temptation (Pokuszenie), 153n31
Terné, Zofia, 16
Thaw, 26, 30, 175, 220–21, 223, 225, 227, 231, 243, 251
Thaw, The (Ottepel'), 223
Theater of Song, 271
Theatre Academy, the, 133n43
Theseus, 109
Thiel, Wolfgang, 23
Third Love, The. See *Woman Who Sings, The*
Thorpe, Richard, 29
Time Machine (Mashina vremeni), rock group, 253, 267, 269–70
Tincknell, Estella, 123
Todorovskii, Petr, 223
Todorovsky, Valery, 30, 293, 294n39
Tokarczuk, Olga, 141
Tolstoy, Leo, 103, 108
Tom Jones, 31
Tom, Konrad, 39n1, 40, 43–44, 47–54, 57–58, 70
Top Hat, 2, 95
Toruń, 70
Touch of Night, The (Dotknięcie nocy), 83n5
Touchstone Pictures, Inc., 145

Tractor Drivers (Traktoristy), 24, 173, 175n11, 177–78, 180–81, 185–93, 202–203, 206n81, 211, 217, 224n10
Trauberg, Leonid, 20
Traviata, La, (Verdi), 6n21
Travolta, John, 5, 161n49
T. Rex, rock group, 289, 292, 295
Trier, Lars von, 160, 166
Troitsky, Artemy, 277, 279n14, 290
Tropillo, Andrei, 275–76
Trystan, Leon (Wagman, Chaim Lejb), 45, 60–63, 65, 67–68, 78–79, 233
Tsoi, 276
Tsoi, Viktor, 31, 32n107, 274–77, 278n13, 279–82, 284–85, 288–93, 295–96
TsSDF. *See* Central Studio for Documentary Film, The
Turovskaia, Maia, 175n13
Tuttle, Frank, 210n88
Tutyshkin, Andrei, 26n93
Tuwim, Julian, 14, 254n16
Twelve Chairs (Dwanaście krzeseł), 12n38
Twelve Chairs (Dvenadtsat' stul'ev), 252n13
Twenties, the Thirties, The (Lata dwudzieste, lata trzydzieste), 16
Twentieth-Century Fox, studio, 1, 13
Twentieth Congress of the Communist Party, 26n92, 175, 220, 242–43, 245
Two Days in Paradise (Dwa dni w raju), 60–61, 69
Tynianov, Yuri, 20, 148

Uchitel', Aleksei, 276
Ukraine, 181, 248–49, 253, 262–63n29
Ukrtelefilm, TV studio, 249
Umbrellas of Cherbourg, The (Parapluies de Cherbourg, Les), 6, 9, 125
Üngör, Osman Zeki, 240
Union of Cinematographers , 175
Union of Soviet Composers, 25
United States, The, 4–5, 9n29, 15, 17, 22–23, 29, 49n23, 55, 83, 133n43, 226n14
United States National Film Registry, 148n21
Universum Film AG (UFA), 40
Urania-Film studio, 60, 69
Urusevskii, Sergei, 223
Usov, Igor', 28
Utesov, Leonid, 22n79, 23, 230n23
utopia, 7, 17, 21, 24, 89, 105, 152, 180, 182

Vanished Empire (Ischeznuvshaia imperiia), 293–94
Varga, Balázs, 119
Variety, the, magazine, 143n8
Vars, Henry. *See* Wars, Henryk
Vartan, Sylvie, 254n16
Vasiliev brothers, 239
Vedishcheva, Aida, 256, 257n20, 257n22
Velvet Underground, The, rock group, 292
Verdi, Giuseppe, 6n21, 23
Vertov, Dziga, 226
Very Best Day, The (Samyi luchshii den'), 32
Veselye rebiata, VIA, 251
VGIK. *See* All-Russian State Institute of Cinematography, The
Victor/Victoria, 9, 153
Viennese operetta, 183n44
Vietnam War, 4, 289n31
Viktor und Viktoria, 9, 153
Vistula, The (river), 52, 54–55, 157
Viva Maria!, 141
Volga-Volga, 22–23, 27, 178, 188, 198, 220, 228–29, 231–36, 238, 240–41, 243n54, 244–45
Volodin, Vladimir, 183
Vologda, 178
Vol'pin, Mikhail, 200

Vysotsky. Thank You for Being Alive! (Vysotskii. Spasibo, chto zhivoi!), 276
Vysotsky, Vladimir, 276

Wagner, Richard, 233
Wahlverwandtschaften, Die (Goethe), 109
Wajda, Andrzej, 16–17, 83, 108–109, 112, 136, 141
Waliszewska, Aleksandra, 149
Walt Disney, studio, 6, 144–45, 160n47
Warner Bros, studio, 1, 13
Wars, Henryk (Warszawski, né Henryk), 11, 13–14, 16, 43–45, 53, 55–57, 59–62, 65, 68–70, 73, 76, 78
Warsaw, 10–13, 15, 17, 39–41, 44–48, 52–54, 57, 59–61, 64–65, 68–74, 76, 78–79, 85, 87–89, 98, 130, 147, 150, 262n29
Warsaw Mermaid, The (Warszawska syrena), 147n20
Warsaw's Parade of stars (Parada gwiazd Warszawy), 40
Warsaw Uprising, 15
Waszyński, Michał (Waks, né Moshe), 10–14, 16, 40, 42, 44, 47–48, 50–51, 61
Wayne, John, 13
Wharton, Edith, 92n32
What My Husband Is Up to at Night (Co mój mąż robi w nocy), 12, 44–51, 55–56, 68, 78
Where Are You, Love? (Gde ty, liubov'?), 266
White, Jerry, 117, 137n49
Who, The, rock group, 295
Wedding in Malinovka, The (Svad'ba v Malinovke) (film), 26n93
Wedding in Malinovka, The (Svad'ba v Malinovke) (operetta), 186
Weill, Kurt, 9
Weldon, Fay, 146
Welles, Orson, 12n41
We're from Jazz (My iz dzhaza), 28, 29n102
We're from Kronstadt, 28n99
Wesby, Ivo (Singer, Ignacy), 48–49
Westerplatte, 82–83
West, Mae, 5n15, 14, 66–68
West Side Story, 8, 89, 106, 166
Wichniarz, Kazimierz, 94
Wife for an Australian, A (Żona dla Australijczyka), 16, 130–31
Wilder, Billy, 14, 112n66
Williams, Linda, 146n16, 148, 156
Wir, 121n15
Wisła, river. *See* Vistula
Wizard of Oz, The, 2, 8
Włast, Andrzej (Baumritter, Gustaw), 60, 79
Wojciechowski, Roman, 121n15
Wolański, Ryszard, 59–60
Woliński, Stanisław, 63
Woman Is a Woman, A, 119
Woman of My Dreams, The (Devushka moei mechty), 174n3, 206
Woman Who Sings, The (Zhenshchina, kotoraia poet), 29, 248, 252n13, 254–56, 258–60, 263, 265, 267–68, 270–71
Women from Riazan' (Baby riazanskie), 226n14
World War I, 10
World War II, 12, 14–16, 25–26, 78, 83, 90, 119, 124, 128, 174, 203, 251
Wrocław, 10
Wrońskie sisters, duo, 157, 161, 165
Wysocka, Tacjanna, 53

Yalla, group, 251n9
Yidl mitn Fidl, 39n1
Yoo, Teo, 277
You and Me, 9
Yugoslavia, 131, 133n42
Yurchak, Aleksei, 275, 287, 294

Żabczyński, Aleksander, 51–52, 59, 78
Zahorska, Anna, 54
Zahorska, Stefania, 12
Zaitsev, Viacheslav, 260
Zakharov, Mark, 229, 252n13
Załuski, Roman, 257n21
Zamiatin, Evgenii, 83
Zanussi, Krzysztof, 83, 112, 159n46
Zaorski, Andrzej, 91
Zatsepin, Aleksandr, 263
Zeki, Erkem, 240
Zel'din, Vladimir, 222
Żeliska, Alina, 51, 63
Zhdanov, Andrei, 25
Zhizn' iskusstva, magazine, 19, 240n43
Ziegfeld Follies, 2,
Ziegfield Follies, The, 60
Zieliński, Andrzej, 18
Zigeunerbaron, Der, 181
Zimińska, Mira (Zimińska-Sygietyńska), 42–43, 46, 70, 126
Zipes, Jack, 145
Znicz, Michał (Feiertag, Michal), 43, 46–49, 52, 58, 78–79
Zoia, 259
Zoopark, musical group, 274, 279, 281, 288, 293, 295
Zorkaia, Neia, 23, 25, 270
Zula. *See* Pogorzelska, Zula
Zveri, musical group, 31
Zwierzchowski, Piotr, 106
Zylska, Natasza (Zygelman), 135

Ingram Content Group UK Ltd.
Milton Keynes UK
UKHW021458030523
421164UK00001B/1